ONE WEEK LOAN

Of Critical Theory and Its Theorists

SECOND EDITION

Stephen Eric Bronner

ROUTLEDGE
NEW YORK   LONDON

Published in 2002 by
Routledge
29 West 35th Street
New York, NY 10001

Published in Great Britain by
Routledge
11 New Fetter Lane
London EC4P 4EE

Routledge is an imprint of the Taylor & Francis Group.
Copyright © 2002 by Routledge

Printed in the United States of America on acid-free-paper.

Library of Congress Cataloging-in-Publication Data
Bronner, Stephen Eric, 1949–
    Of critical theory and its theorists / Stephen Eric Bronner.—2nd. ed.
      p. cm.
    Includes bibliographical references and index.
    ISBN 0-415-93262-9 — ISBN 0-415-93263-7 (pbk.)
      1. Critical Theory. I. Title.

B809.3 .B76 2002
142—dc21

                                                                    2001058917

When the power of synthesis vanishes from the lives of men and when the antitheses have lost their vital relation and their power of interaction and gain independence, it is then that philosophy becomes a felt need.

—G. W. F. HEGEL

CONTENTS

ACKNOWLEDGMENTS

There are many people who have played a role in this enterprise. Luis Eduardo Mendieta generously offered his time, enthusiasm, and invaluable commentary. Samuel Assefa, Edmund Arens, John Ehrenberg, Michael Forman, Micheline Ishay, Kurt Jacobsen, Christine Kelly, Douglas Kellner, Eva Grünstein-Neuman, Jose Maria Rosales, Hong-lim Ryu, Manfred Steger, and F. Peter Wagner also provided me with their insights on various chapters. I would like to thank Eric Nelson, my editor at Routledge, for his support of this new edition. My wife, Anne Burns, was always there when I needed her. Finally, however, I would like to recall the memory of two very different thinkers who inspired my commitment to the critical project: Ernst Bloch and Henry Pachter.

Of Critical Theory and Its Theorists

Introduction
From the First to the Second Edition

In the late 1960s, when I first became interested in critical theory, it was the preserve of a small group of intellectuals. Journals like *Telos* and *New German Critique* had just formed and most academics in America had never heard of critical theory or, with the exception of Herbert Marcuse, its leading figures. The legend that critical theory inspired the movement of the 1960s is, certainly in America, misleading; its major works were translated only in the 1970s. Now, however, things are very different. Jürgen Habermas is everywhere legitimately recognized as a giant of social theory, and there is hardly a literary critic who is unaware of Theodor Adorno or Walter Benjamin. Critical theory has invaded the most prestigious academic journals in disciplines ranging from anthropology and film to religion, linguistics, and political science. In fact, given the new stratum of philosophical professionals, it has arguably become a feature of the very society its proponents ostensibly challenged.

Of Critical Theory and Its Theorists had a measure of success following its appearance in 1994. The publication of this new edition has made it possible to correct minor mistakes, introduce certain stylistic changes, and somewhat revise the structure. Reconstructing the radical aims of the critical project and evaluating its inadequacies along with its legacy for the present, however, remain its purpose. The book was never meant to provide a detailed chronology. Excellent histories had already been written like *The Dialectical Imagination* by Martin Jay and, more recently, *The Frankfurt School* by Rolf Wiggershaus. Important general works had also appeared such as *Introduction to Critical Theory* by David Held and *The Frankfurt School* by Zoltan Tar, along with often magisterial biographies by scholars like Susan Buck-Morss on Walter Benjamin, Daniel Burston on Erich Fromm, Douglas Kellner on Herbert Marcuse, Arpad Kadarkay on Georg Lukács, and Gillian Rose on Theodor W. Adorno. Nevertheless, there is still no other work that speaks to both experts and a general audience about the relevance of the tradition via a critical analysis of its major figures and basic themes.

Of Critical Theory and Its Theorists was an attempt to meet that need. It employs the liberating imperatives of critical theory against the predominant forms in which critical theory is currently expressed. Space constraints prevent the consideration of every important thinker. Considering the contributions of the younger generation in Europe and the United States would surely have been worthwhile and it was not for want of interest that the contributions of Leo Lowenthal and Siegfried Kracauer to the sociology of culture or Otto Kirchheimer, Friedrich Pollock, and Franz Neumann to law and political economy have been omitted. Choosing what to include or exclude involved setting priorities. Questions of length led me to cut essays in the first edition dealing with the critique of ontology and the philosophy of rational choice, which were intended to show what critical theory is not, in favor of two new essays. These older pieces will find their way into other volumes and, even at the time of its publication, I felt that the first edition could have been tighter. Adding chapters on the impact of philosophical idealism and the encounter between critical theory and civil society, I think, not only provides some new insights, but gives this new edition a more cohesive character.

Critical theory is not a system nor is it reducible to any fixed set of proscriptions. Every major figure in the tradition, perhaps for this reason, employed the essay as a stylistic vehicle. The essay, with its inherently unfinished quality, is the logical form for generating antisystemic claims and fostering the exercise of reflexivity. Its use in this volume is consequently within the spirit of the original enterprise. The essay form allows the contributions of one thinker to be treated in one way and those of another in a very different fashion. The point is not to offer a neutral set of judgments. Each chapter provides a new and distinct interpretation of its subject matter. But themes carry over and new ones emerge. There is an open quality to this work, a space for the reader to develop connections, which—again—reflects the original spirit of critical theory. My hope from the beginning was that these essays, like the "constellation" envisioned by Benjamin and Adorno, would coalesce into a book that is more than the sum of its parts.

Of Critical Theory and Its Theorists sought to reinvigorate the interdisciplinary character of the original project, and its essays touch upon fields ranging from philosophy and aesthetics to politics and anthropology to theology and history. Any work on critical theory must recognize its fluid character, the fact that it is no longer identifiable with any "school" or tendency, and that its continued relevance depends upon the willingness to confront old assumptions from the standpoint of new conditions. The present volume presents critical theory as a *cluster of themes* inspired by the quest for freedom. Philosophical idealism inspired this quest, and given the lack of an explicit discussion about the early influences on critical theory in the first edition, I begin the second edition with "Sketching the Lineage: The Critical Method and the Idealist Tradition."

Critical theory in the twentieth century, from the first, expressed an explicit interest in the abolition of social injustice. The aim of its partisans was to show how repressive interests were hidden by the supposedly neutral formulations of science no less than ontology, and, in this way, the movement always retained a commitment to the sociology of knowledge and the "critique of ideology" (*Ideologiekritik*). Its encounter with the existing order, however, retained a transcendent or utopian component. A commitment to the integrity of the individual, and freedom beyond existing parameters, became perhaps the motivating factor. The equilibrium holding between the immanent and transcendent elements of the project was always tenuous. The extent to which one or the other is given more or less weight is an interesting way to consider the development of critical theory and judge individual theorists in relation to one another. Nevertheless, the balance between these two concepts shifts within the different works of any given theorist, and neither is ever sacrificed entirely.

Critical theory preserves this most basic tension behind dialectical thinking. Its objective is to foster reflexivity, a capacity for fantasy, and a new basis for praxis in an increasingly alienated world. Critical theory, in this way, stands diametrically opposed to economic determinism and any stage theory of history. It originally sought to examine the various "mediations" between base and superstructure. It engaged in a revision of Marxian categories and an anachronistic theory of revolution in order to expose what inhibited revolutionary practice and its emancipatory outcome. Critical theory wished to push beyond the stultifying dogma and collectivism of what became known as "actually existing socialism." The ideological and institutional framework of oppression was always thrust to the forefront and made the target of attack. In part, perhaps, this explains the concern with utopia by so many critical theorists and their willingness to experiment with new forms of experience and analysis.

Despite the cluster of themes defining critical theory, however, it retains a certain integrity and coherence. The undertaking emerged in a distinct historical epoch. World War I and the Russian Revolution provided the context in which new and radical departures in dialectical thinking took place. The identification between technology and progress, science and moral development, seemed to have collapsed in the trenches. Progress was exposed as an illusion, and liberalism lost its allure. The "betrayal" of proletarian internationalism by social democracy in 1914, the seizure of power by the communists, and a spate of proletarian uprisings throughout Europe in the aftermath of the war provided the impulse for a critique of orthodoxy and the standard "materialist" interpretation of Marx. The revolution was not supposed to break out in an economically underdeveloped state like Russia, and, in fact, Antonio Gramsci initially termed the communist revolution a "revolution against *Das Kapital.*"

The original preoccupation of historical materialism with the objective development of productive forces surrendered to a new emphasis upon "consciousness" and the vision of a radical transformation of society. A new concern with the connection between revolutionary theory and practice made itself felt. Thus, the relation between Marxism and philosophy became a matter of importance.

Critical theory is usually associated with various members of the Frankfurt Institute for Social Research like Max Horkheimer who became its director in 1930; Leo Lowenthal who joined in 1926; Theodor W. Adorno who began to participate in 1928 but only became an official member ten years later; Erich Fromm who started his nine-year collaboration in 1930; Herbert Marcuse who joined in 1933; and Walter Benjamin who never officially became a member at all. But, in fact, it was spawned by a set of unorthodox thinkers more or less associated with the left wing of the communist movement representing what Maurice Merleau-Ponty would call "Western Marxism." This tendency stood opposed to mechanistic materialism, economic determinism, and all ahistorical forms of interpretation. Its innovative use of the dialectical method and its recognition of the contribution made by philosophical idealism for Marxism, its concern with consciousness and the impact of alienation, turned its thinkers into far more than merely the precursors of the "Frankfurt School." *Of Critical Theory and Its Theorists*, for this reason, opens with chapters treating the contributions of Karl Korsch, Georg Lukács, and Ernst Bloch.

Their philosophical work reflected the radical hopes generated during the "heroic period" of the Russian Revolution that stretched from 1918 until 1923. Bloch's *Spirit of Utopia* was published in 1918, and both Korsch's *Marxism and Philosophy* and Lukács's *History and Class Consciousness* appeared in 1923. This was the year in which the possibility of an international communist revolution was finally laid to rest. It was also the year in which the Institute for Social Research was founded in Frankfurt am Main. The initial research program was developed under the stewardship of Carl Grünberg. It centered around the labor movement, the capitalist economy, and the new experiments with planning in the Soviet Union. Korsch exerted an important influence during this time, and among the important scholars of the institute were Fritz Sternberg, Henryk Grossmann, and Friedrich Pollock. Many members were aligned with the communist movement, and its perspective on the state and monopoly capitalism carried over into certain important writings of the 1930s. A fundamental shift in direction took place, however, when Max Horkheimer became director in 1930. He coined the term *critical theory*, and he used the *Journal for Social Research*, which would serve as the public forum for the institute, to set a new agenda with an emphasis on issues ranging from psychology and aesthetics to philosophy and the critique of technology. The chapter "Horkheimer's Road" is an attempt to explore the contributions and limits of his thought, and certain assumptions behind the intellectual enterprise of what would come to be known as the Frankfurt School.

Critical theory became juxtaposed against all "traditional"—metaphysical and materialist—forms of theory. It was directed against all attempts to construct a fixed system and every attempt to identify the subject with the object, whether conceived in terms of social institutions or the "covering" categories of philosophy. This attempt gave the institute a unique position in the intellectual world of the 1930s. It was a decade in which all hope for the future seemed lost and Walter Benjamin, who would become one of the most prominent thinkers of the century, sought to save it by recapturing "the glow of the profane." He evidenced an extraordinary commitment to freedom, individuality, and philosophical experimentation during the time in which totalitarianism was on the rise. His attempt to construct a negative philosophy of history, substitute a less rigorous constellation for the classical Hegelian concept of totality, and emphasize the particular would ultimately lay the basis for transforming the entire critical project. Nevertheless, while most interpretations stress or even glorify the fragmented quality of his thinking and insights, the essay in this book interprets those very qualities making for his current success as compensations for his failure to fuse the messianic with the materialist elements of his thought in terms of a coherent theory.

Walter Benjamin like virtually every other major figure in the critical tradition was an enthusiastic supporter of modernism. He viewed surrealism, with its emphasis on the transformation of everyday experience, as an essential component of the revolution. With the communist support of the Popular Front and the "progressive" legacy of the bourgeoisie in 1936, however, expressionism and modernism came under sharp attack in favor of "realism." Lukács, who had openly retreated from his youthful avant-gardism in order to propound a standpoint in conformity with the new communist line, set the stage for a debate in which Bloch and Bertolt Brecht offered the most important responses. "Political Aesthetics in the 1930s" provides the background for the "expressionism debate," a quick summary of the arguments made by its principal protagonists, and a preliminary attempt to develop a new critical aesthetic with new categories capable of evaluating the diverse artistic contributions of diverse styles in the face of a new mass media.

For most of the left-wing intelligentsia of Europe, however, exile was the real theme of the 1930s and 1940s. The Institute of Social Research and most of its members, seeking to escape Hitler, ultimately relocated in the United States. There, in collaboration with Theodor Adorno, Horkheimer wrote *Dialectic of Enlightenment*. This marked a sea change in the direction of critical theory. No longer was the proletariat seen as the subject of history, no longer were teleological notions of progress considered sacrosanct, no longer was the liberal Enlightenment legacy taken for granted, no longer was it merely a matter of redirecting technology toward new ends. The new critical theory of society forwarded a more directly anthropological form of inquiry. The possibility of revolutionary transformation was seen as fading in the face of an apparently seamless bureaucratic order buttressed by the "culture industry" and intent on eliminating subjectivity and the reflexive sources of opposition to the status quo. In response, while retaining the dialectical framework of Hegel and Marx, Adorno began integrating the insights of Schopenhauer and Nietzsche in their battle against the collectivist strains within advanced industrial society. The result would prove works of remarkable range and quality including what is arguably the most important work on aesthetics of the twentieth century. It is with the inventor of "negative dialectics," however, that the relation between theory and practice would most nearly verge on disintegration and the connection between immanence and transcendence appear the most tenuous. "Dialectics at a Standstill" analyzes Adorno's rescue of utopia through an "inversion" of reality and his redefinition of critical theory as an antisystemic metaphysic lacking any criteria with which to justify its claims or articulate its purposive aims.

Concerns of this sort are often reflected in the attacks on the difficult style employed by critical theorists. The heritage of dialectical philosophy surely had an impact, and the complex use of complex concepts often justifiably demanded a complex style. Especially in the ideologically charged postwar context, however, it was also a question of employing an "aesopian" form of writing; indeed, often from fear or self-serving purposes, Adorno and others wished to disguise their Marxism and used the highly abstract Hegelian language for that reason. But there is also a more theoretical justification for their abstruse style. Even while concern was expressed with fostering Enlightenment attitudes in works like *The Authoritarian Personality*, which was directed by Adorno, the famous analysis of the culture industry developed in *Dialectic of Enlightenment* had argued that popularity would necessarily "neutralize" whatever radical message a work retained. Only Erich Fromm was really willing to engage this new orthodoxy in practical terms.

Fromm was surely the most lucid stylist to emerge from the institute, and few intellectuals of his time had a larger audience. His concern was with social psychology and its relation to political and clinical practice; indeed, this would continue to serve as a point of reference even in his later attempts to link Freud with Marx. For this reason, when Adorno first insisted on developing the critique of anthropology from the standpoint of Freud's instinct theory, he clashed with Fromm. The dazzling newcomer won the battle. Fromm divorced himself from the institute and proceeded to write a number of best-sellers, including *Escape from Freedom*. Quickly enough, however, he was condemned for the "superficial" quality of his writings. And that judgment has gained the status of a myth. "Fromm in America" attempts to undermine it as the essay explores his significance for postwar intellectual and political life in the United States.

Critical theory reached its zenith in the late 1960s and early 1970s. Its emphasis upon alienation, the domination of nature, the regressive components of progress, the mutability of human nature, and the stultifying effects of the culture industry and advanced industrial society made the enterprise relevant for young intellectuals. Radicalism in theory, however, betrayed what was ever more surely becoming a conservatism in practice. New stalwarts of the establishment like Max Horkheimer and Theodor Adorno, for example, were essentially appalled by the movement their own writings had helped inspire. Even more than Fromm, however, Herbert Marcuse remained faithful to the original political impulse of critical theory. He self-consciously employed it to inform the rash of new movements. He also provided a positive response to what he termed "one-dimensional society." Pessimism concerning the future of a society in which all ideological contradictions were being flattened out combined with the commitment to utopian vision. Marcuse sought to fuse the anthropological insights of the young Marx with the "play" principle of Schiller and the metapsychology of Freud. Contradictions abound in his general theory, and it was viciously attacked by Fromm among others. Nevertheless, this thinker who introduced critical theory to America deserves the respectful yet critical examination provided in "Utopia, Aesthetics, Revolution: Herbert Marcuse and the Radical Imagination."

The passing of the radical wave created a new set of issues for a new generation of critical theorists. Taming its utopian excesses, mitigating its subjectivism, affirming its connection with the Enlightenment, establishing its relation to the empirical sciences, providing its normative concerns with philosophical legitimacy, and infusing it with insights from different traditions—all became matters of concern. Every one of these problems was confronted by the most brilliant modern representative of critical theory, and one of the preeminent philosophers of our time, Jürgen Habermas. A prominent "public intellectual" who has dared to take stands on the most important issues of the age, his thinking underwent a profound change. His innovative emphasis upon the role of critical theory in illuminating the "emancipatory interest" took a "linguistic turn" in which he evidenced a new preoccupation with pragmatism, analytic philosophy, and discourse ethics. Questions linger involving the character of his new approach, its connection with the critical tradition, its claim to provide a "postmetaphysical" philosophy, its ability to deal with questions of material interest, and its relevance to political practice. Indeed, these issues are at the core of "Jürgen Habermas and the Language of Politics."

Critical theory once projected an emancipatory promise and a new interdisciplinary perspective seeking to inform the struggles of the oppressed.

Martin Jay was thus correct in suggesting that the questions raised by the proponents of Western Marxism and critical theory were the right ones even if the answers they offered were not. The continuing relevance of the project depends upon the willingness to make good on its original promise. But this requires an encounter with the political rather than merely the cultural constraints of advanced capitalism "Critical Theory and Civil Society: Political Interests, Private Passions, and the Public Sphere," which has been added in this new edition, is an attempt to refashion various categories and assumptions in order to challenge some of the ways in which public life in advanced industrial society undermines the ability of the less advantaged to pursue their interests. Nevertheless, in my opinion, such an undertaking also demands a confrontation with the apocalyptic assault on "reification," "negative dialectics," and an increasingly academic discourse theory.

Highlighting its political impulse, affirming its practical character, and beginning the formulation of a new critical theory of society were the purposes behind "Points of Departure: Sketches for a Critical Theory with Public Aims." This last chapter focuses on issues ranging from the preoccupation with philosophical foundations and the totality to the status of utopia and the critique of ideology. It emphasizes questions dealing with autonomy and interest, solidarity and the domination of nature, class and cosmopolitanism, reification and aesthetics, and the constraints on democracy and the exercise of arbitrary power in both existing political institutions and the accumulation process. The essay is also based on a standpoint willing to identify critical theory with the democratic and socialist variants of the Enlightenment. Indeed, over time, the ambivalence concerning its connection with the Enlightenment has become ever more wearying and ever less productive. Critical theory must now, once again, determine its priorities and make explicit its political aims. It can no longer afford to play off immanence against transcendence. Any critique worthy of the commitment to emancipation can develop only by reaffirming the connection between them. *Of Critical Theory and Its Theorists* has sought to contribute toward that end. Thus, from the start, it was intended less as a conclusion than as an attempt to provide a new beginning.

STEPHEN ERIC BRONNER

$\mathcal{C}\sim 2 \sim$

Sketching the Lineage
The Critical Method
and the Idealist Tradition

C ritical theory is experiencing a crisis of purpose. It has focused on the price of progress and the fallacies inherited from earlier teleological understandings of historical agency. It has shown how the transformation of culture into a commodity has undermined reflexivity and the exercise of conscience. It has resisted the pretensions of ontology and the incursions of instrumental rationality. In the process, however, its original ability to identify with the suffering of the exploited and disenfranchised has been compromised. Its activist impulse has made way for the aesthetic-philosophic affirmation of subjectivity in the face of a "totally administered society" and an academic and self-referential discourse ethic whose "postmetaphysical" claims veil its conventionally metaphysical character.

Historical events and institutional constraints, movements and ideals of solidarity, have apparently ceased to generate interest for the partisans of critical theory. No longer is it clear what norms should inform the critique of injustice and oppression. There is little sense regarding the salience of universal values independent of the philosophical framework through which they were originally justified. If only for these reasons, without making any pretense of offering an exhaustive examination, it is perhaps useful to sketch the influence of the most important representatives of philosophical idealism on the development of the critical method.

Kant and the Rise of Subjective Idealism
Idealist philosophy may ultimately derive from antiquity, but its modern partisans set themselves a very different task from that of their predecessors, and this task was critical from the outset: it involved refusing to accept the world as the product of God or destiny, or in any terms independent of the knowing subject, and instead choosing to conceive of human history as its own product.[1] Or, to put it another way, reality could now be understood less as an immutable construct than as capable of being transformed by action imbued

with a positive purpose. The emergence of modern idealism was, in this way, related to the existential and practical needs of the rising bourgeoisie to understand reality and provide its critique of feudal society with a positive, ethical standpoint. Nevertheless, idealism also influenced the later confrontation with capitalism: it would shape our understanding of the way in which alienation affects the individual along with the existential and cultural implications of what would ultimately be termed the "inverted world" of commodity relations.

No less than the intellectual representatives of idealism, naturally, the proponents of modern "materialism" also opposed religious dogma and the arbitrary exercise of political power by feudal institutions. But they were unable to provide their critique with a normative basis. In this vein, the idealists highlighted a form of speculative reason whose purpose lay in articulating the universal preconditions for the exercise of individual freedom. This universalism would become ever more pronounced with the development of the idealist tradition. It would indeed provide both a reason for subaltern classes to support the bourgeoisie and an ethical justification for opposing the given order without which revolutionary practice would have been unthinkable.

Justifying this universalist stance, however, required nothing less than the philosophical revolution inaugurated by Immanuel Kant in his *Critique of Pure Reason* and his attempt to confront the radical skepticism of David Hume who had awakened the Königsberg philosopher from his self-professed "slumber." Against Hume's contention that reason is inherently opposed to metaphysics, and that it can only exist as "the slave of the passions," Kant initiated the critique of any unilateral conception of knowledge (*Erkenntniskritik*) and paved the way for the critique of ideology (*Ideologiekritik*). No less than Marx, who would subtitle *Capital* the "critique of political economy," Kant engaged his Scottish adversary through an *immanent critique* predicated on positive aims. This was the method that Kant would contest the assumptions made by Hume and work through the logic built upon them and the problems it raise.

Kant posed the question of how empirical occurrences, or "impressions," from the objective world along with the "laws" of science could be conceived independently of a knowing subject. Once the question was asked in this way the inadequacies of philosophical skepticism became manifest along with the assumptions of traditional philosophy. The claim that perception demanded a knowing subject was the product of a logical deduction. If a knowing subject that obviously transcended any empirical individual was necessary in order to speak about the perception of reality, however, a problem emerged for the empiricist and the skeptic alike. Its existence, after all, cannot be derived from empirical observation or any form of "scientific" causality, which, according to Hume, exhausted the possibilities of "reason" and alone approximated any idea of truth. What's more, if recourse to such a subject was necessary, then an entire realm of possible experience emerged that could not be discussed from the standpoint of skepticism or empiricism.

By asking how perception is possible in the first place, Kant was led to posit a "transcendental subject" defined by a set of a priori categories that enabled perception to occur and made knowledge "possible." Such are the categories of "time and space" whose interactive function allowed them to serve as the "transcendental unity of apperception." But these categories of the "transcendental subject" were not simply mechanically imposed upon the objective world and empirical individuals. Kant claimed instead that this transcendental subject exists only in the constant act of "synthesizing" empirical data and within concrete individuals. The "transcendental subject" was seen as providing the foundation—or, better, the logical postulate—for the subjective constitution of that reality which individuals perceive. It would indeed provide the basis for Kant's "Copernican revolution" of philosophy.

Often ignored is the way in which Kant's thinking retains an *active* element from the very beginning. His willingness to highlight the practical situation of individuals forced with making choices in everyday life, in fact, brings ethics to the forefront no less than the basic value on which it rests. Freedom alone, for Kant, differentiates a subject from an object. Where freedom does not exist, which is in the "objective" realm of nature, "necessity" reigns and "scientific" reason can explore it. Insofar as freedom is not comprehensible in terms of scientific reason other than as the residue of necessity, however, then this realm of "possible" experience requires exploration through a different mode of rationality. A chasm appears between the subjective realm of *noumenal* values and the *phenomenal* realm of objective laws. Thus, Kant can be seen as the premier geographer of philosophy who discovered the boundaries beyond which any particular form of reason cannot venture.[2]

Kant was fully aware that it is impossible to prove the existence of freedom in mathematical or scientific terms. But he was also aware that the concept is a necessary postulate for any discussion of human affairs. This realm of "possible" experience must therefore call forth a variant of reason that differs qualitatively from scientific rationality; illuminating it was indeed the purpose behind Kant's *Critique of Practical Reason*. The quality of knowledge generated by this new nonscientific mode of rationality must logically differ from the "absolute" knowledge that science provides. It thereby became a question of recognizing the integrity of the two realms and navigating between them. Following Kant's lead, in fact, the critical method would confine itself to exploring the realm of social action, the social context in which scientific activity is generated and the uses to which it is put, rather than the internal criticism of scientific claims.

Long before Max Horkheimer and Theodor Adorno wrote their classic work, *Dialectic of Enlightenment*, Kant had intuited that alienation exists at the very heart of reason. Only utopia could overcome it; only aesthetic experience might contest it. But utopia is not the realm in which life is lived, and aesthetic experience ignores the requirements of judgment. Instrumental calculation cannot solve normative conflicts. Judgment demands the exercise of a "practical" form of reason. It is inherently value-laden insofar as it concerns itself with the moral basis for making choices in everyday life. Practical reason therefore retains a speculative character. It facilitates the derivation of universals, which scientific reason employs but whose existence it cannot explain. Practical reason is rational, by the same token, insofar as it provides criteria for guiding and judging the practical affairs of subjects that are not merely arbitrary in nature. Its attempt to contest purely personal interest and arbitrary prejudice no less than the "objective" strictures of science becomes manifest from the start. Nevertheless, there is a way in which speculative reason shares something in common with its scientific adversary.

Reason is universal by definition, and in this sense, according to Kant, what is true of mathematics in the *phenomenal* realm of "necessity" must hold equally true for "freedom" in the *noumenal* realm of speculative reason. Both must retain a universal referent, and either can turn dogmatic if it attempts to overstep its boundaries: when positivist or behaviorist partisans attempt to employ scientific reason for making ethical judgments, or denying the validity of normative judgments, and when practical reason and ethical judgments are used to justify scientific claims. The most telling difference between scientific and speculative, pure and practical reason, is that, in the realm of the subject, this universal requires the will to employ it. The concern for duty rather than the quest for happiness, for this reason, dominates the idealist tradition; it was precisely this substitution that thinkers of the Frankfurt School would contest in their version of critical theory. According to Kant, in any event, every subject will therefore retain an ethical moment of choice whose justification depends upon how his or her decisions correspond to a universal and ideal purpose beyond any determinations of self-interest. This is the basis for Kant's famous "categorical imperative."[3]

Elaborating this imperative in the most radical way involves positing a transcendent ideal capable of normatively regulating immediate practices. Kant could therefore speak about a "kingdom of ends" and promulgate the primary ethical principle that affirms the existence of "man as an end unto himself." Insofar as ethics projects the need for creating a plausible connection between means and ends, even if this connection cannot always be drawn in practical terms, the speculative standpoint suggests that "whoever wills the end also wills the indispensable means thereto." Thus, according to Kant, individuals *should* never be used instrumentally (or as a "means") for any purpose, while all arbitrary attempts to inhibit the exercise of reason become open to criticism.[4]

Kant was no starry-eyed optimist. He believed humanity would never fully incorporate or act upon the categorical imperative in consequent manner: the "crooked timber" of humanity can never be made straight. There is no genuine point of transition between the noumenal and the phenomenal or between "progress," which he identified with the "enlightenment" of the species, and the intellectual development of "maturity" (*Mündigkeit*) by the individual.[5] It was always a question of the individual's exercising his or her freedom in an ethical fashion, and in this respect, practical reason privileged "good will." Kant knew that only with the a priori commitment of "good will" would the person carry out in practice what had been decided upon in theory[6]—purely from a sense of what is morally right and without regard for immediate, material self-interest. Kant was also willing to draw the consequences of his position. Thus, he candidly admitted that his imperative could never be fully realized in practice any more than the notion of freedom itself.

In turn, however, this made it impossible to identify freedom with any empirical condition. The critical method, in this vein, begins with the assumption that ideas are irreducible to any particular historical form of practice and Ernst Bloch later highlighted the way in which they "jut beyond" the reality that generated them. This is applicable to the most radical of Kant's own ideas: "perpetual peace." Perhaps his emphasis on an abstract subject veiled class inequality and the contradictions within the burgeoning economic system of capitalism. His insistence on being able to say what one will, but in the last instance obey authority, was seemingly unequivocal.[7] He was also, surely, less concerned with happiness than duty. Nevertheless, his ideas forward profoundly republican and cosmopolitan commitments[8] and an assault on the feudal world in which the putatively "human" experiences of "honor" and "dignity" were preserved for the aristocracy due to their supposedly "higher" and unique faculties.

Other faculties of reason were also recognized by Kant. Just as he sought to preserve the autonomy of the natural world from metaphysical speculation, and the realm of judgment from the incursion of scientific rationality, he recognized a separate realm for the imagination and the aesthetic experience. Doing even marginal justice to the complexities of *The Critique of Judgment* is impossible in this context. But it is useful to consider the way in which Kant highlights the "reflective" character of the imagination and how, in contrast to either pure or speculative reason, aesthetic experience derives the general rule from the particular. This makes room for the subjectivity of the subject and curtails any attempt to extrapolate from purely scientific or moral insights. In the privileging of experience in the aesthetic realm, moreover, a certain commitment to pluralism makes itself felt. Precisely because Kant feared the collapse of pluralism into sheer relativism, however, even aesthetic judgments necessarily imply the existence of an external referent: form. The value-laden moment of speculative reason, which refers to a particular moral conflict that is inherently purposive, consequently intertwines with the value-free moment of pure reason that derives its law-giving function from its ability to subsume the empirical within the general. Content interweaves with form, particular with universal, subjectivity with objectivity, autonomy with necessity, experience with technique, in the "purposive purposelessness" of aesthetic experience. Just this momentary unity of opposites would later inspire the notion of a tension-filled "force-field" that, according to Theodor Adorno, was most capable of eliciting the "truth content" of an artwork and providing the best opportunity for an individual both to experience his or her subjectivity and resist the incursions of an alienated ensemble of social relations.[9]

Kant would probably not have gone quite so far. He was also aware that the aesthetic imagination did not provide a genuine "grounding" for his philosophy. He would tinker until the end with the possibility of a "fourth critique." But it all came to nothing. He immediately set the record straight and disavowed the effort. There were others in his lifetime, influenced by his work, who sought "grounding" for his thinking. And they did so in the most diverse ways. But he would have none of it: Kant ultimately remained content with introducing a critical method intent upon confronting reality with the ideals it sets for itself, contesting attempts to identify freedom with the status quo, understanding the multidimensional character of reality, exploring the manner in which the arbitrary restriction of freedom takes place, and articulating new possibilities for its expression.

Kant began with the power of the idea: "perpetual peace," which he knew could never exist in reality, provided a utopian standard of harmony with which to confront the conflicts of the present as well as the "temporary" suspension of violence. In the same vein, beyond his own personal prejudices against women, the universalist logic of his argument suggested that freedom should apply equally to "all rational beings" without recourse to products of intuition or prejudice that cannot be justified in a discourse. In an age of growing nationalism, moreover, it is important to consider Kant's commitment to a federated world order and his assault upon provincialism in his attempt to develop the idea of a "universal history with a cosmopolitan purpose." And finally, in his emphasis on the "kingdom of ends," Kant's theory logically opposes a commodity form of production that inherently turns individuals into the "means" of capital accumulation. Indeed, if there is a reason why Marx called Kant "the theorist of the French Revolution," there is also a reason why his work should serve as touchstone for any critical theory concerned with evidencing what Jürgen Habermas termed an "emancipatory interest."

Fichte, Schelling, and the Transition to Objective Idealism

The critical method was initially modest in its ambitions. It rejected the preoccupation with absolutes or the attempts to create a fixed system. Pitting the realm of freedom against the realm of necessity and refusing to give practical freedom the status of justification enjoyed by pure reason, however, proved troubling to Kant's followers. The dualism in his thinking fostered a concern with finding the ontological grounding for the transcendental ego and a system for dealing with the questions of consciousness and freedom.

J. G. Fichte was perhaps the most prominent philosopher among those who would facilitate the transition from the "subjective" idealism of Kant to the "objective" idealism of Hegel. Best known for his *Addresses to the German Nation*, his views on autarky and protosocialist planning,[10] Fichte started as an enthusiastic supporter of the Enlightenment. But his views changed following the French "reign of terror." His first major work of political theory, *Foundations of Natural Law* (1795–96), began the process of subordinating the individual to the will of the state. He ended as an anti-Semitic nationalist who, nonetheless, once retained a profound belief in freedom and its translation into action. Taking a step beyond Kant, in this vein, Fichte argued that the epistemological origin of the subject cannot be separated from the active individual moment of decision concerning the course of a person's existence. Thus, where Kant suggested that the transcendental subject participates in the series of experiences the empirical subject undergoes, the exceptionally complex and convoluted work of Fichte took a seemingly more radical and concrete position.

Fichte begins by conceiving of an absolute subject, or ego, that posits itself along with an infinite range of possibility in which it can act. This infinite range immediately presents the need for its opposite, a finite conception both of the particular ego and of the nonego as "nature." Standing beyond any a priori categories of time and space, the absolute ego is seen as inherently unfinished while underpinning the possibility of employing speculative reason and engaging in ethical activity in the first place. But the empirical ego also evidences an unfinished quality since it can conceptualize the universal and act according to its dictates. Consequently, whether for an individual or a community, the freedom of the subject can never be fully actualized since it "never is, but eternally ought to be."

There is clearly something Promethean about this "absolute ego" that serves as the precondition for any particular consciousness and its active interaction with objective reality. Kant had understood the "categories of transcendental apperception," or time and space, both as the precondition for perception and as activated only in the continuous act of perceiving. Fichte essentially sought to suggest that perception is itself a form of action and, in this vein, the transcendental ego is more than a contingent postulate: indeed, precisely because it posits itself and the world by the act of perception, it can be understood as absolute. Freedom thereby itself becomes a function of the absolute, and the striving to attain it is doomed to remain incomplete: this striving is reflected in the desire to know and the will to act on the part of any empirical subject. Thus, the words of Goethe apply perfectly to his friend Fichte: "In the beginning was the deed!"

Continuous, indeterminate, unconditioned, and free activity defines this absolute ego. Inherently opposed to all that "irrationally" constrains its free development, again, the absolute is seen as constituting those categories of apperception that Kant had more modestly understood as only the logical precondition for perception. Arguably, the old dualism emerges once again, albeit in a new way, between the purely conceptual status action with respect to the absolute ego and the actions empirical subjects undertake in historical reality. Fichte would probably respond by claiming that the absolute ego provides the foundation for the noumenal as well as the phenomenal realms or, putting it another way, subject and object. Such a response would prove inadequate insofar as the separation between the two realms is overcome through a purely metaphysical understanding of action. Nevertheless, in attempting to ground the subject in the unconditioned free act by which it posits itself and its other, Fichte's brand of idealism evinced a contradictory set of qualities that would inspire two distinct philosophical tendencies.

The first is the idealist and dialectical tendency that extends from Schelling and Hegel to the young Marx. For these thinkers not only will the subject posit both itself and its alienated world, thus the proletariat producing and reproducing the alienated set of capitalist social relations in which it functions, but the recovery of this alienated world can only occur through the conscious action of a subject with an interest in freedom. Fichte thereby offers the hidden impulse for developing what Lukács termed the "categorical imperative of revolution" no less than in the free experience of self-reflection highlighted by Adorno and predicated on the relentless resistance against the world of necessity. The second tendency, by contrast, leads over Hegel to Max Stirner, Nietzsche, Heidegger, and Sartre. Existential ontology, which was from the first opposed to the universalist ambitions of idealism, is equally indebted to Fichte both for turning critical philosophy into a system whereby the understanding of reality can be derived from a single fixed proposition, the absolute ego, and for placing primacy on the intuitive recognition of freedom. After all, by definition, freedom juts beyond those modes of speculative and scientific reason that the absolute ego originally posited through its unfettered activity. Intuition of the absolute, in short, can only occur if the individual initially chooses to engage in philosophical reflection. Or, to put it another way, the choice of philosophy still will ultimately depend upon an individual's "inclination."[11]

There is no need to belabor the obvious connection between this view of Fichte and the ruminations over the "use and abuse" of history and the "transvaluation of values" by Nietzsche, the initial "decision" to question one's existence in an "authentic" fashion by Heidegger, and the "fundamental" choice of a "project" in the thinking of Sartre. But it is important to note that Fichte did not simply interpret this "inclination" as the product of irrational intuition. There is a reflective moment involved as well the self-interest of the individual in evidencing his or her "autonomy" against any arbitrary external constraints: thus the importance of law and rights. Or, to put it another way, Fichte sees a basic connection between the individual's interest in freedom, which precedes self-reflection, and those normative claims of speculative reason that differentiate freedom from license. This is the sense in which Fichte could claim that he was indebted to Kantian philosophy not merely for his philosophical categories, but for his character—or, better, the effort to will such a character.[12] Still, the difference between their positions is palpable. Where Kant called upon the individual to make his or her choices with a purely speculative reference to the universal community, Fichte believed that the simple feeling inspiring these choices "will never be mistaken." This form of certainty was asserted rather than justified. It was the kind of dogmatism that Marx often condemned, and the need to combat it would press upon Schelling and other thinkers in the classical idealist tradition.

Various commentators have pointed to the influence of the young Schelling on Marx and the dialectical development of materialist thought.[13] In the present context, however, Friedrich Schelling's importance derives from his concerns over speculative reflection as well as from his claim that transcendental idealism demands an integrated philosophy of nature to avoid the pitfalls of an irrational theory of action.[14] Fichte was unable to provide a historical or concrete referent either for the development of humanity or the moral act that would further it. His thought stood paralyzed in the face of how intentions are turned against themselves. And so, while Fichte raised the issue of reality's constitution in action, he never provided a discussion of the mechanisms by which this occurred. Thus, where his absolute ego may have posited nature, it ultimately remained completely divorced from what it had engendered.

The alienation embodied in the dualism of Kant thereby reasserts itself. The best Fichte could do was offer a more concrete sense of resisting necessity and perhaps provide a check on the dogmatic implications of future teleological theories through his insistence upon the freedom of an experiential subject. It is impossible to derive from his work any notion of consciousness that is historically determinate with regard to real systems of production, and his actionist theory is still framed to suit an abstract individual. Indeed, Habermas was correct in noting how first Schelling and then Hegel could claim that the "spontaneity of an absolute 'I' which posits the world and itself remains abstract; they showed that nature cannot be reduced to the indeterminate material for acting subjects—lest a human world that is itself divested of qualities should shrink down to the blind point of action for action's sake."[15]

Schelling's enterprise involved the attempt to conceptualize the absolute anew and ground the human subject within reality in a new way. Insofar as the absolute is truly absolute, according to him, both consciousness and its "other" must stand in some relation to it. That is why "nature" cannot be excluded from a discussion of that freedom "which is the beginning and the end of all philosophy." Initially, Schelling binds subject and object together in the pure and transcendental unity of the absolute. As a consequence, every determinate and particular distinction between individuals and their world becomes irrelevant to this all-encompassing and infinite fount of activity. Anticipating Hegel's "dialectic,"[16] however, Schelling is still able to link humanity and nature. The "idea" of nature, if not empirical nature itself, becomes the "visible spirit" of the absolute while consciousness appears as "invisible nature." The absolute now provides a transcendental foundation for both the empirical subject and the empirical object.

The idea of nature is seen as both underpinning and unifying its discrete empirical manifestations just as the idea of humanity is seen as underpinning and unifying discrete empirical subjects. But this conscious unity between humanity and nature, which exists at the "free" level of the absolute, is nullified in historical reality by the unconscious manner in which empirical subjects employ the division of labor in dealing with "necessity." People not only transform themselves and nature through work, which harks back to Aristotle and has undoubtedly become a truism through the writings of Marx, but must make sense of that transformation. The historical achievement of that sense takes rational form. History thereby presents itself as the logical arena of inquiry for an idealist philosophy intent upon securing its "foundation" in the absolute. But Schelling did not really carry through on his own insight. Where he did follow through was the way in which the concept of the "good" with its classical roots is connected not merely with natural law but with nature as the external other of the subject.

Or, to put it another way, the idea of freedom is not merely left with the conscious subject but extends as well to the object. A new relationship, which Hegel would develop more fully, now presents itself between necessity and autonomy. Schelling recognized how any concrete interaction between subjects limits the freedom of each in relation to the external world. The human drama of history, as a striving for freedom, subsequently assumes the existence of a subject capable of responding to "necessity" by jutting beyond the particular circumstance in which individuals find themselves and exercising critical reflection with respect to a transcendent understanding of "freedom" inscribed within "practical reason."

Later in life, this critical perspective would appear inadequate to Schelling. He became concerned with formulating a "positive" philosophy of "existence" that would ultimately prove quite important to Karl Jaspers,[17] Heidegger, and other partisans of the existential tradition. This positive philosophy of the older Schelling would highlight intuition, faith, and inner experience of the world in contrast to his earlier willingness to pit freedom and reason against it. No less than for Max Horkheimer, who would emphasize the revelatory experience of the "totally other" as a fundamental element of resistance in his later work, the critical moment is lost in the late work of Schelling. His absolute no longer unfolds through "practical reason," but instead manifests itself to a particular subject and community through myths, religion, and revelation.

Even the early work of Schelling evidenced the philosophical desire to ground time and space within a transcendental absolute, however, and this resulted in an individual abstracted from history. But Schelling clearly anticipated what Marx would later call the "metabolic exchange" between man and nature no less than his theory of alienation. Insofar as "nature" can make itself intelligible to a knowing subject, Schelling breaks its identification with a set of dead empirical facts and purely "objective" laws. This view would serve as the often hidden utopian moment underpinning anthropological criticisms of the domination of nature undertaken in different ways by Max Horkheimer and Theodor Adorno and by Ernst Bloch. Schelling also offered a sense of what might now be termed an "ecosystem" and thereby provided Kant's "kingdom of ends" with not merely an existential but a material correlate. Indeed, whatever the limits of his philosophy, its critical interpretation projects a new set of intersubjective relations with nature—essentially a new set of production relations and values—that serve as the prerequisite for any genuinely emancipated society.

Hegel and History

G. W. F. Hegel marked a breakthrough in the development of the idealist tradition. But his concern was ultimately the same as that of Fichte and Schelling. He, too, sought to provide an absolute foundation for the knowing subject and overcome the dualism inherited from Kant. His innovation lay in turning this absolute into a "world spirit" capable of externalizing itself unconsciously in "space" as nature and in "time" as humanity. History would ever more surely differentiate humanity from nature through work so that Kant's "transcendental subject" would become transformed into both the source and the product of history. The absolute may remain absolute as an idea, but that idea is refracted both in the consciousness of the individual and the philosophical, artistic, and religious determinants of the particular culture in which that consciousness is exercised. Old dualisms fall by the wayside. Nothing is invisible or recedes beyond the grasp of reason. "There is nothing in the essence of an object," Hegel could write, "which does not become manifest in the series of its appearances."

Or, more boldly, freedom evidences itself in the rational unfolding of history. The metaphysical is no longer divorced from the real, the idea is no longer separate from the empirical, autonomy is no longer opposed to necessity. "Truth is concrete," writes Hegel, and thus the world spirit passes through fixed historical stages. These are marked by intense conflict and the emergence of new institutions that impels awareness of the universal notion of freedom that informed practical reason from the very beginning.[18] Teleology is introduced precisely because Hegel is aware that consciousness of freedom is a historical product insofar as it is limited by existing social conditions, and that both individuals and cultures have historically remained in the dark concerning the implications of freedom, or the teleological purpose, that the world spirit is in the process of actualizing. The inability to conceive of the most radical implications of freedom is what must be learned, and this learning, in turn, is seen as deriving from the great clashes between cultures.

Or, put another way, the world spirit winds up realizing the idea of freedom "behind the backs" of those actually involved in the real historical events. These terrible clashes are "necessary" because they serve to further the gradual awareness of freedom's universal character. But reason was aware of its goal, freedom, from the very beginning. The rational purposes and ultimate forms taken by the 'world spirit' have thus been determined a priori. But individuals limited by their historical context remain unaware of this. Consequences of group actions, which have their own immanent logic, transform individual intentions. Such is the sense in which Hegel saw the world spirit actualizing its content over time, and the "cunning of reason" destroying all *arbitrary* forms of domination. The practical purposes of reason and the goal of the world spirit will coincide in a new state under the liberal rule of law through which freedom and responsibility become reciprocally defined and in which it will become possible to speak not about the eradication of the individual but a "multiplicity in unity."

Hegel was unique insofar as he did not mechanically derive consciousness from a fixed transhistorical absolute. He employed Aristotle's notion of *potentia* for his own concept of teleology, whose form exists a priori and whose content will correspond to it with the final realization of freedom by human consciousness within an appropriate institutional setting. Just as Aristotle viewed the polis as the logical extension of the village, which itself derived from the clan and the family, Hegel saw the emergence of the modern state as engendered by civil society and the family. Where the ancient philosopher argued that "contradictions" are purely logical problems that cannot exist in reality, however, Hegel claimed that they do exist, that they emerge in the consciousness of historical epochs, and that they are open to resolution through the march of the world spirit. The *progress* of consciousness is therefore actually nothing more than humanity's awareness of what should have been evident from the beginning: freedom is the purpose of reason. Its realization is the preordained purpose of the absolute idea whose comprehension, or lack of comprehension, itself becomes manifest through philosophy, art, and religion.

As the arena in which reason most fully exercises itself, according to Hegel, freedom can best be grasped by philosophy. He considered it the purest expression of the absolute idea, and, in this vein, it only makes sense that philosophy should evidence the extent to which freedom has been historically realized. Karl Korsch and Georg Lukács, who would later employ the historical method in a critical and self-reflexive manner, endorsed the claim of Hegel that philosophy is its "epoch comprehended in thought." They also embraced the view that history is neither a serial set of discontinuous ruptures nor an expression of simple continuity. The essence of history will manifest itself through the most divergent appearances. Since all history is the ideal movement toward that goal posited by the world spirit, moreover, a new bridge is indeed created between immanence and transcendence. Whereas Kant maintained that the noumenal realm is incapable of revealing the absolute form of knowledge provided by scientific reason, according to Hegel, facts or particular events only assume meaning within the value-laden "totality," or what Marx would call the concrete "ensemble of social relations" that defines a given historical period.

Hegel can, of course, be interpreted in various ways. Many viewed his thought as retaining a fundamental unity, and some considered illusory any attempt to distinguish between his early and later writings. His more radical followers in the tradition of critical theory, however, did not see it that way. They believed that the works leading up to *The Phenomenology of Mind* (1807) essentially provided a critical perspective wherein freedom, which still remains to be actualized, contests every form that claims to have exhausted it: Hegel is seen as conceiving a world state, for example, not unlike the United States of Europe envisioned by Napoleon. Later works like *The Philosophy of History* and *The Philosophy of Right*, by contrast, suggest that speculative musings about a world state are useless, that freedom has been realized in the nation-state, and that philosophy, along with history, has come to an end.

The ability of the world spirit to take new forms, and thereby contest what increasingly appear as the arbitrary constraints of the status quo, generates a critical stance on the part of the philosopher. The normative purposes projected by the method highlight the limitations of the way in which it is used in any given circumstance.[19] Emphasizing the critical method informing the philosophy rather than the system in which it fulfills its positive purpose, however, undermines the ability to specify any philosophical foundations for justifying truth claims or any set of fixed institutional referents. If the critical method is rendered subordinate to the finished system or a state in which freedom has been actualized, by the same token, it becomes possible to ground what appear as merely historical claims and the practical political purposes of the state in philosophical terms.

The defeat of Napoleon forced Hegel to choose between identifying his philosophy with a metaphysic of freedom critical of history or a system capable of justifying his claims through the "truth" of history. Hegel chose the latter. But the tension in his thought between system and method would remain crucial for explaining the split between the "right" and the "left" Hegelians of the next generation.[20] The belief that freedom had not been realized in the bourgeois nation-state, in fact, made it possible to employ the critical method against the conclusions and systematic ambitions of Hegel himself.[21] Early proponents of the critical method did not see freedom as "vanishing" in its battle with necessity any more than they saw the particular "vanishing" in the name of the universal or the given "moment," or determinant of the whole, vanishing in the name of the totality. The young Marx could note, in this regard, how "the nocturnal moth, when the universal sun has set, seeks out the lamplight of the individual."[22]

Most proponents of critical theory were more interested in the method of Hegel than the system he ultimately produced. They were impressed by the way in which he undercut the purely "transcendental" status accorded to both the subject by Kant and the absolute by Fichte and Schelling. They admired how he indirectly bound consciousness to the economic, political, and intellectual forms defining a particular historical epoch. Neither Plato nor Aristotle could conceive of a society without slavery, Hegel could write, and all aspects of reality are historically mutable. Critical theorists also embraced his belief that there can be no history without historical memory.[23] Where they parted company was on the question of progress. Especially Adorno and Horkheimer had little sympathy for his famous statement in *The Philosophy of History:* In the Orient one man was free, in Greece some were free, and in the modern state all will be free.

Progress is progress, according to Hegel, only in the consciousness of freedom.[24] There is truth in that. But there is also truth in his insistence upon the specification of the social, economic, and political institutions in which freedom is best exercised. By emphasizing this, indeed, Hegel robbed "freedom" of its abstract and ultimately subjective character.[25] Institutions *mediate* the ways in which individuals and groups interact with each other and confront "necessity." Freedom thereby becomes not merely the teleological goal, which enables a critique of the present, but the insight into those constraints on liberty produced in a given historical situation and how they might be overcome. Freedom is predicated on the ability to identify the arbitrary constructs that inhibit consciousness of the need for change within the given "totality." Thus, the critical method of Hegel understands the "truth" of freedom as residing in the "negative," in *what is not*, or in what calls the prevailing conditions of "necessity" into question.

Speculative thought incessantly pushes freedom beyond the concrete conditions with which it is popularly identified at any given time. Its partisans therefore exhibit the "unhappy consciousness": these are the prophets unappreciated in their own times and the visionaries who anticipate a new stage of freedom. They contest the "spirit of the times" along with existing prejudices and arbitrary institutional exercises of power. The understanding of freedom is never secure; it produces conflicts of word and deed, and intervening in them, making sense of them, learning from them, is the source of progress. Real progress, once again, takes place in the mind and not in the material transformation of reality. Of principal interest, however, is the contrasting perceptions of historical reality from the perspective of those whose labor constitutes it. This is what leads Hegel to analyze history in terms of the phenomenological conflict between "master and slave." The critical moment is evident from the beginning: only the consciousness of the slave—the most "unhappy consciousness" of all—evidences the "progress" of freedom.[26]

It is here that Hegel most fully differentiates himself from others in the idealist tradition. From the start, he recognized that labor necessarily requires an interaction between one "I" and another "I" through nature. Taking a crucially important step beyond Schelling, Hegel neither set one abstract subject against another nor a single abstract subject against an undifferentiated objective reality. Instead, his argument suggests that only from the *recognition* of a conscious being does it become possible for the consciousness of another to exist. It is merely a question of the terms in which this recognition is given. Thus, Hegel's pregnant statement that language begins when the first subject says "I": such an "I," of course, presupposes another along with the context that defines the relationship between them and that must ultimately be understood as historically produced.

Work in its broadest sense now assumes primacy. The world becomes the product of human thought and the "externalization" (*Entäusserung*) of the idea of freedom insofar as every gain in self-recognition is connected with the particular form of activity in which the individual is engaged. By the same token, however, the work in which people are engaged is alienating since it ever more surely divorces them from the wholeness of nature and also from one another. Abolishing alienation (*Entfremdung*), changing the world, will depend upon the ability to invent institutions capable of realizing the universal implications of freedom. Every subject will become conscious of his or her place within an objective structure, the idea of freedom will pervade reality, and it will finally become possible to speak about the reconciliation between subject and object or what might be termed a subject-object unity.

Before that goal is achieved, however, each subject will remain uncertain about the recognition that others accord him. "Estrangement" (*Verfremdung*) defines the relation between the individual and society because this relation is to some degree institutionally "indeterminate" (*unbestimmt*). Each is therefore intent upon making the other dependent upon him or her, establishing mastery, and gaining a distinct form of recognition. A struggle necessarily ensues that, in its most radical form, initially involves a "trial by death." This struggle will establish the domination of the one who exhibits strength and courage over the other who only manifests weakness and cowardice. The "victor" achieves his "independence" and sense of self through the power that he can impose upon the "vanquished." Willing to capitulate and fearing death, by contrast, the "slave" finds himself condemned to work for his "master," obey him, and become dependent upon him. The master gains freedom from the world of toil and "necessity" within which his dependent slave is confined. This only changes when the slave becomes conscious of the way in which *in reality* the master is dependent upon his work and his obedience. A new struggle now begins to simmer whose outcome will transform the relation between self and other, produce a new stage of freedom, until more *rational* institutions are introduced in which, at the end of history, the *reciprocity* of all citizens will be assured.

Until that time, alienation will define human relations. Anticipating critical theory, Hegel would view the category as mutable, but nonetheless an anthropological reality rather than simply the specific product of a specific historical system. Identifying it with the act of "objectification" (*Vergegenständlichung*), according to Hegel, alienation would thereby define all historical relations infect all who are involved in the historical struggle, and permeates the "totality." Marx would later break this identification between alienation and objectification he would ultimately view the latter as neutral. The more loyal disciples of Hegel, in this regard, were Lukács and the most important representatives of the Frankfurt School who viewed any exercise of instrumental rationality as evidence of alienation. This is the point at which critical theory shifts from Marx to Hegel. Embracing an undifferentiated critique of the totality, and history, its most traditional representatives find themselves forced to choose between the utopian understanding of revolution and the resistance of the individual against an inherently corrupt society. The political paralysis engendered by either position is precisely what demands revision by future partisans of the critical method.

But, for all that, Hegel's dialectic of "master and slave" explodes all romantic myths about a "golden age" of harmonious community since the struggle between them has always taken place. Important is also the way in which his thinking undermines belief in the moral superiority of the victor: he may be more crafty, he may be more intelligent, and he may be more powerful than his adversary, but there is really little ethical difference between them. Neither the master nor the slave evidences any sense of moral obligation to the other: again, this must be learned and history will prove the teacher. The master justifies his position through his historical victory over the slave, while the slave originally accepts his position from fear and a cowardly refusal to call the master's bluff. After all, should the master ever kill the slave, it would ultimately prove self-defeating: such an act would annihilate the very being whom the master needs to assert his status as "master."

Ideology now assumes basic importance. It becomes the way not merely of the master justifying his position but of the slave accepting the arguments that keep him in his place. Since only the slave is engaged in practical activity and directly experiences oppression, however, he can call the prevailing ideology into question. But first the slave must realize that his freedom is not identifiable with his present alienated condition. The critique of ideology (*Ideologiekritik*) thus becomes a fundamental part of the confrontation between critical theory and what Horkheimer termed "traditional theory." The critical method is the tool by which the slave realizes his power as the producer of that particular social order from which his master alone derives real benefit. This realization by the slave ultimately produces the sense that he is living in an "inverted world" (*verkehrte Welt*). Thus, it makes sense to claim that "dialectics is the self-consciousness of the objective context of delusion; it does not mean to have escaped from that context. Its goal is to break out of the context from within."[27]

The slave gradually becomes aware that it is not he who is dependent upon his master, but his master who is dependent upon him. With this recognition, even as the master becomes ever more complacent in his status and luxury, the *self*-consciousness of the slave starts to grow along with his willingness to take risks. This is why the practical fulcrum for change lies in the consciousness of the slave. Only with this kind of critical consciousness can the slave find the fortitude to *act* and ultimately invert the "inverted world." Only then can the real relations between people be made clear, alienation abolished, and a harmony between the individual and his world brought into being through a modern state under the rule of law. Until this time when the dialectic comes to an end, however,

> what is actually happening [the technological unification of the planet] occurs not under intelligent direction, but blindly catastrophically, through wars, evolutions, and the turmoil of conflicting passions, national, social, racial. The half-hidden logic of the process has to be inferred from an accumulation of seemingly pointless disasters. Its human agents—not merely individuals but entire nations—are sacrificed to aims that they had not consciously willed. The "cunning of reason" reasserts itself. Hegel takes his revenge upon the empiricists who consigned his

teachings to the dustbin of history. Science is powerless to control the instrumentarium of death it has let loose upon the world. Statecraft sinks to the level of manipulation. Alternatively, it pursues senseless or utopian aims, then stands appalled at the result. None of this world have surprised the thinker for whom world history was a "slaughterhouse."[28]

Hegel probably understood the price of progress, "the slaughterhouse of history," better than any other thinker. And in this respect, whatever the temptation of viewing the philosophy of Hegel as the culmination of the idealist tradition, it would prove a mistake. Turning Fichte and Schelling, let alone Kant, simply into his forerunners would indulge the worst teleological excesses of Hegel. Such a stance unjustifiably settles matters concerning the enduring philosophical conflict between Kant and Hegel even as it creates blinders with regard to issues ignored by Hegel like the liberation of nature. Earlier thinkers regain their importance precisely because they did not solve the basic problems posed by the idealist tradition. They remain relevant because they resisted teleology in the name of ethics, fatalism in the name of action, and history in the name of nature. There is even a sense in which perhaps the quest for a systematic closure of the sort Hegel sought runs against the grain of the original undertaking. If that is indeed the case then critical theory must resist any form of closure, including utopia, in order to preserve its power.

Transforming the Totality

The critical method was, from the beginning, inspired by a transformative project. Abolishing alienation at the level of consciousness, which was raised by Hegel, generated the hope of abolishing it in material reality. The preoccupation with alienation in terms of consciousness can be seen as insulating it in reality. His insistence on recognizing the subject lurking behind the world of objects, however, expressed the fundamental desire of idealism that the estranged world should be transformed into a human one.[29] Thus, the young Marx could write: "only when the objective world becomes everywhere for man in society the world of man's essential powers—human reality, and for that reason, the reality of his own essential powers—can all objects become for him the objectification of himself, become objects which confirm and realize his individuality."[30]

Such would become the utopian underpinning of critical theory: its method would now speak not merely to the transformation of material circumstances but to the anthropological transformation of human sensibility, or what Lukács would call the "second nature" of human existence. Liberation would be seen as hindered no longer by some conspiracy or the natural limitations of man but instead by the actual course of history. "The idea always came to grief," Marx could note in *The Holy Family,* "insofar as it was distinct from interest." History must now be understood not merely in terms of a presupposed concern with freedom over whose ultimate character the actors in the struggle are unaware until the curtain falls or the owl of Minerva spreads its wings, but by conflicts of interest between oppressors and oppressed, or masters and slaves, that in capitalist society take the form of a struggle between the bourgeoisie and the proletariat—the class that, for Marx, is alone capable of transforming capitalist social relations because it has produced them.

If "the whole is true," according to Hegel, then freedom must manifest itself in each moment of the totality. But the existence of the proletariat, from the standpoint of the young Marx, explodes this assertion. The proletariat is seen as growing poorer even while society grows richer, more spiritually impoverished as more products are produced, because the "objective" economic imperatives of the new capitalist economy oppose the humanitarian imperatives of speculative reason. Historical progress under capitalism is now seen as creating a condition in which not the full flowering of subjectivity, but the subordination of subjectivity to the objective demands of capital, ever more surely takes place. Thus the young Marx could state that the labor of the proletarian "confronts him as another man's property and the means of his existence and his activity are increasingly concentrated in the hands of the capitalist."[31]

Alienation would flourish in what the later Marx called the "inverted world" of "commodity fetishism."[32] All these categories derive from Hegel. But they received a new twist from Marx. He no longer identified alienation with the inability of consciousness to grasp the world constituted by human activity. It would instead become "manifested not only in the result, but in the act of *production,* within the *producing activity,* itself."[33] The inverted world, would find its root in production and fetishism as well. Or, as Marx would put it in *Das Kapital:* "As in religion, man is governed by the products of his brain, so in capitalistic production, he is governed by the products of his own hand."[34] If only for this reason the abolition of private property he sought must be construed less as an end unto itself than as a means for the abolition of alienated labor. And so, while Marx may have stood Hegel on his head, Hegel on his head is still Hegel. His preoccupation with teleology, the unity of subject and object, and the "totality" as the point of reference for practice would provide the framework for the profound shift in thinking—from transforming the totality to resisting it—that would mark the use of the critical method by the most important representatives of Western Marxism and the Frankfurt School.

Lenin had already stated that "intelligent idealism is closer to intelligent materialism than stupid materialism."[35] The Western Marxists took the next step: Lukács, in particular, sought to integrate the most radical elements of idealism into historical materialism. The purpose involved articulating the "totality" of capitalist social relations from the standpoint of its potential transformation.[36] Linking theory and practice in this way, of course, demanded a transvaluation of the idealist tradition. By beginning with a hypostatized subject, an absolute ego or a metaphysical world spirit, according to Lukács, idealism "foundered on the reef" of that very totality which it claimed to comprehend. Given its fundamentally bourgeois character, idealism could not confront bourgeois reality without denying its own premises. That was why the idealist tradition, again according to Lukács, could not come to terms with a production process that turned subjects into objects through the commodity form. It was precisely the inability of metaphysics to deal with alienation and "reification" (*Verdinglichung*) that left the future realm of freedom and the "subject-object" unity hanging in the abstract.[37]

Lukács highlighted many of the themes introduced by Marx in the *Economic and Philosophic Manuscripts of 1844*, which was first discovered only in 1932,[38] even as he linked the teleological moment inherited from Hegel with a new emphasis upon action. The two were not considered mutually exclusive because this new proletarian "subject-object" of history differed from the world spirit. Its *material* position in the capitalist production process provided the proletariat with the opportunity to usher in not merely a revolution with a new economic system, a new political order, and a new ideology, but a classless society in which alienation, the reifying division of labor, and "philosophy" would be abolished. The question was how the proletariat could become aware of its revolutionary "mission,"[39] when it suffered the most from reification.

This seemed to make even more plausible the claim of Lenin that workers, if left to themselves, would only be interested in short-term economic reform: reification prevented them from both seeing what was necessary and acting on the insight. Revolutionary consciousness would therefore have to be introjected into the proletariat from the outside by a vanguard party capable of articulating those "universal" interests which transcend the differences and desires between this or that worker, this or that stratum of the class.[40] A party of professional revolutionary intellectuals, according to Lukács, would be in the best possible position to illuminate the "totality" of reified social relations from the standpoint of its transformation by the proletariat. Such a party would engage in neither reformism nor sectarianism. Serving as the "moral conscience of the proletariat," it would instead endeavor to undermine the impact of ideology and, with respect to program, "impute" a certain consciousness capable of "mediating" the immediate concerns of the working class by linking them to its ultimate mission of revolutionary change.

It is easy to set up a straw man: Lukács formulated the totality, and therefore a total response to the aristocratic and bourgeois legacies of the past that a party, ultimately totalitarian in its ambitions, would introduce with the bloodiest consequences. Such an interpretation, however, ignores the central concern of the entire enterprise: the abolition of alienation and reification. Their persistence would, obviously, undermine the legitimacy of the new regime that Lukács would support with such devotion until the end of his life.[41] In this vein, moreover, his vision of the party should be tied to the vision of workers' councils that dominated the "heroic period" (1918–21) of the Russian Revolution. During this period, for better or worse, not everyone considered communism and councilist democracy mutually exclusive. Lenin's *What Is to Be Done?* may have expressed an authoritarian conception of the centralized vanguard, but many among the left wing of the communist movement saw it as standing in direct and coherent relation with the seemingly radical democratic implications of *State and Revolution*.[42] Inspired by the revolutionary will of the communists, intoxicated with prospect of soviets springing up all over Europe, it made a certain amount of sense for Lukács to conclude that the party would inherently remain committed to fostering what Rosa Luxemburg called the "self-administrative" capacities (*Selbsttätigkeit*) of the working class.

All these themes make their appearance in Lukács's greatest work, *History and Class Consciousness*. It transforms Marxism from a "science" with fixed "laws" into a critical method or, in keeping with the older Hegel, as a "science of consciousness." Marxism turns into a critique of the "totality" and the manner in which social relations—including those of the proletariat— are produced and reproduced. Emphasizing the moment of "class consciousness" in the very constitution of "class" also calls into question not only any interpretation linking Marxism with empiricism or positivism but any attempt to view the proletariat as a prefabricated "objective" entity in the manner of traditional political economy. The work's analysis of reification highlights the increasing dominance of "instrumental" rationality and its subsequent impact on class solidarity and the ability to envision a qualitative alternative.

History and Class Consciousness was blind to the possibility that the vanguard party could evidence its own bureaucratic ambitions and that it might assert *its* interests over and against those of the class, or classes, it claimed to represent. From a postcommunist vantage point, however, the work should be condemned less for its willingness to compromise with what has become an anachronistic set of political commitments than for its stubborn insistence upon transforming the revolution into an assault upon the anthropological residues of oppression and exploitation deriving from the division of labor. The proletariat was changed from a subaltern class striving for economic justice, republicanism, and internationalism into a messianic "subject-object" of history intent upon abolishing economic imperatives, any indirect form of political representation, and any strategy other than world revolution. It now became a matter of bringing the "new man" into existence. This was an old dream with religious roots carried on by secular revolutionaries imbued with a materialist ideology. The utopian temptation was in the air in the immediate aftermath of 1917, and it was embraced not merely by maverick visionaries like Ernst Bloch in *Spirit of Utopia* (1923) but by a host of others including Trotsky who closed his *Literature and Revolution* (1924) with words stating that under communism: "Man will become immeasurably stronger, wiser, and subtler; his body will become more harmonized, his movements more rhythmic, his voice more musical. The forms of life will become dynamically dramatic. The average human type will rise to the heights of an Aristotle, a Goethe, or a Marx. And above this ridge new peaks will rise."[43]

Alienation, Subjectivity, and Resistance

Critical Marxists identified the revolution with freedom, and, no less than Hegel, they opened themselves to criticism by the very method they espoused. But it was different than in times past. Propagandists found it ever more difficult to put the genie back into the bottle. Since reification now marked every moment of both the communist and capitalist totality, and any compromise with the world of alienated social relations would taint the prospect of liberation, radicalism became an existential matter of either/or: it would have to manifest itself either as a "great refusal," using the phrase made popular by Herbert Marcuse, or nothing. The critical method had locked itself into the totality as its point of reference, and with the diminishing prospect of transforming it, a new concern with resisting it took shape.

Other idealist movements had surfaced around the turn of the twentieth century that had little to do with Marxism. But the dominant figure was less Kant, or Hegel, than Nietzsche. Concerned with the subjectivity of the subject rather than a world spirit or class, opposed to teleology and usually indifferent to institutions, these new brands of idealism were infused with a vitalist and protoexistentialist content. This becomes particularly apparent in respect to the *Lebensphilosophie* of Wilhelm Dilthey and Georg Simmel no less than the various forms of neo-Kantianism underpinning certain avant-garde movements like expressionism.[44] Martin Heidegger explicitly sought to explode the idealist tradition by denying the categories of subject and object in favor of his celebrated notion of *Dasein*,[45] whatever its affinities with the absolute of Fichte, and he turned Hegel upside down—far more radically than Marx—by placing primacy upon intuition over reflection and historicity over history in his assault upon teleology in the name of his own phenomenological ontology.[46] A new concern with the experiential unfolding of ideas like liberty, or the persistence of historical patterns, also connected this vitalism with the "neo-Hegelianism" of Benedetto Croce and the gloomy, apocalyptic, and protofascist vision of Oswald Spengler and his followers. It is true: exceptions should be made for the Kantian circle around Ernst Cassirer and the remarkable group of Kantian-Marxist intellectuals who constituted the "Austro-Marxist" group of the Second International. Nevertheless, the most progressive political elements of idealism were emasculated in most of these new tendencies.

As the years passed, communist and fascist totalitarianism, the Second World War and the integration of the Western working class into the postwar situation, and the growing power of bureaucracy and instrumental reason over society made it seem that the implications of reification had not yet been fully elaborated. The very existence of individuality seemed threatened by a bureaucratic society intoxicated with mass culture. The old imperatives of ethics and solidarity rang hollow in a world that had perversely appropriated the most universal concepts to justify oppression. "Science" was expelling all metaphysical and critical concerns from "rational" discourse and seemingly strengthening a "one-dimensional" society intent upon integrating all opposition.[47] Increasingly, for those thinkers associated with the Frankfurt School, it became a matter of preserving the subjectivity of the subject beyond any concern with institutions or movements. This new appreciation for what might be termed a *metaphysics of resistance* was perhaps best articulated by Theodor Adorno when he stated that "philosophy, which once seemed obsolete, lives on because the moment to realize it was missed."[48]

Critical theory changed in its approach and its purpose: a shift would ultimately take place from emphasizing the transformation of the totality to resisting its impact. No longer was it possible to identify history with the growth of freedom, let alone the happiness of the individual or the harmony produced by some metaphysical "subject-object" identity. Quite the contrary. History would now be seen as denoting the realm of unfreedom, the constant subjugation of the subject, and the triumph of "necessity" or instrumental rationality over all metaphysical and utopian concerns. Horkheimer and Adorno considered Kant's belief in the development of humanity's intellectual and inner "maturity" to have proved illusory. But Hegel's vision appeared even worse. Its teleology seemed to justify every sacrifice, and the belief that history moved forward through a constant "negation of the negation" left the individual without any existential moorings. Marx, too, had little concern for the individual amid the march of history. He, too, identified the subject with the working class and understood history in the same dialectical framework as Hegel: the "negation of the negation" would, also for him, mark a positive step in the extension of freedom and project a teleological harmony in which individuals would be reconciled with their world in a "subject-object" identity.

As far as Horkheimer and Adorno were concerned, however, such a "negation of the negation" threw the individual back into the clutches of necessity even as it inherently affirmed an untenable teleological position. In keeping with Schopenhauer and Nietzsche, who highlighted the singular moment of joy and the existential threats posed by mass society, they rejected any attempt to subsume the individual subject under any abstract or historical category. As soon as the individual identified with the given order, from the perspective of Adorno, real freedom was irretrievably lost. It became a matter of maintaining the tension between them. The "positive" moment of historical progress within the "negation of the negation" was no less illusory than the idea of a "subject-object" unity.

There is no "negation of the negation." According to Adorno, who developed the argument most cogently, there is only the "negative" response by the individual to what is "positive": the course of history and the exigencies of "necessity." Such is the real meaning behind the title of *Negative Dialectics*. Its standpoint insists upon restoring the tension between the individual and society or what might be termed the "nonidentity" between subject and object. In this sense, while the critique of alienation and the inverted world is inherited from Hegel and Marx, the work of Adorno remains the most uncompromising defense of subjectivity in a world threatening to engulf it.[49] It serves as a defense of the intellect against the spurious freedom offered by the culture industry. It refuses to consider freedom in terms of anything other than the unique and reflective experience of subjectivity.

Since this kind of freedom eludes all forms of objectification, however, it undermines the prospect of solidarity. Insofar as the whole is false, moreover, it subverts the possibility of distinguishing between movements and institutions capable of fostering and others intent on inhibiting its exercise. The contempt for conformism and the manifold assault upon the hidden violence of advanced industrial society exhibited by Adorno and Horkheimer ironically influenced a student movement with which they ultimately could not come to terms. Just as the critique of alienation by Lukács reflected the "heroic period" of the Russian Revolution, their mature thought was basically the product of a reality defined by Auschwitz, the Gulag, and Hiroshima. Where Lukács identified liberation with an industrial proletariat guided by a vanguard, agents increasingly anachronistic for the new period of globalization, Horkheimer and Adorno extrapolated the extermination of subjectivity by totalitarian regimes into the overriding logic of advanced industrial society. Thus, no less than others in the idealist tradition willing to deal with history, these thinkers also ultimately equated the experience of an epoch with the final product of history itself.

Critique and the Renewal of Critical Theory

Critical theory stands in danger of becoming defined by what it opposes. Its critique of modernity increasingly appears one-sided and, therefore, abstract. Modernity has not only inhibited the possibilities for individual experience or repressed the subjectivity of the subject. The postmodern rejection of objectivity, narrative, and universality in the name of play, diversity, and subjectivity simply reinforces the ideology of an advanced industrial society quite willing to offer random and infantile moments of enjoyment. The moment of action and engagement, so prized by Fichte, drops out. Indeed, while most decry the sophistries and the sacrifices generated by teleological thinking, it remains difficult for even more to deal with a philosophical situation in which guarantees for the success of progressive politics are lacking.

The "stage theory" and the "escalator" view of human development lie in the dustbin of history.[50] But this does not invalidate the idealist legacy. It simply means that the vision of a liberated future has become nothing more than a gamble predicated, in keeping with Kant, upon a set of ethically inspired decisions. Under such circumstances, rather than reject the idea of progress, it might well be time for critical theory to begin thinking about how to specify its indicators and preconditions in new normative terms capable of highlighting the extent to which the exercise of freedom has been expanded.[51] In the same vein, while the working class can no longer be seen as a preconstituted agent of change, critical theory should begin contesting the fragmentation of identities among many of the new social movements with speculative notions of solidarity. Nevertheless, this requires highlighting the transformative character of the critical project and what Jürgen Habermas termed the "emancipatory interest" it should explicitly forward.

Basically the difference between the critical method and the method of the social sciences comes down to the putative relation, or lack of it, between "fact" and "value." From the standpoint of the former, this initially involves differentiating between an empirical fact as such and that fact within the context where it assumes *meaning*. Critical theory must surely continue to expose the manner in which facts are isolated rather than seen as crystallized products of social action. It should explore the way in which any given empirical analysis contributes to a political project intent upon transforming the existing order in terms of the libertarian and egalitarian principles of what Erich Fromm termed "socialist humanism." Nevertheless, it must also reassert the philosophical modesty of Kant and reconsider what has often turned into an unqualified assault upon instrumental reason by its supporters.

Empirical inquiry calls for holding in abeyance or "bracketing" (Husserl) the ensemble of social relations in need of normative judgment. This has legitimacy under certain circumstances. It does not, however, when the self-interest of the investigator becomes interwoven with the analysis. This is the crucial point of departure. The exercise of judgment is viable only in specifying the introjection of self-interest and the implications of the inquiry for the context in which it is undertaken. Kant was correct in insisting that the neutral and inherently reductive criteria of social scientific inquiry cannot apply in the attempt to provide a fact with meaning. But he was also correct in maintaining that instrumental reason has its own logic, its usefulness, and its methodological integrity. Lukács liked to quote Vico's phrase: "the difference between history and nature is that man has created the one and not the other."

Recognizing this difference was an intrinsic element of early critical theory, but it has been forgotten amid concern over the domination of nature and the rise of a new postmodern vocabulary. In this regard, for modern critical theory, the crucial figure again is Nietzsche for whom the "will to power" exists in the realms of both history and nature. Differentiating between them, from his standpoint, is nothing more than an arbitrary procedure. Either interests exist in even the purest method, or that method is blind to them. Knowledge is power, and power is domination. Nietzsche justifies the sociology of knowledge, obliterates universals and neutrality, and assaults any stance intent upon judging interests against one another.

But it is surely one thing to explain the sociological context in which the thinking of Einstein originated and quite another to reduce its value to that context, thereby ignoring any immanent confrontation with the logic informing his accomplishments and their explanatory value.[52] The expertise produced by the division of labor does not disappear because a given theory is averse to some of its applications. Categories used in understanding nature may, of course, be contingent in their truth value and in the range of phenomena they explain. But they are contingent in a way very different from historical categories, and the method applied to them must recognize this difference. Thus, in my opinion, partisans of critical theory were mistaken in simply rejecting the neopositivist idea of "falsifiability" introduced by Sir Karl Popper.[53] Its willingness to highlight the provisional character of scientific truth without abandoning the idea of scientific truth altogether is surely in keeping with the critical method.

Critics of instrumental rationality attack the wrong enemy. It can obviously be employed to eradicate subjectivity and ensure conformity. But that is not necessarily the case: an argument can also be made that the self-critical quality of scientific investigation contributes to the dispelling of prejudice and democratic practice. Under contemporary forms of Western capitalist democracy, moreover, it is simply untenable to maintain that instrumental rationality has either eliminated subjectivity or bred a gray conformity reminiscent of Orwell's *1984*, or Kafka's universe. The range of choices among products, styles, fashions, and ideas broadens as purchasing power increases. In this sense, the practical exercise of subjectivity broadens as well, and it is foolish to maintain that everything is a variant of the same. Such a stance leaves the left in a state of paralysis. If it seeks to constrict consumerism, then is it authoritarian; if it doesn't, then it has caved in to the culture industry. If the left forwards liberal criteria for constraining the exercise of arbitrary power, then it is accepting the world of alienation. Of course, if it doesn't, then yet another testimony to its impotence has been rendered.

Too often, a fundamental confusion has entered the critical discourse. Instrumental rationality does not threaten subjectivity, or existential experience, but the normative moment of decision making and a form of thinking that attempts to provide politics with a sense of political purpose.[54] Those who supposedly stand in the enemy camps of empiricism and positivism do not seek the abolition of passion, sensibility, and subjectivity. Such a claim simply reduces an entire tradition to the most moribund form of behaviorism. The best partisans of scientific rationality merely maintain that while "metaphysical" opinion has its place, it has no bearing on truth claims. The moral relativism generated by a genuinely instrumental rationality can, in this way, even be seen as reinforcing subjectivism. Preoccupation with the "subjectivity of the subject" thus becomes a misplaced response, a form of what Thomas Mann initially termed "power-protected inwardness," to the hegemonic mode of rationality in particular and advanced industrial society in general.

Critical theory must move back from what Goethe called "the small world" of the self into the "great world" outside. Creating the framework for a discourse concerning what is falsifiable is itself a political project. There is no need for a "great refusal" in the abstract, but a concrete refusal of all attempts to impose opinion, justify tradition because it exists, and bow before the notion that might makes right. Resistance is not an end unto itself and the purposes it should serve, such as contesting the arbitrary exercise of power, can no longer be derived from metaphysical postulates or teleological imperatives. We live in a postmetaphysical world and, in my view, it is unnecessary to indulge in discourse ethics to recognize that the extent to which acceptance of the universals underpinning the liberal rule of law and the socialist commitment to economic justice has occurred is the extent to which the exercise of arbitrary power, and ultimately terror, by the state and social institutions has been constrained. Or, to put it another way, it is less a question of validating the claims of idealist philosophy in purely philosophical terms than of thinking about them consequentially in terms of the ideological preconditions required by a genuinely progressive politics.

Better to work from the assumption that history proceeds irrationally insofar as the development of humanity's productive forces has not been commensurate with the growth of conscious control over them.[55] The real should not be considered rational, and the rational should not be considered real. It makes little sense invoking the existence of a metaphysical essence behind history or some faith that the "laws" of history will work themselves out in the end. Partisans of the critical method should instead draw the most radical implications from the claim that the history of humanity is the history of its production.[56] In keeping with the idealist tradition, however, such a claim must include a willingness to engage issues concerning the *comprehension* of that production and the ability to redirect it. Thus, the importance of making interests and principles explicit and specifying both the institutional referents required for the realization of progressive ideals and the material structures that hinder their realization.

Such an enterprise calls upon the partisans of critical theory to cease living in the night wherein all cats are gray. They must speak more *politically* about the state, civil society, and the culture industry. By this I mean that critical theorists must begin to indicate the possibilities for progressive intervention as well as the structures of constraint, the uses as well as abuses of bureaucracy, the importance of positive proposals for constraining the exercise of arbitrary power rather than the usual critique of the whole. And, in the same way, critical theory should not simply forsake the question of agency or indulge in a celebration of difference that, too often, undermines solidarity. It must instead strive to highlight—through notions like the "class ideal"[57]—the common political interests of working people in all of the new social movements, without privileging any, if solidarity is to become concrete.

Renewing critical theory means renewing its commitment to those whom Ernst Bloch liked to call "the lowly and the insulted." But this requires overcoming the self-indulgent notion that affirming one's subjectivity against the "totally administered society" is somehow the best and most authentic form of resistance. It means developing categories capable of informing the purposes of political action, and making critical judgments about legislative issues, movements, and political events. The tension between the universal and the particular, the whole and its parts, is ineradicable other than by repressive means. The pursuit of a unity between subject and object was indeed illusory from the start. There will always be conflict both within the organizations of the disadvantaged no less than between the disadvantaged and the hegemonic elites. New developments in critical theory must illuminate these tensions no less than the changing institutional and ideological preconditions that might further the exercise of freedom. In this sense, then, the future of the critical method rests on the belief that *la lutta continua,* or "the struggle continues."

$$\mathcal{C} \sim 3 \sim \mathcal{D}$$

Karl Korsch

Western Marxism
and the Origins of Critical Theory

Western Marxism" is usually associated with Antonio Gramsci, or Georg Lukács, or sometimes even Ernst Bloch. Karl Korsch is often forgotten. Perhaps that is because his writings were not as suggestive as those of Gramsci, as prolific and wide-ranging as those of Lukács, or as daring as those of Bloch.[1] But like them Korsch viewed Marxism as a theory of praxis, emphasized the importance of Hegel, attacked economism, and placed decisive emphasis on the role of consciousness. There is also something far more concrete about his approach. Indeed, when Korsch died following a long illness in 1961 at the age of seventy-two,[2] he left behind a cogent and self-critical perspective on Marxism informed by a radical notion of proletarian democracy.

Korsch never saw materialism and idealism as antinomial or mutually exclusive. Emphasis on the one over the other may have shifted during his career. Just as the focus on consciousness retained an empirical link with political history in the early work, however, his later and more "positivist" writings were informed by a normative commitment to the empowerment of workers. Anticipating the problems of verification and grounding normative claims, which would arise once the validity of the method became divorced from the truth or falsity of the conclusions reached,[3] Korsch always sought to retain a referent in political practice for his theoretical claims. He was also unwilling to rigidly juxtapose the dialectical "method" of Marxism against its "scientific" character. Korsch often ignored the tensions between them and never systematically articulated the connection between social scientific inquiry and the approach of the natural sciences.[4] The entire thrust of his undertaking, however, suggests that the Marxian "science" retains a critical element. Thus, putting the matter somewhat provocatively, it is possible to consider his interpretation of Marxism as a science of class consciousness.[5]

Korsch's radicalism developed gradually and consistently. An early mem' of the free student movement, he studied philosophy and received his law degree from the University of Jena in 1910. Then, in 1912, he went to England and encountered the Fabian Society. While skeptical of its bureaucratic and reformist politics, he was nonetheless influenced by its antimetaphysical and practical conception of socialism. The Fabians also rejected the fatalistic determinism of orthodox Marxism, and given his early encounter with German idealism, it makes sense that Korsch should have developed an emphasis on consciousness and other subjective factors with respect to the working-class struggle. Such concerns were only reinforced by the Kantian socialist perspective of Kurt Eisner who became close to Korsch when the young man formally entered the German Social Democratic Party (SPD).

But, the political development of Korsch was radically affected by World War I during which he served as a military officer before his antinationalist views led to a reduction in rank. Disillusioned by the opportunism of the SPD, both during the war and in its immediate aftermath, he joined the dissident, pacifist, and revolutionary Independent Social Democratic Party of Germany (USPD), and he stayed with the left wing of that organization when it split to help form the German Communist Party (KPD) in 1919. Rising quickly through the ranks,[6] Korsch became the editor of the party's theoretical journal *Die Internationale*. Then, in 1923, *Marxism and Philosophy* appeared and he became minister of justice in the revolutionary council that briefly controlled the German province of Thuringia.

An "ultraleft" aura was thus cast over the first outspokenly Marxist professor in Germany. But it was probably less his philosophical heresies than the failure of this disorganized uprising and the shifting of political winds in Moscow that led to his condemnation by Gregorii Zinoviev in his famous "professor's speech" at the Fifth Congress of the Comintern in 1924.[7] The complexion of the Comintern changed in that year, and soon enough, the "bolshevization" of the KPD took place under the leadership of Ruth Fischer and Arkadij Maslow.[8] In the process, Korsch became one of the party's most berated figures and the victim of a smear campaign that resulted in his expulsion in 1926. Only then would his "ultraleft" bolshevism begin evolving into anarcho-syndicalism.

This evolution grew more pronounced as the SPD and the KPD gained an ever stronger monopoly on the organizational apparatus of the left, and in the years following his expulsion, Korsch's influence was basically confined to left-wing intellectuals, representatives of the council movement like the philosopher Anton Pannekoek or Rosa Luxemburg's old friend Henriette Roland-Holst, along with a few sectarian ex-communists like Amadeo Bordiga and Lucien Laurat, the editor of *La Révolution Prolétarienne*.[9] Korsch had his own study group, which included important ex-communists like Manabandra Roy, social revolutionaries like Isaac Steinberg, the onetime minister of justice in Lenin's government of 1918, artists like Bertolt Brecht and Alfred Döblin, as well as a number of younger members like Erich Gerlach, Heinz Langerhans, and Henry Pachter.[10] Still, Korsch tried to expand his contacts with workers and workers' movements. He maintained his friendship with Richard Müller, former president of the syndicalist German metal workers' union, and rendered what support he could to the International Workers of the World in the United States and the Spanish anarchists following his exile from Germany.[11]

It was already before the appearance of *Marxism and Philosophy*, which was published in a series edited by Carl Grünberg, that Korsch came into contact with Felix Weil. Grünberg would serve as the first director of the Institute for Social Research while Weil financed it. In 1921, Korsch published the latter's study of socialization in his own series, *Practical Socialism*, which was modeled after the educational undertakings of the Fabians. His own important contribution, "What Is Socialization?", also appeared in this series. Afterward, along with Weil, Korsch served as the guiding force behind the first Marxist Work Week, which brought together Lukács along with Karl August Wittfogel, Friedrich Pollock, Horkheimer, Paul Massing, Julian Gomperz, and others who would assume importance for the development of the institute and critical theory.[12]

But Korsch himself would play only a minimal role in what became the Frankfurt School. His unrelenting concern with the proletariat, his contempt for metaphysics, and his insistence upon maintaining a connection between theory and practice placed him at odds with those who were content to "work but little, and talk a lot."[13] Korsch exerted his influence as an independent Marxist and, perhaps for this reason, his own perspective has often been virtually reduced to his notion of "revolutionary historicism."[14] His theory is, according to this interpretation, content with judging the value of a given theory or practice solely with respect to its immediate relevance for the class struggle. Such is the reason usually given for Korsch's attraction to Leninism and, in this respect, the crucial issue is correctly seen less in the abstract "theoretical" superiority of Leninism than in how it expressed the most radical revolutionary possibilities of the working class in the wake of World War I. The activist moment and the normative purpose of Korsch's thinking makes it somewhat of an exaggeration to link it with the historical positivism of an academic like Leopold Ranke.[15] Nevertheless, the historicist perspective clearly informs all of Korsch's work, including his classic *Marxism and Philosophy*.

Philosophy is not seen as an autonomous realm of intellectual endeavor. Korsch instead understands it as a "moment" within the existing "totality" of social relations that is uniquely capable of "comprehend[ing] its epoch in thought." The roots of the idea derive from Hegel, but Marx employed it in critically analyzing the theory and practice of the bourgeoisie. Still Korsch was the first to self-consciously use "the principle of historical specification" in critically evaluating the theory and practice of the working class.[16] His aim was to analyze its historical practice in terms of its own self-understanding, and this, in turn, meant applying "the materialist method of history to the materialist method of history itself,"[17] Thus, Korsch formulated a critique of Marxism from within the theoretical construct of Marxism itself.

According to his analysis, there are both progressive and decadent periods in the history of a class that are reflected in the particular modes of thought they engender.[18] The philosophy of a class on the rise will justify its activities by articulating transcendent aims, while in a decadent period, when a class has already established itself, these goals will contract as existing contradictions become frozen and projected into the future.[19] The future thereby appears as nothing more than a mechanical elaboration of the present.[20] All this becomes particularly evident in the fate of Hegelian philosophy. Korsch, no less than Gramsci and Lukács,[21] in this vein, believed that the goals of the revolutionary bourgeoisie attained their most explicit articulation in the speculative philosophy of the young Hegel. Through Hegel's projection of freedom beyond the existent, and the inherently "critical" character of his thought, he was seen as making "self-conscious" the most radical possibilities and contradictions of his own class. Its political irrelevance during the latter half of the nineteenth century, however, is reflected in the attack on historical thought by abstract metaphysicians and triumphant positivists. Korsch views the situation with Marxism as essentially no different. It too, as Engels recognized, was the product of a class at a given stage of historical development; it too would experience the introduction of "dialectical" laws along with positivist forms of economic reductionism precisely when the actual, historical possibilities for revolution had begun to dim.

Korsch saw Marxism as falling into three relatively distinct phases and the theory as defined by particular forms of practice.[22] During the first period, from 1843 to 1848, Marx was still in the process of giving his thinking critical shape, which, in turn, reflected the conditions of a proletariat constituting itself in social and political terms. The Marxism of this period, with its decisively Hegelian influence, is subsequently seen as projecting a set of radical goals capable of informing revolutionary practice. That, however, was far less the case with the second phase, which extended from the failure of the Revolutions of 1848 to the close of the century. Marx and Engels's concern with developing a revolutionary form of "scientific socialism" is seen as setting the stage for the positivist interpretation of their work by Karl Kautsky and the foremost thinkers of social democracy. These orthodox Marxists in the social democratic movement are seen as having created a split between the revolutionary implications of the original theory and the reformist practice of their movement. The third phase would consequently result in trade unionists'

rejecting the orthodox theory of social democracy while embracing its practice, and Bolsheviks maintaining—in Korsch's view—a too strict commitment
to the "scientific" character of the theory while attempting to formulate a new
practice.[23] Indeed, this analysis led Korsch to claim that during the "long
period when Marxism was slowly spreading throughout Europe it had in fact
no longer any practical revolutionary task to accomplish."[24]

Korsch's emphasis upon the historical reflexivity of any genuinely radical
approach anticipates what would define the difference between "traditional"
and "critical" theory in Max Horkheimer's famous essay of the same name.
But the transcendent element within Korsch's thinking, his vision of workers'
councils as an alternative order,[25] derives from a misunderstanding of the
Russian Revolution common among many of his radical humanist and anarchist contemporaries in the Weimar Republic. Nineteen-seventeen was judged
by them less in terms of the actually existing dictatorship than the slogan of
"all power to the soviets" employed by Lenin and the ideas of proletarian
democracy articulated in his *The State and Revolution*.[26]

Soviets or councils arose throughout much of Europe in the aftermath of
World War I. They seemed the new alternative organizational form, capable of
overcoming "alienation" by fusing political with judicial and economic decision making. A commitment to proletarian empowerment through this institutional arrangement informed Korsch's later criticisms of the communist
movement, which brought about comment from Stalin in 1926, no less than
his periodic calls for the revolutionary "restoration" of Leninism during the
dark days of the "counter-revolution" from above.[27] Even during the "heroic"
phase of the Bolshevik Revolution, however, the soviets never ruled Russia or
anywhere else for an extended period of time. Korsch's critique of Bolshevism,
ironically, stemmed less from actual historical practice than from his dogmatic affirmation of a transcendent idea. For all his talk about connecting theory and practice, as Korsch's sectarianism evolved, the rift between them
became ever more pronounced in his thought. He was not among those original denizens of the "orthodox" social democratic movement like Rosa Luxemburg, Karl Kautsky, and Léon Blum who provided an early and prophetic
analysis of the revolution. His historical understanding, in fact, militates
against his own convictions: perhaps it was the lack of a realizable organizational alternative following the revolutionary thermidor of 1923, combined
with the growing authoritarianism of the communist movement, which
explains why the majority of the European working class should have
returned to the social democratic movement, or what Léon Blum called the
"old house," from which it might at least derive some practical benefit.

But Korsch himself did not return, not even when he was expelled from the
communist movement. He continued to view social democracy as an atavistic
relic rather than as the only available left alternative to the new authoritarian-

ism. Proletarian "self-administration" (*SelbsttUatigkeit*) was a concept for which its partisans seemingly had as little use as the communists. Excluding a few mavericks like Rosa Luxemburg, in fact, social democrats never had much to say about transforming the production process, introducing new values of solidarity, extending the limits of a purely formal set of bourgeois democratic freedoms, curbing bureaucracy, overcoming a stultifying division of labor, creating new forms for empowering workers, or confronting the instrumental logic of capitalist accumulation which turned them into mere "factors of production." In short, according to Korsch, social democracy lacked a radical perspective on freedom with which to confront either capitalist or communist forms of exploitation. And that was that. Thus, he remained on the outside looking in.

Korsch's commitment to an institutional system of councils continued long after the actual historical possibility for their establishment had passed. The question remains: What justified the retention of that commitment? The belief in a looming crisis? Perhaps. But Korsch always maintained that if surrendering all belief in economic crisis turns the quest for socialism into a purely moral demand, theories postulating an "iron logic" for capitalism's demise are pseudoscientific.[28] Opposed to both the exaggerated faith in crisis theory exhibited by orthodoxy and the optimistic assumptions of reformism, Korsch asserted the need for revolutionary preparation without reference to the political form through which this should occur. And, as a consequence, his transcendent commitment to preparing for a *future crisis* had nothing to do with the *actual crises* in which the working class found itself enmeshed. It chose sides in the Popular Front, the Second World War, and the cold war. But all this seemed essentially irrelevant to Korsch; only the Spanish Civil War—and for good reason—captured his imagination.[29] Thus, he was ultimately left with nothing more than the correct theoretical claim that a "crisis"—as against (say) a mere "recession"—demands the subjective response that will recognize it as such.

"Revolutionary historicism" is useless in understanding any of this. A different perspective is necessary, capable of confronting the fashionable assumption that a historical perspective is somehow inherently critical. It is actually the other way around: not every historical perspective is critical but every genuinely critical perspective is historical.[30] History opposed Korsch's vision, and, ultimately, he was forced to choose between the ideal and the real. And his choice in practice contradicts the dominant interpretations of his theory. Indeed, it was not the historical understanding of reality that would immanently produce his commitment to a particular set of radical ideals; it was rather the transcendent commitment to an unrealized idea of freedom that, for better or worse, informed his historical understanding of reality.

*   *   *

And reality took its revenge. As the idea of soviets became ever more abstract, Korsch's disillusionment grew. Some critics have suggested that this led him to totally abandon Marxism in his later years.[31] At the time of his death, in fact, Korsch was working on a biography of Bakunin; he no longer had much faith in the teleology of Marxism or the attempts to link theory and practice through some particular organizational form of working-class politics.[32] Anticipating the thinking of critical theorists in the 1930s, no less than the radical students of 1968, he was consistent in arguing that the "totality" needed transformation with an eye on proletarian empowerment. The revolutionary perspective from which he sought to confront the degeneration of the proletarian movement never changed. But Korsch was always unconcerned with attempts at "dogmatic calculation [regarding] how the different versions of Marxist theory correspond to some abstract canon of 'pure and unfalsified' theory."[33] Such orthodoxy was, for him, inimical to any commitment to critical and historical thinking.[34] Thus, it is as meaningless to argue that Korsch abandoned Marxism as to argue that Marx abandoned Hegel.

Korsch's criticism was always undertaken from within the dialectical method. Nor did he ever consider Marxism as a set of "iron laws." And the reason is simple. According to him, from such a standpoint, it can never comprehend the society it wishes to transform.[35] Fixated at the level of appearances, unable to view its own assumptions and categories as historically contingent,[36] Marxism turns into a finished system.[37] Economic reductionism necessarily results when the unfolding of "objective" contradictions assumes primacy. The "ensemble of social relations" (Marx) disappears along with the ability to deal with the ideological and practical manner through which a class constitutes itself as such.[38] "Scientific Marxism" consequently cannot serve as a theory of revolution precisely because it neglects the political moment of action. Even while viewing itself as a hardheaded analysis of reality, according to Korsch, "economic determinism" and "vulgar materialism" lose the connection with practice that, for him, makes Marxism unique.[39] He insisted instead that the decisive element within Marxism lay in its ability to recognize that all ideological, political, and economic phenomena were products of specific social relations. Everything had to be seen as a historical product open to critical scrutiny and transformation. Such was the perspective from which the reassertion of control by rational "subjects" over a historical "object" like capital, whose dynamics seemed to possess a life of their own, might take place. Indeed, it was from this perspective that Korsch developed his critique of "alienation" and the "inverted world" of bourgeois society.[40]

Marxism becomes what Gramsci called "a philosophy of praxis" whose vision of revolution and proletarian empowerment is continuously changing.

The transcendent idea of revolution prevents Korsch's historicism from becoming a thoroughgoing relativism even while his commitment to an inherently unfinished notion of proletarian empowerment opens any existing political arrangement to critique.[41] His emphasis on the concept of "concreteness" (*Diesseitigkeit*), in the same vein, led him to reject all ideological justifications for oppression.[42] Just as materialism originally emerged from the critique of religion, for Korsch, so must the critique of capitalist (and even "socialist") ideologies occur through the demystification of production relations.[43] And, at all costs, that criticism demands the commitment to a concrete alternative: workers' councils.[44]

Arguing then that Korsch is engaged in a mechanistic "reduction" of theory to the class struggle, which leads "to the absence of a real critique of ideology," misses the point of his entire undertaking.[45] Exposing how Marxism was employed to veil an oppressive status quo and elaborating a critical historical method, immanently capable of questioning those uses to which it was being put, were the fundamental concerns with which Korsch was intellectually engaged. Nor did he ever view ideology as simply floating about in the superstructure as some reflex of an "objectively" constituted class struggle. Ideology was rather seen by him as a moment of the struggle itself. Thus, anticipating the thinkers of the Frankfurt School, Korsch maintained that it is incumbent upon "modern dialectical materialism to grasp philosophies and other ideological systems in theory as realities and to treat them as such in praxis."[46]

That rubbed against the grain of Marxist orthodoxy, whose thinkers saw the "truth"of reality emanating from the calculable activities of the economic "base" that causally determines the "superstructure" of state activity and the given historical forms of ideological expression.[47] They might admit that political conflict also evidences a moment of "objective" truth insofar as it is directly interwoven with discernible and calculable economic interests. Ideology, however, is nothing more than "pure rubbish" (Kautsky), or "false consciousness" (Lenin), since it veils "objective" reality.[48] Orthodox Marxists thereby reduce their theory to a "science" of economics. Other dimensions of reality are either mechanically determined by its categories of explanation or simply ignored altogether.

Korsch does not interpret Marxism as a "science" whose truth value is equivalent or interchangeable with the natural sciences.[49] He instead understands it as an inherently historical and value-laden approach that seeks to comprehend the existing "totality" and the possibilities for transforming it.[50] In keeping with this idea, which in Hegelian fashion turns historical materialism into a "science of consciousness," the attempt to fragment Marxism into a variety of rigidly distinct disciplines—such as "Marxist political economy" or "Marxist literary criticism"—is seen as denying its very purpose. Once an autonomous character is attributed to any part of the totality, its functioning, along with the structural interests it harbors, becomes impossible to define. Consequently, Marxism is "inherently bound to *praxis* (and self-consciously so) as a total system (*Gesamtsystem*). The critique of political economy is then intrinsically bound to the critique of ideology."[51]

Class consciousness remained decisive for Korsch along with a basic belief in the proletariat as the revolutionary "agent" of history. With the Nazi triumph and the totalitarianism reigning in the USSR, however, Korsch increasingly concerned himself with the notion of "counter-revolution."[52] In a counterrevolutionary period, after all, the proletariat will lack any forces with which to identify its revolutionary interests, thereby justifying the transcendent commitment to revolution in the face of historical reality. But Korsch refused to interpret the counterrevolutionary trend of the 1930s as a simple "betrayal" of the proletariat by the leadership of existing organizations precisely because "the fact of betrayal itself requires explanation."[53] And so, in attempting to analyze this "fact," Korsch began with the conditions that fostered a worldwide response to the most progressive elements within the Russian Revolution. It was a response, of course, which would ultimately infect the USSR itself.

Despite his "principle of historical specification," like Lenin, Korsch was blind when it came to differentiating between existing capitalist regimes. Wishing to highlight the importance of the "critical" moment for Marxism, he never articulated how divergent institutional forms of bourgeois rule could affect the struggle of the working class or the importance of the radical democratic heritage. Nor did he ever confront any serious criticisms of councils or the dangers of radically decentralizing power.[54] It was enough for him that the counterrevolutionary triumph in so much of Europe had created a situation wherein the working class could not express its most radical possibilities. The thinking of the antiphilosopher thus remained, in Hegelian terms, expressive of the "unhappy consciousness." It hung in the abstract, and this situation was only compounded by his belief that the proletariat should not put its faith in any major party since none expressed its real class needs or aims.[55]

Refusing to deal with the actual political and institutional choices of the 1930s and 1940s, no less than the later exponents of critical theory, Korsch lacked any practical referent for his theoretical position and was thereby unable to confront the the "counter-revolution" in concrete terms. Ironically, of course, this was precisely his critique of the dominant working-class organizations. Given that both the communists and the social democrats had abandoned all revolutionary aims, as far as Korsch was concerned, their inability to develop a consistent theory of counterrevolution derived from the fact that they had themselves become part of what demanded criticism. While social democrats were employing Marxism as a purely formal theory, in order to promulgate support for bourgeois democracy and economic reform, the

Soviet Union was using Marxism to postpone introducing the "realm of freedom" and justify the atrocious oppression "necessary" to achieve it.

"Progress" was being uncritically employed by both organizations to justify their policies. It seemingly no longer had anything to do with the degree of empowerment that the working class had achieved.[56] Scientific Marxism now served merely as a way of sanctioning the actions of parties that identified their own needs with those of the class they claimed to represent. And this only made sense, from Korsch's perspective, since this "scientific" interpretation of Marxism placed it in direct connection with the type of "contemplative materialism," inimical to a theory of practice, which was criticized in the "Eleven Theses on Feuerbach." Marx unambiguously maintained in these aphorisms that the political consequences of drawing a sharp line of division between consciousness and its object were quite "real."[57] The implications for Korsch were obvious: the philosophical expression of the revolutionary working class should stand in coherent relation to the most radical philosophical expression of the revolutionary bourgeoisie.[58] All the more strange then that he should have ignored the need to build upon the political legacy of liberalism. Korsch was content to argue that establishing the purpose and meaning of a revolutionary project in the present will depend upon linking it to the unrealized "critical" impetus carried over from the past.

With his belief that "objective" reality was constituted by the particular "subjective" response to it, for Korsch, affirming the Hegelian heritage became a matter of practical importance.[59] No wonder, then, that *Marxism and Philosophy* should have ended with the famous citation of the young Marx: "philosophy cannot be abolished without being realized." Abolishing philosophy would involve institutionalizing direct democratic control by equal human "subjects" over a production process—or "object"— "alienated" from them. With the failure of the councilist movement, however, the possibility of actualizing that goal was lost. Later critical theorists surrendered his political commitments and emphasized instead the freedom of the subject in its unique individuality. But they too preserved the moment of transcendence embodied in philosophy from a dead historicism and a capitalist reality intent upon nullifying its radical character. Philosophy, the tool of reflection and the expression of freedom, would thus—in the words of Theodor Adorno—"continue to exist because the moment for its realization was missed."

Korsch's philosophy continued to exert an—admittedly subterranean—influence. He "believes adamantly in the new. So he loves the young," said Brecht, "and sees them rife in their possibilities."[60] Korsch influenced Lucien Goldmann and the French group "Arguments" as well as Rudi Dutschke and a host of of young activist intellectuals in Germany during the 1960s. He even gained a certain notoriety in Yugoslavia, Hungary, and Czechoslavakia where *Marxism and Philosophy* was distributed underground.[61] His theory not only made it possible to criticize the authoritarian deformations of Marxism but called for opposition against any stance seeking to transfer the old forms of radicalism into the new age.[62] Opposed to bureaucratic hierarchy and supportive of all nondogmatic attempts to develop the self-administrative capacities of the oppressed, his thinking suggests that there is not only one adequate form of socialist organization, nor one immutable theory that will forever inform a movement in terms of what it opposes and what it supports. Open to new categories and possibilities for radical action, whatever Korsch's own preoccupation with the traditional proletariat, his stance legitimated the concern with citizen initiatives and new social movements from a "Marxist" perspective. Nevertheless, the popularity he enjoyed was surely enhanced by the connection between his own political theory and the more general concerns of critical theory.[63]

Korsch's thinking projects the need for a critical and interdisciplinary approach to social issues. Radicals in the European movement felt a kinship with his concern for transforming the "totality" and fusing the ideological, political, and economic moments of struggle in the revolutionary undertaking. They echoed his commitment to the political relevance of social and historical knowledge even as they recognized that socialism, as the projected alternative to the existing order, could not be made by decree. The radicals of 1968 agreed with Korsch that emancipation is a direct function only of the struggles in which the masses participate and that the critical theorist must expose, clarify, and project the most radical possibilities of the existent. With their emphasis on participation, moreover, many were open to the idea of workers' councils and what in France was called *autogestion*. Indeed, with the emphasis on theory as a form of practice, yet another "elective affinity" (Weber) emerged between Korsch's mode of thinking and the student movement.

Ultimately, however, Korsch's isolation from the working class and its parties produced distrust and disappointment. Prizing the idea of revolution above all else, emphasizing the attack on the totality, Korsch saw politics as "all or nothing"; Brecht was indeed right in saying that when framed in these terms, the world is always quick to answer "nothing."[64] The dogmatists laughed at his loneliness.[65] But, in refusing to compromise with reality, Korsch's thought maintained its integrity. His life and work form part of what Ernst Bloch termed "the underground history of the revolution." He preserved the idea of freedom and socialism from the ways in which repressive institutions and philosophies claimed to have realized it, and for that very reason, the enduring relevance of his thought derives from its refusal to relinquish the speculative moment of theory to the dictates of historical necessity.[66]

Marxism in the hands of Korsch evidenced its critical character and positive intent.[67] Stripped of teleology and scientific pretensions, however, the next step is to supplant it with a socialist ethic and transvalue the traditional view of the relation between theory and practice.[68] Korsch never took that step. Perhaps it was because he knew this would result in turning "revolution," the anchor of his worldview, from a strategic end into a tactic relevant under some circumstances and irrelevant under others. But that remains an open question. Its clear only that Korsch was willing to make good on Engels's statement that Marxism is a historical theory and that loyalty to its founders lies not in the commitment to any particular set of propositions, concepts, or parties, but in facing its limits, mistakes, and anachronistic assumptions. New norms and institutions remain necessary in order to confront history with its own unrealized possibilities. Critique has not yet lost its importance. And that is because, if the age of freedom has not yet dawned, the time of dogma is still far from over.

ৎ 4 ৡ

Philosophical Anticipations
A Commentary
on the "Reification" Essay of Georg Lukács

Georg Lukács was still a communist when he died in 1971 at the age of eighty-six. He had become reconciled to the limitations of the Soviet Union, and his thinking had taken a conservative and ontological turn. All the more ironic that Rudi Dutschke and other intellectuals of the student movement should have resurrected his masterpiece, *History and Class Consciousness*, which introduced the two concepts most notably associated with critical theory: alienation and reification. The book offered an innovative foundation for the critique of ideology, generated a new concern with the "totality," and provided critical theory with a sense of radical purpose. It conceived of the proletariat less as an empirical than as a logical category whose ethical primacy derived from its role in thematizing the structure of capitalist society. Lukács's interpretation of alienation and reification transformed materialism into a theory of praxis. It deepened the understanding of revolution, highlighted the role of consciousness, resurrected the vision of utopia, and influenced any number of diverse philosophical developments. No longer would Marxism prove identifiable with party dogma or arbitrarily chosen citations from the masters capable of justifying any particular political exigency. It would now appear as a method capable of incorporating the insights of new thinkers and meeting the problems posed by new historical conditions.[1]

History and Class Consciousness, contrary to myth, was not the first book to link Hegel with Marx.[2] But it was the "charter document of Hegelian Marxism," and it "almost single-handedly succeeded in raising [Marxism] to a respectable place in European intellectual life."[3] The work proved a remarkable philosophical achievement whose most ambitious, and ultimately seminal, chapter was titled "Reification and the Consciousness of the Proletariat." The book, however, was marred in a number of ways. An adherence to Leninist principles, whatever the influence of Rosa Luxemburg,[4] led to an underestimation of civil liberties and hampered the development of a socialist theory of democracy. An exaggerated emphasis on consciousness also bred indifference to the specification of institutional constraints and the politics of power. Its voluntarism, similarly, undercut the emphasis on historical determination, while its utopianism burdened political action with a completely unrealizable set of expectations. Lukács's preoccupation with achieving the "identity" between subject and object, in this regard created the conceptual framework wherein even his staunchest critics like Theodor Adorno would become defined by what they opposed.

Metaphysical prejudices make a contemporary reading of the "reification" essay quite difficult. A more concrete interpretation that might make the appropriation salient is also hindered by the fact that Lukács himself used "alienation" (*Entfremdung*) and "reification" (*Verdinglichung*) interchangeably.[5] These concepts retain their relevance. But they require reinterpretation in light of the teleological collapse, which has become evident to all except the most dogmatic partisans of the past. Differentiating alienation from reification is a matter of some importance. First, however, it is necessary to clarify the historical background of these concepts and their traditional philosophical connotations. Only then will it become possible to confront their implications for modernity.

*   *   *

Alienation has a long history. Its most radical sense already appears in the biblical expulsion from Eden.[6] The story of paradise lost precedes the loss of objects to the world of exchange, which originally defined its social usage.[7] The biblical allegory justifies the fallen state of humanity and explains why people are condemned "to earn their bread by the sweat of their brow." It also shows why trust between individuals has been lost, nature appears as an enemy, and—interestingly enough—redemption becomes possible. Unity and harmony are forfeited, and humanity is stripped of its organic connection to the world with the banishment of Adam and Eve. Human choice has produced the fall and, with the expulsion of Adam and Eve, the hope of re-creating paradise. Prometheus may have sought to make good on that hope, but he was thwarted for all eternity by a "wicked god" bent on condemning human hubris.[8] Hope becomes fused with the recognition that its fulfillment will never take place. Thus, utopia serves as the only response to alienation.

Alienation is the experience of "estrangement" (*Verfremdung*) from others,[9] and the intimation of an alternative. This becomes apparent in different ways in the *civitas dei* of Augustine and the *cur deus homo* of Anselm. Alienation appears in Maimonides and Dante, the desire of Hobbes to escape from a condition in which "life is nasty, poor, solitary, brutish, and short" as well as in the more beneficent conception of the "state of nature" offered by Locke.

Nowhere, however, does the problem of alienation become more evident than in the early essays of Rousseau. Wealth and the creation of artificial needs corrupt the "natural" virtues like decency, simplicity, kindness, and honesty. Civilization is seen by Rousseau as subverting the communal values that make life worth living. And so, if he had little use for the nobility or its trappings, he was also aware of the way in which the bourgeoisie was cutting people loose from the security of the past. The loss of tradition by "simple souls" was what rendered a radical response necessary. Science was as responsible as the arts, materialism was as much to blame as metaphysics, for fragmenting the community. Anomie no less than despotism or inequality generates the need for determining a "general will."

Society must prove reducible to the individuals composing it. Only in this way is it possible to restore the self-respect of the individual. Rousseau makes his plea for a small community of individuals with similar backgrounds and traditions in which authority is accountable and each has the right to participate in making decisions. No confrontation with provincialism or cultural prejudices, however, can really take place. Any such attempt would obviously usher in the conditions of alienation he so dramatically sought to mitigate. Cosmopolitanism and technological progress, individualism and occupationally differentiated notions of identity, become the enemies of an organic community. Rousseau would undoubtedly have identified with the critical tenor of the following lines from Hölderlin:

You see craft-workers, but no people; thinkers, but no people; priests, but no people; lords and servants, youths and persons of property, but no people. Is this not like a battlefield on which hands, arms, and limbs of all sorts lie strewn amid one another while their spilt life-blood runs into the sands?[10]

In this vein, especially with the irretrievable passing of the ancien régime, contesting alienation would ever more surely spur what the young Lukács called "romantic anti-capitalism." But the first systematic encounter with alienation occurred in the writings of Hegel. His concern was with the way in which action occurs behind the backs of individuals. Alienation exists insofar as humanity is estranged from nature and its creations escape its conscious control. World history is the stigmata suffered by the absolute spirit (*Geist*), whose goal is to reappropriate its "estranged" objectifications.[11] Alienation, or the experience of this "estrangement," is overcome insofar as such an appropriation takes self-conscious form through the constitutive categories of the spirit's "absolute idea": religion, art, and philosophy.

Alienation is the experience of a world beyond the control of those who created it. The concept initially is reducible neither to psychology nor economics. The problem with alienation indeed has less to do with any reductive definition than with its all-encompassing character. Every form of objectification, according to Hegel and the Lukács of *History and Class Consciousness*, results in alienation. The spirit of freedom is estranged in the material world, and only teleological faith in the possibility of cleansing the stigmata of history can bring about its ultimate recovery.

Alienation is experienced in every facet of the "totality," and in keeping with the sources of the concept, the ultimate confrontation with it must prove total as well. Transcending alienation involves transcending objectification. And, for this reason, a new identity between subject and object must dissolve what Marx later termed "pre-history." New conditions of empowerment must subject the world to human control, and its estranged character must vanish. Utopian and anthropological preoccupations will thereby inform any response to alienation, and the partisans of critical theory would embrace them even when they no longer accepted either the teleology of Lukács or his view of the "totality."

Abolishing alienation should be understood less as a matter of overcoming capitalism than of redeeming the miseries of history, which Hegel conceived as the "calvary of the absolute spirit." But he was no utopian. The act of cognition was, for Hegel, the culmination of a process wherein the universal implications of reason are actualized in a new state governed by the rule of law. Conflict and existential alienation remain even at the "end of history" insofar as individuals are still confronted with scarcity and their own mortality. His political vision of a rationally ordered society, a state reproducing itself under the rule of law (*Rechtsstaat*), simply creates the space in which people can deal with their most private concerns free of external interference. In keeping the exploitative class relations of civil society intact while privileging an essentially unaccountable bureaucracy, however, subjectivity is withdrawn and individuals are treated philosophically as objects.

Hegel took bourgeois philosophy to its limits, but he never transgressed them. Lukács, for this reason, sought to create a direct link between Hegel and Marx without reference to the impact of Feuerbach. He was already aware of Marx's comments concerning the "contemplative" character of traditional materialism.[12] But there remains something ironic about the fact that Western Marxists could only highlight the revolutionary moment of historical materialism by emphasizing its idealist rather than its materialist roots. This is all the more strange since Feuerbach essentially criticized Hegel for ignoring the religious source of alienation without providing anything other than purely formal ideas for its resolution.

Alienation, according to Feuerbach, derives from the externalization (*Entäusserung*) of human powers upon a nonexistent entity: God. An imaginary world comes into existence, which is the richer, the poorer this one

becomes. Reality appears alien to the individual as responsibility for its genesis and progress shifts to an Other. Religion is seen as the source of alienation and atheism insofar as it projects an existential empowerment and
becomes the foundation for a new humanism. Feuerbach deals with the
experience of alienation in a way that Hegel does not. His anthropological
critique of alienation, of course, has nothing to say about practical empowerment; history vanishes and the human essence is comprehended in terms
of a "dumb generality" that *naturally* unites individuals. Resurrection of the
individual occurs through the contemplative resurrection of the species.
Marx could thus correctly claim that Feuerbach failed to grasp the significance of "revolutionary" or "practical-critical activity" and that "the highest
point attained by *contemplative* materialism . . . is the contemplation of single individuals in 'civil society.'"[13]

The "Eleven Theses on Feuerbach," which Engels termed the "first document" in which the "germ" of a new worldview appears, were written in 1845
but published only in 1888 as the appendix to *Ludwig Feuerbach and the End
of Classical German Philosophy*. They mark the point at which Marx breaks
with the abstract humanism and idealism of his youth, not in the sense that he
simply abandons old concerns but insofar as he invents a new set of categories
with which to interpret the "inverted world."[14] Such is the source for the
famous chapter on "commodity fetishism" in *Das Kapital*, which describes
how capitalist production transforms subjects into objects for the accumulation of profit, and develops the "material" basis of "reification."

Marx never used the word. He was content to differentiate alienation from
objectification in the *Paris Manuscripts of 1844*.[15] In that work Marx essentially derived alienation from the division of labor and explored its three-fold
estrangement of the individual from his community, from his product, and
from his own potential. These writings were never published during his lifetime. They appeared only in 1932 after being smuggled out of the Institute for
Marxism-Leninism with the help of its director, David Rjazanov, who would
later pay with his life for this and other acts of intellectual integrity. The early
manuscripts became seminal to the thinking of the New Left and, before then,
to the development of critical theory. Nevertheless, for once, it is perhaps useful to consider why Marx might have chosen not to publish them.

He never retracted the democratic commitments expressed in the *Paris
Manuscripts*. But their utopian bent and anthropological form of argumentation are another matter. The class categories, the logical rigor, and the institutional insights of the later works are obviously lacking. There are ways in
which the thinking of Marx moves beyond Hegel and Feuerbach. He notes the
role of wealth and, for example, how it can make smart the stupid and render
beautiful the ugly. This insight is appropriated from Shakespeare, however,
and the structure of capitalist production is never delineated. The response to

alienation, furthermore, is left at restoring what in *The German Ideology* he termed the "species being" of humanity or the wholeness repressed by the division of labor. An organic connection between humanity and nature, the individual and the community, is now projected into the future rather than conceived as having been lost in the past. The abolition of private property is highlighted. But the meaning is vague, and the romantic impulse remains. The image of a "new man" arises as utopia is placed within an indeterminate end of history in which all the anthropological conditions of repression are abolished. Transcendence supplants immanence, speculation supplants the need for institutional referents, and consciousness overcomes material constraints. Thus, there are good reasons why Marx should have moved beyond these legendary early works even as he began to contest all forms of "contemplative" materialism with the "Eleven Theses on Feuerbach."

What Marx in his later years might have deemed the failings of his youthful writings, however, seemed to fit the revolutionary mood during the years when *History and Class Consciousness* was being written. The messianic moment of redemption seemed to have arrived with the Russian Revolution and the suffering endured by the masses during World War I, and its aftermath seemed to prefigure the apocalyptic transformation of reality. Empires had crumbled, forty million had been slain or crippled, and, between 1918 and 1921, an offensive had been launched to spread communist revolution throughout Europe. Workers' councils were springing into existence with each revolt. Enthusiasts thought that "popular justice" was making legal institutions anachronistic and that money was being eliminated in the USSR. Cultural experimentation seemed ready to combine with the inexhaustible radicalism of a communist vanguard in expressing the general will of a "new man." This was the historical crucible in which the new revolutionary agent, the "subject-object" of history, was apparently taking shape. Indeed, finally, it seemed possible to speak concretely about the abolition of philosophy.

The subject would now no longer be seen in terms of the isolated entity of bourgeois materialism or the purely formal category of transcendental idealism. The individual of old is sublated (*aufgehoben*) by the agent responsible for the unfolding of teleology. A new subject speaks to the reified totality in a way the individual subject could not. Structural constraints and historical crises vanish. The world becomes a pre-existing complex of ready-made and unalterable objects. "For the individual, reification and hence determinism are irremovable. Every attempt to achieve 'freedom' from such premises must fail, for 'inner freedom' presupposes that the world cannot be changed."[16]

The individual ceases to serve as the measure of all things because, from such a stance, historical change becomes impossible to conceive. Kierkegaard and Nietzsche, who so influenced the young Lukács,[17] subsequently make way for Hegel and Marx. Alienation as the inalterable condition of social existence becomes open to historical transformation. Hegel's "world spirit" (*Weltgeist*) might have been engaged in working its way to universal consciousness through the the the culture of nations. Now, however, the proletariat of Marx—as interpreted by Lukács[18]—will take on the mission of historical change and create something far more radical than a bureaucratic state under the rule of law or a *Rechtsstaat*.

During the time when the "reification" essay was written, the proletariat appeared on the verge of ushering a classless society into existence and bringing "pre-history" to a close.[19] Its aims seemed similar to those of the world spirit: Both seemed intent upon abolishing the exercise of arbitrary power and a world in which history is made unconsciously or behind the backs of individuals. The difference is merely that the proletariat of Marx and Lukács is material in the sense that it is generated by the production process and that a reified or alienated form of production itself becomes the object of transformation. Thus, Marx could write that "when the proletariat proclaims the dissolution of the previous world-order it does no more than reveal the secret of its own existence, for it represents the effective dissolution of that world-order."

The self-understanding of the proletariat, for this reason, becomes the objective understanding of the nature of society.[20] It perceives the mediations that differentiate the effects of a reified totality on different classes. The proletariat rejects both the determinism of vulgar materialism and the moralistic "ought" of Kant. It overcomes the dualism by seeking to discover "the principles by means of which it becomes *possible in the first place* for an 'ought' to modify existence."[21] The revolution thus can no longer occur merely in thought even if its "objective possibility" is itself determined by thought. It becomes apparent that:

> a *new* element is required: the consciousness of the proletariat must become deed. But as the mere contradiction is raised to a consciously dialectical contradiction, as the act of becoming conscious turns into a *point of transition in practice*, we see once more in greater concreteness the character of proletarian dialectics . . . [N]amely, since consciousness here is not the knowledge of an opposed object, but is the self consciousness of the object, the act of consciousnesss overthrows the objective form of its object.[22]

The greatness of Marx now appears in his synthesis of idealism and materialism in such a way that it renders concrete the claim of Hegel that dialectics must present itself as "the immanent process of transcendence." But there was still the matter of explaining why so much of the proletariat was incapable of recognizing the need for unity along with its revolutionary mission. Reference to its inherent economism, in keeping with Lenin, only begged the question. A given form of thinking with certain assumptions was involved even if it derived from a particular mode of productive activity. Making sense of this connection between theory and practice meant contesting not merely alienation, a world outside the control of those who had created it, but the logic informing its production and reproduction. Lukács, in this way, would take up the famous claim of Marx that "social life is essentially *practical*. All mysteries which mislead theory to mysticism find their rational solution in human practice and in the comprehension of that practice."[23]

*   *   *

The experience of alienation called forth the inquiry into the conditions for its production and reproduction or what might be termed the process of reification.[24] The unyielding emphasis on subjectivity and the unique experience by the modernist avant-garde was in part a reaction against standardization, mechanization, rationalization, and the leveling or equalizing tendencies of what would become advanced industrial society. Similar concerns appear in the work of the neo-Kantian philosophers in Germany.[25] Lukács was close to many of them including Max Weber, Georg Simmel, Wilhelm Windelband, and Emil Lask who helped inspire the concern with reification.[26] For its part, however, orthodox Marxism was basically unconcerned with such concerns. There was little discussion of the "inverted world" of commodity fetishism in which workers are treated less as subjects than as tools for the creation of profits.[27] The production process itself was primarily identified with technology. The unrelenting development of technology would supposedly—of itself—increase competition among firms, mechanically increase the "industrial reserve army," depress purchasing power, and generate revolution. Its deadening impact on consciousness and the creative interaction with nature was underestimated.

Lukács wished to consider economic categories in terms of their political implications. And, in so doing, he transformed technology from a governing principle into the product of given social relations, which then defines them in turn.[28] His point is not that technology or the sciences are irrelevant. It was merely that bringing technology under control must involve opening it to historical inquiry and revolutionary transformation from the standpoint of the proletariat. Both are expressions of the division of labor wherein subjectivity is fragmented through rationalization and specialization destroys every image of the whole.[29] The division of labor is the material expression of a purposive rationality predicated on calculability and efficient routinization of tasks.[30] Calculability inherently involves transforming qualitative differences between objects into quantitative ones and, insofar as production involves the objectification of subjectivity, reducing natural resources and people to the same mathematical units of analysis. Only with assumptions of this sort is it possible to conceive of selling commodities for more than the price of producing them.

Contesting capitalism from the standpoint of the proletariat must mean contesting the division of labor and the commodity form that robs workers of their subjectivity and turns them into objects, or instruments, for the creation of profit. But the division of labor preceded capitalism. Along with the commodity, in fact, it reaches back into the beginnings of the interchange between humanity and nature. Both reach fruition under capitalism by touching every moment of the totality. None of this, however, was ever really an issue for orthodox Marxism. Its partisans were content to criticize capitalism for its unequal distribution of commodities rather than for its production process; indeed, Marx himself had castigated the nascent social democratic movement on precisely this point.[31] The problem with capitalism was seen as stemming from an anarchic market erupting in periodic crises. Planning and nationalization, which the partisans of the labor movement would undertake within a parliamentary framework and use in conjunction with certain market mechanisms, basically defined "socialism" in the thinking of Karl Kautsky and the other dominant theorists of orthodox Marxism. Only Rosa Luxemburg and certain of her supporters ever really developed a more radical outlook. Even their criticisms, however, never really extended to issues concerning the division of labor.[32]

Lukács gave revolution, which he viewed as the categorical imperative for a theory of practice,[33] a new meaning by fashioning a dialectical link between the historical critique of capitalism and the anthropological critique of exploitation. Even before Fichte condemned his age as one of "absolute sinfulness," the followers of Sabbatai Sevi, the "false messiah" of the Jews in the seventeenth century, believed that only after every sin was performed would the messiah come. In the same vein, approximately one hundred and fifty years later, Lukács would pronounce the proletarian revolution possible only once the commodity form had become dominant. His *Theory of the Novel* had already displayed a preoccupation with the apocalypse and, inspired by Martin Buber,[34] sought to show that modernity had not dried up the "metaphysical source" of Judaism. Now, in *History and Class Consciousness*, only under the conditions in which subjects have been most fully transformed into objects by the production process can the abolition of reification by the proletariat occur.

Of course, Lukács did not mean that the revolution would have to await the moment at which reification defined every person on the planet. It was, following Hegel and Max Weber, a matter of *tendency* and an ability to recognize the point at which society is learning to satisfy all its needs in terms of the

commodity.[35] The point is not whether more or less commodities exist in capitalist society but whether the commodity form dominates all other possible
forms of production. Anthropological tendencies from the past become newly
rationalized insofar as the ever more powerful market transforms the *subject*
of production into an *object* for consumption.[36] The very "compulsion"
toward objectification (*Vergegenständlichung*) under capitalism makes it possible for a worker to become "conscious" of the class context. Indeed, this was
why Lukács could claim that "the objective theory of class consciousness is the
theory of its objective possibility."[37]

History and Class Consciousness provides a hermeneutic. The extent to
which the working class recognizes its objective condition results in the
changing of that condition.[38] The method of historical materialism, for this
reason, privileges the moment of consciousness. Later forms of critical theory
would, in fact, retain this hermeneutical imperative even when the interpretation of society became based on nothing more than the "constellation" constituted by a particular individual. The ability to fashion this constellation, or
exert the normative claims of reflexivity in comprehending the object, would
also rest on resisting the identification of reification with progress. A theory
self-conscious about its relation to practice is thus "essentially the intellectual
expression of the revolutionary process itself."[39] Indeed, for this reason,
"bourgeois" theory must stand in opposition to that process.

Explaining reification, and the ability to deal with it, are flip sides of the
same coin. The dialectical character of Lukács's teleology becomes apparent
insofar as "intellectual genesis must be identical in principle with historical
genesis."[40] Alienation thereby becomes the point of departure for developing
the critical consciousness of the proletariat.[41] Confronting capitalism calls for
confronting the history of exploitation, while confronting the history of
exploitation requires class consciousness. Looking at Marx with the eyes of
Hegel, breaking the identification of dialectics with the economic or technological determinism of Engels, Lukács introduced a messianic conception of
teleology into a supposedly materialist worldview. The revolution became the
apocalypse: the goal was now not merely the abolition of capitalism but the
elimination of reification. Anything less could only be considered a betrayal of
the revolution. Lukács gave a new meaning to the notion that capitalism creates its own gravediggers: providing history with meaning becomes dependent
less upon the philosophical constructions of some philosopher than the revolutionary commitment of a proletariat born of modernizing processes intent
on "disenchanting the world" (Max Weber).

Reification is the material expression of this "disenchantment." It is the
framework within which facts gain their meaning and thus the barrier against
which the variants of metaphysics and positivism constantly struggled. Both
equated reason with natural laws capable of covering all empirical contingen-

cies, and in this way, they relinquished any concern with the subjectivity of the subject no less than the material constitution of the unique event. Scientific rationality and metaphysics both veiled the contradictions of reality by focusing on either the phenomenal *or* the noumenal dimensions of reality. Both assumed an abstract or "reified" character as form became divorced from content and subject from object. Incapable of recognizing the framework in which the given fact gains meaning, seeking to isolate the datum from the conditions of its constitution, both prove incapable of contesting the reifying conditions in need of transformation.[42]

Understanding reification is possible only by bringing to bear those categories that reification denies. For this reason, according to Lukács, the materialism inherited from Marx must differentiate itself from all the older versions and, in keeping with the Hegelian notion of totality, contest the given system rather its mere empirical expressions. Natural laws and the criteria of the natural sciences, which uncritically employ transhistorical categories and thus freeze reality, have no place in a historical inquiry intent upon dealing with social issues. The point is no longer, for example, to "prove" whether a "transformation" of value into price takes place. The "labor theory of value" now assumes phenomenological form,[43] and the empirical investigation into the commodity dissolves into a critical analysis of the social relations "hidden" within it. Marxism thus becomes a critical theory of society grounded within a philosophy of history rather than a science based on fixed claims about the workings of the economy.

History and Class Consciousness is an attempt to subsume the empirical forms of capitalism within an analysis of its "real life-process."[44] The framework within which facts gain their meaning thus becomes the object of criticism for the new revolutionary subject. Reification defines that framework. It enters into each moment of the totality. The moments are not reduced to economic class interests, but rather become defined in their constitutive dynamics by the same form of instrumental rationality. Reification is seen as ever more surely reducing production to its constitutive elements and turning specialization into the principle of life. It increasingly transforms the product into an "objective synthesis of rationalized special systems whose unity is determined by pure calculation."[45] Even space and time are reduced to a common denominator: the latter is "degraded" into a calculable dimension of the former.[46] Indeed, from within what is itself a reified ontological framework, this is precisely what Martin Heidegger would so stubbornly seek to resist both in *Being and Time* and in his lecture given at Marburg University in 1924 titled "The Concept of Time."[47]

Interiority crystallizes into a fundamental concern. The externalization of the interior (*Entäusserung*) is seen as occuring within an increasingly prefabricated and ever more deadening form of everyday life. Activity becomes the pursuit of self-interest and the manipulation of abstract laws.[48] Personal responsibility and legitimate authority fade behind the network of institutional systems and subsystems. No one rules even while all are ruled without genuine accountability or discursive determination of priorities. The person becomes a mechanical part of a mechanical system, which exists independently of him or her and thus demands attitudinal or intellectual accommodation.[49] The fragmentation of the object is mirrored in the subject. Memory itself is endangered to the point where, paraphrasing Walter Benjamin, even the dead will not escape the grasp of the victor. The "second nature" of humanity, which is the anthropological product of reification, makes reflection on the mutability of the existing order impossible.[50]

Breaking that "second nature" is possible only through an act capable of providing new and coherent definition for the relation between continuity and discontinuity or, to put it another way, anthropology and history.[51] The position of the proletariat within the production process, its preconstituted existence as the revolutionary subject of history, anchors the moment of revolutionary transcendence within the production process and its immanent contradictions. With the integration of the proletariat, however, the moment of transcendence assumed legitimacy in its own right. An immanent contestation of reification from within capitalism would ever more surely vanish from the work of the Frankfurt School. Affirming the sociological, for this reason, became more important than ever before.

But the historical failure of the proletariat has not necessarily invalidated the need for drawing an epistemological connection between thought and action, consciousness and being, theory and practice. Investigating the relationship between them remains as necessary as before. With the rejection of such concerns, in fact, philosophy retreats into forms of thinking associated with the time before Marx. Ironically, this is the sense in which alienation remains what Lukács called "the specific problem of the age."

*   *   *

Alienation played a role in all the works of Lukács. His search for salvation from "transcendental homesickness," the anxiety generated by the unyielding demands of society in conflict with those of the spirit, pervaded his remarkable *Soul and Form*. Despair over the cultural decadence of modernity, the demise of the epic notion of life and its fragmentation expressed by the bourgeois novel, mirrored the descent into World War I that Lukács described in *Theory of the Novel*. The apocalyptic strain, the obsession with a world on the brink, did not disappear in *History and Class Consciousness*.[52] It faithfully reflected the thinking of the "ultraleft" of the Communist International during the "heroic" years of the Russian Revolution. Communism would end the era of "anarchic individualism" and recreate human society in the form of an "organic whole."[53] All things seemed possible. Only the proper consciousness of proletarian unity seemed necessary for the abolition of alienation and the introduction of a new world.

But such consciousness was impossible to assume. Unity is not a natural phenomenon for workers, most of whom were concerned with improving their own particular economic situation. A vanguard "party of a new type" was seemingly required to foster revolutionary consciousness and contest the constraints on the revolutionary enterprise. Reification was such a constraint. Its specific impact on the proletariat turned it into *the* theoretical and practical barrier to action. The importation of consciousness "from the outside" (Lenin) became the logical practical consequence for an argument predicated on the idea that reification infects the totality of social relations. Lukács warned against the party's acting as a "stand-in" for the proletariat.[54] But his criticisms were halfhearted. Only a party of committed "revolutionary intellectuals," reflexively privileging the moment of transformative action, might contest the objectivity to which the working class is structurally consigned. The vanguard, for this reason, according to Lukács and Lenin, exhibits the "true" consciousness of the proletariat. It alone can rise above the empirical interests of particular groups of workers, which are articulated by trade unions, no less than the utopian fatalism of the social democratic labor parties whose promises of "the day"—always in the future—of a socialist transformation would begin to ring ever more hollow in the years following World War I.

Lukács would, using his party name, forward the notion of a "democratic dictatorship" in the "Blum Theses" of 1928.[55] To him as a youthful bohemian, however, parliamentarism was anathema even before his association with the anarcho-syndicalist Ervin Szábo from whom he learned his revolutionary Marxism.[56] Empiricism and determinism were, in the same vein, seen as incapable of inspiring revolutionary action since they uncritically reflected the very reification in need of abolition.[57] Both tended to subvert the normative character of the radical enterprise. Fostering action involved linking the subjective and empirical interests of workers with their objective and scientifically predetermined mission, which, in turn, made it incumbent upon the vanguard to "impute" a certain consciousness to the working class in the articulation of a program or a tactic.[58] The vanguard thus manifests an "aspiration to totality,"[59] which sets the framework for judging any particular action[60] and renders it the actual subject-object of history.

Herein lies the totalitarian strain within *History and Class Consciousness*. The integrity of the individual subject is subsumed by the subject of history,[61] the working class, whose revolutionary consciousness is incarnated within the vanguard. Checks on its power are irrelevant by definition, and its revolutionary character is presupposed. The vanguard need define itself neither by illegality or legality. Its teleological commitment to the radical goal of communism would justify opportunism in meeting the needs of one exigency and then another as the organization saw fit. Necessity was turned into a virtue. The organizational question was resolved, but metaphysically. There is something quite legitimate about suggesting that Lukács "willingly asserts his idealism in order . . . the better to secure it against attack."[62]

Ethics surrenders to teleology, which, in turn, becomes the preserve of the vanguard. A different interpretation of the relation between ethics and teleology, however, is also possible. Aristotle had, after all, developed an ethic based on teleological assumptions. The uncertainty and contingency associated with ethics are usually seen as being precluded by teleology. For better or worse, however, Lukács sought to create a new linkage between them. He turned the "standpoint of the proletariat," itself teleologically generated by history, into a universal ethical formulation intent on subjecting to criticism all institutions—including the vanguard party—that might seek to constrain its capacity for self-administration. Class consciousness, in keeping with the thinking of Rosa Luxemburg, would thus turn into the "ethic" of the proletariat, and this interpretation gains particular credence insofar as the vanguard party plays no role in the most famous chapter of *History and Class Consciousness.*

The critical method is applied to the critical theory: the method of Lukács calls his own political choices into question. In keeping with its earliest essays, which sought to balance the soviets with the party, the chapter on reification tends to militate against the totalitarian views articulated in other parts of the book.[63] The soviets, of course, had already lost even the semblance of independence before the book appeared in 1923.[64] But its "utopian surplus," to employ the phrase of Ernst Bloch, contested the authoritarianism of communist politics, and the commissars sensed it. Indeed, it was not merely because Lukács was aligned with the wrong faction at the Fifth Congress of the Comintern in 1924 that Zinoviev called for the censure of *History and Class Consciousness* along with the various Hegelian interpretations of Marxism by Karl Korsch and others.[65]

This congress reflected the end of the "heroic" phase of the Russian Revolution. It recognized that the proletarian revolutions in Europe had failed, accepted the need to "bolshevize" the communist parties of Europe, and asserted that industrialization rather than "socialization" should take priority in the Soviet Union. *History and Class Consciousness* harbors a rejection of these policies, and while Lukács ultimately recanted his heretical book, he did not go quietly into the night.[66] The work's transformation of Marxism into a critical method, a theory of society rather than a science, also made it an obstacle to implementing a new fixed and finished communist dogma. Where a new turn toward productivism was taking place, along with an uncritical admiration of technology,[67] Lukács maintained his belief of 1920 that "liberation from capitalism means liberation from the rule of the economy."[68] His concern was with instituting new forms of "self-administration."[69] His emphasis on the abolition of alienation ensured that for the genuine revolutionary, it was no longer a matter of one class supplanting another, or one form of state substituting itself for another, but the introduction of a new form of life.

This ultraradicalism also has its problems. Determinations vanish, and the modern notion of revolution is sacrificed to what is actually a premodern and apocalyptic conception of change. The theory of praxis thereby turns into its opposite: a purely contemplative radicalism. [70] The failure of the proletariat to fulfill its role as a revolutionary subject not only strengthened this tendency toward what might be termed an "antipolitical politics" but also shattered the symbiotic connection between the bourgeoisie and the proletariat on which the entire teleological conception of *History and Class Consciousness* ultimately rests. The logic involved in making freedom concrete in universal terms, which served as the impetus behind philosophical idealism, collapses along with the promise projected by liberalism for socialism. Once the framework of Lukács dispenses with its revolutionary proletarian subject, indeed, resistance against the reified totality can only take place from the standpoint of the individual subject. The result is an abstract negation in which the particular is pitted against the universal.[71]

A new point of departure for critical theory, by contrast, would suggest that just as alienation is different from objectification, so are both different from reification. All this, at first glance, is relatively simple. Marx himself had criticized the Hegelian attempt to conflate objectification with alienation by noting that while the former is neutral and transhistorical, the latter is inherently negative and occurs only under distinct historical conditions. A nonalienated alternative to the status quo is possible for Marx, and in keeping with the refusal to reify theoretical concepts, it becomes illegitimate to naturalize existing social relations. Nevertheless, if nonalienated activity can occur only outside capitalist social relations, the ability to make judgments or employ "practical reason" in the realm of "prehistory" is severely compromised.

There is a hidden truth to this error. Alienation speaks not merely to rendering institutions accountable, or resurrecting the subjectivity lost in the assumptions of the existing accumulation process, but to what Walter Benjamin appropriately termed "the poverty of the interior." Responding to alienation politically is consequently far more difficult than rectifying the unequal distribution of wealth or existing conditions of linguistic distortion. Alienation has an existential component. It is more than a reflex of "social conditions" and irreducible to the division of labor. Intellectual works of the past beginning with the Bible show how the concept is connected with loneliness, mortality, unrequited love, unfulfilled hopes, expectations denied, and a host of other personal and communal concerns. Alienation is an experience of society as "other." Its multifaceted character renders it inherently indeterminate and more than the sum of its historically constituted parts. Alienation escapes every formula and reconstitutes itself with every piece of legislation—especially since "progress" achieved in one arena of social life may produce regression in another. No institutional arrangement can promise its abolition. This demands utopia. And, precisely because alienation is a *felt need,* utopia is kept alive by its persistence. Ernst Bloch was correct in suggesting that the only response to alienation is the utopian vision of a global "home," without estrangement and grounded in real democracy, "which has appeared to everyone in childhood and which no one yet has visited."[72]

Alienation should be understood as different from reification, in my view, and responding to the latter should not require the introduction of utopian aspirations. Reification is based on rationalization, but the one should not be reduced to the other.[73] Rationalization involves dealing with nature in an instrumental or mathematical fashion, and there is a connection with reification insofar as reification turns individuals into "things" insofar as it undermines their reflexive capacities and gives their world a fixed and finished, or "natural," form. But reification takes place only insofar as purposive ends are closed to critical scrutiny in the employment of such techniques and profits become more important than people. If the theory of reification is not itself to become reified then the concept must be understood not merely as mutable in terms of some future apocalyptic action but flexible in its impact.

Or, to put it another way, reification must be seen as capable of being intensified or diminished under different regimes and through different policies; it is worse in a concentration camp than a republic, for example, and shorter hours for better pay increase the possibilities of self-realization by individual subjects. The point for a contemporary movement is not whether to employ instrumental rationality or the newest and most advanced forms of computer technology. It is now a matter of choosing what priorities to privilege and exercising accountability over social and political institutions. If the difference between alienation and reification is not to assume a purely academic or semantic form then the difference must rest with whether the *practical* response to the phenomenon requires the realization of a utopian vision or the—always inadequate—pursuit of regulative ideals concerning economic justice and political liberty. Neither liberalism nor socialism, nor the two in combination, offers a solution to the manifold problem of alienation. Either or both in combination, however, can mitigate reification.

Neither alienation nor reification deserves to be forgotten. The utopian concern with alienation can generate action, make us aware of new experiences of oppression, and inspire the imagination. Just as those committed to justice cannot dismiss the utopian concern with alienation, however, so must utopian radicals recognize the importance of confronting reification. The transformation of people into things is not a matter of theory, but rather an urgent concern of everyday life. It occurs whenever workers are turned into a "cost of production" and political authoritarianism denies their integrity as subjects of law. Alienation will always remain with us, it escapes reform, but an assault on reification occurs with every institutional attempt to further the accountability of all social institutions and the empowerment of working people. Differentiating between these concepts is a matter of crucial importance. In this sense, even if many assumptions made by Lukács have lost their relevance, the future of freedom still depends upon dealing with the categories his work made famous.

~ 5 ~

Utopian Projections
In Honor of Ernst Bloch

"The true genesis is not at the beginning, but at the end."
—*The Principle of Hope*

Ernst Bloch is only now becoming known in the United States. Especially toward the end of his long life, however, he was one of the best-known intellectuals in Europe. His extraordinary literary output, which always oscillated between art and philosophy, was marked by a unique metaphorical and expressionist prose. His students revered him, and during the 1960s he served as an inspiration. But with the rise of neoconservatism and the collapse of communism, his influence began to wane. Utopia became a word of derision. Nor is it legitimate any longer to speak of a "teleological suspension of the ethical" (Lukács). Alternative systems have lost their appeal; socialism and utopia seem ready for the dustbin of history. But there is no denying the existential price for the new philosophical moderation. People feel "hollow," paraphrasing T. S. Eliot, in a modernity seemingly bereft of vision and purpose. Thus, it is still worthwhile to consider the thinking of undoubtedly the greatest of utopian philosophers, who died in 1977 at the age of ninety-two.

From *Spirit of Utopia* and *The Principle of Hope* to collections of stories, essays, and the last great works like *The Problem of Materialism* and *Experimentum Mundi*, one idea preoccupied Ernst Bloch: the "dream of the better life." The content of that dream, the goal inspiring human action, led to disquisitions on everything from reincarnation to alchemy. His "romantic anticapitalism" was fundamentally premodern, cosmological, and eschatological, and the attempt to fuse it with Marxism and the Enlightenment expanded the boundaries of emancipation more than any thinker before or since. Martin Jay was surely correct in noting how the philosophy of Bloch shows that Western Marxism was more than just Hegelian Marxism. There is also something strangely esoteric about his way of thinking. For all that, however, his basic ontological claim was simple enough: "everything existing retains a utopian glimmer and philosophy would be nothing were it not capable of furthering the intellectual solution to the creation of this crystalline heaven of a regenerated reality."[1]

Ernst Bloch was a prophet like Marx and Thomas Münzer. His restless life gave meaning to the identification of philosophy with "transcendental homesickness." His work, however, provides new content for an idea as old as humanity itself. Past utopias, especially of the political variety, were concerned with pacification, order, and symmetry; they were usually far more culturally conservative than most radicals would care to admit. But there was never anything boring about the utopian conception of Ernst Bloch. Its freeflowing character became part of his expressionistic literary style. Its cosmopolitan nature was reflected in his extraordinary intellectual range. Its inherently unfinished quality left open the new experience of tomorrow. His utopian conception, of course, retained residues of repression and confusion. Its teleological elements led Bloch to identify with Stalin and often compromise his political judgment. Seeking to build on the example of Marx, he wished to make his utopian philosophy relevant for the present and a prefiguration of the future. But prophecy is not the stuff of politics. Even with the benefit of hindsight, his lectures made it apparent that he had little real political insight, and many contemporary attempts to somehow preserve him from his past are dishonest. There was nothing ambiguous about his support for the Moscow Trials.[2] Nevertheless, it was an exaggeration for Jan Robert Bloch to claim that the work of his father constituted nothing more than a "philosophical and propagandistic cover for Stalin's bloody terror."

Ernst Bloch knew that the value of a work is not exhausted by the politics of the author. And, in contrast to Martin Heidegger, there is a critical and reflexive moment within his philosophy that *immanently* calls into question the particular judgments on policy he made. Bloch's thinking was genuinely that of a maverick. Oskar Negt might have called him the "German philosopher of the October Revolution," and Bloch's lifelong admiration for Lenin was undoubtedly genuine, but most communists—in Germany no less than the Soviet Union—considered him an outsider and a mystic. Even within the Institute for Social Research, with which he was loosely associated, few took him seriously. Bloch's thought never jibed with the pessimism of Adorno and Horkheimer. He was older. His philosophy harked back to intellectual tendencies existing prior to World War I when cultural radicalism was defined by a commitment to the "new dawn" foreshadowed by Nietzsche, the visionary communitarian socialism associated with figures like Gustav Landauer, the concern with reification and alienation exhibited by neo-Kantians like Emil Lask and Georg Simmel, the rebirth of interest in Jewish mysticism and Christian chiliasm, and the manifold experiments of the modernist avant-gardes. Bloch's thinking incorporated elements from all these sources and others as well. Indeed, the result would prove uniquely his own and jut boldly into the future.

Utopia, in the thinking of Ernst Bloch, ceases to exist as "nowhere," or as an other to real history. It is a constituent element of all human activity and, simultaneously, historical. It becomes manifest in the quest for meaning, the thrill of sports, the desire for love, the daydream, the wonder of a child, and the experience of lightness before a genuine work of art. Each is a dim prefiguration (*Vorerscheinung*) of its existence. The question becomes how to articulate and realize the hopes unconsciously shared by humanity. And here, whatever the influence of neoromantic and mystical currents from the turn of the century, revelation is inadequate to the task at hand since "the forward glance becomes all the stronger, the more lucidly it becomes conscious. The dream in this glance seeks to make itself clear and the premonition, the right one, quite plain. Only when reason begins to speak can hope, in which there is nothing false, blossom again. The not-yet-conscious must become conscious in action, *known* in its content."[3]

Utopia is at the core of human existence. But humanity appears in an endless variety of forms, and so it follows that utopia will receive articulation in an endless variety of ways. It is no accident then that the gaze of this most European of thinkers should have extended to Zoroaster, Confucius, and the stories of the mythical Scheherazade. Bloch retained what Kant termed a "teleology of hope," but considered material equality as the precondition for actualizing utopia. If this obviously led him to Marx, however, the recognition that various forms of experience provided a sense of the *novum* also led him to medieval mystics like Meister Eckhart, Jakob Böhme, and Paracelsus. A rationalist concerned with determining the "ratio of the irratio," the critical character of mystical experience, he undertook the construction of a "left Aristotelianism" extending from Avicenna over Giordano Bruno to Leibniz and Marx. Ernst Bloch may have believed he was integrating the insights from this tradition into the "warm current," rather than the scientistic "cold current," of Marxism. Ultimately, however, he was engaging in a peculiar form of eclecticism. And so, it makes sense that he should have been criticized from virtually every angle. Bloch was rigorous after his fashion. His cosmological theory of nature was built on a knowledge of physics, and it anticipated what would become a new preoccupation with the ecosystem and animal rights. His belief that human emancipation presupposes a new form of interaction with nature, which involves recovering its repressed subjectivity, has now become a commonplace within the ecological movement. Nevertheless, many of the technical and political criticisms of his work remain valid.

His philosophical stance was never bound to praxis as he claimed, and especially now, in an avowedly antispeculative age, his utopian theory seems anything but "concrete." His neo-Platonic claims were too often asserted rather than argued, and his categories generally lack precision. The theological strain in his work and its eschatological character call for a suspension of disbelief. Few criteria are provided for the formulation of ethical or aesthetic judgments. He has little to say about the constraints on revolutionary transformation, the structure of emancipated production relations, or the democratic institutions necessary for maintaining a realm of freedom. In his analysis of death and resurrection, daydreams and utopian symbols, the line between fantasy and logic often becomes blurred. His daring attempt to reintroduce a radical telos into dialectical thought and ground it within an ontology of Being, however, extends the tradition of natural law and Marxism beyond purely economic or even regulative concerns. In this vein, whatever his own political commitments, his philosophy was a response to the manner in which goals commonly agreed upon were displaced into an ever more distant future by the communist vanguard. There is an inherently critical element to his way of thinking, which rests on a positive vision of emancipation. Its sophistication and quality have little in common with the dogmatism promoted by the communist states he supported. Its willingness to unearth the moment of freedom and happiness in everyday experience also confronts what has become a deadening philosophical pessimism among intellectuals.

Ernst Bloch wished to provide an ontological foundation for utopia. His philosophy thus retained an eschatological view of history. But it was one without the certainty of salvation or redemption. Realizing utopia, according to Bloch, can occur only through the creation of conditions capable of guaranteeing humanity's reflection on what has been ignored.[4] It depends ultimately upon an act of will and the commitment to, in the words of his friend Walter Benjamin, "never forget the best." Categories for determining the "best" were, for Bloch, never forthcoming. It was enough for him to emphasize that the best will only appear where it is least expected. Tolerance and civil liberties are thus immanently demanded by the philosophy of the man who once defended Stalin's show trials. Unacknowledged works by the most diverse cultures, "traces" (*spuren*) of forgotten lives, fragments of historical production retain untapped perspectives on the "best life," which never simply "vanish" (Hegel) into immediate forms of practice. Indeed, "the waking dream everywhere feeds on what has been missed."[5]

Realizing the utopian *novum* depends upon tapping the potential from the past. And this, in turn, is dependent upon the degree of consciousness generated in the present. The future is thus no mechanical elaboration of the present; nor does it emerge from a series of "steps" or "stages" deriving in linear fashion from the past. The future is open. Determining the "horizon" of the present is possible only through unearthing the "anticipatory consciousness" embodied in the cultural achievements of the past. Utopia is not seen by Bloch as an abrupt break with what exists; thus, in contrast to critical theorists like

Adorno and Horkheimer, history becomes more than the unrolling of "necessity" and "freedom" more than the affirmation of "negativity." That is why Bloch could say: "To the *novum* there belongs, in order that it really exist as a *novum*, not only an abstract opposition to a mechanical renewal, but rather in fact a specific type of renewal: namely, the not-yet-realized total content of that goal which is itself meant and intended and processed out of history's progressive novelties."[6]

Of course, for all Bloch's claims to materialism, his remains a fundamentally idealist vision. The "objective contradictions" within the existing order are not entirely forgotten. But the essential point, important enough, involves a commitment to *deideologize* ideology and articulate a utopian hermeneutic capable of building the content and furthering the realization of a "realm of freedom." That having been said, however, the philosophy of Bloch harbors a unique view of ideology that flies in the face of Leninist orthodoxy. Without any organizational referent, whatever Bloch's attempts to employ the language of communist orthodoxy, his thinking inherently rejects any mechanical distinction between "true" and "false" consciousness.

His approach also rejects the popular idea that the potential within any form of social practice is exhausted by examining the historical context from which it arose. A reaffirmation of the dialectical relation between immanence and transcendence occurs as cultural products become more than mere "artificial social constructs." They can "jut beyond" the historical conditions of their emergence, or, in reactionary and regressive fashion, retreat behind them. And Bloch draws the theoretical consequences. A perspective takes shape in which, against all dogmatic forms of dialectical "stage theory," it becomes impossible to assume that a reconciliation of *all* the contradictions defining a given epoch will take place before the next appears on the scene. Unresolved problems as well as unfulfilled hopes carry over from one phase of history into another. And the form, no less than the function, of these "non-synchronous contradictions" will change within the dominant social, economic, and political structures of the new period. A single unresolved concern like salvation can manifest both positive utopian and negative disutopian characteristics in different ways in different historical epochs. The implications of Bloch's approach are important for analyzing manifold phenomena including racism, sexism, the "cult of the personality," and the role of atavistic classes like the peasantry and petty bourgeoisie. Indeed, even while Bloch considered the proletariat immune from "non-synchronous contradictions," the concept would prove crucial for his remarkable analysis of German fascism.[7]

Once again, however, the political underpinning of his argument was naive. There was simply no serious possibility of developing a "triple alliance" of the workers, peasants, and disgruntled petty bourgeoisie against the Nazis. This perspective obscures the mass base of Nazism, and mistakenly, in keeping with the communist line of the period, tends to equate it with the interests of "monopoly capital." There is also something questionable about the claim that Marxism was being stripped of its utopian ideals in the 1920s even while the Nazis were employing a corrupt notion of the apocalypse in furthering their quest for power. Nor is it ever really made clear, except when referring to the most extreme circumstances, how the categories of "false" and "true" utopia are ultimately grounded in anything more than goodwill: the Nazis surely reaped enormous propagandistic value from mutilating the past and establishing their particular forms of utopian symbolism. This becomes as apparent in the marching songs, in the films of Leni Riefenstahl, and the torchlight parades. Coincidence alone, according to Bloch, cannot explain why Möller van der Bruck should have taken the notion of a "third reich" from the humanist and utopian vision first articulated by the medieval philosopher Joachim di Fiore.[8]

Ideology becomes a fungible concept. It is neither fixed nor finished. Ideology may obscure and justify the oppression of the status quo. But since human practice inherently retains a teleological component, it will also retain an emancipatory moment. A ruling ideology is for Bloch, in more concrete terms, the ensemble of ideas of a ruling class. But a universal interest, generally articulated while a class is on the rise, can coexist with a particular one in any given work. "Liberty, equality, fraternity" is an example; "we the people" or "the right to life, liberty, and the pursuit of happiness" is another. Every articulation of a universal interest projects the desire for justice, harmony, freedom, and the like. Usually, the dominant class will become alienated from the radical implications of its ideals by its oppressive activity. Without the existence of the utopian element in ideology, however, it is impossible to explain the allure of these ideals or why they can transcend the context in which they arose.[9]

Radical analysis is then not just a matter of sociological reduction or explaining the "immanent" historical roots of ideas. It also involves unearthing their "transcendent" potential as well. The ideology of a given period is subsequently never entirely "false," as in "false consciousness," since a set of "not-yet-realized" utopian possibilities remains "latent" and waiting for self-conscious appropriation by the lowly and the insulted. The new society will not just "objectively" appear. "Subjective" action is necessary to interpret the unfulfilled possibilities of the past and reshape the repressed needs of humanity as they become evident in the manifold set of cultural products through which history is understood.

Gone is the determinism of "scientific socialism" and the willingness to ascribe an inflexible class content to a given idea or work. The "cold current" gives way to the "warm" one. The sober emphasis on modernization gives way before the mission articulated by the young Marx and the Lukács of *History and Class Consciousness*. Visions of anthropological transformation, the employment of dialectics as a critical method with a humanistic intent, the creation of a fuller, richer, more meaningful existence become the purpose of the socialist enterprise. The aim is "to lift the world and inwardness, in their new interaction, out of their alienation and reification. Marxism is thoroughly realistic, but definitely not in the sense of a banal schematic copy of reality; to the contrary, its reality is actuality plus the future within actuality. Through its own concrete change, which it ever holds open, Marxism demonstrates that there is still an immeasurable amount of unused dream, unfinished content of history, unsold nature in the world."[10]

Just this—the "unused, the "unfinished," and the "unsold" is what critical inquiry must clarify. Reflection and critique never lose their primacy in the work of Bloch. But the importance of fantasy and the experience that explodes the constraints of the given is never lost either. Dealing with such concerns, in fact, becomes obligatory for the cultural critic. Aesthetic criticism cannot remain content with either political or sociological pronouncements. Nor will purely formal judgments get to the heart of the matter. Art, for Bloch, is a mode of enjoyment and of experiencing the world in a new way. And the implication of his position is clear enough. Chaining either cultural production or criticism to the traditions of the past is inherently illegitimate. Art, for Bloch, *must* experiment with new forms of expression that overcome the limitations of the past. The value of art appears in its simultaneous ability to serve as a "utopian laboratory" and a "feast of elaborated possibilities" for the future.[11]

There is no stasis. The possibilities of a work change through its interaction with a changing public. In fact, Bloch considers it necessary to judge even "unpopular" works, which might initially appear as irrationalist and fragmented, with an eye on the new and the unexplored. Bloch thus does not see "decadence" in the surrealist and expressionist attempts to merge dream and reality, perceive the world in a new light through distortion, or juxtapose dissimilar objects through montage. He looks for more. He delights in the new color of the fauves, the fantastic imagery of the surrealists, the irreverent fun of the dadaists, and the free play of the expressionists. This Stalinist always remained a modernist. And he wasn't a snob either. Indeed, just as he took exception to the "realist" position favored by Lukács in the famous set of debates between them during the tail end of the 1930s, his interest in a variety of popular forms ranging from the detective novel to nursery rhymes placed him in opposition to the stance usually associated with the Frankfurt School.

Experimentation with new forms and the aesthetics of fantasy make for, in the view of Bloch, a "dream which looks ahead" (*der Traum nach Vorwärts*) and confronts the "way things are." This dream is not commensurate with a retreat into childhood fantasies. And so, in contrast to Freud, Bloch refuses to concentrate upon the "night-dream" whose truth emerges in memories of the past or the "no-longer-conscious." He instead emphasizes the role of the "day-dream" with its projection of the "new," the "not-yet-conscious," and its loose connection with the situation in which the individual finds himself. Hope appears in the day-dream; happiness is envisioned as "the shape (*Gestalt*) of things to come." The day-dream, for Bloch, is capable of surmounting the censoring qualities of the superego and thus inherently retains a utopian kernel.[12]

Arguably, in analyzing the subjective presentiment of utopia, Bloch ignores how social repression is introjected into the very substructure of the individual, and the freeing of rage that can occur once objective referents are exploded. Also, in his emphasis on the "anticipatory consciousness," the "day-dream," and the "not-yet-conscious," he turns the concept of possibility into the property of pure consciousness. This would obviously place him in opposition not only to the followers of Marx and Lenin but also to adherents of Martin Heidegger and Jean-Paul Sartre.

Phenomenology and existentialism had gained in popularity during the 1930s. They emphasized the "concreteness" of individual existence and drew a connection between the concept of "possibility" and death. The central category of "authentic" experience was "anguish" or "dread." Bloch was aware, however, that hope is as legitimate a fundamental mode of experience as anguish once a "possibility" of existence is encountered. With any "concrete" possibility, after all, there is the hope of its being fulfilled as well as the anguish at the thought of its remaining unfulfilled.[13] Death is unavoidable. Only through a philosophical sleight of hand does it become a "possibility." And so, once again, Bloch draws the consequences. Real possibility, for him, "does not reside in any finished ontology of the Being of that which is already existent, but rather in that ontology of the not-yet-existent (*noch-nicht-Seienden*) which is continually grounded anew as it discovers the future in the past and in all of nature."[14]

The "possibility" of utopia remains. Bloch's ontology is neither fixed nor finished. And, precisely for this reason, the unfulfilled promises of the past and the untapped sources of consciousness in the present prevent any *absolute* denial of utopia in the future;[15] indeed, once again, a famous line from the "Theses on the Philosophy of History" by Walter Benjamin comes to mind: "every second of time is the strait gate through which the Messiah might enter." And so, a "militant optimism" comes to define Bloch's worldview. Optimism of this sort bears no relation to the passive and naive variant so often encountered. Rather, it assumes the existential commitment to make good on the "latent" possibilities existing in the present and help in actualizing a new world for the future.

Now, Sartre once wrote that the question of whether history has a meaning is foolish: the real question involves what meaning is given to it. Perhaps Bloch was too quick in dismissing the contribution realism might make in determining the concrete conditions wherein the "new" can serve as an "interruption." But he was surely correct when he wrote that "man does not live by bread alone—especially when he doesn't have any." Idealism is essential for the emergence of any political movement. And this idealism has palpably dissipated. The reaffirmation of ideals is no small matter in today's world. But that does not call for the suppression of the unpleasant or a self-imposed blindness regarding the mistakes of the past. This was a point of which Bloch was aware. Human nature may be malleable, but evil runs deep. And yet, "in the negative there are also constructs of the unconstructable, the absolute question: there are unbearable moments of wonder."[16] A writer like Kafka, who describes the existential no less than the bureaucratic nightmare with such precision, thus makes a utopian contribution by defining what must be overcome. His work did not lack an "anticipatory consciousness": Brecht indeed captured this when he said that Kafka "saw what was coming without seeing what was there."

Perhaps this "anticipatory consciousness" is not inherent within every cultural construct. Bloch, in his ontological justification of aesthetic claims, may well have overstated his case. But he is willing to address the unacknowledged question. What is the worth of art? And his answer juts beyond its immediate impact. He knows that every great work of art remains, "beyond its immediate manifestation, imprinted upon the latency of the other side; that is, upon the content of the future which had not yet appeared during its own time, if not upon the content of a yet unknown final state. For this reason alone, the great works of all times have something to say and, in fact, a far-reaching *novum* which is not noticed in any of them by the previous age."[17]

A project, inherently new and fresh, presents itself in the philosophy of Ernst Bloch. It is founded on hope and a willingness to recognize that the potential for emancipation breaks the constraints of every fixed and finished system. It is the same with art and philosophy. Of all the philosophers within the tradition of critical theory, he is the most generous when it comes to aesthetic experience and so perhaps best understands what it means to speak about the integrity of an artwork. His is an essentialism that does not exclude; it doesn't serve the purposes of sexism, racism, or any other form of oppression. His thinking refuses to accept anything as simply given. The articulation of what it means to strive for the "best life" can be found in a hundred rivers and a thousand streams. It calls for a cosmopolitan frame of mind and a refusal to chain the meaning of a work to any set of political aims or provincial experiences. Critical interpretation breaks the chains of dogmatism and that enterprise, no less than the quest for utopia, is unending. Thus, following the African sages, Ernst Bloch insisted toward the end of his long life that "if a story is nothing then it belongs to him who has told it . . . but it is when it is something that it belongs to all of us."[18]

⌒ 6 ⌒

Horkheimer's Road

Max Horkheimer was born in Zuffenhausen, a suburb of Stuttgart, in 1895, the son of a wealthy Jewish businessman. His early school years were undistinguished and he left the Gymnasium to work as an apprentice in his father's textile factory. In 1911, however, he made the acquaintance of Friedrich Pollock who would become an important political economist, an early member of the Institute for Social Research, and a lifelong friend. It was Pollock who introduced Horkheimer to the world of the mind, traveled with him, and supported his desire to marry Rose Riekher, nicknamed Maidon, a non-Jewish woman, against the wishes of his family.[1] Even in his youth, however, Horkheimer was influenced by a sense of being Jewish.[2] Still his views were assimilationist and critical, which in keeping with a certain enlightenment tradition of Judaism, he considered two moments in the same process of emancipation. This indeed allowed him to judge the existing order in terms of its own professed ideals of liberalism.

His interest in Kant, especially given the popularity of neo-Kantianism in Germany around the turn of the twentieth century, thus makes sense. Horkheimer's dissertation would concern itself with the relation between teleology and the capacity for normative judgment (*Urteilskraft*) in the philosophy of the great Königsberg thinker. The young man would inherit from him the idea of freedom as pertaining to an individual subject resisting the encroachments of instrumental rationality, a fundamental commitment to reflexivity, and skepticism concerning all absolutist claims. Another thinker from the early days, however, would also exert an influence: Schopenhauer. His pessimism combined with his ethical emphasis on compassion and hatred of violence fit the historical experience of Jews, and it would shape Horkheimer's entire intellectual development. Schopenhauer's *Aphorisms for Worldly Wisdom* had a pronounced impact on the early collection of jottings and impressions, published in 1934 under the pseudonym Heinrich Regius, titled *Dawn*;[3] indeed, the aphoristic form would later become a hallmark of critical theory.[4] Schopenhauer's *The World as Will and Idea* would also inspire Horkheimer's critical encounter with the Enlightenment. Finally, the striking pessimism of Horkheimer's later essays evidences traces of the philosopher he already admired in his youth.[5]

Horkheimer had his differences with both Kant and Schopenhauer, and scholars differ over the respective degree of influence exerted by them. Arguably, especially during the 1930s, the influence of Marx was greater than either.[6] Kant and Schopenhauer, however, always remained with him; one gaining temporary predominance, the other never disappearing entirely. A tension existed from the beginning between his commitment to speculative inquiry and fear of the irrational and his preoccupation with "concrete" experience and the yearning for an indefinable alternative that would prove both utopian and existential. But this tension became more pronounced following World War II. Most interpreters suggest, in this vein, that the later philosophical problems encountered by Horkheimer were directly related to his reliance on Kant.[7] In my opinion, however, it was the influence of Schopenhauer that helped lead his thinking into a cul de sac. Either way, of course, this oversimplifies the matter. It was probably more a matter of the incompatibility between their respective approaches no less than the social values dividing the Enlightenment tradition from that of its critics.

Attempts to construct new philosophical standpoints always involve a degree of experimentation with the past. But there is a difference between integrating insights from different thinkers into an articulated framework and simply conflating mutually exclusive assumptions or traditions. Kant emphasized reflexivity, the universal subject, republican values, and a "teleology of hope" while the philosophy of Schopenhauer is framed around intuition, subjectivity, elitism, and a profound pessimism. Reconciling them was problematic from the start, and Horkheimer's rejection of epistemology and all "systematic" forms of thinking involved a price. Thus, his theory would perhaps best exemplify the most crucial philosophical problem with critical theory.

Horkheimer's thinking changed over the years. But he never surrendered his commitment to critical theory. A concern with the negation of suffering and the liberating force of subjectivity never left him. It was there in the beginning, even before he was drafted into the service, where his time was spent in a Munich health clinic. There he heard of the Russian Revolution, experienced the disintegration of the monarchy following Germany's defeat, and anticipated an "association of free people" in the council movement. The war seemingly forecast the cataclysmic end of bourgeois society and radical hopes were being inflamed by the new Communist International. And so, for a while, the determinate negation seemed to supplant the indeterminate. The influence of Schopenhauer receded into the background as Horkheimer sought to forge a critical theory fundamentally committed to the idealist strain within the Enlightenment tradition and Marxism. His metaphysical pessimism was tempered by historical optimism. Horkheimer perceived the "objective tendencies" for transforming capitalist society. Nevertheless, from the start, a doubt remained about whether this transformation would ever occur.

* * *

It was in the aftermath of the war that Horkheimer, together with Pollock, returned to high school, received a diploma, and decided to pursue academic work. Following a semester at the University of Munich, Horkheimer transferred to Frankfurt where he studied gestalt psychology, economics, music, and philosophy. Ultimately, after taking courses with Edmund Husserl and meeting Martin Heidegger in Freiburg, he wrote his rather routine dissertation—on Kant's *Critique of Judgment*—for Professor Hans Cornelius in whose seminar he also encountered his later collaborator: Theodor Adorno. But the crucial event occurred in 1923. Felix Weil, whose family had made its money as wheat merchants, had long been Horkheimer's friend, and in that year, he funded a new institute to study the history and theory of the workers' movement.

Carl Grünberg, a professor of law and politics at Frankfurt University, became its first major director following the death of Albert Gerlach, who did not live long enough to make an imprint. The Institute for Social Research would become the first independent Marxist institute in Europe.[8] During the early years it reflected Grünberg's somewhat traditional Marxist emphasis on political economy. While Horkheimer worked on *Dawn*, a novel posthumously published as *Out of Puberty* (1974), and started on a book tentatively titled *The Crisis of Marxism*, which he never finished, the institute committed itself to works like Henryk Grossmann's study on capitalist laws of accumulation and collapse, Karl August Wittfogel's inquiry into Chinese economics and society, and the first systematic study of Soviet economic planning by Pollock. The focus only changed after Grünberg suffered a stroke in 1927.

Pollock ran the institute for a few years. But the real shift from political economy to critical theory began when Horkheimer took over as director in 1930. That he should have been chosen for the post came as a shock. Horkheimer held no academic chair.[9] Also, outside of a few articles, very little of his work had appeared up to that time; in fact, it was only in 1930 that Horkheimer finally published the *Beginnings of the Bourgeois Philosophy of History*. But, the only others who could have assumed a leadership role, Grossmann and Pollock, were preoccupied by their political activity with the Communist Party. Then, too, Horkheimer knew the administrative workings of the institute.[10] He had also already become a genuine influence on the young scholars who attended its seminars and who ultimately comprised the "inner circle" of the Frankfurt School—Theodor Adorno, Walter Benjamin, Erich Fromm, Leo Lowenthal, and Herbert Marcuse.

Horkheimer's inaugural lecture was published in the institute's *Journal for Social Research*.[11] There he articulated a new philosophical and practical project for the institute: its "supra-disciplinary" approach, which, in fusing philosophy with empirical social scientific research, would produce a new materialist enterprise guided by normative assumptions.[12] This standpoint would inform the major undertakings of the institute during the 1930s. It presupposed a concern with historically situating phenomena as well as an awareness of philosophy's role in shaping the society it seeks to describe. Positivism and all appeals to ontology—or what, in short, might be termed "traditional philosophy"—thus came under attack from the perspective of his new antiphilosophical critical theory.[13] And yet there remained a commitment to the autonomy of theory beyond its relation to any particular worldview as well as a utopian concern with the abolition of all repressive social relations. All this would receive further definition in a series of articles, also originally published by the *Journal*, which included perhaps *the* seminal work for the new philosophical enterprise: "Traditional and Critical Theory."[14]

Aware with Marx that practice alone could evidence the truth content of philosophy, and that idealism veiled the existence of economic exploitation, Horkheimer ultimately recognized that the proletarian revolution had betrayed the truth it was meant to actualize. It would prove difficult since Horkheimer was committed to the Communist Party throughout the 1930s. Its more orthodox notions, like the mistaken belief that fascism was the product of "monopoly capital," often appeared in his writings. His work during this time also did not evidence any antipathy to science or technology per se[15]; it merely made the claim, which was admittedly radical at the time, that science was mediated by the contradictions of society at any given phase of historical development. There remained the concern with suffering and, like Schopenhauer, Horkheimer he believed ethics should be grounded in "concrete" needs rather than universal precepts. At the same time, Horkheimer maintained that the alleviation of suffering in the future demanded a recognition of "necessity" in the present. But the Hitler-Stalin Pact of 1939 was the last straw. The critical method would now increasingly divorce itself of practice and its primary concern would become the individual.

Critical theory was originally conceived by Horkheimer as a materialist enterprise. But his version of materialism did not reject the moment of critique inherited from idealism.[16] "Critical theory," in this sense, was arguably itself a by-product of the theoretical innovations undertaken by Georg Lukács and Karl Korsch in the early twenties.[17] After all, they had already argued that Marxism was not some dogmatic form of economic reductionism with a catechism of theses and predictions. It was instead understood by them as an inherently "critical" method dedicated to examining the "totality" of social relations and so, in the words of Korsch, committed to "the application of the materialist conception of history to the materialist conception of history itself."[18] Both thinkers provided a "dialectical" critique of "vulgar materialism," by which they meant empiricism and positivism, as well as a rejection of all fixed and finished philosophical systems. Their historical approach also resurrected the connection between Marx and Hegel. It placed consciousness, as well as the practical role of ideology and reification, at the forefront of the theory. Indeed, while committed to a "ruthless critique of everything existing" (Marx), Korsch and Lukács sought to influence political practice with an eye toward abolishing the alienating effects of the division of labor along with all forms of exploitation.

So where then does Horkheimer's philosophical contribution lie? It is most important, perhaps, in giving the critical method a genuinely independent status. No longer tied to a party or a given institutional arrangement as a goal, surrendering any connection to teleology or ontological grounding, his critical method brought the unrealized aspects of human freedom to the foreground and raised the question of "compassion" in terms of an anthropological ethic.[19] Horkheimer also sought to explore, without reference to the "privilege" accorded a supposedly preconstituted proletariat, the manner in which consciousness was the product of various practices connected with a broad definition of civil society in its historical unfolding. No less than for Lukács and Korsch, in his view, the standards of neither positivism nor a metaphysics based on the primacy of intuition were adequate for justifying truth claims.[20] Facts would now gain their validity only when historically situated and linked to the ideal of the "good society." Horkheimer's critical materialism, moreover, would manifest a highly original understanding of philosophy insofar as he sought to link it with social scientific techniques, which interested neither mainstream social scientists nor associates like Marcuse and Adorno, and thereby anticipated what has become known as post-metaphysical thinking.[21]

Critical theory would now involve the attempt to actualize the materialist content of idealist philosophy.[22] But such an undertaking was hindered by teleological thinking as well as the increasing hegemony of instrumental rationality and a pragmatist outlook. All these forms of thought assumed the "identity" between reason and reality. The response would come in the form of a new emphasis upon preserving the "non-identity" between subject and object. Horkheimer's essays from the 1930s, materialist though they were, perhaps best articulate the roots of what would become the hallmark of the new tendency, a preoccupation with the subjectivity of the subject, even as they lay the foundations for the metaphysical turn of "critical theory."[23] This desire to protect subjectivity (*Selbsterhaltung*) from an increasingly rationalized world of commodities and instrumental thinking, in turn, required a new emphasis on the autonomy of theory from political practice. And so, without reference to specific conditions or institutions, Horkheimer found himself criticizing both reform and revolution in pursuit of the "totally other." Alienation and the concerns raised by the young Marx became ever more paramount in his thinking. By the same token, however, the postwar period was beginning to take on strongly reactionary characteristics both with McCarthyism in the United States and a stifling conformism in Germany. "Critical theory" became a code word for Hegelian Marxism, which enabled its partisans to enter the prevailing academic discourse.[24] But it retained a fundamentally radical quality in the postwar period. Critical theory would outstrip the thinking of both traditional working-class parties just as the elite university of times past was turning into a mass institution with a new constituency ready to appropriate its insights. Thus, the most profound impact of critical theory would be exercised on the radical intellectuals of 1968.

*   *   *

Most critical theorists were engaging in a critical assessment of Marxism, of course, before the 1930s came to a close.[25] Horkheimer and his colleagues began emphasizing social psychology over political economy if only because, in various empirical studies on the working class and the nature of authority, research had shown that only a small minority of members from left-wing political parties displayed a coherent ideological orientation and were disposed to revolutionary engagement.[26] Works of this sort were obviously meant to explore the conditions that inhibited the revolutionary process. It was increasingly the "totality" that had to be changed. But this appeared ever more difficult as the Soviet thermidor made way for Hitler's triumph. The utopian demand to change life rather than simply transform society surrendered to a new pessimism as Horkheimer sought to relocate the institute in exile.

But, for all that, these were the years in which members of the institute made their greatest contributions to the development of social theory. These were inspired by the work of Horkheimer. "Traditional and Critical Theory," along with a host of other philosophical essays seeking to delineate the stance of the Frankfurt School, were complemented by works like *Studies on Authority and the Family* (1936),[27] on which Horkheimer collaborated with Erich Fromm, as well as his own essays like "The Jews and Europe" (1938) and "The Authoritarian State" (1940).[28] The collaborative enterprise essentially argued that the transfer of socializing functions from the family to various political institutions had produced an increase in sadomasochistic tendencies, and a loneliness that craved authority.[29] Developments of this sort were complemented by the analyses of how liberalism was giving way to authoritarian institutions and atavistic racism was emerging from capitalism. Each of these works explores a different dimension of repression. In viewing them as a whole, however, Horkheimer suggested that the traditional connections existing between civil society and the political realm were being destroyed while ideology was becoming a direct expression of the state. Thus, already in this period, Horkheimer claimed that a form of unaccountable bureaucratic control was weaving all realms of public life into a seamless web of domination.[30]

All these works rested on the belief that liberal capitalism did not and could not fulfill its promise of liberation. The Enlightenment notion of progress, implicit in Hegelian teleology and inherited by Marxism,[31] was increasingly called into question along with the ability of the proletariat to break from its ideological bonds and institute a new order. Qualitative differences between regimes and institutions began to fade in the thinking of Horkheimer. But the budding tendency to provide a "critique" of the "whole," without any "positive" institutional referents other than some passing references to the need for workers' councils, immediately produced political and analytic problems.[32] If communism is merely the "negative reflection" of what it wishes to oppose, and fascism is a direct product of bourgeois society in which social democracy has been integrated,[33] each can express nothing more than a structurally distinct version of the same authoritarian state.[34]

Totalitarian society becomes the model for advanced industrial society.[35] In the totalitarian world of bureaucratic rationality run amok, the relevance of principles and normative criteria for judgment diminishes. Such a belief was obviously buttressed by the Munich Agreement of 1938, which sacrificed Czechloslovakia to the Nazis in order to secure an illusory "peace with honor," and the Hitler-Stalin Pact of 1939 that would unleash the Second World War. Enemies became allies as political principle vanished before the overwhelming impact of strategic exigencies. Ideological differences between regimes seemed to give way to an instrumental willingness to deal with one another and sanction repression.[36] Ever more surely, the relatively uncritical perspective on the Enlightenment of earlier days, the once firm belief in the Soviet Union, and the revolutionary mission of the working class, fell away. Emphasis on the individual and critique, even without a positive referent, received new historical justification. Horkheimer influenced a new philosophical perspective in which individual freedom is inimical to the *form* of bureaucratic domination existing within advanced industrial society.[37] The original commitment to emancipation divorced from any agent would thereby become capable of bringing it about.

And, in fact, there was no longer such an agent. Maintaining the commitment to liberation therefore required turning away from historical reality. This is where the real break with the tradition of Hegel and Marx, the real beginnings of what Adorno would later call "negative dialectics" and what Herbert Marcuse termed "the great refusal" appears. Freedom, from this time on, will no longer appear as the "insight" into "necessity" or the attempt to confront a given period with a determinate "negation."[38] It would instead become the rejection of "necessity" and the denial of determinacy. Seeking to preserve the lost moment of experience, and the revolt against an all-encompassing reification, Horkheimer collaborated in developing what might be termed a new "negative" philosophy of history. The historical character of the original "critical" enterprise thus gave way to a new approach intent upon differentiating between the "potentiality of freedom and the actuality of repression."[39] That is what received expression in *Dialectic of Enlightenment.*

Begun in the early forties, completed in 1944, first published in 1947, this book is surely the most important product of the Frankfurt School and the most influential work of critical theory. It was essentially the product of ongoing debates between Horkheimer and Adorno, which were taken down in dictation. The work also retains numerous unresolved contradictions, and Horkheimer was wary of republishing it after the institute moved back to Germany. It might well have seemed too radical for the new chancellor of the University of Frankfurt (am Main). His activity on the project, however, was no aberration from his other intellectual undertakings.[40] Quite the contrary. Its most basic themes appear again and again. Indeed, for all the shifts in emphasis, *Dialectic of Enlightenment* stands in coherent relation with Horkheimer's earlier works.

Debating whether Horkheimer or Adorno played the leading role is a matter of purely pedantic interest. It was a common effort, and both authors must ultimately take responsibility for its content no less than a style in which loosely connected essays and cutting aphorisms eschew any systematic mode of presentation and brilliantly juxtapose insights from radically diverse fields. For all that, however, the purpose of the book is clear. Horkheimer and Adorno wished to situate the critique of bourgeois society within an "anthropology of domination" (*Urgeschichte der Herrschaft*).[41] They wished to show how progress resulted in barbarism and how the very mythology of domination the Enlightenment sought to destroy reappears as its own product.[42] Regression rather than progress is seen as defining human development so that fascism is understood as surpassing "the conditions that prevailed before its coming to power, not in a negative sense, but rather in their positive continuation."[43]

All this initially emerges from the dazzling reading of *The Odyssey* where the "cunning" of instrumental reason is employed by Odysseus, who changes his name to "no one" in order to escape death at the hands of monsters. Sacrifice lies at the base of rationality; the repetition of sacrifice disempowers the gods it seeks to exalt even as it undermines subjectivity and freedom. And so, *from the very inception of civilization*, individuals appear condemned to preserve their existence by denying their subjectivity. Subjects are now, according to Horkheimer and Adorno, indeed interchangeable. This is not the result of any particular social or political system. It is rather a product of the instrumental attempt to dominate nature and deal with others.[44] This tendency would become full-blown in the historical epoch known as the Enlightenment. Myth had originally sought to control nature and now, in the age of full-blown barbarism, enlightenment would itself become a myth. This is the real if unacknowledged legacy of the enlightenment which, according to the authors, extends from Kant over Sade to Nietzsche. After all, if Kant undercut the verities of all mythical or normative claims in the name of scientific rationality, Sade could take the next logical step and view all subjects as instrumental means for personal gratification even as Nietzsche, ruthless in the critical application of his skepticism, would ultimately consider history and nature as subordinate to the arbitrary will of the subject.

Commodity production is seen as underpinning this development and, insofar as exchange value transforms qualitative differences into quantitative ones,[45] it turns technical rationality against all forms of metaphysics and normative concerns. The exercise of arbitrary power complements a process which renders subjects ever more subordinate to the mercy of objective forces and strips them of the capacity to make normative judgments. The apogee of this development lies in anti-Semitism and the gas chambers.[46] But the dynamic exists just as surely in the modern era with its conformist and profit-driven "culture industry," which seeks the "lowest common denominator" for its products, and subverts the very possibility of reflection or revolution. Thus, "humans pay for the increase of their power with alienation from that over which they exercise their power. Enlightenment behaves towards things as a dictator toward men. He knows them in so far as he can manipulate them."[47]

Dialectic of Enlightenment is clearly a critique of the Enlightenment undertaken from the standpoint of Enlightenment itself; indeed, there is even a certain connection between this book and Adorno's later defense of metaphysics and its unfulfilled promises. The problem for both of them lies in the dominance of closed philosophical systems and the imperialist ambitions of instrumental thinking. Horkheimer and Adorno believed that, in jettisoning the speculative component of reason, instrumental rationality actually winds up insulating itself from criticism and becoming a new dogma akin to myth.[48] It only makes sense then that their joint effort wished to preserve the reflexive moment of language from practice, which, in turn, became the theoretical justification for the complexity and density of their prose. In opposition to Nietzsche and the thinkers of postmodernism, however, Horkheimer and Adorno never collapsed cognition into power and consistently rejected a relativism they saw as connected with historicism and positivism. Quite simply: They believed that Enlightenment rationality violated the reflexive component of language and thus ineluctably aided in the creation of a totalitarian society.

Deluded by assumptions of unilinear progress, the sentimentality of human-ism,[49] intoxicated by scientific rationality, complacent in their utilitarian quest to dominate nature, the proponents of Enlightenment were seen as engender-ing precisely what they wished to suppress.[50] The resurrection of Schopen-hauer's influence along with the new pessimistic strain in Horkheimer's thought is evident in this new critical attitude toward the Enlightenment and a view which, here in contrast to the earlier writings, holds that "technical rationality is the rationality of domination itself."

Horkheimer expanded on the consequences of this claim in *The Eclipse of Reason* (1947). Speculative philosophy might still hold out the idea of a final reconciliation between humanity and nature, the possibilities of the individ-ual and a society that might actualize them. But he maintained that reality was increasingly being made immutable and "self-identical"—or equivalent to the objective categories that define it—by pragmatist and positivist successors to Enlightenment philosophy committed to eliminating all utopian or specula-tive criteria of judgment and identifying technological progress with progress as such. Nor is idealism free of sin; viewing progress as a phenomenon of the mind, subordinating concrete experience to abstract categories and the theo-retical imagination to fixed modes of thought, its metaphysical presupposi-tions led to the surrender of any power it might have had to protect concrete individuality against the incursions of instrumental reason. Indeed, these were the ways in which Enlightenment turned reason into what David Hume called a "slave of the passions."

*   *   *

Dialectic of Enlightenment unquestionably remains a landmark in radical thought. Placing the individual at the center of a dialectical analysis, employ-ing metaphor and rejecting positivist criteria of truth, Horkheimer and Adorno forwarded an anthropological perspective that revealed how the instrumental domination of nature expelled freedom from the historical process even as it threatened to invade the realm of the subject. Their analysis of the "culture industry" would profoundly influence the discourse on media and society. Horkheimer and Adorno turned conformism into more than a merely bohemian concern and the instrumental colonization of everyday life into a political issue. Then, too, anticipating postmodern philosophy, their work constituted an assault on the need for epistemological congruence and a corrective for the lavish praise traditionally accorded Enlightenment thought by the labor movement. The book also provided one of the earliest attempts to link Marx not only with Freud but with Nietzsche, and perhaps for the first, the price demanded by all teleological notions of progress was deemed too high.[51]

Dialectic of Enlightenment remains a *chef d'oeuvre manqué*. It extrapolates conditions pertaining in the 1930s and 1940s into the future. Its elitism is undeniable. It sunders the connection between theory and practice, and it substitutes an "anti-political politics" for a politics predicated on interests, organization, and common ideals of solidarity. The image of the Enlightenment becomes distorted, and the authors play fast and loose with its historical legacy. Horkheimer and Adorno viewed the Enlightenment as the most advanced ideological expression of a rising bourgeoisie seeking to establish a new production process and solidify its political control. But they also viewed it as part of an anthropological "enlightenment" intent upon waging an assault against superstition, myth, and prejudice. They never recognized, however, that it is more than either or the two in combination. Identifying "enlightenment" merely with a debunking of what stands beyond the scientific domination of nature and what Kant called "pure reason" ultimately reproduces the very reductionism and "reified" form of philosophical inquiry that Horkheimer and Adorno putatively sought to oppose. Their picture of the historical Enlightenment is arbitrary and one-sided. Emphasizing its connection with technological rationality, they never undertake a genuine political analysis.[52] Horkheimer and Adorno ignore how the Enlightenment concern with universality became the foundation for republicanism, socialism, and internationalism;[53] how its new emphasis upon the liberal rule of law was based upon protecting the individual and constraining arbitrary power; and how its commitment to scientific knowledge fostered tolerance and openness to change rather than mere contentment with the status quo.[54] Enlightenment political philosophy was predicated on the accountability of state power, while its greatest figures such as Lessing and Locke, Hume and Kant, Diderot and Franklin were fundamentally committed to liberal beliefs. The famous claim of Horkheimer and Adorno that the Enlightenment gave rise to Nazism and totalitarianism is simply wrong: its proponents were those whom the Nazis fought against and the Stalinists despised, and there is hardly a single modern antifascist value that does not stem from the period of the great bourgeois revolutions that extended from England to America to France.[55]

Just as it is a mistake to locate the ideological source of fascism in the Enlightenment, however, so is it mistaken to view the phenomenon as a simple outgrowth of bourgeois civil society. Not only was fascism a self-conscious ideological response to liberalism and Marxism, democracy and socialism, but the atavistic anger of its mass base—located in *precapitalist* classes like the petty bourgeoisie and peasantry—was fundamentally directed against the two dominant classes of the modern production process: the capitalists and the proletariat.[56] From the standpoint of neither intellectual nor political history, let alone class analysis, does the interpretation offered by Horkheimer and

Adorno make sense. Their interpretation of what Hegel termed "the cunning of reason" (*list der Vernunft*), by which instrumental rationality subverts the normative values originally inspiring it and thereby opens the way for the eradication of conscience in the totalitarian state, ignores the obvious. It was not instrumental reason that brought about fascism and destroyed the ability of the individual to make normative judgments, but rather real movements with one set of values intent on eliminating those committed to *qualitatively* different ones.

Horkheimer and Adorno obscure all this with their anthropological and metaphysical approach. Even if historical reconstruction were simply a hermeneutical project, mediated by inherited guilt and allegorical or utopian modes of reasoning, it would still require points of historical reference. Without such referents, social interests become obscured and politics becomes a purely arbitrary enterprise. Horkheimer and Adorno, of course, wished to offer a "radical" transcendent perspective with which to contest all competing internal historical standpoints. But, from the start, their attempt to unify qualitatively different phenomena under a single rubric could only lead to pseudo-dialectical sophistry.[57] Communist theoreticians, interestingly enough, were always masters at this game. They liked to see fascism, committed to the destruction of parliamentary democracy, as the product of "monopoly capital"—which nevertheless also supposedly ruled the bourgeois democracies of the interwar period.[58] Then too, all "superficial" differences notwithstanding, such a stance allowed them to castigate social democrats as "twin brothers" of the Nazis in the years preceding the Popular Front of 1936: Léon Blum and Charles Maurras or Rudolf Hilferding and Joseph Goebbels could thereby be seen as "really" one and the same. [59]

Even after surrendering any lingering belief in the revolutionary character of the Soviet Union, Horkheimer provided a new twist on this former way of thinking.[60] The "integral statism" of his deeply pessimistic essay "The Authoritarian State,"[61] with its suggestion that socialism has lost its internal connection with historical progress and that a burgeoning bureaucracy is eradicating qualitative differences between governmental forms and ideologies, anticipates the claim of *Dialectic of Enlightenment* that liberalism engenders totalitarianism.[62] Ignored is the way in which ideological critique and the commitment to civil liberties are crucial elements of the Enlightenment enterprise. Institutional differences between regime types also vanish in favor of philosophical and anthropological abstractions. And these are only reinforced by the decision of the authors to consider Sade, Schopenhauer, and Nietzsche as an extension of Enlightenment thought.[63] That they considered themselves opponents of the underlying values of Enlightenment political theory appears irrelevant. The "idea" is always privileged over the event, and if Horkheimer and Adorno indeed claimed that "social freedom is inseparable from enlightened thought," their real aim was to illuminate the way in which a "self-destruction of the Enlightenment took place."[64]

Perhaps, ironically, their enemies understood the reality much better. The Nazis knew that materialism no less than idealism was connected with liberal political thought and that, whatever the degree of purposeful misinterpretation, the roots of their ideology lay in the vitalist critique of both by many of the same thinkers embraced by Horkheimer and Adorno. Dismissive of the "superficial" differences between intellectual representatives of diverse traditions, however, the authors of *Dialectic of Enlightenment* sought to broaden the "enlightenment" to include its greatest and most self-conscious critics. Those they include are also "critical" in their approach, but the authors too often forget that critique can be leveled from different political perspectives and that it can serve different purposes. There is no inherent connection between critique and emancipation: the former is necessary to further the latter, but the latter is not required to engage in the former. That is why situating the given critique of the status quo within a political or philosophical tradition becomes very important.[65] John Stuart Mill and Antonio Gramsci had both observed the trivialization of culture and—perhaps because they never lost track of their political projects—did not fall prey to elitism. The modernist critique of mass culture and the "culture industry" developed in *Dialectic of Enlightenment*, however, is not really indebted to them. It rests instead on the thinking of Nietzsche and a host of anti-Enlightenment critics, all of whom evidenced a peculiar brand of aristocratic radicalism and "romantic anti-capitalism." They too wished to preserve subjectivity from the "lowest common denominator" and a world increasingly dominated by crass materialism and technological rationality. They too were quick to note the false sense of immediacy produced by various fads and what was termed "the loss of niveau." They expressed their contempt for "the masses" and were, at best, unappreciative of "the democratic ethos . . . " No less than Horkheimer and Adorno, they despised conformism and obsessed over modernity's manifold threats to subjectivity.[66]

Dialectic of Enlightenment viewed cultural developments, by way of contrast, as interconnected with a given system of production. If its authors were critical of popular culture, that was because they believed it subverted genuine autonomy and deadened the spirit of emancipation. Horkheimer and Adorno may have looked to "classic" and technically complex works,[67] but that choice was dictated by their belief that such works alone fostered the capacity for reflexive discernment and the remembrance of past horrors in the face of declining educational standards and perpetually changing fashions.[68] Artworks seeking to express radical political messages were seen by them as merely fueling the hegemonic power of the status quo, creating a false sense of liberty, and fostering a relativism in keeping with what Herbert Marcuse would term "repressive tolerance." Thus, for them, the extent to which a given work of art is made popular by the culture industry is the extent to which its critical or liberating potential is absorbed.

Talk about the "integration" of such works only begs the question of whether they were really rendered impotent or whether they actually helped change the "hegemonic" system and were only then turned into museum pieces. Questions of this sort, however, are never entertained in *Dialectic of Enlightenment.* Is it really the case that the commodity form exhausts the critical potential of an artwork? It is true enough that the public realm of discourse has narrowed, that there is a literacy crisis, and that the general level of cultural production has fallen. Most artistic works produced by the culture industry debilitate the intellect. But that is not true of all of them. With Horkheimer and Adorno, however, the analysis always remains stuck at the level of form and presentation. And so, in line with the philosophical thrust of *Dialectic of Enlightenment,* Adorno later write that "every visit to the cinema leaves me, against all my vigilance, stupider and worse."[69] He would later qualify the statement. But that doesn't change the fact that the metacritique developed by him and his coauthor has little room for categories capable of differentiating between works: Is Charlie Chaplin really no different from the Three Stooges? Without categories capable of drawing distinctions between popular works, ironically, the aesthetic vanishes within the sociological. It was enough for Horkheimer to note that if the culture industry comes to define the public realm, then the moment of resistance must enter the tenuous domain of a private experience constantly threatened by the extension of technical rationality.[70] Thus, interestingly enough, he was actually less sanguine about the liberating role of aesthetics than either Adorno or Marcuse in their later writings.

The whole was what counted and, increasingly, it was seen as being defined by a reifying form of instrumental rationality. Political attempts to transform the existing order and its network of significations, from such a perspective, become useless by definition. Solidarity through any form of organization is conformity. Enlightenment of the masses can prove nothing more than "mass deception." A single option remained, and Adorno embraced it with his claim that "only insofar as it withdraws from Man can culture be faithful to man." With the articulation of this stance, however, critique reproduces the very conditions it claims to contest. Normative judgments can only appear ad hoc. Even the concept of utopia, from which critique ultimately derives its power, becomes subverted. Originally the concept retained a sense of the institutional prerequisites necessary for the construction of an emancipated order. It was as much a regulative idea for action as a vision of emancipation. Somehow, however, Horkheimer identified it with a quasireligious "longing for the totally other" (*Sehnsucht ganz Anderen*). Thus, his commitment to freedom became coupled with the most debilitating pessimism.

*   *   *

Horkheimer was scarred by the war and the revelations about the concentration camps. He had observed the weaknesses of Weimar. He had been exiled by Hitler and betrayed by Stalin. The totalitarian state with its concentration camp universe led him to emphasize concepts like "marginality" and look to "admirable small groups" whose irrelevance to the "apparatus of oppression" made possible their "escape to truth." Solidarity would, he believed, become universal only by empathizing with "those standing outside" and, in accord with Schopenhauer, compassion must serve as the foundation for an ethics. It is irrelevant whether some of his later speeches and radio talks had an optimistic ring, whether the totally administered society projects vague tendencies toward universal solidarity, or even whether the father of critical theory called upon the rebellious students of the sixties to recognize the freedom offered them by the West in contrast to the East.[71] His postwar view of advanced industrial society, even as it derived from his earlier collaboration with Adorno, lost its radical sense of purpose. His skepticism in the postwar era now extended to democracy itself. He may have continued to think of himself as "radical," but, in fact, he sought stability rather than revolutionary transformation or even structural reform. This half-hidden desire often gave Horkheimer's political admonitions in the years to come a sanctimonious and conservative quality.

His social position had changed from the time he first left Germany. Horkheimer's academic standing in the United States grew after the institute published a five-volume series titled *Studies in Prejudice*, for which Horkheimer—collaborating with Samuel Flowerman of the American Jewish Committee—wrote the foreword. The *Studies* would result in at least three classic texts: *Rehearsal for Destruction* by Paul Massing, *Prophets of Deceit* by Leo Lowenthal and Norbert Guterman, and *The Authoritarian Personality* by Theodor Adorno and numerous other collaborators. It made sense, then, that the newly constituted West German state should have eagerly sought the return of the institute. The offer was generous and, after much agonizing and haggling, Horkheimer agreed. The Institute for Social Research, amid a good deal of fanfare, relocated to Frankfurt in 1949.[72] Horkheimer and Adorno then in 1955 decided to publish the *Frankfurter Beiträge zur Soziologie*[73] and thereby made popular the previously unknown publications of the *Journal for Social Research*. They became major intellectual figures in the postwar order, and Horkheimer, who ultimately became chancellor of Frankfurt University, collected a coterie of remarkably talented students that included Jürgen Habermas.

The influence of critical theory on young radical intellectuals like Rudi Dutschke and Hans-Jürgen Krahl, two of the most prominent figures in the

European uprisings of 1968, would prove profound. They admired the stance that seemingly called upon them to contest both liberal reformism and soviet communism; they believed that the power exerted by bureaucratic rationality demanded a new emphasis on participatory democracy, normative judgment, and what Herbert Marcuse appropriately termed a "new sensibility." They saw the culture industry and its mode of manipulation as eliciting the need for a radical transformation of everyday life, a genuine "cultural revolution," and an openness to the contributions of the Third World in which various movements were undertaking the difficult struggle for national self-determination. They agreed with Adorno that "the whole is false." But when radical students shouted slogans like "Power to the Imagination!" or "Be Realistic, Demand the Impossible!" Horkheimer reacted angrily. Again and again, his *Notizen* evidenced concern with the supposedly totalitarian threat engendered by the student uprisings and the fear of impending chaos brought on by excessive democracy.[74] A caricature of the movement appears in his writings. There is little enough said about the civil rights movement; what Eisenhower himself saw as the threat from the "military-industrial complex"; poverty; the dynamics that led to Vietnam; the tumbling of de Gaulle; or the attempt to transform everyday life.

Horkheimer's arguments were actually no different from those raised by a host of less philosophically talented mainstream conservatives. They too warned of abandoning values by those wishing to raise them. They too talked about political realism with respect to a foreign policy, a war, and a defense budget that made no sense. They too employed old-fashioned communist sophistry with their hysterical claims that the critics of the West, naively and unconsciously, served the interests of the East. In search of stability they too raised the banner of family, religion, community. Indeed, forgetting the criticisms that he himself had once leveled against these same ways of thinking, Horkheimer no longer wished to argue that "the critical theorist's vocation is the struggle to which his thought belongs. Thought is not something independent, to be separated from this struggle."[75]

It was as if, like Luther, he came to fear the practical implications of his own ideas. The critical perspective withered. The arguments sounded less and less original. And so the rebels could only shrug their shoulders when, in articles like "Critical Theory Yesterday and Today" (1970), Horkheimer claimed that a fundamental contradiction existed between the quest for individual freedom and the call for equality.[76] The more discerning knew that this argument had already been made—and made better—by the most important exponents of laissez-faire capitalism like Friedrich von Hayek and Milton Friedman. Nor were they misled. They could point to a host of figures like John Stuart Mill who knew that the practical exercise of democracy is facilitated by economic equality and that freedom is not furthered by treating individuals as means to an end since inequality will then follow logically. But Horkheimer ignored Mill along with the rest. Conveniently, in complete agreement with the ultra-left, Horkheimer's stance allowed him to condemn all action by the mainstream left as not radical enough. His own politics during the postwar era reflected the truth of his insight: "*les extrêmes se touchent*."[77]

Horkheimer justified his political conservatism through philosophical radicalism. He maintained his hatred of nationalism and militarism, and there were still isolated moments of bravery; thus, in spite of his support for the state of Israel, Horkheimer never surrendered to the more extreme forms of Zionism and openly criticized the Eichmann trial.[78] In keeping with his new prominence, however, his writings on returning to Germany generally reflected a decidedly cautious and antipolitical tone.[79] He ignored his own influence. He had little use for Marcuse's "marginal groups' theory," the "new sensibility" of the rebels, "surplus repression," or theoretical attempts to break with the "reality principle." Horkheimer neither embraced ontology, which explains his distance from Ernst Bloch, nor retreated into aesthetics in the manner of Adorno. Nevertheless, he was unwilling fully to abandon utopia or surrender the idea of a radical alternative to instrumental rationality.[80]

There is a sense, then, in which the end lay in the beginning. The moment of indeterminacy that had plagued critical theory from the first now reached fruition. And so too did the commitment to allegory. With all aesthetic and strictly philosophical avenues closed, remembering the betrayal of one revolution and fearing the next, with thoughts of Auschwitz and the atomic bomb indelibly etched on his consciousness, with progress still an illusion and subjectivity still endangered, he saw only religion as maintaining the vision of "the wholly other." Such is the solution to the "enigma" of his final theoretical choice and his philosophical decline.[81] Horkheimer looked to the Old Testament, which taught that just as the attempt to portray God is prohibited, knowledge of the true and the good is inaccessible. The injunction against idolatry is an injunction against false idols; Horkheimer's theological stance thus retains certain elements of the demystifying and defetishizing stance originally associated with critical theory. Nevertheless, while the younger Horkheimer was too much the materialist to believe that a perception of the absolute is the condition for judgment, the old man now wished to employ the sacred to preserve a moment of hope from the profane.[82]

The yearning for God[83]—for the "wholly other"—would evince a happiness denied by the world and the lack of a common interest in abolishing suffering. The social function of this theological standpoint was obviously to provide a new foundation for morality.[84] Solidarity would somehow translate into a "community striving for a better existence"; Horkheimer thus anticipated the concern of a contemporary communitarian theorist like Michael Walzer with establishing the "moral sentiment" and what Richard Rorty now conceives as a common desire to eliminate "cruelty." But Horkheimer's stance is more systematically elaborated and more existentially concrete. The image of the Other, confirming the insight of Schopenhauer that earthly happiness always remains incomplete, both makes existence bearable and maintains the inability to end suffering in secular terms.[85] This indeterminate yearning for an inexpressible alternative was meant to provide the individual with consolation in an otherwise hopeless world. Horkheimer continued to reject all ideologies the individual that reconciled to suffering and he employed a notion of "complete justice" to challenge the reality of injustice. But, for all that, a profound pessimism obviously inspired the "negative theology."[86] His new morality never translated into an ethic capable of dealing with practical problems. There are no categories of judgment; it forwards no positive injunctions nor foundations for institutional criticism. At the same time, whatever its debt to Judaism or Christianity,[87] the new standpoint offers neither the prospect of salvation nor the reality of community grounded in ritual. Horkheimer's "negative theology," for this reason, can neither meet the existential needs of religiosity nor the secular demands of the dialectician.

There is a sense in which the principal concern of his later years had not changed: it was still a matter of preserving the self under conditions of total administration. And the argument proceeds apace. For where there is barely a self to preserve and no historical or political vehicle to secure its happiness, dialectically—or, better, paradoxically—reason projects the need for faith. Only through faith can the victims of progress gain something for their sacrifice; only through faith is it possible to maintain the "yearning that the murderer not triumph over his innocent victim."[88] But this "yearning" translates into nothing concrete. It lacks a critical edge and, frankly, verges on the trite and the sentimental. The world is left as it is. Thus, far more than the philosophy of the Enlightenment, Horkheimer's critical theory with its initial commitment to reflection and emancipation ultimately turned into its opposite.

But it would be a mistake to remember him only by his later efforts. Horkheimer influenced every major current within critical theory by championing the moment of negativity in transforming the understanding first of philosophy, then of history, and then of theology. His enterprise was marked by genuine cosmopolitanism, extraordinary intellectual range, and a profound humanism. He was among the first to confront the radical implications of the divorce between theory and practice in the dialectical project. He also drew perhaps the most honest consequences of Benjamin's insight that emancipation must involve a break with progress and history. Even if others remained more true to the radical implications of the original project, Horkheimer remained consistent in his contempt for systematic philosophy, authoritarian strictures, and ideological sophistry. He always prized the individual rather than an abstract revolutionary "subject" like the class or the nation. And with this concern in mind, he employed the critical method to assault the shibboleths of enlightenment, science, the family, and the bureaucratic state. Willing to call the most basic values of modernity into question, both organizationally and philosophically, he helped create a framework in which intellectuals might further the original critical undertaking. Nor did he ever lose his love for the treasures buried in the great philosophical traditions of the past. And the commitment to an alternative, even when he could no longer find its secular anchor, stayed with him to the end. In fact, until his death in 1973, Max Horkheimer always sought to capture that speculative moment of knowledge which shows how reality falls short of what we can imagine and what the powerless so often unknowingly demand.

Rescuing the Fragments
On the Messianic Materialism
of Walter Benjamin

We know that the Jews were prohibited from investigating the future.
The Torah and the prayers instruct them in remembrance, however.
This stripped the future of its magic, to which all those succumb who
turn to the soothsayers for enlightenment. This does not imply, however, that for the Jews the future turned into homogeneous, empty time.
For every second of time was the strait gate through which the Messiah
might enter.
           —*Walter Benjamin,"Theses on the Philosophy of History"*

W alter Benjamin knew what he wanted. In 1930, he could write of his
wish "to be considered as the premier critic of German literature."[1]
His output was already impressive. The translator of Baudelaire
and Proust, he had authored *The Origin of German Tragic Drama*,[2] some
unique autobiograpical writings for what would become *Berlin Childhood
around 1900*, a compilation of aphorisms entitled *One-Way Street*, a few scholarly books, a remarkable set of literary studies, and numerous articles for
major newspapers. But his greatest work, the thousand-page compilation of
notes and citations for *The Arcades Project*, was never completed.[3] Similarly,
while his acquaintances ranged from Brecht and Hofmannsthal to Gide and
Valery, he was always on the verge of poverty and died fleeing the Nazis in
1940 at the age of forty-eight, virtually unknown. Only due to the efforts of
friends like Theodor W. Adorno, Hannah Arendt, and Gershom Scholem—
who themselves only rose to genuine fame after the war—was his work redis-
covered.[4] They published his correspondence, individual works, and volumes
of his selected writings in the 1950s. They wrote reminiscences and spread his
name around academic networks. Nevertheless, it was only with the popularity gained by the Frankfurt School during the student movement of the 1960s
that this wish of Walter Benjamin was truly fulfilled.

His intellectual standing has now reached almost mythical proportions, and it is not Marxists alone who quote him like "holy writ."[5] Quite the contrary. Benjamin has become a pillar of the literary establishment. He is embraced by everyone from linguistic structuralists to fashionable Marxists and postmodernists. Excellent work on his legacy has, in fact, been done by a host of scholars. Ironically, however, his extraordinary fame does not simply derive from that. Other factors are at work: his spirituality, his personal idiosyncracies, his preoccupation with the most varied esoteric interests, his Marxism, his submersion in everyday life, his life as an outcast. And then there is a prevailing intellectual cultural climate that not only prizes these values but renders suspect the very attempt to formulate an internally consistent argument. Indeed, beyond the intrinsic worth of his works, external factors of this sort have helped turn Walter Benjamin into an intellectual cult figure.[6]

All this would be well and good if the reception did not subvert the critical quality in his thinking. It has. Too many admirers avoid dealing with the gaps in his thought as well as the specific nature of his contribution or the contradictions in his peculiar form of messianic materialism. Simply enjoying his diverse insights into the seemingly insignificant details of everyday existence, suggesting that he is engaged in a postmodern form of "playing with language," dishonors his achievements. Ignoring the epistemological character and political intent of Benjamin's approach undercuts any determination of how his enterprise furthers or hinders the critical enterprise. Superficially viewing Benjamin's work as a "tapestry," while forgetting about his inability to weave together the diverse strands of his thought, becomes only a backhanded compliment. Nor is it enough to note that his political naivete and epistemological weaknesses created the interpretive space for appreciating the singular and the unique. Praising the fragmentary and idiosyncratic qualities of his work has only tended to liquidate any sense of what is really at stake.

Exploring these epistemological and political concerns is a thankless, perhaps even a hopeless, task. Hopeless because no article can possibly assimilate his extraordinary range of interests; thankless because, even on the epistemological level, a multitude of intellectual forces were at play in which the appropriate expertise of the critic is weak with respect to one or the other. That, however, is precisely the allure of dealing with Benjamin. His thinking does not follow a "one-way street." It shifts gears and often stops short. Then it starts and again and takes on speed through each encounter with a new viewpoint or discipline. Benjamin makes good on the promise of the Frankfurt School for an interdisciplinary approach in perhaps the most radical possible manner. His method calls into question the strategies and abstractions of "traditional" theory and, whether it succeeds or not, projects a sober and flickering image of emancipation. Reflection takes on new objects of concern; it turns upon itself. Materialism receives a hermeneutic underpinning while the messianic encounters history. Benjamin's thinking exposes the problems associated with simultaneously seeking to follow paths that, even while they occasionally intersect, still ultimately separate as they recede from view. His was a perilous intellectual undertaking. Nevertheless, if his "hermeneutics of danger" provided him with an existential way to survive fascism,[7] his intellectual biography does not simply follow a chronological sequence.

Active in the youth movement, Benjamin breathed its air of "romantic" opposition to bourgeois conformity. The experiments of the modernist avant-garde also became known to him early in life through his association with dadaists like Hugo Ball and expressionists like Kurt Hiller, Ludwig Rubiner, and Franz Pfemfert. Also in his youth, Gershom Scholem, Martin Buber, and Hermann Cohen exposed Benjamin to Jewish theology, which, in turn, profoundly influenced his later hermeneutics and theory of language. Neo-Kantianism, furthermore, fostered his desire to overcome the tension between reflexivity and experience, the metaphysical and the material, abstraction and the particular. As for Marxism, Benjamin's interest was awakened after Scholem left for Palestine in 1923.[8] Around that time he met Asja Lacis, a communist and innovator of children's theater, with whom he fell deeply in love.[9] Already influenced by the messianic radicalism of Gustav Landauer and Ernst Bloch, Benjamin was introduced by her to Bertolt Brecht and Karl Korsch.[10]

Utopian speculation played a role in all these traditions, and Benjamin never surrendered the insights and perspectives of earlier days.[11] The concerns of his dissertation entitled "The Concept of Artistic Criticism in German Romanticism," for example, stayed with him. Immanent criticism, utopian longing, spiritual crisis, historical rupture, the importance of tradition and the dangers of its manipulation, as well as the self-renewing set of intepretive possibilities within the work of art, would prove crucial for every aspect of his work.[12] Perhaps, in the future, he would give up on the attempt to develop a standpoint "on the ground of the Kantian system."[13] But he preserved the theological terminology and symbolism no less than the preoccupation with experience beyond the rational.[14] This interest, in fact, led Brecht to criticize his friend for retaining elements of "mysticism in spite of an anti-mystical attitude." The concern with experience, however, enabled Benjamin to maintain his commitment to subjectivity in a world increasingly dominated by totalitarian terror and the commodity form. Thus, his attempt to "re-function" dialectical materialism and messianism while fusing the facticity of the historical with the experience of myth.[15]

An emphasis on "experience," the limitations of traditional "systems," and "concrete" philosophy defined the intellectual climate of his youth.[16] The similarities with the exponents of existentialism and phenomenology, who were gaining popularity in the 1920s, is striking. In fact, whatever their protestations to the contrary, that is also the case for many within the camp of critical theory. With Benjamin's thinking in particular, however, "the philosophical faculty is extended to non-philosophical objects, to seemingly blind, unintentional materia."[17] And this interest in bringing the objects of everyday life into the purview of philosophy stayed with him even after his conversion to Marxism. Thus, Ernst Bloch could note that "Benjamin had the quality which was so extraordinarily lacking in Lukács. He had a unique eye precisely for the important detail, for that which lies by the wayside, for the fresh element, which breaks open in thinking and in the world, for an unusual and unschematic disconnected singularity which doesn't fit any preconceived purpose, and which therefore earns a completely private attention that turns one inward."[18]

Walter Benjamin called upon dialectical thinking to confront the particular and the exception to the rule. It was the "rubbish" of history that a radical messianism should reclaim. The experience of a boulevard, postage stamps, children's books, unpacking one's library, eating, and untold other elements of everyday life became the objects of critical scrutiny and manifold associations; each takes on an allegorical, mythical significance. A view of this sort obviously set him in opposition to official Marxism and placed him squarely within a certain current of critical theory best exemplified in the writings of Siegfried Kracauer and Theodor Adorno. Their unique form of analysis wished to show how the macrocosm is mirrored in the microcosm. Unique to Benjamin, however, is that he always let the object speak for itself; its singularity never gets lost. The fine English critic Terry Eagleton was correct in maintaining that for Benjamin:

> The thing must not be grasped as a mere instantiation of some universal essence, instead, thought must deploy a whole cluster of stubbornly specific concepts which in Cubist style refract the object in myriad directions or penetrate it from a range of diffuse angles. In this way, the phenomenal sphere is itself persuaded to yield up a kind of noumenal truth, as the microscopic gaze estranges the everyday into the remarkable.[19]

No less than his friends, however, Benjamin was never tempted by empiricism; indeed, he wished to preserve the dialectic. But while he might have had that sense of the singular and the exceptional lacking in Lukács, he also lacked what Lukács had. Rejecting the structured and mediated concept of "totality" in favor of a constantly shifting "constellation," Benjamin neither situated his object of concern within what Marx termed the "ensemble of social relations" nor invoked abstract categories to structure it. As usual he put his interpretive position metaphorically. Thus, he could write:

> Ideas are to objects as constellations are to stars. This means, in the first place, that they are neither their concepts nor their laws ... It is the function of concepts to group phenomena together, and the division which is brought about within them thanks to the distinguishing power of the intellect is all the more significant in that it brings about two things at a single stroke: the salvation of the phenomena and the representation of ideas.[20]

The relation between objects and the perspective of the viewer are left in a constant state of flux. That can have its value insofar as it undermines the sense of certainty and provokes reflection. It renders Benjamin's approach inherently antisystemic and experimental. But there is also a danger insofar as what he views as an "essential corrective to a narrowly totalizing ideology at the same time [risks] hardening, like certain contemporary theories, into no more than that ideology's inverted mirror-image, replacing a theoretical myopia with a corresponding astigmatism."[21]

What remains as epistemological organizing principles are allegory and the commodity form.[22] But the former will lose its theological and the latter its historical meaning. Insofar as the one is transcendental and contemplative while the other is historical and is active, linking them requires ripping them from their original philosophical context so that both lose their objective referents: the one in terms of God's order and the other in terms of historical development. This prevented Benjamin from producing the internally consistent worldview of Lukács or, for that matter, even Bloch. Which is not to say that Benjamin didn't want one. Rejecting fixed systems is not the same thing as denying the need for coherence.[23] Centering on the experience of the object immanently calls for uniting history with the conditions that make such experience possible and comprehensible.[24] Such an undertaking, central to neo-Kantianism, is actually part of a tradition extending from Fichte to Lukacs. It implies overcoming the tension between immanence and transcendence or the metaphysical and the historical. And this attempt was already made in what is perhaps his greatest essay: the study of Goethe's *Elective Affinities*.

Gershom Scholem was correct in noting the importance of this work for Benjamin's career insofar as "his speculative talent was aimed no longer at devising something new, but at penetrating something existent, interpreting and transforming it."[25] Prior inquiries into language and the form philosophy should take in the coming period give way to a standpoint dependent upon the existence of an empirical object. His essay thus notes that "critique" is intrinsically related to unearthing the transcendent "truth matter" (*Wahrheitsgehalt*) of the work while "commentary" is concerned with its immanent "subject matter" (*Sachgehalt*). Originally, in the production of a work, the two are bound together. They divide, however, once it enters the public realm. How to reconnect them was never made clear. Benjamin claimed that the more compelling the "truth matter" the more intimately is it bound up with the "subject matter" of the work. Thus he could write:

> the expression that is linguistically most existent (ie. most fixed) is linguistically the most rounded and definitive; in a word, the most expressed is at the same time the purely mental. Exactly this, however, is meant by the concept of revelation, if it takes the inviolability of the word as the only and sufficient condition and characteristic of the divinity of the mental being that is expressed in it.[26]

Truth resides within language. And the "true," in this sense, is the "whole": thus, the attempt to shift revelation from the ineffable experience to the word. But this wholeness is precisely what modern history has rent asunder. This "totality," not the infinitely mediated category of Hegel and Lukács, is the one Benjamin initially wished to restore. It is a wholeness associated less with the notion of "species being" in Marx than the ideas of Benjamin's contemporaries like Martin Buber and Karl Jaspers about the mystical and the Godhead. In contrast to these thinkers, however, Benjamin never assumed its existence "behind" reality. In fact, according to him, it is the very loss of this wholeness that necessitates language. Only in language can the comprehension take place of an experience which "makes uniform the continuous multiplicity of knowledge."[27]

Allegory is to language what ruins are to things.[28] It gives power to memory and creates the "horizon" wherein transcendence becomes possible.[29] Allegory, or so it is argued in *The Origin of German Tragic Drama*, provides a structure for conceptualizing the past no less than the mutability of all significations. It allows the shapelessness of materia to take an eternally mutable shape within an immutable context. Allegory makes a continual substitution of disparate particulars possible precisely because "things and occurrences do not meaninglessly stand next to one another, but rather refer to one another."[30] The concept, after all, has scholastic roots, and it was traditionally used to explain the manner in which secular reality is linked to the beyond and, epistemologically, how a conception of the beyond can arise.[31] Indeed, through the ability of allegory to provide every particular with symbolic properties, language presents the possibility of both giving and transforming the meanings of things.

Neither "political" nor "formal" analysis can then exhaust the meaning of an artwork. That belief would separate Benjamin from many of his more Marxist contemporaries; it would also inform *The Arcades Project*, which in its attempt to provide an "*ur*-history of modernity" entirely through the use of quotations, necessarily presupposes the existence of transcendent possibilities within works of the past as well as a sociological standard with which to judge their relevance for the emergence of the "modern." Benjamin was no relativist. More open than others in the Frankfurt School to film and popular culture, he nevertheless told Scholem of his need for "texts of canonical importance in order to develop his philosophical ideas adequately to comment on them."[32] Nor was he afraid to thematize reality; *The Arcades Project* is an attempt to offer a "grand narrative," albeit built on fragmentary foundations, which also evidences his desire to connect transcendence with immanence. The belief in the existence of such a connection indeed created the basis for his famous claim that there is no cultural artifact of civilization which is not at the same time an expression of barbarism.[33]

Commentary, in short, is unthinkable for Benjamin without critique. His aim was not to engage in word games but to overcome the academicism of literary criticism and give it a political purpose: "the art of the critic in nuce," Benjamin could write "offer slogans without betraying ideas."[34] His purpose was less negative than positive, not deconstructive but reconstructive.[35] The past becomes a set of "ruins" in need of restoration, and the present more than what first meets the eye. Or, put another way, these ruins harbor an untapped content. Works of art no less than philosophy forward a truth in need of judgment. But the evaluation is never final. Judgments and verdicts, as Benjamin said in the prospectus for his proposed journal *Angelus Novus*, always remain open to renewal.

The critical essay, in keeping with the Lukács of *Soul and Form*, transforms itself into an artwork deserving of further commentary. Translation, for example, is understood by Benjamin as a form sui generis.[36] It is an attempt to grasp the transcendent potential within an artwork. An emancipation from the original linguistic assumptions immanent to its creation thus necessarily takes place: this enables it to speak to a new audience in new conditions. But, in turn, this implies that the salience of the translation will prove transitory and that a new one will become necessary.[37] An ongoing process of constituting and reconstituting the connection between the immanent and transcendent properties of an artwork takes place. Thus, Benjamin could write that "the critic inquires about the truth whose living flame continues burning over the heavy logs of what was and the simmering ashes of life gone by."[38]

Without some form of prior or contextual justification, however, his claims appear tautologous since the critic seems engaged only in determining the content of concepts arbitrarily imposed on the object in the first place. Which way to turn? Epistemology might define their logical standing, but it is inherently abstract and Benjamin knew that a theory of knowledge can provide neither an ontological nor a material foundation for any particular form of inquiry. Ontology, of course, would ground his project; but, the undertaking of Ernst Bloch notwithstanding, it would do so only in the "systematic" terms against which Benjamin always rebelled. As for the teleological assumptions of dialectical materialism, they had proved false. With respect to a purely heuristic justification, whatever its benefits, he knew it would turn his categories into little more than ahistorical techniques. Not many doors remained open.

Jewish theology provided a way out. And Benjamin would employ it in a far more innovative way than either Max Horkheimer or Erich Fromm. This form of thinking neither presupposes a teleological structure within history nor a formal abstract epistemology. Benjamin's theology is not merely the unintegrated component of a fragmentary worldview developed by a philosophical iconoclast.[39] That is reading the story backward. Theology served a positive function in Benjamin's theory. His aim was to show how aesthetic experience and then historical insights are bound up with theological categories. And for good reason. His method, by relying on the theological moment, gained a foundation of sorts without recourse to an articulated ontological system. Given what Benjamin termed his "epistemologico-critical" approach, it becomes evident why the theological component should have remained with him *even after* he had lost his belief in God around 1927 and turned to Marxism.[40]

God, for the young Benjamin, existed as the unattainable center of a system of symbols intended to remove Him from everything concrete and everything symbolic as well.[41] It would only make sense then that insofar as philosophy participates in such a system, it will reflect an absolute experience symbolically deduced in the allegorical context of language.[42] What remains without God, which explains the superficial allure Benjamin holds for various postmodernists, is thus an allegorical world of symbols capable of endlessly transferring and multiplying the signification not merely of objects but of categories and philosophical systems as well. The existence of such a world legitimates his fusion of diverse insights from a multitude of sources and what would originally appear as mutually exclusive systematic claims.

Only montage can, in literary terms, adequately reflect a world dominated by rupture and incoherence. It becomes the theoretical point of entry into the content and the form of *The Arcades Project* as well as his earlier *Origins of German Tragic Drama*. Both demonstrate a preoccupation with spiritual rupture and the possibilities of using montage to construct a sense of coherence. Disciplinary boundaries fade. The blending of the historical, the theological, and the epistemological produces a constantly shifting foundation for the critical inquiry. Justified by the existence of a metaphorical world, however, the fusion of Marxist materialism and messianic Judaism offers a standpoint for Benjamin with which to overcome relativism. Both philosophies seek a harmony lost to the modern world. Utopia remains. Only, with Benjamin, it is a speculatively comprehensible yet materially unattainable condition ripped from any interconnection with traditional understandings of progress. In order to make his point, he introduces his now famous image from Paul Klee's painting titled *Angelus Novus:*

> [It] shows an angel looking as though he is about to move away from something he is fixedly contemplating . . . His face is turned toward the past. Where we perceive a chain of events, he sees one single catastrophe which keeps piling wreckage upon wreckage and hurls it in front of his feet. The angel would like to stay, awaken the dead, and make whole what has been smashed. But a storm is blowing from Paradise; it has got caught in his wings with such violence that the angel can no longer close them. This storm irresistibly propels him into the future to which his back is turned, while the pile of debris before him grows skyward. This storm is what we call progress.[43]

Progress does not simply extend into the future, according to Benjamin, but depends upon the manner in which the past is appropriated. The affirmative notion of unlinear progress, subverted in any event by the experience of World War I and the rise of fascism, is contested in the name of lived history and a more critical perspective. The unrealized potential of history gives utopia its content and, in turn, provides a utopian foundation for critique. For Benjamin, however, this means that every element of the past becomes open to redemption. This makes it possible for him to claim:

> Nothing that has ever happened should be regarded as lost for history. To be sure, only a redeemed mankind receives the fullness of its past— which is to say only for a redeemed mankind has its past become citable in all its moments. Each moment it has lived becomes a *citation a l'ordre du jour*—and that is Judgment day.[44]

Giving the apocalypse secular shape permits reintroducing an emancipatory point of reference just as the possibility of instituting a genuinely classless society was becoming ever more remote. A theological notion of remembrance, which finds its way into the thinking of Marcuse and Adorno as well, contests the perversion of history by totalitarianism. It becomes the only way to deal with that "single catastrophe" on which one gulag after another "keeps piling wreckage upon wreckage."[45] Such a view places new responsibility on the critic; Walter Benjamin was aware that "the task of history is not only to give the oppressed access to tradition, but also to create it." The past stands in need of "reawakening," which is precisely where the theological moment enters and converges with the modernist emphasis on montage and the unconscious. A critical intervention is necessary to shake the audience from its complacency. Benjamin considered the "*mémoire voluntaire*" of Proust inadequate for turning history into "the object of a construction whose foundation is not that of homogeneous and empty time, but rather that of a time filled and informed by the present time (*Jetztzeit*).[46] A reflexive and experiential "tiger's leap" into the past was required to crack open what is usually considered dead within the continuum of time and reaffirm it for a contingent future. This is the sense in which Benjamin could maintain that: "Only the historian is firmly convinced that *even the dead* will not be safe from the enemy if he wins. And this enemy has not ceased to be victorious."[47]

Ignored in much of the aesthetic discussion about Benjamin is the political purpose of his enterprise. He was clear about his wish "to interpret phenomena materialistically meant not so much to elucidate them as products of the social whole but rather to relate them directly, in their isolated singularity, to material tendencies and social struggles."[48] Whether he ever made good on this intention, however, is a highly debatable proposition. Walter Benjamin wished to retrieve what Hegel had thrown into the historical dustbin. He sought to discover an unrealized emancipatory potential from the facts considered useless and irrelevant by the dominant classes. The question involved how to make their salience or "concrete potential" recognizable. And, in this respect, Benjamin never had a clue. Revolution, for him, was always a messianic projection or a romantic longing. Reform and organization were tedious and boring. "Never in politics," he could lament in January of 1913, "does the Idea appear, always the party." And so, in his youth, Benjamin became interested in Sorel and reached the preposterous conclusion that "law"—in contrast to "justice"—is an order capable of being established only in a world of myth.[49] His naivete regarding the world of politics was extraordinary. His analysis of fascism was blind to conflicts between political parties, economic imperatives, and institutional interests. Indeed, Benjamin never understood anything of institutional constraints or the concrete options for change.

His response to the petrification of theory and practice under Stalin was to argue that each moment held a revolutionary potential and that it was time to reconsider the legacy of Blanqui.[50] There is barely a word in his *Moscow Diary* on the momentous struggle between Stalin and Trotsky, nor did his sojourn in France show any insight whatsoever into the politics of the Popular Front. Benjamin basically opposed it in favor of the spontaneous strike wave of 1936. But he seemed completely unaware that the strikes were purely economic in character, that France stood on the brink of civil war, that the parties of the working class neither constituted a majority nor were prepared for military conflict, or that the overwhelming majority of workers embraced León Blum's call for a "reform of the structure." His position was sectarian from the start and evidenced a bohemian romanticism common to others of his circle like Brecht and Bloch.[51]

Given his immersion in the history of nineteenth-century France and his admiration of Blanqui, always a favorite of Lenin, and of Marx to a lesser extent, Benjamin's thinking reflects a tentative left-Leninist critique of Stalin.

Benjamin's discovery of "the eternal prisoner," in conjunction with his messianism, led him to argue that an immanent revolutionary possibility presented itself with each moment in time.[52] Attacks on "contemplation" abound in Benjamin's work. But his thought yields no insight into the relation between theory and practice. Mistakenly, in the "Theses on the Philosophy of History," he even identified Marx's idea of revolution with "a leap into the open skies of history."

It was a strange form of Marxism embraced by Benjamin.[53] His interpretation involved the puzzling combination of a rather orthodox technological reductionism with an exaggerated conception of the method's utopian capacities. The point of Marxism for Benjamin was less to inform the creation of a "socialist" society than to provide the foundation for a utopia ultimately brought in from the outside. And to speak of a "materialist theology," in this sense, is merely playing with words. Neither the proletariat nor any other earthly agent could help in realizing what Benjamin wished to achieve. Marxism is gutted of its content and purpose. Its usefulness is relegated to certain key concepts like the commodity form and perhaps the manner in which it can function as a "myth" (Sorel).[54] The romantic conception of "violence," the exaggeration of revolutionary possibilities, becomes a temptation for all who don't have to deal with power, and it was prevalent in the thinking of Bloch and most members of the Frankfurt School as well. Benjamin, however, gave it a particularly radical stamp and was unafraid to expose the theological foundations for a Marxism of this sort. Scholem was surely correct when he called his friend "a theologian marooned in the realm of the profane."[55] Benjamin's attempt to fuse theology with historical materialism, for all its grandeur, was questionable from the beginning. Indeed, one of the finest scholars on Benjamin, Rolf Tiedemann, quite properly suggested that the theological terminology of the "Theses on the Philosophy of History"

> attempts to preserve the content of the proletarian revolution within the concept of the Messiah, the classless society within the messianic age and class struggle within messianic power. At the same time the revolution which does not come is supposed to be standing at the gate at any moment, like the Messiah. There, in some historical beyond, it can quickly put together a classless society, even if it is nowhere to be seen around here. The retranslation of materialism into theology cannot avoid the risk of losing both: the secularized content may dissolve while the theological idea evaporates.[56]

The "secular" is only metaphorically compatible with the "beyond."[57] The proletariat may have had "no goals of its own to actualize," which was probably meant as a call to realize the unrealized democratic goals of the bourgeoisie.[58] Whatever Marx meant by the phrase, however, he surely did not wish to claim that everything in the past—including the dead—is capable of resurrection through some apocalyptic moment of redemption.[59] Benjamin, for his part, wished to confront the unlinear and teleological views of history inherited by Marxism from the Enlightenment. His undertaking was marked by compassion for what had been irretrievably lost and a new view of the past as open and capable of constant reconstruction.[60]

What might be termed a *messianic hermeneutic* renders whole or gives cohesion to what has become fragmentary and redeems the suffering of the past. Utopia, previously conceived by Marx as immanent within history, is now transformed into an external standpoint with which to judge progress.[61] It becomes, in keeping with Sorel, a form of myth. As for history, in keeping with Nietzsche, it appears as a product of the subjective will. Arbitrary, without derivative categories for coherent interpretive judgment, its employment is an experimental exercise without any coherent relation to economic development, actual movements, or even cultural traditions. The historical standpoint thus retains assumptions that provide an insight into the sympathy so often expressed by Benjamin for the revolutionary voluntarism of Blanqui. Just as voluntarism confronts history, apocalypse confronts revolution; the end of time is not equivalent, except metaphorically, with the substitution of one class for another and one order for another. Nor is qualitative change the same as rupture, especially since, from a dialectical perspective, the counter-concept of continuity alone gives it meaning. Rendering a judgment about quality, or defining the empirical content of such change, becomes impossible since everything outside utopia is necessarily painted with the same shade of gray. And, for that reason, Benjamin must envision a new messianic form of appropriating the past. Unfortunately, however, the determination of the conditions under which such an appropriation can occur is abolished in the same instant that the wish materializes.

Remembrance is introduced into the science of orthodoxy. But its actual relation to critical interpretive work remains unclear since the criteria for employing it are never brought into play. Nor is it sufficient to remain content with the truism that all attempts at liberating the past must remain fragmentary. The plea to forget nothing turns into its opposite. Coherent attempts to appropriate the past assume a systematic view of history, which Benjamin's "Theses" render impossible. Materialism has subverted everything except the messianic will to redemption. Theology, for Benjamin, thus offers the last desperate expression of human freedom under conditions that, with the onset of the war and the failure of the radical uprisings in France and Spain, rendered hope impossible. Thus, the connection between these last jottings of Benjamin and the essay on Goethe's *Elective Affinities* that ends with the beautiful and oft-quoted line: "Only for the sake of the hopeless is hope given us."[62]

*   *   *

Walter Benjamin wrote much about the social condition of the writer. For him, however, he "remains the figure on the fringe who refuses to take part."[63] Benjamin was aware of the danger Western concepts of consumerism and egoism posed for the ideology of a newly emerging workers' state, but unaware of how the communist strategy of modernization would introduce precisely these values. Along with Bloch, he recognized the role of utopian motivation in revolutionary commitment and, following Lukács, anticipated the manner in which the commodity form would produce a "poverty of the interior."[64] But while his call to reinvigorate revolution with the surrealist spirit of revolt may have later endeared him to the *enragés* of 1968, it was little more than a metaphysical gesture from the very beginning. His desire to offer an alternative mode of praxis remained at the intellectual level of challenging the dominant notion of progress, reaffirming "the radical concept of freedom," obliquely criticizing the Communist Party apparatus, and demanding revolution for its own sake. And when it was finally too late, anticipating works like *The Dialectic of Enlightenment*, Benjamin extrapolated one terrible moment of horror into the future.[65]

Most assume that unlike Adorno, Benjamin sought to find the potential for transcending the given order immanently or from within its contradictions.[66] Actually, however, this was more a wish than a reality. The "dialectical image," through which the past offers itself to immediate experience in the present, is insufficient for such a task. Not only does it presuppose a revelatory "shock" of recognition on the part of the audience, whose unity and ability to appropriate the object depend upon a vaguely defined notion of collective unconscious, but it does nothing to help define the criteria for constructing a new history that "brushes against the grain." More is involved than Adorno's criticism that metaphysical essences do not become immediately manifest in facts. The real question is whether such essences exist at all or whether a prior worldview, external to the derivation of any potential within the image, is necessary to set the *political* context for appropriating the unrealized utopian potential within the object.

Marxism provided an "epistemologico-critical" context of this sort. Only from within such a normatively inspired and concrete context would the audience gain an "interest" in the work and a "reason to think" (Brecht); only with such a set of presuppositions could "crude" dialectical images begin to speak for themselves.[67] The problem, however, was that Benjamin could not completely embrace the necessary assumptions. He may have used Marxism to illuminate the commodity form, but he doubted its teleological claims. He may have stood in solidarity with the proletariat, but he was skeptical with respect to the party; he may have publicly embraced materialism, in his own unique way, but it was always qualified with theological messianism. His life and work were undoubtedly marked by empathy with suffering and the exploited.[68] But he never articulated even the beginnings of an ethic or a theory of socialist democracy. There are only the ongoing references to freedom and the power of fantasy.

Dialectics may have been Benjamin's preferred mode for reconstructing the lost possibilities within the phenomenon. But, in his theory, the particular is neither open to appropriation through transcendent categories nor situated within contradictions projecting determinate emancipatory possiblities. The transcendent potential of the material object, in messianic fashion, is simply presupposed. Making that potential manifest is thereby, in keeping with Blanqui, turned into a matter of arbitrary decision. The two perspectives complement one another. Existing in a metaphoric universe, wherein each element of the past is recoverable in messianic terms, the signification of an object appears immediately in its relation to that of other objects. There is no place for "mediation." Thus, in keeping with Benjamin's refusal to accept ideas that did not somehow take an immediately outward shape,[69] it makes sense that he should have sought to relate elements of the superstructure directly to one another and sometimes even to the economic base.

The Arcades Project was an attempt to create an objective context of signification wherein the subject might orient his or her choices.[70] Benjamin may well have sought to explode the immediacy of the present and any sense of linear development by creating "constellations" of dialectical images; he knew that recovering the past is a political act. But his approach was incapable of determining specific contradictions or any positive way of resolving them. Any connection between the physical and the metaphysical, the historical and the speculative, the historically concrete and the allegorical, falls asunder. Each cancels the other, so to speak, and what remains in the chasm are fragments, objects within an experiential "horizon," seemingly unviolated by the imposition of external categories and open to a relentless continuum of transformation disguised as historical appropriation by the oppressed. Thus, Lukács could note that:

> after all, in such actions interchangeable things and details are only sublated (*aufgehoben*) in their being-as-they-are (*Geradesosein*). The act of sublation directs itself only to their character at the particulat time and substitutes something which is exactly the same from within their inner structure. Thus, insofar as it is only a particular which is being replaced by something just as particuar, this sublation is nothing more than the restless reproduction of their particularity.[71]

Benjamin's theory divides against itself by mirroring the object under consideration from two irreconcilable positions simultaneously. Allegory provides the object with signification and the endless possibility of transformation even as it subverts the concern of historical materialism with determinacy and mediation. Dealing with such concerns, by the same token, robs the object of its allegorical transcendence. Thus, while the need for a concrete appropriation makes an allegorical interpretation impossible, the emphasis on allegorical transcendence undercuts the ability to offer anything other than an arbitrary and subjective mode of appropriating the object. That is perhaps because Benjamin was content to "show," not to tell; the objects were to speak for themselves.[72] But the problem is that usually they don't and, even if they do, the language will change with each attempted appropriation by any particular group. This will either relativize the importance of the phenomenon in question or, even worse, turn it into little more than an object of contemplation.

"Interest" cannot serve as the criterion of "truth" since, as Horkheimer liked to note, truth will then always remain in the service of the strong.[73] The choice, however, is not restricted to either imposing abstract categories or letting the object speak for itself. Perhaps aesthetic inquiry, whatever its unique practices and claims, is always informed by a broader social theory whose empirical and ethical justifications are external to it. The inadequacies of Benjamin's approach make clear how the valid use of a genuinely interdisciplinary standpoint will depend upon the ability to differentiate between disciplines and the areas of their relevance. Benjamin, however, did not see that. The inability to deal with this systematically derived from Benjamin's opposition to the totalizing impulse. But, interestingly enough, his most important contribution emerges from his particular form of resistance to it: his willingness to offer a material explanation for the aesthetic experience. Rereading his early essay on "Experience" in 1929, Benjamin noted: "In an early essay I mobilized all the rebellious forces of youth against the word 'experience.' And now that word has been carried over into much of my work. I nonetheless remained true to myself since my attack cut through the word without destroying it. It forced itself into the center of concern."[74] And he was right. His aesthetic ultimately highlighted the metaphysical experience of the commodity form, the interplay between technological development and fantasy, and his original preoccupation with transcendence.[75]

Nowhere does this become more evident than in the famous analysis of the "aura." The concept is difficult and it underwent a series of permutations before receiving its final elaboration in Benjamin's study of Baudelaire and his essay "The Work of Art in the Age of Mechanical Reproduction."[76] Especially the latter, for all the criticism it has undergone, is a landmark in the history of aesthetics. Never before did the moment of aesthetic experience become open to such radical scrutiny in material terms. It is not merely that the experience of an artwork becomes interwoven with the conditions of its production and reception. Even more important is the way in which Benjamin sees that:

experience of the aura rests on the transposition of a response common in human relationships between the inanimate or natural object and man. The person we look at, or who feels he is being looked at, looks at us in turn. To perceive the aura of an object we look at means to invest it with the ability to look at us in return.[77]

André Malraux liked to tell the story of how peasants fell to their knees before religious masterpieces when they were paraded through the streets, thinking that these were not simply representations of holy figures but rather their living embodiments. Benjamin understood how the singular experience of the work, in a religious context, provides it with a nimbus, a glow, as well as an anthropomorphic quality. The primacy placed on revelation, on faith, and on noninstrumental forms of thought under premodern circumstances—the embeddedness of the work within a tradition and an organic community—make this possible. There is no mediation. The work of art communicates with the audience even as it becomes imbued with their experiences.

Technology beginning in the "age of mechanical reproduction" abolishes the singularity of the work and renders traditional aesthetic forms obsolete. A new cultural situation presents itself in which the experience of the work no less than the work itself is ripped out of context and the preconditions for an organic community are destroyed.[78] Photography and then film, for the historical creation of the one "dreamed" the other, made the reproduction of the original work possible: its singularity is lost and a new disenchanted world inimical to tradition and organic forms of society presents itself. Thus, Benjamin could write:

One might subsume the eliminated element in the term "aura" and go on to say: that which withers in the age of mechanical reproduction is the aura of the work of art. This is a symptomatic process whose significance points beyond the realm of art. One might generalize by saying: the technique of reproduction detaches the reproduced object from the domain of tradition. By making reproductions it substitutes a plurality of copies for a unique existence. And in permitting the reproduction to meet the beholder or listener in his own particular situation, it reactivates the object reproduced. These two processes lead to a tremendous shattering of tradition which is the obverse of the contemporary crisis and renewal of mankind.[79]

In this new age, art becomes an object for the masses. The conditions for its production no less than for its distribution are made more democratic. A scientific worldview and the application of technology create a secular attitude that impinges upon the interaction of the individual with the work. The religious quality of awe vanishes and the aura is conquered. The immediacy of aesthetic experience takes on a new character and the aura gives way before something new. Fashion substitutes itself for the myths of old and the movie stars replace the demigods. But this does not mean that the mythical element is eliminated. Quite the contrary. The technological ability to detach the object from tradition creates new possibilities for propaganda. This becomes particularly evident with film wherein the alternatives of the new situation present themselves most starkly. It all depends upon a commitment by the audience and the artist that is at once philosophical, political, and aesthetic. With the loss of aura and the rise of the secular, after all, it only follows that the traditional notion of the masterpiece should make way before the work of "intervention." An "organizing function" thus defines the artist in the new era since art is now a mass phenomenon. A choice between conformism and individuality, irrationality and reflection, also presents itself to the audience. Often it is forgotten that, just as technology makes possible new forms of mass manipulation, the loss of aura opens the way for political analysis and what Benjamin termed a "heightened presence of mind."

Of course, in the beginning, new methods of production are still interwoven with the old and "dialectical images" still arise from which it is possible to deduce various collective ideas of wish fulfillment. The past still retains its utopian residue. With the increasingly pronounced effect of technology upon art, however, the ability of older forms to elicit experience becomes ever more precarious. And Benjamin was, in keeping with Brecht, not inclined to be sentimental. Thus, he could write: "Novels did not always exist in the past, nor must they necessarily always exist in the future; nor, always, tragedies; nor great epics; literary forms such as the commentary . . . we are in the midst of a vast process in which literary forms are being melted down, a process in which many of the contrasts in terms of which we have been accustomed to think may lose their relevance."[80]

Benjamin had enormous respect for Brecht and the latter's notion of "epic theater." Not merely did the author of *The Three-Penny Opera* emphasize the need for "crude thinking," which might make the determination of "dialectical images" somewhat easier, but his "estrangement-effect" (*Verfremdungseffekt*) also prized reflection, concentration, and sobriety in coming to grips with reality. Making the audience aware of how it is being fooled creates an interest in knowledge; keeping it simple enables it to comprehend the complex; forging a sense of distance from the action and the characters increases the outrage over oppression; politics mixes with fun; indeed, commenting on Brecht's technique, Benjamin put it nicely when he wrote that "there is no better starting point for thought than laughter; speaking more precisely, spasms of the diaphragm generally offer better chances for thought than spasms of the soul."[81]

Reflection and social reality are not simply juxtaposed against experience and fantasy. If Benjamin illuminated the manner in which a structural transformation takes place between experience and the productive forces of society, he also recognized that commodities hide a desire that takes new shape with each change in fashion; the commodity is always "bathed in a profane glow."[82] An analysis of commodity fetishism cannot rest at the economic level of production but must also include the experience of consumerism. The experience of commodity fetishism, by the same token, appears only in the analysis of the particular phenomenon. Critique, for Benjamin, always demands an empirical object. And here, in contrast to so much contemporary literary discussion, Benjamin stood with Schlegel when he wrote that "in what is called philosophy of art usually one of two elements are missing—either the philosophy or the art." The experience demands its material referent. This insight led Benjamin to make reductivistic claims regarding the relation between a poem or an image and the existing productive forces.[83] Nevertheless, it helps explain why he did not unequivocally condemn the entire realm of mass culture in the manner of Horkheimer, Adorno, and Marcuse.

"The separation of the true from the false," Benjamin could write, "is not the starting point, but rather the goal of the critical method."[84] It is with the particular object rather than with a judgment of the general form that an inquiry must begin. The culture industry engages in manipulation but produces works incarnating forgotten dreams. Reconstructing those dreams seemingly crushed beneath the boot of fashion is the only way to rub history "against the grain." There is nothing too small, too insignificant, from which to draw pictures of unfulfilled wishes. Such is the injunction behind the aphorism from The Arcades Project that runs: "Those who are alive at any given time see themselves in the midday of history. They are obliged to prepare a banquet for the past. The historian is the herald who invites those who are departed to the table."

But the banquet is composed of leftovers. It is not meant for those who "sit at the golden tables" (Brecht). An undertaking of this sort will employ an allegorical frame of reference to interpret the commodity form. Only then will the inquiry into the commodity illuminate a repressed desire that confronts the course of history. There is no theoretical mesh between these two constructs, and it is true that incompletely integrated into either perspective, the object ends up suspended between them. That was why, whatever his antisystemic tendencies, Benjamin wished to fuse the messianic with his own brand of materialism. Only in that way would it become possible "to rescue the metaphysical experience of the objective world."[85]

He felt his hermeneutical undertaking justified insofar as the loss of aura is symptomatic of what Max Weber termed the "disenchantment" of the world. Did Benjamin then wish to reenchant it? That depends. Affirming possibilities of experience endangered by the reification process is an obvious aim of his approach. Benjamin was fascinated by the thought processes of children; hashish fostered visions; the occult held an allure. But his more basic point was that the quest for new experiences makes it incumbent upon artists to exploit new technical innovations. Just as photography forced painting in the directions of cubism and expressionism, and film transformed the meaning and experience of the photograph, so will holographs provide a new impetus for film.

Fashionable claims about the "end of art" appear foolish from Benjamin's perspective. Artistic innovation, now interwoven with the development of technology, will survive so long as technology survives. Nor should there be any mistake. Benjamin's materialist insight is not some paean to technology. He does not claim that every artistic innovation is positive because it employs new technological forms. He is aware that innovations can be introduced from any political perspective. Exploring the relation between artistic and political judgments thus becomes of crucial importance, especially since the new mass media tend to blur the distinction between art and politics.[86] Disentangling the one from the other, rather than engaging in some form of postmodern resignation, becomes the task of the critic whom Benjamin termed "the strategist of the literary struggle."[87] Without a framework for evaluating the existing political situation or the emancipatory potential within an object, however, judgments will become arbitrary. And the fact is that Benjamin the critic was not exempt from such arbitrariness. Thus, he could appreciate Leskov and Gide but summarily dismiss Bulgakov by claiming that "the tendency is completely counter-revolutionary."[88]

The need for criteria to render judgments thus, once again, asserts itself. Benjamin knew that neither epistemological categories nor aesthetic standards can arise from literary criticism "commenting" on itself or trying to appear as philosophy in a new guise. Nor was he content to accept criteria derived a priori. Especially in his early writings, but also from a certain view of *The Arcades Project*, they emerge only from an analysis of the particular text. Benjamin's emphasis upon the object in its uniqueness, the particular text and the practices capable of being inferred from it, is the strength—the genuinely materialist aspect—of his method. But his work offers neither the necessarily transcendental coordinates with which to make sense of the particular nor an insight into the sociological dynamics of its constitution. How then to secure the conditions for a "rescue"?

The answer emerges from the conditions for mechanical reproduction defining the new age. Given the new connection between technology and art, he believed, a "political tendency which is correct [will] comprise a literary tendency which is correct."[89] Benjamin did not wish to argue that the positive judgment of literary works depends upon the manner in which they provide a "correct" depiction of political concerns. Quite the contrary. In keeping with his emphasis on technical innovation, and the "organizing function" of the writer, he emphasized that:

> Commitment is a necessary, but never a sufficient condition for a writer's work acquiring an organizing function. For this to happen it is also necessary for the writer to have a teacher's attitude. And today this is more than ever an essential demand. *A writer who does not teach other writers teaches nobody.* The crucial point, therefore is that a writer's production must have the character of a model: it must be able to instruct other writers in their production and, secondly, it must be able to place an improved apparatus at their disposal.[90]

The implications of this statement confront the notion that form alone counts as well as the belief that the content of the work is the criterion upon which a judgment rests. Bob Dylan is a case in point. Judging the singer on his various religious conversions or the manner in which he does, or does not, offer a pathway to revolution is to employ criteria outside the practice in which he is engaged. The extent to which he articulates utopian wishes and dialectical images, the degree to which he makes other artists aware of technical innovations, and the ways in which his songs evidence transcendence by changing their function become the criteria by which critics can judge his work and that of others as well. Progressive use of literary technique and the identification with a progressive political position, however, are not intrinsically connected with each other; T. S. Eliot or Ezra Pound employed progressive literary techniques and believed in reactionary politics. Anatole France or Romain Rolland, on the other hand, employed less sophisticated techniques even as they associated themselves with more progressive political positions. Benjamin could deal with this situation, however, because he saw the work of art as a "living center of reflection."[91] This indeed is what enabled him to shift the terrain of radical criticism from a judgment about the politics of an artwork to a judgment of its utopian, critical, and redemptive potential.

Times have changed. Perhaps, to use a phrase from Leo Lowenthal, the sparks of an artwork illuminate only what once was possible.[92] No matter. What ultimately made Benjamin a great critic was his knowledge that the work is always new and fresh. It remains an assumption with which any intellectual inquiry must begin. Endless paths may lead back into the past. But there are others, unnoticed for now, that lead into the future for people with clear eyes and a free imagination. Walter Benjamin did not shut his eyes or close his mind. Indeed, such was the nature of his genius.

$\mathcal{C}$ 8 $\mathcal{O}$

Political Aesthetics in the 1930s

In Memory of Christopher Johnson

Left-wing political aesthetics in Europe during the 1930s always had an eye on the Soviet Union. This was surely the case with the evaluation of modernism. The problem among the more culturally conservative communist intellectuals was whether it built proletarian solidarity and contributed to unifying the masses behind the industrialization of the USSR. This enterprise had begun with Stalin's "left turn" of 1928 and his use of the slogan "socialism in one country." They foreshadowed the horrible Five Year Plans and the terror at home but, abroad, they were less signals of revolution than testaments to the seeming stabilization of capitalism. They reflected the fact that communism had turned inward, away from the West, and the onset of what Korsch termed the "counter-revolution." Under Stalin, soon enough, authoritarian control became totalitarian, artistic innovation ceased, and Marxism became transformed into the dogma of "dialectical materialism" or "diamat." Cultural freedoms were constrained. Divorce and abortion became difficult to obtain in the new police state. Emphasis was placed upon the family, and with the introduction of Stakhanovism, a puritanical provincialism was extended to the artistic arena. Tolerance for radical modernist experiments, like those undertaken by the constructivists and suprematists, vanished. Art would now directly relate to the immediate needs of the party. Thus, "socialist realism" came to define its official line.[1]

If socialist realism fit into the burgeoning totalitarianism of Stalin in the Soviet Union, however, the "line" embraced by communists abroad took a somewhat different and, arguably, more flexible form. Understanding why is possible only when the cultural line is situated in a political context. The 1920s had witnessed an increasing sectarianism on the part of the communist movement; its member parties, licking their wounds from the defeat of the revolutionary offensive mounted throughout Europe from 1918 to 1923, denounced the new republics in Germany and elsewhere as surely as the new fascist parties and states like Italy. With the inward turn of 1928, in fact, came the "twin brothers" thesis that identified social democrats with Nazis. But the triumphs of Hitler, combined with fears of the growing fascist threat in France, forced a change of "line" in the mid-thirties. A new concern with forging alliances with all "antifascist forces" became reflected in a new preoccupation with the connection between "bourgeois" and "socialist" realism. No longer would the communists proclaim their intention of destroying bourgeois culture. The communists were now set upon inheriting its most "progressive" aspects and employing them against the more "decadent" petty bourgeois ideas that had helped the fascists to power.

An International Writers' Conference for the Defense of Culture took place at the Paris Mutualité in 1935. This meeting of antifascist, but not necessarily communist, writers occurred in the wake of the Comintern directive to build a popular front, which was issued at its Seventh World Congress under the leadership of Georgii Dimitrov. Its most visible member was Heinrich Mann. But a host of other luminaries took part: Malraux, Gide, Plivier, Huxley, Ehrenburg, Benda, Döblin, Feuchtwanger, Bloch, Madalaine Paz, Brecht, Seghers, Waldo Frank, and others. While the congress expressed the unity among antifascists, however, many participants were left with the bitter feeling that dogmatism was running rampant and that those who had not accepted the new line, or who believed that no line should be imposed, were unwelcome. It was in this political atmosphere that what came to be known as the "expressionism debate" took place.[2] But it could just as easily have been labeled the "realism" debate. Its content derived from the first attempt to stamp a uniform orientation on socialist art and culture.

Most of the debate was carried on in *Das Wort* (The Word), which grew out of this antifascist conference. The journal appeared for the first time in 1936 with an editorial board composed of Bertolt Brecht, Willi Bredel, and Lion Feuchtwanger. The debate achieved an almost legendary status among intellectuals of the European left, especially during the 1960s and 1970s. Its major disputants were dominant intellectual figures like Georg Lukács, Ernst Bloch, and Brecht. Even the secondary contributors, however, were of importance. Alfred Kurella, for example, was one of the most influential communist critics of the age. Johannes R. Becher had been a famous expressionist poet and later became one of the leading cultural commissars of East Germany. Anna Seghers, author of *The Seventh Cross*, had also become a major figure in communist cultural politics. It was the stature of the participants, the quality of argumentation, and the context in which the debate developed that contributed to the aura surrounding the expressionism controversy.

There is still something to be learned from it. Cultural politics has grown increasingly popular since the 1960s, and the connection between modernism and radical politics still exerts a certain fascination. Now, whatever the use of fashionable terms like "fascist modernism" or "technological paganism," the Nazis wanted nothing to do with a modernist movement like expressionism.

Admittedly, usually from their armchairs, certain avant-garde intellectuals intitially supported fascism. They identified with its irrational, violent, and apocalyptic tendencies. They believed it would bring a "new man" into existence and make an end of bourgeois society. Once in power, however, the fascists retreated from much of the rhetoric they had used while their movement was on the rise. As the Brownshirts of the SA gave way to the Blackshirts of the Gestapo, as order came to rule, the fascists' tolerance for these bohemians waned. The artists either became servants of the new order or engaged in an "inner emigration" following their inclusion in the infamous "Degenerate Art Exhibition" of 1938.

None of this, however, says much about the extent to which expressionism shaped the climate in which the Nazis came to power. It had been the dominant avant-garde tendency in Germany just before and after World War I. These were the years of *Die Brücke* and *Der Blaue Reiter*, of the transformation of theater by figures like Ernst Toller, Erwin Piscator, and Brecht, and of the revolution in music by Schönberg. Expressionists, whatever the stylistic and political differences between them, basically harbored similar feelings. They felt alienated from established society, and they yearned for a better world. They protested against what they considered a sterile rationalism and a vapid materialism with heightened emotion and metaphysical despair over the "death of God."

The modernist assault on bourgeois society had started much earlier. The beginnings occurred in romanticism with its emphasis on the autonomy of experience and the grace of nature. It gained momentum through symbolism, fauvism, cubism, and futurism and came to generate ever more vehement statements of secession from the constraints of convention in ever-accelerating cycles. The modernist movement fought hard for its triumphs, withstanding ridicule and staunch opposition during those periods in which its most radical aesthetic innovations were developed. And, in aesthetic terms, it was successful. Modernism changed art: its subject matter, its modes of representation, its public, and even its boundaries.

Arguably, however, the years of aesthetic vitality are not necessarily the most important for a movement. Its effects and definition generally come about only when the owl of Minerva has spread its wings. The 1920s were the time in which expressionism came into its own. The movement had initially been confined to a small group of bohemian artists and intellectuals. The 1920s, however, saw its assimilation by the same bourgeoisie it had originally held up to ridicule. Economic dislocation, ideological disillusionment, a pervasive sense of decay, and a new republican order with liberal convictions helped create a somewhat broader public for artists like Wedekind and Munch, Kirchner and Becher, Kandinsky and Klee. Oskar Kokoschka, who was called the "Austrian terror" in the years preceding World War I, received a professorial chair, while Alban Berg's *Wozzeck* was performed by the State Opera.

Expressionism was incorporated into the cultural constellation of bourgeois taste. Among that thin stratum of the "modern" bourgeoisie who voted for the German Democratic Party (DDP), snorted cocaine, and underwent psychoanalysis, expressionism was in vogue. Bankers paid thousands of dollars to have their portraits done by expressionist painters, while the National Gallery and the Neue Pinakothek greedily bought paintings by Barlach, Kandinsky, Kirchner, Marc, Pechstein, and others. The satirical papers had great fun with this symbiosis of wealth and self-laceration. The sad truth is, however, that modernism had few political defenders. The Nazis denounced it as "cultural bolshevism" and part of a deliberate design by the Elders of Zion to demoralize the German people. Their own populist protest against the machine age had found its expression in popular (*völkisch*) kitsch, "heroic realism," and sentimental lyricism. Nor did the organized labor movement, even prior to the birth of Stalinism, have much sympathy for modernism in general or expressionism in particular. High cultural critics pointed proudly to Courbet and Millet, Anatole France and Gorky, Käthe Kollwitz and Heinrich Zille. Cézanne or Matisse, however, were alien to both the socialist and communist press. It was by accident of personality, rather than ideology, that a few intellectuals like Paul Levi should have appreciated modern art. Thus, the major expressionist journals *Der Sturm* and *Die Aktion* found their audience among ultraleft bohemians and intellectuals rather than in the working class.

Expressionism and modernism seemed to hang suspended between the major classes and the existing political formations. This is what made their political message and their social impact so difficult to decipher. Modernism had not yet become classical, Marxism played a very different role, and the fascist threat was far more real than today. Many of the issues bitterly contested in the expressionism debate may thus seem somehow anachronistic. Questions concerning the nature of a "revolutionary" or "progressive" art, however, retain their relevance. Nor have issues concerning the social impact of cultural products lost their importance. Thus, while various unwarranted political and epistemological assumptions become evident in the debate, even the errors of the participants can help in orienting future forms of critical aesthetic inquiry.

Georg Lukács: Expressionism and Critical Realism

The stage for the expressionism debate was set in 1934 with the publication of Georg Lukács's 'Grosse und Verfall' des Expressionismus in *Internationale Literatur*. His earlier pre-Marxist works, like *Soul and Form* and *Theory of the Novel*, had themselves been reflections of the modernist sensibility. Following his retraction of *History and Class Consciousness* in 1924, however, Lukács engaged in an ever more critical reevaluation of his development.[3] His philosophical shift away from vitalism and idealism, in fact, mirrored his growing attachment to bourgeois or "critical" realism. Thus, especially given the new "popular front" line of the Communist Party, it only made sense that he should have defended this tendency against its decadent counterpart: expressionism.

Grounding himself within the tradition beginning with Walter Scott, which found its greatest twentieth-century proponent in Thomas Mann, Lukács claimed that a work of art grows out of a given society and "mirrors" it. This mirroring, however, is not simply based on the artistic accumulation of facts, impressions, and experiences. It occurs insofar as the realist work presents the dialectical "totality" of mediations, contradictions, and interconnections defining a given order. A work of "realism" consequently exposes the "objective" social context so often ignored in the subjective experience. Ideological veils are stripped away as it reveals the difference between the way society "really" functions and the way it merely "appears."

Lukács draws the distinction between essence and appearance and, in doing so, defines himself in the tradition of the most progressive representatives of the rising bourgeoisie on which Marx himself relied. Kant gave the essence-appearance relation its first modern epistemological expression. Appearance, or the "phenomenon," took on a dual meaning. It was simultaneously an "object of empirical intuition" and the product of an essence, or a "noumenal" thing-in-itself, which remains closed to rational investigation. Kant's cleavage between essence and appearance, however, was overcome by Hegel, who maintained that the essence of an object will become manifest in the series of its appearances. History evidences the "essence," or "idea," underlying all purposive human activity: freedom. Marx, however, strips away the trappings of idealism. A historically specific system of production is seen as giving rise to objective class contradictions, which constrain the exercise of freedom and subjectivity, and the essence of society becomes the "totality" mediating given "moments" of action. No less than Kant and Hegel, however, Marx maintained that discovering the essence of reality involves a rational form of critical inquiry: only through a concrete analysis of the totality is it possible to comprehend the particular in the mediations constituting it. Thus, for Lukács, the prime purpose of literature presents itself.

> If literature is indeed a special mode of mirroring objective reality, then it is of the utmost importance that it comprehend this reality as it is actually constituted and that it not limit itself to a rendering of that which immediately (*unmittelbar*) appears.[4]

An articulation of the mediated totality is precisely what Lukács finds in the work of the great realists. In Tolstoy, for example, the characters and their interactions, the changes they undergo and the opinions they form, are seen as emerging from within a changing context. By contrast, modernism in general and expressionism in particular favor an unmediated rendering of experience. An emotive, unreflective, irrational, and subjective apprehension of reality confronts the progressive legacy of the bourgeoisie no less than the method of Marx. This is why, from the first, Lukács championed objective and realistic aesthetic forms against the subjectivism of modernism. He was not blind to the importance of the inspirational element in artistic creation. But he maintained that the inspirational and emotive factor could not be considered by itself or in a reified fashion. Inspiration, from his perspective, first becomes artistically viable only when it becomes a "moment" within the cognitive process as a whole. Consequently, the categories seeking to make sense of the creative process in art must stand in coherent relation to those employed in understanding the world of production.[5]

The ability to comprehend society in terms of its totality ultimately separates the realist from the modernist. Without an explicit dialectical relation between the particular and the totality of which it is a part, the work cannot, for Lukács, offer a cogent and rational worldview.[6] The inability or, better, the refusal to develop such a worldview is precisely what is seen as defining the "decadence" of modernists in relation to the realists who preceded them. The inherent relation between "essence" and "appearance" breaks down along with the way the world is experienced and the way subjectivity is itself constituted within a context. And this was seen as having political consequences. Where the expressionists might subjectively have considered themselves free from bourgeois influences as the avant-garde initiating the "regeneration of man" (*die Erneuerung des Menschen*), objectively they appeared to Lukács in a different light. Though preoccupied with attacking conservative social mores, militarism, and the bourgeoisie itself, he maintained that these issues were never framed concretely and that, instead, they were ripped from their historical context. So, for example, expressionist dramatists tended to label their characters "The Son," "The Friend," "The Father," in order to cloak them in universality. The expressionist critique, according to Lukács, remained a purely abstract form of humanism embodied in the cry "*O Mensch.*" Subjectivism and moralism, in his view, infected the expressionist worldview. So, whether consciously or unconsciously, they proved unable to confront the reality they sought to expose and judge. Their criticisms reproduced the problems they sought to confront. Thus, no matter how "radical" the expressionists may have thought themselves, their opposition to bourgeois life was merely "romantic" and "petty bourgeois."

Life, from the expressionist perspective, becomes a conglomeration of experiential fragments. Insofar as they are preserved from "interconnection" with the social totality, and closed to dialectical reason, reality becomes a "chaos" or a "riddle" to which an answer becomes impossible a priori. The world is robbed of values and meaning even though, from the perspective of Lukács, it is possible for the subject to situate himself or herself through a rational examination of the given historical conditions. The avant-garde, however, rejects that alternative and thereby turns its back on the progressive heritage of the bourgeoisie. Consequently, for Lukács, it is no accident that various avant-gardists like Barlach or Kandinsky should have embraced a vague spiritualism or even that the more politically inclined dadaists like George Grosz and John Heartfield should ultimately have turned from expressionism to the "new objectivity" (*Neue Sachlichkeit*).

Apocalyptic visions play an important role in expressionist art. For Lukács, this is just another example of the way in which its partisans ignored the "concrete potential" for qualitative change. Abstracting itself from the existing society prevented expressionist art from "mirroring" it, which, in turn, assured the irrational response toward it. Social reality could appear only as an indecipherable "chaos." And, for this reason, it was no longer capitalist society to be overcome but rather the "chaos" as such. Revolution gave way to the apocalypse, and, according to Lukács, it is precisely in this expressionist syndrome, "often unrecognized by its victim," that the danger appears. For, in the mysticism and the abstract use of categories, the left-wing attack on the status quo can easily veer to its opposite extreme. It can turn into "a critique of bourgeois values from the right, into that same demagogic critique of capitalism to which fascism subsequently became indebted for its mass base."[7]

Expressionism, in this vein, is seen as helping create the cultural climate in which fascism could thrive.[8] Irrationalism turned the avant-garde into a symptom of the crisis rather than a cure.[9] The issue is consequently not merely the "abstract" quality of their work. The realists, after all, also employed abstraction. But their use of abstraction stands opposed to the expressionist or modernist abstraction away from reality (*Wegabstrahierung*). A twofold creative as well as ideological (*weltanschauliche*) effort takes place: "namely, first the intellectual discovery and creative formation of the interrelations [of reality—trans.] and second, yet inseparable from the first, the artistic concealment of these abstractly worked through interrelations: the sublation (*Aufhebung*) of the abstraction."[10]

Lukács is aware that the realist will "abstract" from the everyday individuals in order to create a character. The special emphasis placed upon him or her will render the character "atypical." Insofar as the character is brought back into a milieu, however, he or she regains an element of "typicality" even while remaining "atypical." A character like Hans Castorp in *The Magic Mountain* or Pierre Bezuhov in *War and Peace* is then "atypically-typical" with the sublation (*Aufhebung*) of the initial abstraction.[11] A character in a modernist play by Pirandello or an expressionist work by Ernst Toller, by contrast, *can* never appear in this light since the context in which experiences occur is never fully defined. Modernist works *can* therefore never distinguish the "appearance" from the "essence" of reality and, precisely to this extent, they reproduce the ideology they claim to criticize.

Putting the particular in context, according to Lukács, is what validates the initial abstraction and the use of fiction to expose truth. And so, where the abstraction of the modernist or expressionist can produce only illusion, the abolition of the initial abstraction by the realist employs illusion to reveal the objective reality veiled by ideology. The strength of realism subsequently derives from its ability to destroy the illusions of its characters by confronting them with the social processes in which they are formed. Tensions therefore emerge within an organic whole, or a "closed" totality, that enables the audience to contemplate "objectively" the actions taking place. The intrinsic clarity of realism makes the work accessible to the masses in a way the works of modernism are not with their subjectivism, formal difficulty, and often purposeful obscurantism. Realism thus projects a certain relation to the life of the masses (*Volkstümlichkeit*) even as it retains a pedagogic function.

Lukács surely stressed the *Volkstümlichkeit* of realism in order to salvage the concept from the Nazis who employed it merely as an ideological tool to justify their own "heroic" forms of pseudoclassical kitsch. By the same token, however, he probably also sought to accommodate the new cultural policy of Stalin. Lukács spoke positively of certain "socialist realist" works.[12] But in emphasizing the legacy of "critical" realism, he undoubtedly also sought to preserve the Enlightenment legacy for Marxism. Thus, it is possible to suggest that he was engaging in a type of literary "guerrilla war" against the dogmatism of Andrei Zhdanov and his more rigid comrades in the communist movement. [13]

Realism, according to Lukács, is "critical" precisely insofar as it objectively explicates the specific conditions of capitalist social relations and the manner in which they impinge on individual experience. But there is no reason to think that this "critical" quality cannot extend to "actually existing socialism" itself; indeed, there is nothing ironic about the fact that Lukács should have praised the early work of Alexander Solzhenitsyn. His basic point is simply that any work seeking to perform a critical or pedagogic function must situate itself within the historical and artistic traditions of a particular society. Nor need such a stance result in an "evolutionary" conception of either history or art. Quite the contrary. Indeed, following Hegel, Lukács claimed that only in relation to the most progressive innovations of the past can the liberating possibilities of the present become concrete.

Not realism is aligned with "evolutionary" conceptions of change, according to Lukács, but modernism insofar as it undialectically opposes all traditions and proclaims with Antonin Artaud: "*A finir avec les chefs d'oeuvres!*" It sees only ruptures and catastrophes so that, instead of serving as a genuine negation, it becomes merely the anarchistic opposition of evolutionary reformism.[14] Again following Hegel and Marx, Lukács views history as the "living dialectical unity" between continuity and discontinuity. Insofar as the avant-garde is incapable of grasping the social totality, however, it remains blind to this "unity." Modernism in general and expressionism in particular cannot help but mystify reality and distort the historical crisis of bourgeois society. Thus, for Lukács, there remains little the oppressed can learn from an irrationalist and elitist avant-garde that constituted a "subordinate" (*unterge-ordnete*) moment of the fascist victory.

Lukács, in articulating these views, initiated the "expressionism" debate. Both Ernst Bloch and Bertolt Brecht took exception to his unqualified defense of realism, his reductivist approach, and the often mechanistic nature of his analysis. In this context, their response was informed as much by the attempt to preserve the need for a novel and experimental art as to justify expressionism itself.

Ernst Bloch: Expressionism and Liberation

Ernst Bloch was also critical of privileging the irrational, and he liked to call mysticism the "ignorant caricature of profundity."[15] But he still believed there was much to be gained from an "anticipatory movement" like expressionism that projects emancipation beyond the constraints of the existing discourse. The totality cannot remain confined to the sphere of "objectively" discernible interactions for, if it is really total, it must also incorporate fantasy and the imaginative components of subjective experience.[16] According to Bloch, in fact, analyzing expressionism sociologically results in an "academic" standpoint incapable of appreciating what is most important: the anticipation of emancipation, the experimentation with new forms, and the experience of "artistic joy" (*Kunstfreude*). Transcendence confronts immanence in the more subjective forms of modernist art like poetry, music, and painting. The omission of these forms of expression from Lukács's analysis in favor of literature subsequently skews the analysis. It is, in fact, "all the more surprising since, not only were the relations between painting and literature of the closest kind at the time, but the expressionist paintings are far more indicative of the movement than the literature."[17]

The chord that Bloch had already struck with the publication of his *Spirit of Utopia*, a work he later termed a "testament to the original expressionist impulse," is carried over into the expressionist debate. In this earlier work, he had written: "We are starting from scratch. We are poor and have forgotten how to play."[18] This was the time when an an extremely close personal as well as working friendship still existed between Bloch and Lukács that ended around the time of the latter's self-criticism for *History and Class Conscious-*

ness. Bloch, too, was a communist. But he never retracted his association with the avant-garde, and, ironically, his position in the debates was obviously influenced by the early work of Lukács. Nevertheless, while Lukács emphasized the role of naturalism in the emergence of the avant-garde,[19] Bloch saw the power of expressionism in its liquidation of the "real."

Against those content with equating the empirical with the real, according to Bloch, it is necessary to confront reality in its dynamic movement.[20] But this requires the ability to portray the "exact fantasy." The "true"—the non-alienated and nonreified, exists outside the calculating logic of capitalist reality. "Mirroring" existing forms of social relations consequently does not exhaust the criteria for evaluating art. It was less important that expressionism should have reflected what "is" than that it should have provided a sense of "what is not" by indicating a new set of unrealized emancipatory hopes and fantasies. There, in the "dream content" of expressionism, lies its radical indictment of the status quo and its connection with the revolutionary inheritance of the past. The revolution, in accordance with certain radical tenets of modernism, must move beyond the economic and the social realms. It must also speak to the cultural and the psychological. Expressionism makes that move, according to Bloch, by exploding the possibility of objective contemplation on the part of the audience. It distorts objects, juxtaposes unrelated fragments of reality, subverts syntax, and transvalues time. All this tends to force the onlooker to see reality in a new way and draw his or her own conclusions.

Modernism also sought to free the unconscious and give voice to fantasy. It fostered a return of the repressed and generated new forms of empathy through attempts to "transfer" oneself into what resists "progress." Nowhere is this more apparent than in the use of montage, which necessarily involves the spectator in a mode of comprehension that changes his or her perception of the world. A qualitatively different idea of reality emerges as montage reveals a richness within existence that cannot be discovered in the usual ways in which it is perceived. There is, of course, a naive and romantic quality to all this. A naive idea, however, can have very sophisticated consequences. Just such emotions, for example, fostered a new cosmopolitan concern with African art and inspired the wonderful animal paintings of Franz Marc. Modernist art was informed by revulsion against the suffering inflicted by capitalism even as it expanded the realm of aesthetic expression.

Confused theories were often offered to justify experiments in montage and nonrepresentational painting. But their philosophical weaknesses are irrelevant, according to Bloch, if such writings—like *Point and Line* by Kandinsky—helped clarify certain problems of artistic production. Nonrepresentational works in particular may generate the need for constant reinterpretation in light of the self-renewing fantasy they throw in the face of repression. But that is all to the good. Abstraction gains justification in its own right. Liberation from the constraints of the given opens a space for fantasy and the experience of "artistic joy." All of this, however, presupposes a willingness to "experiment" with the content of reality. Modernists and expressionists could not have created anything, according to Bloch, had they simply relied on the forms handed down to them by bourgeois realists like Goethe, Balzac, and Tolstoy. They chose different masters like Grünewald, El Greco, and Büchner: they refused to consider "tradition" as some type of organic or "objective" phenomenon. Indeed, it was the modernists who first recognized that tradition is always "invented."

Nor did the break with representation occur by chance at that particular point in time. The crisis of capitalism had its effects. The totality changed its face. Traditional values and forms were overthrown by the experience of war.[21] They lost their relevance, and, according to Bloch, the attempt to retain them becomes reactionary from the start. Maintaining the classical totality thus becomes a prejudice, which perhaps explains why Lukács should have turned

> . . . against every artistic attempt to bring about the dissolution of a world-view (even when this world-view itself was capitalistic) . . . He sees nothing except subjectivistic ruptures in an art which interprets the actual ruptures of the surface interrelations of the existent, and which attempts to discover the new that already exists in reality's crevices. Thus, he equates the experiment of dissolution with the state of decadence.[22]

Realism, from the standpoint of Bloch, is not treated historically. It is not the unalterable aesthetic norm by which decadence should be judged. Art should not be judged through externally imposed categories or solely in terms of its implications for practice. The priority given by Lukács to the totality, moreover, condemns art to follow precedent even as it undermines the anticipation of new conditions. Franz Marc's painting *Fate of the Animals* and the works of other avant-gardists seem, in retrospect, to have foreshadowed the horrors of World War I. Bloch admits that expressionism evidenced an abstract pacifism and neglected real class contradictions. But he considers it illegitimate to judge the activities of the past by the results of the present, especially when so many expressionists opposed the war.[23] It was just this kind of thinking, according to Bloch, that enabled Lukács to relegate any noncommunist resistance to the ranks of the bourgeoisie or petty bourgeoisie. Indeed, for Bloch, the pacifism of the expressionists and even their moralism constituted a valid political response.

But, in a way, he overstates the case. Support for the communist cause was not a basic criterion of aesthetic judgment for Lukács. Thomas Mann, for example, publicly supported World War I in a particularly vile manner, and Lukács never wavered in his admiration for him. By the same token, enough expressionists aligned themselves with the reaction. Gottfried Benn, Hans Johst, Emil Nolde, Wyndham Lewis, D. H. Lawrence, the Pound-Eliot clique, and the futurists all expressed support for right-wing dictatorships at one time or another. The real sociological question is not *who* was a fascist but which literary form best tends to promote what values. And here Bloch made it too easy for himself. He could thus praise the futurists for their "passion for frenzy, dynamism, and all-pervading sense of immediacy," while neglecting to mention the other protofascistic ideological concerns with which these qualities were intertwined.[24] The defense of expressionism is, by the same token, seen as a defense of experimenting in the name of the "concrete utopia." Its "horizon" is what art projects, and where the "prospective horizon is left out, there reality appears only as what it has already become, as the dead, and here it will be the dead—namely the naturalists and empiricists—who will bury their dead."[25]

Art is an experiment, for Bloch, and he wants to highlight its reliance on fantasy. Lukács was correct, however, in claiming that his former friend confused the fantastic with the real and the concrete with the abstract. In asserting that nonobjective painting retains an object—namely the color itself (*Farbigkeit*)—Bloch falls into precisely this mistake. It is impossible to provide a negation for the real without a perception of its mediated historical content. Emphasizing the importance of fantasy, in this vein, need not involve denigrating the value of naturalism. These different artistic forms project very different possibilities for criticism and liberation. Fantasy can illuminate reality from the perspective of what it could or should become. But fantasy cannot substitute for an explanation of reality. Its projection of utopia creates a gap with reality, which cannot be bridged at will.

Emancipation was the goal of expressionism, and, for this reason, it only made sense to Bloch that the Nazis should have decried modernist art. Its emphasis on the imagination and fantasy always spells danger for repressive regimes cloaking themselves in cultural provincialism. No wonder then, from the standpoint of Bloch, that even the artists who had originally expressed support for fascism should soon enough have been vilified. Expressionism contested the banality and provincialism of the *Spiessbürger* and the *Bildungsphilister*. Those were the cultural values on which the Nazis relied, and they had little to do with the complex technical innovations of the avant-garde. Expressionism was appalled by the existing society. Its cries of despair projected a new sensibility, a different world, and a utopian mode of experience. Bloch was ultimately correct in portraying expressionism as a movement "which the philistine spat upon, an art wherein human stars—however inadequate, however singular—burned or wished to burn."

Bertolt Brecht and the Laboratory of Art

Bertolt Brecht approached the expressionism debate in a very different way than either Lukács or Bloch. He detested irrational excesses, prided himself on his "realism." He conceived of his work as part of the attempt to transform the existing order, and he was always concerned with keeping close ties to the Communist Party; indeed, for precisely this reason, Brecht never published most of his contributions to the debate. He was also more skeptical about the idealist legacy than Lukács, and he was never enthusiastic about the Popular Front or the aesthetic line of the party. Whatever his differences with Lukács, however, it is mistaken to suggest that Brecht's views were the same as those of Bloch. Brecht was far less concerned with utopian theory than the need to change traditional aesthetic assumptions in order to meet the contemporary needs of artistic production.[26] Nor was he ever a great friend of either the modernist avant-garde in general or expressionism in particular. *Baal*, his very first play, was quite openly directed against Hans Johst's expressionist work titled *The Lonely One* (*Der Einsame*). The unleashing of emotion (*Eindrucksauslösung*), the pathetic scream of "*O Mensch*," the plaintive appeals in the name of "poor little humanity," and the excessive emotional baggage of expressionism were all repulsive to Brecht. The emotional attempts of expressionists to elicit empathy from the audience also had little in common with Brecht's famous "estrangement-effect" (*Verfremdungseffekt*). Surprise, shock, playfulness, and distortion all occur in his plays. In his own way, however, Brecht was an aesthetic puritan.[27] He always felt that the impact of an art relying principally on exciting and manipulating the emotions would prove fleeting. Thus, "the most extreme effect of a work of art occurs but once. The same tricks won't, on any account, go over a second time. To a second invasion of new ideas which make use of familiar, more or less proven devices, the spectator is already immune."[28]

Brecht wrote this in the context of criticizing dadaist happenings and futurist soirées. But the statement also had consequences for the discussion of realism. Any fetishism of technique, for Brecht, is anathema due to the constraints it imposes on artistic production and the experience of an audience. No less than Bloch, he saw the work as "open." Its aim is to begin and then recommence a dialogue with its public. In contrast to Bloch and the expressionists, however, Brecht was unconcerned with articulating some abstract utopian potential.[29] For him, it was rather a matter of forcing the public to confront political and moral choices that stem from the contradiction between the way social forces appear and how they actually function. Brecht's notion of the relation between "essence" and "appearance" is subsequently derived neither from the objective presentation of the "totality" nor from an exclusive concern with the utopian *novum*. It emerges instead from an immanent critique of existing ideology and the existing possibilities for political practice.

Realism is, for him, less a matter of form than an ability to render historical class contradictions concrete for a particular public in a particular society.[30] Forms are seen merely as products of changing social and aesthetic needs. It is thus misguided to speak of "decadence" in art, according to Brecht, since this implicitly identifies the highest form of cultural production with the historical development of the bourgeoisie. Nor is it possible, even if such an identification is made, to demarcate the "vigorous" art of the nineteenth century from the "decadent" art of the twentieth. The periods marking the high points of expressionist popularity, for Brecht, required new modes of experimentation precisely because the prewar no less than the immediate postwar period harbored new revolutionary opportunities. It is consequently a matter of building not on 1789 and 1848 but on 1917. Naturally, Brecht realized that this potential was never fully realized or even reflected in modernism or expressionism. But condemning artists like Picasso or Döblin in the name of realism, from his point of view, simply binds art to the past and constricts its ability to illuminate new contradictions in new ways in the future. Chaining the concept of realism to a nineteenth-century mode of depicting objective conditions, moreover, reifies the concept of realism and the category of totality as well. Tradition is, for Brecht, no rigid set of precedents or rules: it speaks to the needs of cultural production in the present. Consequently, even though he was never an expressionist, Brecht made use of certain formal devices initiated by the movement. Why not?

> We cannot allow ourselves to be held up too long by the problem of form or, at least, we must be exact as to what we mean and speak concretely. Otherwise, as critics, we will become formalists, no matter what vocabulary we use. It disconcerts our contemporary writers when they have to hear, all too often, "that's not the way grandmother used to tell it." Okay, say that the old woman was a realist. Assuming that we are also realists, would we then have to recount something in exactly the same way grandmother did? There must be some misunderstanding here.[31]

"Form" and "content" are not, for Brecht, realities unto themselves. They are merely heuristic categories useful in analyzing a work that is itself an organic unity. Separating form from content can only occur abstractly. Calling for the retention of old forms narrows the ability to deal with new issues of content. Art must keep pace with history. The comprehensibility of any given work is, furthermore, not assured by taking on the style of Balzac or Tolstoy. Brecht was always skeptical of highly abstract art and sought to keep his own language simple and concrete. But, in his opinion, a viable art "should bring forth the thing-in-itself, the incomprehensible. Yet, art should neither depict things as self-evident (seeking an emotional response) nor simply as incomprehensible. Rather it should depict them as comprehensible, but not yet comprehended."[32]

The audience, for Brecht, should never feel too comfortable. Art requires concentration. Marxists always maintained that consciousness does not change with the same speed as the infrastructure. As a Leninist, however, Brecht could consider it legitimate for art to remain a step—"but only a step"—ahead of existing cultural forms reinforcing the ideology of the status quo. This might make for a certain difficulty regarding the comprehensibility of the work and its accessibility to the masses. Brecht, however, never saw this as a problem. Rather than accept what has already been made comprehensible as the only authentically "popular" form, the future socialist culture must, in his opinion, experiment with new forms. Indeed, this is the sense in which Brecht views art as a "laboratory."

A truly socialist art in his view must develop new *forms* of hearing, seeing, and understanding the world along with a new content. One of his primary aesthetic concerns as a playwright, in this respect, involved undermining old forms of experience and showing how they hampered the class consciousness of the masses. The point is not simply to copy bourgeois realism from a socialist perspective. It is instead a matter of bringing this "new art" into existence. That is only possible, however, by learning from the past rather than dismissing it in the manner of the most radical or anarchistic modernists.

> The new exists, but it arises out of the struggle with the old, not without it, not out of thin air. Many forget about learning or treat it disdainfully as a formality, and some even take the critical moment for granted, treating that as a formality as well.[33]

Unlike Bloch, in this vein, Brecht is concerned about the implications of relativizing "realism," and he attempted to counter this from a class standpoint. But the "standard" he used was different from the one employed by Lukács. Referring to the past is inadequate. The critique of ideology provides a point of departure; the realistic work must expose how "the reigning views are the views of those who reign."[34] But it must also focus on the concerns of those who do not reign. This twofold undertaking is what, according to Brecht, marks a realistic art. It is in this way, without rules or precedents determined a priori, that art can inform political practice.

Notes for an Emancipatory Aesthetics

An emancipatory aesthetic cannot begin by choosing between realism and modernism. Both have become part of our cultural currency, and both have had partisans on both the left and the right of the political spectrum. The work is the issue, not the style. Just as it is illegitimate to subsume the quality of a work under the judgment of a style, so is it illegitimate to equate any given style with a political position, identify the political position with a particular class standpoint, and then use that standpoint to evaluate the work. Any style, moreover, can be appropriated in various ways: it makes little sense, for example, to consider an essentially internationalist and pacifist movement like expressionism in the same "petty bourgeois" terms as an avowedly protofascist movement like futurism. What Karl Korsch termed "historical specificity" disappears in this kind of thinking. Finally, there is also no reason why art must presuppose answers within its formal ways of framing questions. A work of art is not a manifesto or analytic construct in which the answers simply derive from the way in which the questions are posed.

An emancipatory aesthetic that is practical must derive its categories from the changing practice of artistic production. Imposing categories, or turning the form of one period into a standard for judging art in a new period, simply reifies the interpretive enterprise. Such a stance undermines the possibility for developing new interpretations, and it readies the artwork for the museum. It also undermines the ability to perceive contradictions in an unreconciled state and expand the range of experience. Reified forms of criticism, furthermore, make it impossible to *deideologize the ideology* within a work and extract the insight buried beneath the mystifying worldview of a particular artist.

Kandinsky is a case in point. His nonobjective paintings shatter the empirical world of appearances supposedly in order to determine what lies beneath it. The "essence" he finds is the movement of an inexplicable "spirit" whose presentation demands a radical break with artistic traditions of the past. The affirmation of "objective" reality is impossible, from the perspective of Kandinsky, without its denial. The philosophical argument is unbelievably confused. But, still, his work rescues the experience of subjectivity threatened by the reified world of production in advanced industrial society. Perhaps, in his own way, it even "mirrors" the indeterminate labor power lost in the object. Critical interpretation can, in any event, employ Kandinsky to inspire a memory of the lived moment.

Critical insights of this sort do not simply present themselves in a work. Kant recognized the problem when it came to the philosophy of history. To find evidence of progress or freedom, the critic must initially make the commitment to look for them; indeed, this is precisely what calls into question the drive toward a purely formalist notion of aesthetic inquiry. The semiotic isolation of elements or codes, in this vein, is merely the flip side of a stance condemning interpretation as such. Criticism without an "emancipatory interest" (Habermas) either engages in a sterile reflection upon itself or consigns art to the realm of immediate experience. Neither stance can confront the interests in interpretation or the prevailing relativism perpetuated by a culture industry concerned with appealing to the lowest common denominator in order to generate the greatest possible profits.

Critical cultural criticism has its own aim. It speaks to the new needs of cultural production no less than the unrealized possibilities for expanding the realm of experience. It should not violate the integrity of the work by imposing political or philosophical criteria external to it. A typology of categories thus becomes necessary to define the internal dynamics (*Eigendynamik*) of a given work and open it to political or cultural appropriation as a moment within the totality. Not every work of art will fit squarely into one or another category, and, of course, the employment and relevance of categories will differ with differing genres. More than one category might apply to any given work of art. A critical aesthetic must also assume that the "anticipatory" interpretation provided through its categories will speak less to the immediacy of private experience than to a public sphere in which its claims become open to discourse. There are other provisos. But it remains necessary to begin. Thus, the following is an attempt to sketch the most basic interpretive categories of a critical cultural criticism.

Immediacy

All works of art, including the products of "mass culture," evidence the desire for experience and gratification on the part of an audience. But, as in the case of television sitcoms or certain rock songs that harp on sex or love, the presentation of such desires can prove neither reflective with regard to prior forms of expression nor exhibit an awareness of the constraints inhibiting their fulfillment. In the works of art that produce the most immediate emotional impact, moreover, any possibility of judging the desire itself is precluded. Works of intense immediacy, again, can mirror the existence of real needs. But their indeterminate mode of utopian anticipation makes them particularly prone to manipulation by commercial advertising and the culture industry. The critic's role in dealing with works fitting into this category would first involve subjecting to critical scrutiny the need or plurality of needs for which the particular work is the condensed expression. Only then can it prove possible to show the gap existing between the need and the structural conditions denying its satisfaction.

Indeterminate Reflexivity

A second form of anticipatory consciousness occurs in the critical confrontation with the prevalent forms of the genre in which the given work is situated. Artworks of this sort reflect a preoccupation with new experience and the limitations on expression of earlier styles even if they don't evidence any comprehension of the contextual sources for their own content or concerns. They are indeterminate even while they often evidence a profound reflexivity. Modernist works, for example, tend to ignore questions of immanence, historical genesis, and social context in favor of issues pertaining to formal innovations. A major task of the critic therefore involves specifying the value of the technical contribution while placing the work within a meaningful context of interests.

Unreflexive Determinacy

The "realist" or "naturalist" works of Balzac and Zola provide a useful counterpoint. These might very well comprehend a given sociohistorical complex and perhaps even mirror a mediated totality, but they don't necessarily question traditional forms of aesthetic production or illuminate what Benjamin termed "the poverty of the interior." They provide a sense of historical determination without necessarily confronting the aesthetic forms with which history is perceived in a critical or reflexive fashion. Employing the logic of representation while examining the structures of the existing order, the vision of an emancipated alternative sensibility and a new ordering of social relations tends to vanish. The role of the critic thus becomes particularly difficult. He or she must question the formal assumptions taken for granted and subject the work to a criticism capable of defining what remains unexpressed.

Reflexive Determinacy

There are, of course, also artworks capable of confronting formal traditions of presentation while illuminating a given social complex. The plays of Shakespeare or even Brecht, the poetry of Eliot or Yeats, the operas of Mozart or Verdi, might serve as useful examples. Reflexive in their ability to transvalue the formal inheritance of the past in an emancipatory fashion they also render determinate the material conditions making necessary such an undertaking. The principal function of the critic in dealing with such works thus involves elaborating the manner in which the given vision of social and aesthetic self-comprehension can radicalize existing cultural, social, and political forms in different ways.

A work of art, once finished, separates itself from the author. It becomes an "objectification" (*Vergegenständlichung*) or autonomous entity in which original intentions become moments of the organic whole. The work can, in this way, turn against the prejudices of the author; Engels could thus respond to an inquiry concerning his admiration for Balzac, an ardent supporter of the petty nobility, that "his irony is never sharper than when he employs it against the class he loves." Even the work of a political reactionary can retain critical or emancipatory elements. But no work ever fully escapes its genesis. History remains; there is always a *contextual residue*. The critic must, for this reason, confront both the immanent potential within the work and the external forces that shaped it. This was made clear in the expressionism debate. Nevertheless, the terms in which such an effort should be undertaken have changed.

It is no longer a matter of deciding on a style consonant with a correct political stance; the communist movement is a bad memory and anticipation of liberation calls forth the reinvention of tradition. The issue is rather one of choosing a conceptual framework capable of clarifying the diverse contributions different works can make in different ways to clarifying and intensifying an interest in freedom. No work of art ever exerts even its indirect effects in an autonomous manner. They are always mediated by the effects of coexisting works and styles no less than the institutions structuring the existing public sphere. Neither the realist nor the modernist work exists in a vacuum; where there is Kafka there is also Thomas Mann, and where there is Klee there is already Daumier. A willingness to recognize the differing contributions of diverse works in different styles thus only reflects the actual conditions in which criticism must currently operate.

Critical cultural criticism has no choice other than to view art as an experiment. This means balancing the awareness that every technique can be employed in the most regressive way with the knowledge that only the innovative use of form prevents art from becoming repetitive. Montage, for example, is constantly used in the worst television commercials. By the same token, however, it is surely more than a "subjectivist" disortion of reality. New meanings can become manifest as objects take on new relations to one another. Nor need montage involve an arbitrary throwing together of fragments. Even if the bond between objects is often purposively withheld, montage can generate a narrative and, while engaging the audience in the construction of the work, also create an awareness of what is assumed in the restructuring of reality. This is precisely what occurs in the photo-montages of Barbara Kruger or, even more impressively, John Heartfield.

Modernism may engender subjectivity and the autonomy of art from reality. Many of its partisans, however, also highlight individual responsibility especially insofar as the audience is made to take part in the active construction of something new. This is as true in the plays of the expressionists as in the dramas of Brecht; it is as much the case in the great surrealist works as in the works of Döblin. Modernism proclaimed in a new way that freedom is only freedom for the subject. Lukács, however, was not simply "academic" in noting how such concerns can engender formalism and aestheticism. It was realism generated a concern with redressing the repressive institutional and material conditions in which the actual exercise of freedom takes place, and, arguably, a space for the "exact fantasy" only appears through the interpretive interplay of these styles.

Critical aesthetics rests on a radical understanding of tolerance. It seeks to grasp the "horizon" of a work even as it recognizes that the ability to illuminate repressive and utopian trends may not occur in the same work or even in the same style. It militates against closure and constantly calls for reinterpreting works whose meanings are considered fixed and finished. Above all, however, its version of tolerance contests the dogmatism of a critic who criticizes an artist for not writing the book he or she would like to read. Critical aesthetics also opposes arbitrariness and the type of unthinking relativism generated by the culture industry. Indeed, for this reason, critical aesthetics requires criteria for making judgments regarding the quality and standing of different works.

Tradition is one such category, genre another. There is, for example, no sense in comparing Beethoven with Louis Armstrong or James Joyce with Francis Ford Coppola. It is, however, extremely instructive to compare any of them with any number of less talented artists working within their own particular traditions and genres. Setting a work in context is important for making aesthetic judgments, and this requires the willingness to render them concrete and precise through qualifications and determinations. Transcendent concerns have their place. The formal elements of a work can anticipate the interpretive assumptions of a future public. An experimental work of art can anticipate the sensibilities and the interpretive assumptions of a future public. Because modernist movements were separated from the struggles of the masses does not alone invalidate their progressive qualities. Nor does it deny the possibility that the masses might ultimately become a public for their works. Not a single critic would ever have thought in the prewar era that a million people would come to see an exhibition of Picasso or Matisse.

Nor is it legitimate to maintain that their popularity somehow nullifies their utopian or radical qualities. The culture industry may well turn works into commodities, and critical theory was correct in emphasizing its more debilitating effects. But the extent to which works become commodities is not necessarily the extent to which they lose their artistic quality. Charlie Chaplin's films provide a perfect case in point. The particular work, once again, gets lost in the all embracing character of the formal claim made by Max Horkheimer and Theodor Adorno. Contesting the power of the culture industry, however, does not depend upon a work's internally generating tensions capable of maintaining what Adorno considered the "non-identity" of subject and object. It is rather a matter of recognizing that pockets of cultural resistance can emerge on the periphery of society and that critical education—perhaps even through the culture industry—can mitigate the dulling of reflexive capacities and what Russell Jacoby once called the "falling rate of intelligence."

Cultural relativism becomes reactionary in a context wherein the bulk of artistic stimulation for the great bulk of the populace is overwhelmingly supplied by the culture industry. It is no longer a matter of creating art for the masses. Capitalism has already realized that goal, and the idealistic emphasis upon the need for a "popular culture," organically grounded within the community, is anachronistic. Believing seriously that the working class and the poor have either already read Kafka and Thomas Mann, or alternatively that they have no need of them, results only in idealism or elitism. Critical aesthetics must instead insist upon providing the broader public with what the culture industry ignores and a framework for judging the quality of different works within an increasing number of traditions and genres.

Critical cultural criticism should also begin thinking more concretely about the various publics with which different works have what Max Weber termed an "elective affinity." The public for a given work can, of course, change over time, and Brecht was correct in maintaining that "difficulty" in the present does not preclude the possibility of fascination in the future. It is a serious mistake, in this vein, to neglect the intelligentsia in the name of "reaching" the masses or constantly preach the need for "simplicity" when the "popularity" of even Sartre or Camus pales before that of Stephen King or Danielle Steele. Nor is it sensible to believe that the impact of a work is always commensurate with the degree of its popularity. Multiple publics exist beneath the smooth surface of advanced industrial society. Their boundaries are fuzzy, and while their values often conflict, they sometimes overlap. Analyzing the complex of values held by each is of exceptional importance for a genuinely critical cultural criticism. But this should not detract from the political intention. Building an emancipated culture is a manifold act, and critical cultural criticism must begin with the assumption that there are manifold ways of influencing what Marx called "the material level of culture." Articulating new categories for appropriating the differing contributions of differing works is, for this reason, a pragmatic necessity. Indeed, such is the principal task of any new critical aesthetics with practical aims.

$$\curvearrowright 9 \curvearrowleft$$

Dialectics at a Standstill
A Methodological Inquiry
into the Philosophy of Theodor W. Adorno

He was perhaps the most dazzling of them all. His dialectical style, his command of the aphorism, and his uncompromising assault on banality and repression turned Theodor Wiesengrund Adorno into the most alluring and surely the most complex representative of critical theory by the time he died in 1969 at the age of sixty-six. His range seemingly knew no bounds. He was a musicologist who had studied with the great Alban Berg, a composer in his own right, a philosopher with expertise in the intricacies of phenomenology, a social theorist steeped in the tradition of Western Marxism, a sociologist engaged in complicated empirical studies, a connoisseur of literature and poetry, an anthropological thinker, and an aesthetician committed to the new and the technically innovative. He incarnated the interdisciplinary perspective of the Frankfurt School, and made contributions in all his fields of endeavor. He, above all, played a decisive role in shifting the interest of Horkheimer and the institute away from its political and economic preoccupations of the 1930s. Adorno, in his own way, transformed the meaning of critical theory. It was Adorno, after all, who asked whether writing poetry was still possible after Auschwitz. It was Adorno who railed against the "liquidation of the subject." It was Adorno who claimed that the whole is false.

His thinking stands and falls on his confrontation with the "ontology of false conditions" in the name of an endangered subjectivity. Reacting against this ontology led him, "in opposition to Hegel's practice and yet in accordance with his thought,"[1] to explode the moment of positivity in favor of an unqualified emphasis on negation. Affirming the "non-identity" between the individual and his world was the logical consequence. Conceptualizing this threatened subjectivity and preserving it involved Adorno in what would become an attack on virtually every major philosophical school. He left nothing unscathed: not phenomenology with its ontological flattening of the very experience it claimed to valorize; not empiricism with its blindness to the context of oppression; not positivism with its expulsion of normative values; not instrumentalism with its sanctioning of what exists; and not even Hegel or Marx with their teleological commitment, their affirmation of progress, their vagaries concerning revolutionary change, and their concern with the "negation of the negation."

No reductionism would infect the mature theory of Adorno, no theological remnants of the Other, no soft humanism,[2] no retreat into "play." This time there would be no illusions. Or, better, illusion, the semblance of reality, would serve both a critical and a utopian purpose. Embedded within art, created by technique, illusion confronts the impoverishment of experience generated by the "inverted world" of the commodity form. Adorno stands up against the "ontology of false conditions" with the emancipatory truth demanded by negative dialectics and retained in works of art. He knew that this truth is politically impotent, that its ability to contradict the unfreedom of the social whole exists only in the fleeting glimpse and the momentary experience. That is why Adorno simultaneously rejected the category of totality, elicited the evanescent and the fragmentary, and still called for a systematic reading of his own work and a contextual understanding of all social phenomena.[3] He would, for better or worse, define freedom by the ontology it denies. The dialectic would grind to a halt and, in this way, remain true to the reality it sought to comprehend. Adorno could not draw the practical conclusions. Nevertheless, through exposing the inverted "truth" of an "inverted world," illusion provided his "negative dialectics" with its uncompromisingly critical thrust.

Reification and Its Inversion

Negative dialectics was, from the start, a confrontation with the "false condition" of things. It thus always presupposed the commitment to a vision of truth critical of the way in which they were presented. History is that presentation. It develops through the rational domination of nature with its expulsion of subjectivity and value-laden concerns from the scientific process. Instrumental rationality, for example, underpins the transformation of capital from the object of production into its subject and the actual producers of wealth into objects for the creation of profit.[4] With its eradication of "use value" by "exchange value," moreover, capitalism becomes the highest expression of an anthropological development dedicated to dominating "inner" and "outer" nature while turning qualitative distinctions into quantitative ones. Externalization of what is internal to the subject impoverishes the subject: that is the key to alienation.[5] Rationalization is thereby rendered equivalent to alienation and reification;[6] the objectifying "form" of productive activity produces it.

Reification becomes the fundamental fact of human existence, which is then read back into each historical epoch and every facet of human experience. Such a stance contests the claim that objectification is an anthropologically neutral phenomenon and that contingent historical conditions, rather than interaction with nature per se, create alienation. An anthropological standpoint, albeit of a "negative" sort,[7] begins to take shape. No wonder that in contrast to Erich Fromm, Adorno should have called upon the institute to place less emphasis on attempts to "sociologize" psychology and more on an independent appropriation of the instinct theory and the metapsychological inheritance of Freud.[8] The domination of nature through history would now receive grounding in the repressive forms of sublimation offered by civilization. Maintaining any genuine commitment to happiness would then involve contesting the ways in which instinctual gratification is offered, delayed, and distorted. The metapsychological and anthropological standpoint would make the need for a "total" break with reality evident.

Adorno won Max Horkheimer over to his new metacritical position and thereby supplanted what had been Fromm's important role in the institute. This metacritical perspective would directly influence the "dialectical logic" of *Dialectic of Enlightenment* and, in a way, the metapsychological utopianism of Marcuse no less than the later work of Horkheimer. If ontology exists, it will define the "false condition" in which freedom has no place. That false condition is history. No reform is capable of altering its structure any more than the effects of a reification process identified with objectification. Liberation must therefore involve an apocalyptic transformation in which a new order will emerge capable of preventing the conflation between subject and object while introducing a new harmony between humanity and nature.

An inversion of the traditional understanding of liberation must take place. The response to reification cannot occur in terms of "what lies beyond" it. The impossibility of bringing about such a change, making "present" what inherently lies beyond, thus complements the ethical need to confront the encompassing reality of repression. Not simply an identification with suffering[9] but guilt at the inability to eradicate its pervasiveness is what produces the commitment to negative dialectics. Practical pessimism thereby comes to stand in "dialectical" tension with a certain variant of philosophical utopianism in the thinking of Adorno no less than the others whom his thinking influenced. Critical theory, in his opinion, cannot deny this tension. Quite the contrary. It should intensify the "force-field."

Contesting the hegemonic claims of mainstream sociology subsequently becomes imperative. Its "scientific" prejudices are inverted as its point of departure is less the happiness of the individual than the quest for objectivity. Not only do empiricist and positivist forms of sociology, according to Adorno, ignore how subjectivity remains unexhausted by the processes supposedly constituting it, but their partisans also remain blind to the manner in which society is itself constituted by subjects. Remaining stuck within the realm of "social facts" necessarily produces a form of thinking in which the subject or individual is collapsed into the object or society. Mainstream sociology, by stripping the social outcome from the value-laden conditions of its constitution, thus contributes to the reification of the very subject it ultimately seeks to study.

A new "critical" approach to sociology is introduced by Adorno. Such an approach would prove as useful for empirical studies of authoritarianism as for criticisms of astrology. But these do not fulfill its methodological purpose. The point of his new "critical" sociology is to highlight the "intrinsic tension" between the need to understand the structures of society, which are open to reflection, and the ways they inhibit subjectivity and the individual's desire for happiness and freedom.[10] It is in order to explore this tension that Adorno has recourse to the categories of idealism, like totality and mediation, which were ignored by the mainstream. Of course, these categories undergo a fundamental change of purpose and quality from the way they were employed by Hegel, Marx, Weber, and Lukács.

"Mediation," for example, becomes a way of preserving experience by undercutting any sense of "false immediacy," while the "totality" loses its validity as a "comprehensive principle of explanation";[11] grasping it is no longer possible from the standpoint of the proletariat.[12] Adorno turns both "mediation" and "totality" into conceptual tools with which to indicate the subjectivity that escapes social and historical objectification. The indeterminate metaphysical character these concepts assume is precisely what justifies their determinate sociological employment. This is the sense in which inversion as a strategy of opposition underpins the entire enterprise. Inverting the "inverted world" of the commodity form, without reference to the proletariat as the revolutionary agent of history, will demand that critique assume the existence of a realm external to the object of analysis. Only in that way is dialectical tension maintained. Potentiality, for this reason, denies actuality while the subject confronts the object. Critique must contest all forms of identity thinking, which Adorno once called the "*Urform*" of ideology, even those of Hegel and Marx. Indeed, this occurs in the name of that "non-identity" between subject and object wherein freedom is experienced.

Given its involvement in the domination of nature, of course, history is seen as undermining this nonidentical relation between subject and object. That is why Adorno wants to break the identification of history with categories such as progress. And this is also undertaken from the perspective of a radical inversion. Progress is turned against itself, freedom is expelled from history, and the individual is pitted against a reality itself of human making. Adorno thus employs an "inverted historicism" to confront various Enlightenment versions of the philosophy of history with their teleological assumptions.[13]

Universal history must be construed and denied. After the catastrophes that have happened, and in view of the catastrophes to come, it would be cynical to say that a plan for a better world is manifested in history and unites it. Not to be denied for that reason, however, is the unity that cements the discontinuous, chaotically splintered moments and phases of history—the unity of the control of nature, progressing to rule over men, and finally to that over men's inner nature. No universal history leads from savagery to humanitarianism, but there is one leading from the slingshot to the megaton bomb."[14]

Heilsgeschichte, or redemptive history is transformed by Adorno into a history of damnation.[15] This reflects the claim made in *Dialectic of Enlightenment* that just as myth served as a premodern form of enlightenment, enlightenment retreats into "myth."[16] In principle, either philosophically or historically, no "reform" is possible: the negation of the negation cannot produce anything "positive."[17] History is a boot in the face. Nor does this derive merely from class contradictions. It is rather a result of the constraints imposed by instrumental reason from the very beginnings of human history.[18] Reality is a constant assault on freedom. Only as an illusion is it possible to reassert the freedom lost in the reification process. And this demands a different language capable of asserting its "sensuous" quality for a subject that must remain irreducible to either philosophical categories or any set of objective conditions. No wonder then that for Adorno, the "mimetic" language of artworks should most directly express what is, in the terms of a reified reality, the illusion of freedom. Illusion projects emancipation. Its "truth content" (*Wahrheitsinhalt*) provides illusion with an element of truth, which propels it beyond magic and make-believe. This truth, however, has nothing in common with the assumptions of logic or instrumental reason. That is precisely what separates aesthetic illusion from ideology and preserves its critical character. Adorno, following the dialectical thinking of the Western Marxists, he knew that "it is not ideology in itself which is untrue, but its pretension to correspond to reality."[19] Nevertheless, he gave their original historical criticism with a political intent a very different twist.

Adorno refashioned the confrontation with reality. Freedom, for him, is no longer in need of formulation or grounding; its concrete and secular quality (*Diesseitigkeit*) is lost since aesthetic illusion, wherein the repressed potential of subjective experience is preserved, can only exist outside reality in the "beyond" (*Jenseitigkeit*).[20] Inversion provides the standpoint of Adorno's "immanent criticism." Only from outside reification is it possible to engage in a defetishizing of reality. Artworks incorporate the subjectivity expelled from history and thus the quality of transcendence. They are, of course, created from the elements of the real. Adorno, for this very reason, could claim that artistic innovation is a "counterpart to the expanding reproduction of capital in society."[21] Indeed, it is the emancipatory inversion of that process.

Emancipation conceived in this way can never receive any concrete determination. Negative dialectic sunders the wish from the deed. And it does so in a very particular way. The "determinate negation" emanating from within the contradictions of a given historical epoch must, in terms of aesthetic critique, appear one-sided and insufficient.[22] The seemingly indeterminate critique of reality projected by aesthetic illusion becomes determinate precisely because it realizes that "the whole is false."[23] Rationality with its technical fetish stands open to critique only from the standpoint of what it denies. The negation, for this reason, can become manifest only through the inversion of reality. Illusion is that inversion. Its manifestation in art offers the palpable indictment of history that Adorno always sought. Philosophy makes sense of that indictment; it is illusory precisely because the illusion of emancipation is preserved from history. The totality is real only in its negation by aesthetic illusion. As a consequence, totality should cease in its attempts to encompass the subject and, instead, be understood as its creation. The concrete does not precede the abstract and the object does not precede the subject. Truth will not appear within history, as its intentional product, but in its "intentionless" manifestations.[24] The point is to assemble the whole, in a form of "parataxis," from a series of partial complexes whose relations are not hierarchically defined.[25]

Generating the idea from these propositions and partial complexes of elements, making connections without creating a system, is the "higher praxis" of which Adorno's supporters tend to speak.[26] It is not a matter of rejecting concepts in the name of irrationalism, but of using them to comprehend a freedom beyond concepts.[27] Subjectivity is preserved as the "constellation" becomes the category with which to expose the dynamic character of reality. Naively, Adorno can assume that "out of the construction of a configuration of reality the demand for its real change always follows promptly."[28] His aesthetics shows how artworks become "constellations" and "unintentionally," or in a "purposefully purposeless" manner, evidence their "truth." History has, in any event, thrown philosophy on the defensive; it continues to exist only because the historical moment for realizing its emancipatory truth—presumably during the workers' revolts of 1917–23—was missed.[29] The legitimation of metaphysics proper, not the creation of a "materialist metaphysic of modernity,"[30] is what takes historical form. Adorno wished to render metaphysics "negative," antisystemic, and capable of discerning the threat to subjectivity through its metacritical inversion.

This undertaking was directly influenced by his friendships with Walter Benjamin and Siegfried Kracauer, no less than his encounter with Edmund Husserl wherein—whatever his criticisms of phenomenology—he defended him for seeking to "destroy idealism from within," for maintaining a commitment to philosophical truth against relativism, and for preserving subjective experience from the "concrete" ontology of Heidegger.[31] Adorno had originally given his study on Husserl, which can be literally translated as *Towards a Metacritique of Epistemology*, the working title "Dialectical Epistemology."[32] He always insisted on the *logic* behind his immanent subversion of concepts.[33] Adorno was as little engaged in formulating an "anti-epistemology," the official English translation of this work, as in denying the truths embodied in the "untruth" of idealism. The issue for him involved recognizing the impossibility of identifying particular objects with concepts even while thinking always crystallizes in particulars.[34] A concern with the unregimented and the spontaneous, which manifests itself in art as well as in "non-identical thinking," is the basis for Adorno's assault on idealism. Critical reflexivity, however, remains the only way to uncover the "untruth" of identity and the manner in which subjectivity is repressed. Adorno maintained his commitment to immanent criticism.[35] Indeed, he did so in the name of what always served as both the foundation and goal of idealism: freedom.

His own "metacritique of practical reason" followed certain currents of Husserl's work.[36] It would, admittedly, emphasize the ignored antinomies of traditional phenomenology. But it too would seek to preserve philosophy from the incursions of social theory and historicism, reject ontology, radicalize idealism by exploding its formalism, and subject its positive assumptions to critical scrutiny. None of this has anything to do with materialism unless that concept is configured in the most abstract terms. Habermas is therefore correct when he writes that "the Marxist theory of society is recast into pure philosophy through the form of Adorno's negative dialectic."[37] A severing of the relation between "theory and practice" occurs as well.[38] Adorno feared the subordination of theory to the exigencies of practice. To a certain extent, furthermore, this was understandable given his experiences in the interwar period.[39] Arguably, Adorno's later works build on Horkheimer"s materialist writings of the 1930s and the anthropological stance elaborated by the two of them in the 1940s. In sealing the divorce between theory and practice, however, Adorno's later works break with the earlier attempts of the institute to influence the struggles of the oppressed. His career from the postwar era tends to legitimate what Leo Lowenthal considered Adorno's motto: "don't participate."[40]

Philosophical reflection continues to project emancipation even if only, following Walter Benjamin and given the argument of *Minima Moralia*, by asking how things might look from the perspective of their redemption. The importance of understanding freedom in terms of unqualified autonomy remains. "Freedom," writes Adorno, "is really delimited by society, not only from outside, but in itself. We no sooner put it to use than we increase our unfreedom; the deputy of better things is always also an accomplice of worse ones."[41] The historical process, in Adorno's view, has expelled freedom, while the hegemony of instrumental reason threatens subjectivity. The goal of critical thinking, however, thereby becomes clear. Reason must project freedom in the *form* of new images so that "in the age of the individual's liquidation, the question of individuality [can] be raised anew."[42]

Adorno is closer to Kierkegaard in this respect than he would probably care to admit.[43] The universal does not vanish; it is merely inverted regarding its relation to the particular. Both philosophers understand that "the principle of individuation, while encapsulating the demand for aesthetic particularization, is of course, itself a universal. What is more, it inheres in the subject that seeks to free itself. In short, it has a universal—spirit—which is not beyond the particulars, but in them."[44] The singular becomes the universal. And the need for such an inversion is the same in the realm of culture. Consequently, even in music, "the collective powers are liquidating individuality, which is irrecoverable—but against them only individuals are capable of consciously representing the aims of collectivity."[45]

A crucial difference, however, does assert itself. Adorno believes that the tradition of existential phenomenology stemming from Kierkegaard obliterates real subjectivity by subsuming it within an ontological framework. Individuation substitutes itself for subjectivity, under these circumstances, in the same way that prefabricated and standardized forms of entertainment supplant the immanent elaboration of genuine artistic concerns.[46] A philosophical critique of subjectivist ontology, if not the ontological character of external reality, complements Adorno's aesthetic critique of the culture industry. Both have as their goal the reassertion of this repressed subjectivity. Thus, contesting Kierkegaard's notion of inwardness, Adorno assumes that "the constitution of the domain of art resembles the constitution of an inner space of ideas in the individual."[47]

His position, however, is defined less by an attempt to develop a "materialist reincarnation of the Kierkegaardian subject"[48] than by a traditional emphasis on immanent critique and an unwillingness to identify subjectivity with anything external to it. This makes it possible for Adorno to suggest that a dour irrationalism, predicated on the experience of "dread" (*Angst*),[49] is merely the flip side of the "happy consciousness" (Marcuse) generated by advanced industrial society. Again, in keeping with the idealist spirit, it becomes apparent that freedom demands transcendence. Theory must "rise above the individuality that exists as well as above the society that exists."[50]

Art embodies that transcendence; it rejects the "pure immanence" of positivism. The artwork, whose various moments exist in constant struggle with one another,[51] becomes the most obvious way of contesting the given petrified arrangment of reality. Every genuine artwork, according to Adorno, "exposes something which is lacking." Art makes the individuated person aware of his or her repressed subjectivity. It follows from Adorno's modernist convictions, in fact, that a genuine artwork always produces a "tremor."[52] The aesthetic inquiry must begin with the object and its critique of the world in which the subject is enmeshed. For this reason, art must "hurt." Pleasure and entertainment, even when transfigured within the artwork, lose their validity: "entertainment and art are antithetical to each other."[53] The specter of false immediacy presents itself, and insofar as pleasure and entertainment are rationalized, severed from the critique of repression,[54] they become the enemies of aesthetic appreciation. "The value of a thought is," according to Adorno, "measured by its distance from the continuity of the familiar. It is objectively devalued as this distance is reduced."[55]

Alienation from the alienated social relations of the whole, the "ontology of actuality," is the aim of art. And that is only possible by emphasizing the formal, rather than the substantive, character of the work. Adorno's first cultural essay, "Expressionism and Artistic Truth," already emphasized that the form employed by this movement rather than its rebellion against the "father" or its political ambitions projected its emancipatory character.[56] By highlighting the question of form, however, Adorno necessarily places particular weight on the specialized knowledge of artistic technique. Initially, of course, the critical theory of society developed by the Institute for Social Research was "supradisciplinary" in character; it was meant to serve as a propadeutic with which to inform the specialized empirical sciences and maintain the commitment to the unrecognized concerns of humanity as a universal. In the later writings of Adorno, however, "art can realize its universal humanity only working within the framework of specialization. All else is false consciousness."[57] What occurred in response to the traditional philosophy of history with its teleological assumptions now takes place in terms of specialization. Adorno engages in another inversion. Specialization is changed, when employed by critical aesthetic inquiry, from a servant of alienation into a rebel seeking to contest its power.

Obscured by the increasing division of labor, without a subject to thematize its transformation, and thus incomprehensible from the standpoint of social theory, the totality becomes the focal point of a critical aesthetic built upon specialized knowledge. What sociologically appears as emphasis on subjectivity, from the standpoint of the aesthetic, gives "primacy to the object." The artwork offers a critique of the whole precisely because its rejection of direct political commitment prevents it from leveling a critique of anything in particular. Its illusionary quality confronts the real, and its indeterminacy supplants meager determinations of freedom, so that "praxis is not the impact works have; it is the hidden potential of their truth content."[58] Freedom covers its face. Adorno, like Max Horkheimer, rejects any attempt to provide the most radical illusion with a content. He, too, will embrace the Jewish injunction against seeking to depict God—and extends it to the Holocaust and utopia.

Aesthetic Inversion and Illusion

Adorno never surrenders the concept. So, for the hopeless, he holds out a moment of hope. But, in his view, utopia rests upon a "compact with failure." His is a telos without teleology. Emancipation thus becomes a floating opposition to a reality ontologically structured by reification. The truth of illusion contests the untruth of repression. It was for this reason he could write that "truth is inseparable from the illusory belief that from the pictures of the unreal one day, in spite of all, real deliverance will come."[59] The unreal and the nondiscursive confront the reification of the real and the rational. This deliverance is neither articulated with respect to its meaning nor justified in terms of its "concrete possibility" (Lukács). It is really, for want of a better term, a myth, and thus the inversion of what the Enlightenment sought to dispel.

Such is the manner in which art evidences what Stendhal termed its *promesse de bonheur*. Philosophy once proclaimed a similar promise. History, however, remained deaf to it. Philosophy, for this reason, lacks foundations, and even negative dialectics recognizes that its status has become indeterminate.[60] Contradiction must therefore become redefined in terms of opposition to reality per se.[61] Illusion alone, generated in the form of art, can contest the real. It alone can secure the moment of transcendence by remembering the past.[62] Indeed, with the unceasing assault on philosophical reflection by technological rationality and reification, "art may be the only remaining medium of truth in an age of incomprehensible terror and suffering."[63] The aesthetic inversion of reality now serves as its negation. Art redeems truth by illuminating its sensuous quality. It does not, like philosophy, assume that "the authentic question will somehow almost always include its answer."[64] Emancipation lies in fantasy and the language of experience irreducible to linguistic rules: mimesis. Freedom is sensed beyond the conditions defining it while experience is preserved from closure in fixed philosophical categories and formulas.[65] Philosophy loses the unassailable primacy given it by Hegel; it now complements or "overlaps" with art in the idea of truth content.[66] Philosophy receives a new task. It must now discursively shape the nondiscursive and "mimetic" elements of art.[67]

The fusion between art and philosophy is, however, impossible to achieve.[68] Their identity is little more than a utopian longing predicated on the "nonidentity" between them. It is the same with the "logical essence," the internal coherence of an artwork,[69] which underpins the ongoing conflicts between the elements composing it. Tension of this sort is always felt. It is what disrupts the sleek and smooth unfolding of technological rationality and secures the unrealized potential of freedom. The internal volatility of art is what resists the world and fosters the "non-identity" between subject and object.[70] An inversion of the relation between universal and particular thus takes place within it; the object must highlight the subject in the realm of the aesthetic, if

not in reality per se, which is why Adorno can claim that "art speaks in universals only when it moves away from universals to specific impulses."[71] This, in
turn, renders art incapable of being defined ontologically or by any determinate set of logical, philosophical propositions.[72] The artwork stands apart. It
has no external referent; its autonomy testifies to its freedom; it is always sui
generis.

Adorno is no traditionalist. The innovative and the new, inverted in the
aesthetic realm, confront the tricks and the fads of the culture industry. Judging the innovative character of a work, however, presupposes a knowledge of
artistic technique. Artworks may not be reducible to technique, they may
threaten the nonconceptual "language" of art,[73] but only technical knowledge
provides an objective referent for criticism and a corrective to interpretations
based on experiential or historicist criteria.[74] Technique, whose origins derive
from the external world that the artwork contests, becomes internal to its
effect. The manifestation of reification turns into the criticism of it. Thus,
with its inversion, technique "alone guides the reflective person into the inner
core of art works, provided of course he also speaks their language . . . It is
rational but non-conceptual, permitting judgment in the area of the non-
judgmental."[75]

Aesthetic form, precisely insofar as it transfigures empirical being, "represents freedom whereas empirical life represents repression."[76] The truth content of an artwork is thus necessarily transcendent.[77] The illusion generated
by technique projects a promise beyond the suffering produced by the hege
mony of technical reason. That is the sense in which works of art "want us to
become aware of what is true and what is false in them."[78] In this way, according to Adorno, technique helps elicit the "meaning" of the work:[79] the hidden
moment of reconciliation demanded by the unreconcilable opposition to
reality. Aesthetic negation thus suggests positivity, which, within the terms of
a reified reality, remains always negative. This is the sense in which Adorno's
later work fulfills the earlier desire to provide a "positive concept of enlightenment."[80] The work is that positive concept. It is the central concept of the
aesthetic; "art," Adorno can write, "is as inimical to 'art' as are artists."[81] For
this reason, in contrast to Benjamin or Marcuse, he seeks to introduce categories of aesthetic judgment. Intensity, accomplishment, depth, and articulation become the conceptual tools with which to divine quality.[82] Categories
such as these are meant to rescue the work from submersion within the experience of the subject. Indeed, given these categories, it makes sense for him to
claim that "aesthetic experience must pass over into philosophy or else it will
not be genuine."[83]

Aesthetics becomes metaphysical.[84] So it must if experience is to resist reality and remain immune to relativism.[85] Adorno, unwilling to surrender the
concept of reflection,[86] maintains its intrinsic connection with a thematized

object. He is not intent merely on deconstructing reality, denying the need for categories of differentiation, obliterating universals, or promulgating subjectivism. Quite the contrary. Adorno may have opposed the neoclassicism of Igor Stravinsky and Paul Hindemith along with "new objectivity" (*Neue Sachlichkeit*) and its belief that the composer is a "musical engineer." Nevertheless, the problems with his own aesthetic derive precisely from an objectivism of a different sort.

"Dialectics is not some rule on how to handle art, but something that inheres in it."[87] The artwork, so to speak, takes on a life of its own. It retains a set of dynamics from which possibilities arise for reconciling internal tensions while contradicting the external reality from which it arose.[88] While interpretation, commentary, and criticism are necessary to elicit the truth content of the work, however, they are little more than midwives. They only articulate what is already extent, the elements of quality, within the work as a work. It is rather a matter of employing reflexivity to "retrace" the dynamic of a work by examining its particular aspects and how they are "wanting." The autonomy Adorno seeks implies that "works of art are their own standard of judgment. They themselves stipulate the rules they then follow."[89] The influence of Benjamin is again apparent in Adorno's refusal to divorce categories from the empirical objects they describe.[90] Universality makes itself felt in the particularity generated by the aesthetic monad. The artwork lives, assumes its most critical character when it first appears, and then dies buried in the museum. Indeed, "neutralization" is the social price art pays for its autonomy. Once artworks are buried in the pantheon of cultural exhibits, their truth content deteriorates.[91]

Amor fati: The authentic work of art, no less than Nietzsche's authentic individual, loves its fate because it determines that fate. Art pulsates for Adorno. The work of art, with its appropriated materials and dynamic capacity for engendering reflection, produces its own temporality. Adorno knows, of course, that art participates in the history of society. It is a product of social materials; there is also no way in which a genuine work of art will not put those materials to critical use. No matter how art is mediated, then, art will constitute itself as autonomous beyond its existence as a social fact.[92] But the participation of an artwork in history is only partial: it derives from its appropriation of technology from the external world.[93] Progress in art, which is legitimate to discuss only because "there is no progress in the real world,"[94] is comprehensible in terms of an inherently contingent form of such appropriation. It is neither linear nor apparent in the arbitrary comparison of particular works. Fashion indeed makes sense of Adorno's claim that artworks die.[95] The discontinuous progress of art, which actually subverts the concept, differs qualitatively from that of social development. The only point of continuity within art history is the constant rejection of that domination inherent in the social conditions making for its own genesis. Thus, the work of art internally sets its technologically appropriated devices in motion so that they transcend the merely functional.

The moment of art within the artwork accomplishes that in the name of freedom.[96] Adorno never rejects the concept of "essence," even if only as the "irreducible" differentiating subject from object.[97] He does, however, back away from the irrationalist implications of what initially appears as an inverted form of aesthetic *Lebensphilosophie*. Metaphysics provides the corrective in a world dominated by instrumental reason on the one hand and irrationalism on the other. Adorno's point is to assert what has been lost. The question of whether metaphysical experience is still possible, which animates *Negative Dialectic*,[98] receives its answer in *Aesthetic Theory* where experience is preserved in the work of art. Thus, in order to explicate works of art, Adorno can claim that "they have to be honed to the point where they become philosophical. It is in the dynamic of the internal constitution of works and of the relation that particular works have to the concept of art in general that we obtain proof of the fact that art, its monadic essence notwithstanding, is an aspect of the movement of spirit and social reality."[99]

Philosophy prevents art, with its ability to generate an irreducible experience or a "somatic moment" of cognition, from slipping into "the abyss of relativity."[100] Metaphysical reflection preserves the work from purely historical interpretation and illuminates the moment of universality projected by the monadic "essence" of the work. Just as philosophy makes the truth of art comprehensible, according to Adorno, art makes the truth of philosophy concrete.[101] The moment of reflection, however, is itself interwoven with experience. Adorno does not ignore the excitement of art or its elemental attraction. Thus, while praising the manifold possibilities for new experience offered by the circus, he can eloquently describe fireworks as the "prototype of art."

This is the key to understanding his commitment to art and the manner in which it embodies freedom. "The work of art," he can write, "is both a process and an instant."[102] Fireworks evidence the evanescent, the fleeting moment, which prods memory; indeed, Adorno can write that "the tendency to objectify what is evanescent rather than what is permanent may well be one that runs through art history as a whole."[103] Subjectivity experiences itself in that moment.[104] Even this, however, does not simply belong to the subject. Adorno maintains his rejection of "false" immediacy, of enjoyment,[105] in the name of a structured experience capable of grasping the utopian. Aesthetic feeling, even in the case of fireworks, retains its critical and reflexive edge. Consequently, he can write:

> Aesthetic feeling is not what is being aroused in us. It is more like a sense of wonderment in the presence of what we behold; a sense of being

overwhelmed in the presence of a phenomenon that is non-conceptual while at the same time being determinate. The arousal of subjective effect by art is the last thing we should want to dignify with the name aesthetic feeling. True aesthetic feeling is oriented to the object; it is the feeling of the object, not some reflex in the viewer.[106]

Fireworks demonstrate the idea of art as a tour de force. The display is defined by antinomies. Its particular elements rebel against unification even as they form a unity without a fixed center. Colors clash, mosaics form, the work lives and then it dies. Fireworks are not reducible to the interpretive description, and the meaning of the event occurs only in the attempt to "retrace" it. The work retains its own internal discipline,[107] creates its own "mimetic" language, and binds people together while leaving the singularity of their experience intact. The prototype of art secures the nonidentity of subject and object in the experience of a nonobjectifiable freedom, which begins to vanish as soon as it appears, like utopia. Reality can never measure up to the illusion. For that reason, however, reality takes its revenge.

Exploding the Inversion

"The gentleman does not find the world to his liking? Then let him go and look for a better one."[108] Adorno hated this kind of talk. But he protested too much. For, while such a view might well shackle artistic experimentation and limit the range of experience, its relevance for politics is obvious. Adorno, however, could not—or would not—make the distinction. And this has profound implications. The question is whether the cult embracing Adorno, identifying his ideas with those of critical theory per se, is willing to draw them. It is irrefutable that Adorno made seminal contributions to aesthetics by reaffirming the centrality of the work, exploring its inner dynamics, and opposing its reduction to psychology and historicism. Early in his career, admittedly, he argued that transcendental philosophy must give way before a standpoint predicated on the "critique of ideology." He had claimed then that the function rather than the manifest content of philosophy demands analysis. Nor did he ever really retract that claim. There was no need. It would inform his negative dialectics, his defense of an idealist tradition betrayed by history, and his decision to emphasize the primacy of the artwork. Consequently, it is only fair that Adorno's own standpoint be confronted with the same standard of criticism he embraced.

There is no question about it: Adorno's thinking became increasingly marked by a retreat from the concrete and an affirmation of the status quo he always putatively rejected. His critique of ontology ultimately stands defined by what it opposes. The "truth" of illusion is pitted against the "untruth" of reality, the determinate against the indeterminate, metaphysics against history, and aesthetics against anthropology. A divide results. The theoretical architectonic and the concrete reality are separated in terms of an *ontological chasm*. Nor does it help to claim that Adorno is turning dialectics against itself, whatever that means. The result is not dialectics, but stasis wearing the costume of radical change. It provides neither a method of concrete analysis nor a theory of practice. This is, indeed, what Walter Benjamin termed "dialectics at a standstill."

Adorno's theory, whatever its contributions, does not constitute a useful response either to the collapse of Marxist teleology or to the world of "late" capitalism.[109] The character and aims of his thought, even while predicated on the reinversion of a world inverted by the commodity form, are different. There is no objective referent for solidarity,[110] and no immanent analysis of the production process. Adorno may occasionally have spoken about his commitment to a "genuine liberalism." But there is no institutional analysis of the divergent political systems representing advanced industrial society. The philosophical importance of his work thus derives from its greatest sociological weakness: an exaggeration of the integrative power of advanced industrial society and the impossibility of practical resistance.[111]

The extraordinary integrative power of modern society makes aesthetics alone capable of resisting it in the name of freedom. In the process, however, freedom is robbed of its content and subjectivity becomes just as nebulous as in the most reactionary of phenomenological approaches. Adorno's unwillingness to engage in discussions of "grounding" is no excuse. Neither is his fear of "systems." His refusal to justify the status of aesthetics or philosophy left him in this unenviable theoretical situation. And its implications become manifest in a variety of ways. Adorno claims, for example, that a progressive work of art provides an immanent critique of the formal limitations of existing artworks and, simultaneously, a rejection of repression. His justification, however, is based on little more than a previous definition of form as embodying freedom and an identification of empirical reality with repression.[112] The argument thus becomes tautological.

Tautology legitimates the supposedly radical use of inversion. Intervention is consequently equated with the inversion of reality. The formal moment of aesthetic freedom, indeterminate from the perspective of social interaction, is identified with a determinate response to repression by Adorno;[113] any concrete response to oppression is, by the same token, criticized from the utopian stance for its indeterminate and partial character; indeed, this explains the link between his aesthetic radicalism and his fear of concrete political change.[114] Other inversions follow from this one. Aesthetic objectification ensures subjectivity while work in the social realm demeans it. Concrete praxis, or a theoretically informed political intervention into the status quo, loses its standing in favor of a "higher praxis" lacking in any material effect whatsoever. Thus, Adorno can write:

Concrete and positive suggestions for change merely strengthen [the power of the status quo], either as ways of administrating the unadministratable, or by calling down repression from the monstrous totality itself. The concept and the theory of society are legitimate only when they do not allow themselves to be attracted by either of these solutions, when they merely hold in negative fashion to the basic possibility inherent in them: that of expressing the fact that such possibility is threatened with suffocation. Such awareness, without any preconceptions as to where it might lead, would be the first condition for an ultimate break in society's omnipotence."[115]

No concrete practice is ever radical enough. Theory turns its back on the reality it is to transform and detaches utopia from history. Art metaphysically puts "an advance on a praxis which has not yet begun."[116] But it can do so legitimately only insofar as the work does not project anything concrete in its vision. Adorno never provided even the hint of an institutional alternative like the workers' councils, which informed the sectarian thinking of Korsch, from which to launch his critique. He was content to affirm that "a free society would situate itself beyond both the irrationality of its false costs and the means-ends rationality of utility. This ideal is encoded in art and is responsible for art's social explosiveness."[117]

Whether such an encoding is actually in a painting by, say, Mondrian is debatable. Whether such an ideal is relevant for an emancipated order, especially given any serious commitment to nonrepressive interaction with nature, is not. Given this stance, it is no wonder that Adorno should have been unable to develop any institutional referent for his thinking or any notion of the public good. If Adorno is correct in maintaining that materialism eliminates epistemology by fiat, which is surely the case, his aesthetics does the same with politics. It is simply insufficient to speak of the "unfulfilled promise" of the Enlightenment without direct reference to the social values and political institutions envisioned by its most important representatives. Adorno is right in insisting that the old teleological unity between theory and practice has broken down. It is no longer a matter of the "future appearing as present." But, in principle, theory remains capable of speculating about the new conditions necessary for realizing its promises and intervening in the given order. Unfortunately, however, he shied away from the implications of this claim. He came to believe that:

The call for unity of theory and practice has irresistibly degraded theory to a servant's role, removing the very traits it should have brought to that unity. The visa stamp of practice which we demand of all theory became a censor's placet. Yet whereas theory succumbed in the vaunted mixture, practice became nonconceptual, a piece of the politics it was supposed to lead out of it; it became the prey of power.[118]

Power is inherently evil: it speaks only to the realm of "necessity." Identifying reification with objectification obscures how power exists as a relationship in which contingency always plays a role. Power is identified with the "system" by Adorno rather than the struggles between people and institutions within it. A reified notion of domination substitutes itself for power, and as dialectics becomes little more than running in place or an engine idling, metaphysics supplants social theory. Breaking the relation between theory and practice, while associating autonomy with the one and repression with the other, defines the new brand of critical theory. The problem derives from the way in which metacritique is initially elaborated in *Dialectic of Enlightenment*. In that work, after all, freedom is expelled from history. It loses both its form and its content. Freedom becomes anchored in the subject. What this means, however, remains open to question. With freedom as the "other," any concern with expanding the range of individual choices is rendered irrelevant. Freedom is now content to contest power and thus forgets that power is necessary to constrain its arbitrary exercise.[119] The ethical and practical function of freedom is lost. It becomes transcendent and loses its immanent connection with human affairs. Freedom, from the standpoint of social reality, must appear as an illusion. Thus, politics is liquidated in the name of a methodological critique incapable of either specifying the conditions needing transformation or positing an alternative form of institutional organization.

In *The Authoritarian Personality*, of course, Adorno and his collaborators developed an "f-scale" for testing the degree to which authoritarian values have taken hold in an individual. In contrast to *Dialectic of Enlightenment*, learning becomes a possibility and fascism is seen more as a probable than as a necessary outcome of liberal society. Enlightenment and education can mitigate the worst forms of racism and intolerance. The study was a major contribution and, with its quantitative techniques, caused a great deal of controversy. Adorno, however, never integrated the results into his general theory. And for good reason. Extending its sociological insight would have involved subverting his broader enterprise. *The Authoritarian Personality* indeed calls into question the formal identification between alienation and objectification as surely as the claim that "mass enlightenment" will only result in "mass deception." Adorno might reply that the general formal claim can never fully encompass the particular. That is, in fact, precisely the point of Adorno's "negative dialectics." It resists the distorting power lurking in concepts as surely as in institutions. But the question is whether the particular and the empirical contradict the general and the formal. Mediating categories are necessary to show the connection if they don't. These, however, are never supplied. There is consequently only one conclusion to draw: the empirical analysis in *The Authoritarian Personality* excludes the formal analysis forwarded in Adorno's philosophical studies.

It is the same with the famous inquiry into the "culture industry" first articulated in *Dialectic of Enlightenment*. The purpose of Horkheimer and Adorno was undoubtedly a noble one. They wished to examine the effects of the commodity form on culture. They had seen how the state could employ the new media in advanced industrial society. They had recognized its potentially negative effects on political consciousness no less than on what Marx had termed "the material level of culture." The issue was its form. The increasing power of the culture industry was a direct reflection of the expanding power of the commodification process and instrumental reason. And, from the perspective of the general theory, the commitment to a criticism of the culture industry must prove uncompromising. That is why Adorno could write that, no less than dissonance, "black as an ideal"—the color devoid of colors—would alone enable art "to stand its ground."[120] This makes it logical to assume that a particular type of reflexive discernment is necessary.[121] The proper experience of a work as a tour de force,[122] in contrast to the false immediacy propagated by the culture industry, is interconnected with a technical knowledge of its form. *Guernica* by Picasso is, from this standpoint, meaningless to a person who knows nothing of its context or techniques. Adorno might have been elitist in his views on the existing "material level of culture." Nevertheless, there is much valid in his critique of those who would simply glorify "experience" in judging a work of art.[123]

Subjectivity is preserved by aesthetic form, and given the need to contest the culture industry, the more complex and innovative the better. Even when emptied of its most expressive content, the form recalls—without redeeming—the horrors spawned by progress along with those aspects of individuality weakened by the incursions of the culture industry. The subject experiences his subjectivity then in response to the "slaughterbench of history" and his freedom in the rejection of prefabricated forms of "entertainment." This only makes sense given that "the emancipation of the subject by art was co-extensive with the shift towards autonomy in art itself." [124] Nevertheless, if subjectivity is freed to the extent that art becomes autonomous, then the extent to which art can fulfill its purpose is the extent to which it contests and breaks free of its subservience to the commodity form.

In making this kind of general argument, Adorno's attack is directed against the culture industry. But this industry has many branches, and as a consequence Adorno was willing to consign all sports to the realm of "unfreedom" and maintain that jazz is simply a "commodity in the strict sense."[125] Of course, like anyone else, he had his likes and dislikes: Adorno often made positive comments about various forms of popular entertainment, including the circus, fireworks, and even the Marx Brothers. But he provides no viable categories for justifying his tastes. A bizarre situation thus results in which even the "prototype of art," fireworks, must be embraced as a formal principle and then rejected when employed—in what is actually their most flamboyant form—by the "systems" on occasions ranging from Independence Day to Chinese New Year. It is the idea of "fireworks," not the reality, which Adorno enjoys. Nor is the use of fireworks by Walt Disney Productions to introduce its programs ever mentioned. The idea of fireworks is lifted above its real manifestations just as freedom is defined outside its immanent exercise. The situation is similar with the Marx Brothers. Sensitive literary critics can note that Adorno praises the simple and the outrageous qualities of their skits,[126] which often make use of modernist and expressionist devices. Radical differences of quality, however, define their films no less than the rapid-fire delivery and the relentless routines within them; Adorno does not have even the most general categories for distinguishing between them, judging the Marx Brothers against imitators like the Ritz Brothers, or evaluating them in relation with other comic giants of the culture industry like W. C. Fields. Concrete discussions of this sort would contradict Adorno's more general claims about the culture industry through suggesting that its products deserve the same analytic treatment as "higher" works of art. The chasm looms once again, and in the absence of procedures and categories of evaluation, his judgments often appear arbitrary. Habermas may have overstated the case in claiming that Adorno calls the very commitment to rationality into question. Nevertheless, there is something legitimate in the suggestion that his former teacher followed Nietzsche in turning what should be discursively justifiable validity claims into mere preferences.[127]

A new preoccupation with the individual subject marked the change in critical theory initiated by Adorno. It surely inspired the cultural rebels of the 1960s. But he remained outside the movement. Adorno chastized his students like Hans-Jürgen Krahl and others for ignoring the dangers of "non-conformist conformity,"[128] underestimating the authoritarian sources of their tactics, and viewing terror as the only response to a situation in which "the whole is false."[129] Still, he had nothing positive to offer them as an alternative. Fearful of mass action, opposed to terror, his ideal of genuine subjectivity was left hanging in the abstract: it becomes the preserve of the connoisseur. Adorno's insistence on "no emancipation without that of society"[130] even today rings hollow. His theory nullifies its promise. All that remains is the long trek inward and a bitter memory of what was left behind.

○ 10 ○

Fromm in America

America embraced Erich Fromm like few other émigrés. But, ironically, the man who made so many tenets of critical theory part of the American vocabulary was never really associated with that philosophical tendency in the public mind.[1] Most intellectuals knew him as a social psychologist and one of the founders, along with Karen Horney and Harry Stack Sullivan,[2] of the neo-Freudian "culturalist" school. But no mass public read the wealth of specialized papers he produced or the technical arguments underpinning his "analytic psychology." His fame rested on *Escape from Freedom* and what many intellectuals considered "how-to" tracts like *The Art of Loving*, "feel-good" books like *The Heart of Man*, or "dilettantish" incursions into the field of politics and social theory like *May Man Prevail*. Perhaps, in the 1950s, important sociologists like his students David Riesman and Paul Lazarsfeld took him seriously; in fact, sociological journals were rife with citations from the work of Erich Fromm. By the 1960s, however, Fromm had turned into a merely "popular writer." Few considered him an intellect on par with someone like T. W. Adorno, and he neither became a titan of academic affairs like Max Horkheimer nor the guru of a movement like Herbert Marcuse. He never prized the aesthetic like Adorno and, in contrast to Horkheimer, employed his organizational talents outside the university; in contrast to Marcuse, furthermore, he was dissatisfied with "the great refusal" or any utopian conception inimically separated from reality.

Aside from Horkheimer, arguably, Fromm was the most important theoretician during the early years of the Frankfurt School.[3] Later, however, its leading representatives would somewhat patronizingly regard him as the "idealist," the "mystic," the "naif," and—above all—the humanist. Jealousy was surely involved. More than any other member of the Frankfurt School, even Marcuse, Fromm touched a nerve in the progressive reading public beyond the university. But that was not, as most commentators maintain, because he "abandoned" critical theory and a "radical" perspective. In fact, far more than most of the others, Fromm consistently and openly identified himself with the left during the dark days of the cold war. He neither denigrated social theory in favor of aesthetics like Adorno nor used religion to justify political paralysis like Horkheimer. Not even Marcuse identified his aims with a practical political tradition or presented ideas for concrete change as forthrightly as Erich Fromm. His writings attest to the fact that popularity does not preclude political commitment any more than clarity of style precludes clarity of thought. Fromm's influence derived from his willingness to reassert the original tenets of the critical enterprise, reformulate them after his own fashion, and present his views in such a way that they might contribute to the broad-based progressive movement that was surfacing in the America of the 1950s and 1960s.

*   *   *

It was said of Charlie Chaplin that he never discarded a single piece of film; he used everything. Erich Fromm never forgot anything either. That was the case with the Talmudic tradition in which he grew to maturity no less than the critical theory into which he was introduced during the late 1920s. Born in 1900, even as a child he was drawn to the great prophets of the Old Testament like Isaiah, Amos, and Hosea less for their warnings of catastrophe than for their utopian visions. Fromm helped establish the legendary *Freie judisches Lehrhaus*,[4] and his association with rabbis like Ludwig Krause, Nehemiah Nobel, and especially Salman Baruch Rabinkow inspired a commitment to humanism that would last until his own death in 1980.[5] Fromm's earliest works treated religious themes, like *The Sabbath* (1927) and, with a Marxian twist, *The Dogma of Christ* (1930), while his dissertation, written for Alfred Weber at the University of Heidelberg, dealt with "The Jewish Law: Toward a Sociology of the Jewish Diaspora" (1922); in fact, the theological strains within his thought would later strike a popular chord in radical works of biblical reinterpretation like *You Shall Be as Gods*.[6] Nevertheless, in America, it was as a social psychologist fusing the thought of Marx and Freud that he first achieved success.

He emigrated early in 1933. Already friendly with a number of important intellectuals, having set up a psychoanalytic practice, he immediately became a guest professor at Columbia University and later taught at the University of Chicago, Bennington, Yale, and the New School for Social Research. *Escape from Freedom*, originally published in 1941, reached an enormous popular audience. It would most likely not have had such impact in an earlier period. During the depression, in the words of Edgar Friedenberg, the populace "did not take any form of psychoanalytic thought to have serious social implications, but tended to dismiss it as a rich man's toy."[7] The onset of World War II, however, forced the nation to confront totalitarianism and recognize that Nazism was not merely the work of a clique and that it retained a mass base of millions willing to sacrifice themselves for its goals. *Escape from Freedom* inaugurated what would become a spate of studies on the "authoritarian personality" and the "origins of totalitarianism" even as it gave readers a handle with which to confront Hitler's "new man" and the "SS state."[8]

Fromm considered himself engaged, especially during the 1930s, in developing a "materialist psychoanalysis." His social psychology, in this vein, rested on an appropriation of critical theory. It is true that by 1939 he had already broken with his former comrades of the Institute for Social Research.[9] Fromm was angered by what he perceived as a growing discourtesy on the part of Horkheimer,[10] the refusal of the latter to publish *The Working Class in Weimar Germany*, and the problems of collaborating with him on *Studies on Authority and the Family*.[11] Then, too, there was the growing influence of Theodor Adorno, whom Fromm heartily disliked.[12] Most important, however, the Frankfurt School changed its view of Freud as well as its political perspective when Fromm left and Adorno became a full-fledged associate in 1938.

Attempts to expose the mediations between the psychological and the sociological in order to overcome economic reductionism, and explore the manner in which revolutionary change was being hindered, now surrendered before Adorno's desire to secure an anthropological foundation for critical theory by employing the instinct theory and metapsychology of Freud. The original program of the institute had called for the development of an interdisciplinary perspective capable of connecting philosophy and empirical analysis. It was believed that social scientific inquiry would thus become imbued with a normative component and overcome the position of those who would separate "fact" from "value." The original project sought to situate all forms of activity within a totalistic view of social relations, confront the implications of the commodity form, foster a dialectical perspective, and maintain the commitment to an emancipatory alternative.

Fromm's social psychology always highlighted its connection with practice.[13] None of his future work, even his preoccupation with Nietzsche and various "philosophers of life" in seeking a foundation for his psychological arguments, evidences a break with the past. All of it builds on two of his earliest contributions to the *Journal for Social Research*. These essays, dating from 1929 and 1931, already emphasized that the psychological neither is divorced from the sociological nor is its mechanical complement. They already raised questions about the links between the economic and the psychic realm, the manner in which the ego is organized, how the psychic apparatus affects the development of society, and the extent to which psychology can aid the political confrontation with inhuman conditions.[14]

Escape from Freedom employs this interdisciplinary perspective in order to analyze a specific historical occurrence: Nazism. Much to the chagrin of Fromm's former comrades in the institute,[15] most of whom were still virtually unknown, the book created a sensation with its depiction of the sado-masochistic character as the specific historical response to the loneliness and alienation caused by capitalism and the political institutions it engendered in Weimar Germany.[16] Identifying neurosis as a social product whose mitigation or intensification depends upon the transformation of living conditions,[17] the book culled insights from work undertaken with Horkheimer during the 1930s in which the family was seen as a primary agent of repressive social-ization. Inaugurating what would become a virtual obsession with the "authoritarian personality" among American intellectuals, this study provided a concrete example of the manner in which socioeconomic conditions are translated into a particular "social character."

And, with this, Fromm began his "revision" of Freud.[18] The work of Karen Horney and Harry Stack Sullivan on the role of interpersonal interaction in producing anxiety never resonated with other members of the Frankfurt School. But the idea that behavior was shaped by cultural norms was embraced by all of its members. That philosophical tendency, after all, had emerged in response to the failure of the proletarian uprisings following the First World War and the inability of that class to make good on the "objective conditions" for revolutionary transformation provided by the economic col-lapse of 1929. The reasons for the failure of successful revolutionary action were not simply reducible to questions of economics. Cultural issues also required analysis, and Fromm's writings, in this regard, proved important for critical theory.

He often criticized the mass media. But his criticisms lacked the dogmatic and arrogant tone so common with his former colleagues at the Institute for Social Research. This, in turn, made it possible for him to engage American public life in a way that they could not. Fromm never really developed a gen-eral theory of the culture industry. Perhaps he was fearful of directing his cri-tique at the form of cultural production in advanced industrial society. Fromm was wary of claims suggesting that it inherently appealed to the low-est common denominator or suggestions that all radical impulses become absorbed or invalidated once they become popular.[19] His approach was dif-ferent; it built upon a different set of assumptions. Thus, his most sustained critique of alienated consumption was built upon the category of "social character."[20]

This concept derives from the original desire of the institute, in keeping with the thought of Korsch and Lukács, to situate all phenomena within the context of the totality, and it affirms Fromm's commitment to the original critical enterprise. The category of social character militates against viewing consciousness from the standpoint of simple institutional manipulation from the top down and reaffirms its sociological connection with practice.

The concept of *social character* refers to the matrix of the character structure common to a group. It assumes that the fundamental factor in the formation of the "social character" is *the practice of life as it is consti-tuted by the mode of production and the resulting social stratification. The "social character" is that particular structure of psychic energy which is molded by any given society so as to be useful for the functioning of that particular society.* The average person must *want* to do what he *has* to do in order to function in a way that permits society to use his energies for its purposes.[21]

Too many misconceptions still surround the intellectual relationship between Freud and Fromm.[22] It was not that Fromm flatly denied the validity of categories like the Oedipus complex, or the unconscious, or the existence of a certain instinctual energy. His concern was rather that Freud's instinct theory, his patriarchal bias, and his focus on sexuality led to interpretive dis-tortions of the oedipal myth. Fromm rejected all claims regarding the univer-sality of the oedipal complex and believed that each society retains a certain libidinal structure that has an impact on the lives of its inhabitants.[23] He was also willing to speak of human nature—though one that is neither fixed nor infinitely malleable. Were it static, change would prove impossible a priori; were human beings totally malleable, the need to resist oppression would be sociologically extinguished.[24] Fromm's approach maintains that a "dynamic adaptation" of human nature to the contradictions of a given social complex will occur.[25] The result can prove beneficial under stable circumstances and explosive when the economic infrastructure is in a state of rapid change. Under any circumstances, while modifying the somewhat functional or mechanical view of the relation between the psychological and the sociologi-cal apparent in his earliest essays, Fromm rejected Freud's emphasis on a fixed, libidinally centered, ahistorical theory of the instincts in favor of the histori-cally unique "social character."

Generally overlooked is the way in which Fromm's revision of instinct the-ory made possible an interpretation that most nearly renders Freud, Marx, and even Nietzsche for that matter theoretically compatible. This had been one of the central concerns of the Frankfurt School almost from the begin-ning. But the ahistorical character of Freud's instinct theory and Nietzsche's vitalistic subjectivism created a logical stumbling block for those seeking to integrate their thinking with that of historical materialism. No accident then that the attempts by Wilhelm Reich should have foundered on the reef of vitalism even as freeing the subject for Adorno and Horkheimer would ulti-mately involve breaking not only with history but society as well.

According to Fromm, by contrast, society remains at the center. Rejecting Freud's ahistorical characterization of individuals through distinct structural categories like the id, ego, and superego, he chose to view the individual from the perspective of an integrated being grounded within society.[26] And so, if the existence of psychic energy is recognized, it is no longer identified as biological or with sexual libido. This energy, which Nietzsche also emphasized, becomes manifest in the living of life as a social being. A logical connection emerges with the anthropological perspective of the young Marx wherein "the eye becomes the human eye, the ear the human ear."[27] It is the complex of existing institutions that, according to Fromm, either inhibits or facilitates the expression of subjective potentialities Nietzsche understood in the reified form of a "will to power." The existential need to overcome loneliness and find meaning can thus occur in a "productive" or "destructive" fashion.[28]

Opposing the metapsychology of Freud, especially with respect to the power accorded the transhistorical "death instinct," seeking to employ categories like the Oedipus complex to explain forms of social action,[29] Fromm's approach stands in accord with the critique of metaphysics developed by Korsch and Lukács and in the writings of Horkheimer prior to World War II. Repression, from such a perspective, retains an intrinsically historical dimension and can take a manifold set of social forms. In fact, unless the death instinct and repression are seen historically, the existence of the one can always be used to justify the maintenance of the other. The "ruthless critique of everything existing" demanded by the young Marx thereby becomes necessary in order to confront authority and actualize the full potentiality of each individual. Thus, it only makes sense why Fromm should have maintained that "understanding the unconscious of the individual, presupposes and necessitates the critical analysis of his society."[30]

His attempt to establish a unified social psychology placed him at the center of postwar debate in his discipline and opposed to the desire of his former comrades at the institute to preserve an arena of autonomous psychological subjectivity from society.[31] Marcuse, for example, argued that individuality must be understood "either" in terms of a repressive social order "or" in transcendent utopian terms. According to Fromm, however, such a standpoint is reified from the start. Freedom cannot appear as some state of pure otherness beyond any positive determinations or as predicated on the existence *ex novo* of a new biological infrastructure for humanity.[32] Indeed, since subjective freedom is a social phenomenon, maintaining sanity depends upon the ability of the individual to fill a social role and affirm his or her fullest potential.[33]

Fromm's belief in the need for some objective referent in the discussion of subjectivity is the principal reason why his "revisionism" was condemned and seen by his former associates as a betrayal of the radical impulse within Freud's thought.[34] Adorno, in particular, believed that the libido theory provided a substratum for subjective experience and a way of attesting to the "non-identical" character of the individual in relation to society. Only in a society where all contradictions are abolished is a methodological integration of subject and object legitimate.[35] But this would necessarily sever any connection between theory and empirical research as well as the freedom of the individual and the determinate conditions in which he lives.[36] Fromm subsequently had little use for a "negative dialectic" that views the freedom of the subject from "outside" the existing order, an avant-gardist notion of "the great refusal" (Marcuse), or some quasireligious commitment to what Horkheimer termed "the totally other."

According to Fromm, in keeping with Aristotle, only when freedom is identified with the potentialities of the subject within society can it inform political struggles. The attack on Marcuse's utopian interpretation of Freud's metapsychology, in this vein, distanced him from the radical minority. But his critique certainly does not subvert the need for an alternative; "social character" was, after all, intended to offer criteria to distinguish between the social interactions of the existent and those of an emancipated order. Nor is it legitimate to claim that Fromm engaged in some capitulation to the forces of exploitation and conformism. Against various exponents of ego psychology, in fact, Fromm never stressed adaptation by a "rational" ego to the repressive values of the status quo, and, in the name of the "social defect," he explicitly opposed the idea that a "consensual validation" of norms by the members of society attests to their truth or emancipatory value.[37] "Conscience," Fromm could write, "by its very nature is nonconforming; . . . to the degree to which a person conforms he cannot hear the voice of his conscience, much less act upon it."[38] By the same token, no less than Freud, he retained a willingness to examine collective neurosis and social pathologies.[39] Indeed, Fromm's belief that a profound alienation existed beneath the affluence of America in the 1950s and 1960s made for his popularity and animated his controversial contention that "destructiveness is the outcome of the unlived life."[40]

*   *   *

Erich Fromm's work did not achieve such influence merely because it provided a psychological analysis of a totalitarian regime. *Escape from Freedom* was not just a book about what the United States was fighting against but also raised the existential question of what it was fighting for. The defeat of the fascist enemy left a world dominated by two superpowers and what would soon become a type of spiritual malaise. The onset of the nuclear arms race poised humanity at the edge of the abyss and seemed to render the life of the individual meaningless. The experience of Hitler coupled with the revelations about Stalin's concentration camp universe, and his policies in Eastern Europe, simultaneously produced cold war politics and a left culture in which Kafka, the existentialists, and the "beats" claimed center stage. The growing British movement to abolish nuclear weapons would become an important influence on the new social movements of the 1960s, and many were thrilled by the great struggles for national self-determination in the Third World. Beyond the burgeoning civil rights movement in the United States and the anticommunist hysteria inspired by Senator Joseph McCarthy, however, a new intellectual absorption with the self coupled with a seemingly unqualified belief in the promise of science and technology gripped the United States.

Fromm's popularity in this period, no less than the one that followed, is directly attributable to the manner in which he confronted these concerns. While Horkheimer began his retreat from any kind of radical political involvement, warning against political activism or turning philosophy into "propaganda,"[41] Fromm was playing an important role on the political left. A cofounder in 1957 of the National Committee for a Sane Nuclear Policy, he helped develop a critique of both West and East that would further the commitment to a "socialist humanism"; indeed, his international symposium on that topic brought together the thinking of more than thirty of the world's leading socialist scholars in a quite influential volume that appeared in 1965.

Erich Fromm was a "public intellectual" par excellence. He was involved with various progressive organizations like Amnesty International and the Socialist Party of America and with a number of small journals on the left. But it was not as if Fromm suddenly became a "party man." For example, his association with the Socialist Party, which he joined in 1960, was tumultuous. His political activity was as an intellectual, and when he offered his well-known platform for the movement, it was harshly criticized. American social democracy, far more than on the continent, was animated by an uncritical economism. And so, when Fromm's "Let Man Prevail: A Socialist Manifesto and Program" was published during 1960 in *Socialist Call*, its insistence that the movement "aim at a goal which transcends the given reality" was perceived as a slap at the traditional wisdom.

Whether it actually was or not is an open question. His comrades like Irving Howe, Lewis Coster, H. Stuart Hughes, Sidney Lens, Norman Mailer, and A. J. Muste on the editorial board of *Dissent*, the leading social democratic journal in the United States, had in 1953 basically reached the conclusion that the socialist movement could not effectively intervene in American political life and that a new educational project to instill critical ideas was on the agenda.[42] For all the talk of democratic socialism, it was not so much that they abandoned trade union economism as that they saw the need to provide a new intellectual justification for it in a particularly reactionary climate. Staunchly anticommunist, essentially conservative on cultural matters, and always wary of spontaneous activism from below, *Dissent* was not particularly enamored of Fromm's existential psychological concerns any more than his critique of technology. There were real and bitter differences between him and other editors on Israel and a host of other issues. He was always on the outside. But in countless articles and numerous books, Fromm presented a set of forward-looking positions with a clarity and rationality that is enviable. Thus, even while no expert in political science or foreign policy, he stood in the forefront of those committed to nuclear disarmament and willing to distinguish between ideology and reality in the foreign policy of the Soviet Union.

With the passing of the Soviet Union and the recasting of the cold war in terms favorable to the victor, it is important to consider what Erich Fromm had to say. That is particularly the case with respect to his contention, underpinning his entire position, that the Soviet Union was neither "revolutionary" nor "expansionist" but rather cautious in terms of its foreign policy and concerned with maintaining the status quo.[43] Without in any way excusing the repressive policies pursued by that nation,[44] particularly when it came to the lack of independent trade unions,[45] this implied the need to distinguish between ideology and reality. The difference between the two was what ideologues like Joseph McCarthy sought to abolish. Fromm believed that the ability to make such a distinction is impeded by "paranoid thinking," "projection," and "fanaticism."[46] By now, these psychological terms have entered the mainstream political discourse on international relations. Fromm gave them a relatively precise meaning, however, which is often forgotten. Paranoid thinking, in his view, is not simply a form of irrational fear; it is the willingness to substitute an abstractly deduced logical *probability* for *possibility* the that a particular form of action will occur. Developing a realistic and sensible foreign policy is difficult when that occurs. And the difficulty is only increased when the intentions of one party are unconsciously identified with those of its enemy. This kind of projection, no less than the ability to hold two contradictory beliefs at the same time, is justified by fanaticism in the form of some particular idolatry. And Fromm knew that such prejudices can taint technocratic thinking that is presumably value-free. It is subsequently no accident that he should have criticized the notion of "tactical nuclear war" developed by Henry Kissinger, which would thrust the future secretary of state into the limelight and turn him into an object of satire in Stanley Kubrick's *Dr. Strangelove*, as well as the insane attempts by Hermann Kahn to calculate the effects of thermonuclear war in terms of cost/benefit analysis.

As always, however, Fromm's critique was informed by the vision of a positive alternative directed to a broad progressive public. He believed that foreign policy is a strategic rather than a tactical enterprise which, holding in abeyance whether it should be or not, is highly debatable.[47] Henry Pachter, a socialist political theorist and friend of Fromm's, was probably more on target in suggesting that even the aims of foreign policy are inherently specific to a particular moment in time. And that moment passes. Judging Fromm's views thus becomes difficult under circumstances when the assumptions underpinning the cold war are no longer valid. Even when viewing the past from the perspective of the present, however, he was clearly correct in opposing any monolithic view of communism and maintaining that the split between the USSR and China was real.[48] Recognizing that splits did exist in the communist world prevented Fromm from falling for the "domino theory" and, without romanticizing Mao or national liberation movements like those in Vietnam, made it possible for him to take seriously the groundswell of support for them no less than the way in which backing right-wing dictatorships throughout the Third World undermined the credibility of American foreign policy. Anticipating thinkers like Paul Kennedy, for better or worse, Fromm suggested that a "multi-polar" world loomed on the horizon. Still, he knew that a certain threat from the USSR existed. And so, he did not simply embrace the calls by a minority for total unilateral disarmament by the West. His commitment to arms control anticipated the "nuclear freeze" movement of the early 1980s, while his criticism regarding the economic stake of the given system in a high defense budget retains its relevance in the present period.

Fromm did not see how the cynical exaggeration of the expansionist threat posed by the USSR served to create an arms race that would economically weaken the USSR; nor did he extend his critique of the United States to the incredibly foolish priorities created by the Soviet establishment. In this respect, perhaps, he was a man of his times, but no less so than those committed to the "totalitarianism" thesis who maintained that no change had occurred from the time of Stalin, that the possibility of internal reform was nonexistent, and that the Soviet Union would forever ruthlessly hang on to its empire unless attacked from the outside. Finally, Fromm's belief in the need for a modus vivendi between East and West was justified insofar as internal pressues were actually creating conditions for reform in the Soviet Union and Eastern Europe as well.[49]

Fromm's general stance on foreign policy, no less than his interventions on specific issues like Cuba and Vietnam,[50] fit nicely with what would become the basic worldview of the New Left. More is at stake than his support of the presidential candidacy of Senator Eugene McCarthy or the apocryphal story that *The Sane Society* was one of the four or five books that inspired Tom Hayden in formulating the founding document of Students for a Democratic Society, the Port Huron Statement. Fromm was able to emphasize certain fundamental strands that, whatever the crucial differences, tied the political theory of the Old to the New Left. Interestingly enough, he accomplished this by drawing on the origins of critical theory. And here perhaps it is important to mention that prior to the publication of *One-Dimensional Man* by Herbert Marcuse in 1964, most intellectuals were totally unaware of the Institute for Social Research.[51] Camus, Hesse, Sartre were Europeans who exerted a real influence on America in those years. But not the Frankurt School. The notion that critical theory was somehow of importance to the formation of the New

Left is a myth.[52] The only exception is Herbert Marcuse, whose *One-Dimensional Man* was published in 1964. *History and Class Consciousness* by Georg Lukács appeared only in 1971, Korsch's *Marxism and Philosophy* was first published in 1970, and a severely edited version of Benjamin's *Illuminations* only in 1969. Horkheimer's collection titled *Critical Theory* and his and Adorno's *Dialectic of Enlightenment* were published in 1972, and Adorno's *Negative Dialectics* in 1973, while Ernst Bloch's *Principle of Hope* appeared in 1986. None of these works were known when the movement was on the rise, or even when the future of Martin Luther King's Poor People's Movement was on the agenda, but rather only when the original flame had begun to flicker.

Long before 1968, however, Fromm was already a figure. *Escape from Freedom, The Sane Society*, and *The Art of Loving* were acknowledged best-sellers when *The Revolution of Hope* appeared. All these works were animated by the concept of alienation and a humanism fundamentally inspired by the writings of the young Marx. In fact, it is probably fair to say that Erich Fromm's *Marx's Concept of Man* introduced the young Marx to America and provided the dominant interpretation of this thinker. Marx had been a casualty of the cold war, identified in America with vulgar materialism and economic determinism, the laws of *Das Kapital,* and the dogma of Lenin. Fromm revived him with an enormously popular presentation of the *Economic and Philosophic Manuscripts of 1844.* His critique of Marx was very different from the claims of the mainstream that his thought intrinsically led to totalitarianism. The problems for Fromm were that Marx did not fully acknowledge the moral factor in social relations, that he underestimated the resilience of capitalism, and that he considered the socialization of the means of production a sufficient condition for the transformation of the capitalist into the socialist society.[53] But, ultimately, Fromm gave the humanitarian, idealist, and romantic proponents of the New Left a Marx they could love. His interpretation emphasized Marx's contribution to establishing a philosophical anthropology and a "critique of political economy," which presupposed that people are not driven merely by pursuit of narrowly "rational" or material interests.[54] Indeed, from this perspective, it is precisely the dependence on such interests that the socialist project must confront insofar as it distorts and alienates all social interactions.[55]

Was it the "real" Marx who came to life? That is framing the question poorly. Revolution and economic contradictions, class struggle and political institutions, vanished from Fromm's analysis.[56] But no less than in the time of the First International, or the Second or the Third, Marx was interpreted to fit the needs of the time. The roots of Fromm's Marx lay in a liberal tradition whose promises had been betrayed by the USSR even more than by capitalism. This Marx gave primacy to the creative fulfillment of individual potential and the creation of a "free association of producers" predicated on social equality and participatory democracy. Indeed, the Marx of Erich Fromm provided a critical perspective with which to confront the "military-industrial" complex and the affluence bought through a deadening standardization of production and consumption, work and leisure.[57]

Tradition, organization, style, and some basic values separated the New from the Old Left. Fromm was unique in that he bridged the gap. Along with most partisans of the New Left, he no longer believed that the working class constituted a revolutionary subject. He also mistakenly assumed that the business cycle had run its course and that American economic supremacy would remain as it had been since the close of the Second World War. Enough social democrats, however, tacitly held similar views. Admittedly many progressives from the Old Left were skeptical about the new critique of consumerism.[58] But they saw that Fromm had no use for the type of mysticism and irrationalism propagated by elements within the New Left or the burgeoning commitment to cultural relativism;[59] Fromm's commitment to the Enlightenment never wavered.[60] He was outspoken in his conviction that democratic regimes like those in the United States demand basic support even should they not live up to their promises.[61]

Nor did Fromm ever abandon his commitment to basic socialist demands. He was completely committed to the need for vigorous independent trade unions and programs that would provide national health insurance and a guaranteed income. Above all, however, he insisted upon understanding capitalism as a system of suprapersonal market forces wherein individuals must treat others as potential competitors and so become estranged from themselves and their own possibilities.[62] Where he differed from others like Daniel Bell, a thinker then equally concerned with the effects of inequality and even alienation, was in his skepticism about the priority accorded a technocratic resolution of grievances.[63] This did not make Fromm Luddite. He recognized the need for large-scale enterprise organizational planning. Nevertheless, in keeping with the New Left, Fromm feared that a mechanized society with a centralized bureaucratic apparatus might turn its members into automatons despite the institutional foundation for a multiplicity of interest groups and formal democratic guarantees.[64]

Lacking in the vision of the Old Left was a perception of how the technocratic-consumer society debilitated the internal lives of individuals and a program that stood for something beyond piecemeal reform from above. Where, Fromm wondered, was the "whole human being" of whom Marx and a host of visionaries before him had spoken? Where was the concern with a new emancipated relation between man and nature? Socialism, for Fromm, was not reducible to an economic enterprise. It was rather a quintessentially moral project capable of providing a system of orientation and devotion so that every person might deal with what the meaning and aim of his life might prove to be.[65] Indeed, according to him, the validity of socialist thought for the modern age would depend upon its ability to answer the question: What kind of society is fit for unmutilated human beings?

*   *   *

An answer to that question could only emerge through an attack on "alien-ation." No concept gripped the white student radicals of the 1960s like that one. The score of academic books and articles dealing with the concept pale before the degree to which it became manifest in popular movies like *The Graduate*, which turned Dustin Hoffman into a star, or the music industry and the first great hit by the Rolling Stones: "Satisfaction." In the process, of course, alienation tended to become a pose. Still, the search for personal meaning and the creation of an emancipated social order had real sources, and they were an intrinsic part of the movement. Fromm, in fact, was surely correct in claiming that such concerns play a role in every genuine movement.

In a way, he had already tackled the problem of alienation in *Escape from Freedom*. There, in keeping with Max Weber and the Frankfurt School, Fromm noted how technological society had "disenchanted the world" and eradicated both religious faith and the humanistic values bound up with it. Freed from feudal bonds, the individual now stood isolated in the market without roots in the world. Fromm's interpretation of Marx, however, resulted in a broadening and deepening of alienation. It was now no longer confined to the objective effects of the division of labor or any particular class.[66] Fromm made the concept live by analyzing how it affected personal life. The issue for him was not merely the mechanized society over which humanity has lost control, though that was important enough, but the internal passivity and mental dullness that it fostered. His works spoke to the young people sick of the men in gray flannel suits and fearful that a mechanized society had put them "out of touch" with their own feelings and those of others as well. Public administration, which simply reduced social concerns to particular issues, could not possibly provide an adequate response. A new emphasis on civic participation and social interaction alone seemed capable of confronting the crisis. And that is precisely what Fromm provided in his notion of "communi-tarian socialism."[67]

His vision of a decentralized and egalitarian order anticipated and then converged with the type of Jeffersonian populism associated with the New Left.[68] It gave Fromm something in common with Paul Goodman, the great anarchist educator who was nevertheless also a long-standing member of the *Dissent* editorial board until his tragic death, as surely as with the thinking of Martin Buber, to whom he is so often compared.[69] Critical of hierarchy, con-temptuous of the ideology behind an all-pervasive consumerism, Fromm sought a new spirit to actuate human relations. He was concerned neither with the introduction ex nihilo of a "new man," in the manner of Herbert

Marcuse or Frantz Fanon, nor with finding some way in which to "escape from authority." Just as he distinguished authoritarian ethics from humanistic ethics, insofar as the former assumes the inability of the mass to know what is good or bad and so answers the question in terms of what benefits authority itself,[70] so does he differentiate "rational" from "irrational" authority. Such a distinction is deeply lacking in the main proponents of critical theory.

Fromm's view on rational authority lacked an adequate analysis of the relation between law and ethics. Nor did his theory have an institutional referent or a coherent view of the constraints on freedom produced by the existing logic of accumulation.[71] But this only makes sense given that the most important influence for his social theory derived from the tradition of anarcho-socialism exemplified by figures like Buber, Gustav Landauer, and Augustin Souchy. None of these anarchists was "revolutionary" in the sense that they believed in imposing their will through violence and the centralization of authority like Lenin or insisted on an explosive moment of transformation like Bakunin. Indeed, the point was rather to extend socialism "from the center to the periphery" precisely because "the freedom of all can only be achieved when realized in the self-consciousness of each."[72]

How that would occur always remained open to question. These communitarians were utopian insofar as they stressed the responsibility and goodness of individuals without really discussing the impact of ideology, the institutions required by a free society, or the limits of spontaneous action. And so, indebted as Fromm was to the anarcho-socialists, he shifted the focus. He was unwilling to accept the notion of a radical rupture between present and future,[73] and he was ready to question whether the mere existence of a subjective need was a sufficiently valid reason for its fulfillment. Nevertheless, his ill-fated call to project the "voice of the American conscience" through public councils composed of leading citizens and intellectuals in towns and cities throughout the United States was assuredly naive in its own right.[74]

But, for all the sarcasm it spawned, the idea fit nicely with a burgeoning populist set of attitudes in America. It was an attempt at reform, but not from above. His suggestion was not viewed as elitist. He was trusted. He was recognized as a spokesperson for the idea of community and the need for every individual to assert himself through it. Everyone knew that the learning process Fromm had in mind was directed at the heart as well as the mind. He liked to speak of "being" rather than "having"; a person, according to Fromm, was more than what he accumulated, just as education was more than the minimum knowledge necessary to function properly at work.[75] Then, too, in keeping with the original thrust of critical theory, Fromm believed in happiness and always maintained that "every increase in joy a culture can provide will do more for the ethical education of its members than all the warnings of punishment or preachings of virtue could do."[76]

All this endeared him to the counterculture. And, surely, he had a good influence on its proponents. His interest in the Third World was serious rather than fashionable. Helping found the Mexican Pyschoanalytic Association in 1962, beyond his activities in opposition to the Vietnam War and on behalf of numerous organizations, he would become one of the most influential figures in the development of Latin American psychoanalysis.[77] His openness to Eastern philosophy was also carried on with seriousness and dignity. His philosophical emphasis on faith and hope was never dogmatic or somehow opposed to rational inquiry any more than his search for the good life was reducible to the mystical quest for "the totally other" (Horkheimer). No less than Martin Buber, the Baal She'em Tov, or the great exponents of the Talmudic tradition, he treated religious experience as a type of "wisdom" capable of being employed in the world no less than as a mystical experience by which an individual can transcend his selfishness and separateness;[78] Fromm's "religiosity" never came at the expense of the world, and, thus, his concern with exploring the possibilities of subjective experience was never self-indulgent.

The Art of Loving, perhaps his most popular book, also evidences this quality, and there is something snide about viewing it merely as some "how-to" manual. Lapses into the type of pseudophilosophical language that reflects the most syrupy excesses of the counterculture occur.[79] In the consumer society of the 1950s, however, his book served an important and legitimate purpose.[80] Not only did it attempt to help individuals confront the emptiness of their lives by bringing out the best in themselves, it also finally overcame the vacillation between subjectivity and solidarity that had plagued the thinking of the Frankfurt School from its inception.[81] The book emphasized the existential relation between autonomy and dependence. Fromm's view of love was not based on narcissism or social conformity, sentimentality or sexual attraction. Quite the contrary.[82] His concern, no less than that of the early Horkheimer, involved developing an ethical perspective that was not confined by formal rationalism. But where Horkheimer sought to employ Schopenhauer's concept of "compassion," Fromm emphasized a notion of love that has much in common with the concept developed by Feuerbach. The love between two people ultimately rests on a generalized notion itself predicated on a sense of individual self-worth along with a moral willingness to care for humanity;[83] Fromm liked to quote the famous Rabbi Hillel: "If I do not stand up for myself, who will; but if I stand up only for myself, what am I then?"

It only makes sense, from such a perspective, that violence should have been anathema to him. Fromm opposed guerrilla tactics not only for their practicality but also on principle.[84] Similarly he sought a "sane society" rather than a utopian one that might solve every basic existential dilemma.[85] The unqualified claim that "Fromm, in short, is a revolutionary and a utopian" is misleading.[86] Rejecting any stance that would view the individual as something other than an end unto himself, maintaining the original pacifism of the social democratic movement, and never showing contempt for the masses, his humanist philosophy dovetailed nicely with the concerns fostered through the grassroots organizing of the civil rights and antiwar movements of the 1950s and 1960s. Nor is it any wonder that Fromm should have had so little influence on the abstract utopian thinking of that "revolutionary" minority existing on the political fringes of left-wing politics which, around 1968, was able to steal the limelight precisely because the truly radical potential of the older movement had already begun to wither.[87]

The passing of Fromm's influence can be understood in the same terms. With the fragmentation of the New Left and the rise of postmodernism, his work now appears almost quaint.[88] The old concern with inner development and the emancipatory content of new social relations is no longer what it once was. What John Kenneth Galbraith termed "the affluent society" has changed. America has become poorer for its poorest citizens following the triumph of conservatism in the 1980s and the boom of the 1990s. A rollback of the welfare state has taken place, a new militarism is now on the rise, and an ideological counteroffensive against the 1960s has proven remarkably successful. "Issues" have supplanted the concern with alienation and the like. Many are legitimate. Too often, however, they appear only as the demands of "special interests"; the moral spirit that enabled activists to believe that they stood with history and justice is conspicuously absent in the new pragmatism. Erich Fromm has a role to play in rekindling such convictions. The critics were wrong; his socialist humanism defies what has become the dominant logic of both the left and the right. As for that "logic," as Kafka might have said, it "is doubtless unshakable." No less than Kafka, however, Fromm always believed that "it cannot withstand a man who wants to go on living." Such is the hope that keeps the spirit of progressive politics alive.

11

Utopia, Aesthetics, Revolution
Herbert Marcuse and the Radical Imagination

Resistance has many sources. There is the sense of injustice produced by economic exploitation, the indignity resulting from the arbitrary exercise of power, the contempt for stupidity, and simple aesthetic disgust. Ideas can inspire resistance; the aesthetic imagination can inflame it. But some thinkers wish to explore its roots in the psychological infrastructure of the individual and the anthropological development of the species. Herbert Marcuse was such a thinker. His was an attempt to resist the affluence, appeal, and integrative power of advanced industrial society in the name of an unrealized, and perhaps unrealizable, utopian order. Freedom and happiness, as he understood the terms, involved a break—an impossible break—with the logic of progress. Marcuse sought to employ critical theory for the cause of solidarity and political practice,[1] but he knew the project of emancipation would never fulfill its aims. This utopian was a pessimist.

Progress for Hegel and his followers had always implied an ability to shape the world in terms of its unrealized potentiality for freedom.[2] The concept inherently retained a moral definition. According to Marcuse and his comrades at the Institute for Social Research, however, this ethical element was ever more surely in danger of being eradicated by the commodity form and the alienating logic of instrumental rationality.[3] It was not merely capitalism that threatened subjectivity and reflection on the possibilities for the "good life." Horkheimer and Adorno's *Dialectic of Enlightenment* had already suggested an anthropological basis for reification. Their analysis produced the practical pessimism and flight from political engagement so obvious in their later work. Marcuse proceeded differently, however, and it only makes sense that his politics should have taken a different turn. He sought to counter the anthropological basis of alienation and the repressive character of progress in a positive fashion.[4] Marcuse never surrendered the totality to some subjective notion of the constellation or the speculative vision to the theological comprehension of the "totally Other." He rather attempted to fuse the speculative, the aesthetic, and the political moments of the critical enterprise. How well he succeeded is open to question. Nevertheless, in the process, he made good on the most radical implications of critical theory and provided it with new relevance.

Nowhere else in the postwar works of the Frankfurt School is either the aesthetic question discussed in such directly political terms or the need for a break with "the dialectic of necessity" (Adorno) argued from a perspective outside that of the individual subject. Marcuse called upon theory, once again, to inform practice. He knew that the proletariat was no longer the "revolutionary subject" of history and that the old motivations for political action did not suffice for the new era. He believed, in fact, that advanced industrial society was increasingly projecting a "closure of the political universe."[5] For that very reason, however, Marcuse called upon partisans of the dialectical method to "risk defining freedom in such a way that people become conscious of and recognize it as something that is nowhere already in existence."[6]

An anthropological break would become the goal of a speculative theory that seemed to have reached a crossroads. In fact, with progress having expelled freedom from social reality, it appeared that only two ways remained of preserving the quest for liberation. Theology, which never held the same allure for Marcuse as for Horkheimer,[7] was one possibility. Aesthetics, which intrigued Marcuse from the beginning of his career, was the other.[8] He was not content, however, to emphasize the character of the artwork in the manner of Adorno. Nor did he wish to treat liberation as a moment of experience withdrawn from an advanced industrial society intent on turning art into

> part of the technical equipment of the household and of the daily work world. In this process, [artistic works] undergo a decisive transformation; they are losing the qualitative difference, namely the essential dissociation from the established reality principle which was the ground of their liberating function. Now the images and ideas, by virtue of which art, literature, and philosophy once indicted and transcended the given reality are integrated into the society, and the power of the reality principle is greatly extended.[9]

The reality principle becomes, according to Marcuse, the barrier to an anthropological break. It underpins the existing technological notion of progress no less than the ability of the culture industry to nullify all emancipatory alternatives. The culture industry performs this task in a particular way. Its concern is not merely with portraying social conditions and individual life positively in the manner of traditional propaganda and so strengthening the "happy consciousness." The culture industry is more insidious. Conservative fashion may prevail at one time and radical fashion at another. The sole concern of the culture industry is to turn every cultural object into a commodity for sale. Relativism is its philosophy, and the creation of a fad or a scandal just another way to maximize profits. The culture industry is a business, and in keeping with the prerequisites of the accumulation process, matters of political principle and aesthetic quality become secondary. Such developments undermine the power of reflection and the commitment to emancipatory concerns. Negative thinking, the only viable source of creativity in Marcuse's view, is thus constantly threatened with elimination as even the most radical and bohemian works are condemned by the culture industry to

> suffer the fate of being absorbed by what they refute. As modern classics, the avant-garde and the beatniks share the function of entertaining without endangering the conscience of the men of good will. This absorption is justified by technical progress; the refusal is refuted by the alleviation of misery in the advanced industrial society. The liquidation of high culture [thus becomes] a by-product of the conquest of scarcity.[10]

Progress renders the aim of artworks irrelevant. The experience of them— following the logic of Walter Benjamin—becomes increasingly prefabricated; indeed, the endless production of one fad after another robs art of its ability to highlight the memory of past suffering.[11] The autonomy of the artwork is thereby rendered illusory. Necessity, however, can be turned into a virtue. Insofar as art still projects the illusion of freedom, it confronts the reality of unfreedom, and insofar as it embodies the wish for beauty, it confronts the reality of ugliness and repression. This beautiful illusion (*schöner Schein*) does not derive from the "content" of art but rather from the ability to shape that content. The illusion is instead generated by the "form" of art, which, in turn, affirms the resistance of the subject to becoming integrated by objective reality. Aesthetic form, according to Marcuse, inherently seeks a break with the logic of progress. Projecting both the potentialities for a genuine experience of subjectivity and what Stendhal called a utopian "*promesse de bonheur*," it highlights the normative component of progress increasingly subverted through its appropriation by advanced industrial society. Or, put another way, aesthetic form manifests the "truth of the human condition [which] is hidden, repressed—not by a conspiracy of some sort, but by the actual course of history."[12] Thus, echoing Schiller, Marcuse could write that "the realm of freedom lies beyond mimesis."[13]

Utopia can only be conceived as an anthropological break with the reality principle. The repressed wish for its realization, by the same token, is seen as lying at the anthropological core of art. Its projection in aesthetic form assures the transcendence of art and affirms the fact that a "rational transgression [of the existent becomes] an essential quality of even the most affirmative art."[14]

The ongoing commitment to formal experimentation thereby becomes the logical consequence of Marcuse's position and, in keeping with Adorno and Bloch, ties him to the tradition of the modernist avant-garde. Experimental use of aesthetic form functions to keep "words, sounds, shapes, and colors insulated against their familiar ordinary use and functions: thus they [are] freed for a new dimension of existence."[15] Even in the case of representational works, however, the same dynamic is involved. With Flaubert or Balzac, for example, the possibility of any resolution between existential demands and a repressive external reality "can only be illusory. And the possibility of a solution rests precisely on the character of artistic beauty as illusion."[16]

Utopia resides in that illusion. The crystallization of this illusion, beauty, inherently serves as "the negation" of the commodity world along with the values and attitudes required by it. That negation is necessarily "indeterminate." Still, for Marcuse, the "beautiful illusion" is precisely what helps "render incorrect even one's own assertion that one is happy."[17] Existing outside reality, aesthetic experience is understood as retaining a "truth content" beyond philosophical demands of falsifiability or verification. It is a truth, in keeping with Adorno, which unifies what are usually seen as the mutually exclusive demands of sensuality and reason. Such is the real character of a freedom now comprehensible only in the realm of the imagination.[18] Art is thus the most radical way of presenting "a negation of the principle that governs civilization ... [Art] is attained and sustained fulfillment, the transparent unity of subject and object; of the universal and the individual."[19]

Solidarity and the wish for a "pacification of existence" are built into the aesthetic. Marcuse is less preoccupied with the tension-filled relationship between technique and experience than Adorno. His concern is rather the illumination of a "second nature" (Lukács) beneath the conflict and exploitation on which civilization has been constructed. Justifying the existence of this second nature is impossible in empirical terms or from the teleological perspective of Hegel or Marx. It requires instead a "negative anthropology." It was for this very reason, following the concern generated by Adorno and opposed by Erich Fromm during the late 1930s,[20] that Marcuse entered into a critical encounter with the metapsychology of Freud.

*   *   *

Civilization, according to Freud, is "first of all progress in work—that is work for the procurement and augmentation of life."[21] Work, however, is predicated on a denial of "Eros" and the life instinct's desire for immediate gratification. The "pleasure principle" is constrained when humanity first confronts economic scarcity and the "reality principle," which, in capitalist society, is commensurate with the "performance principle" so that "under its rule society is stratified according to the competitive economic performance of its members."[22] Socialization will consequently emphasize competition as progress becomes identified with instrumental rationality and the domination of nature. It only follows that concern with the "pacification of nature" will fall by the wayside, fantasy will ever more surely become circumscribed within the aesthetic dreams of the individual subject, and a blunting of speculative reason will take place. Additional limits on gratification, well beyond the minimum level of repression indispensable for human interaction, will also take institutional form in the patriarchal-monogamic family, the church, the hierarchical division of labor, the bureaucratic state, and a mass media inherently desirous of subverting a genuinely private sphere of life.[23] Institutions such as these become the instruments through which "surplus repression" is extracted and maintained for the benefit of the given order.[24]

Derived from Marx's notion of "surplus value," "surplus repression" seemingly has its objective basis in the "false needs" that are endemic to the production process of advanced industrial society. "Planned obsolescence" provides an example of how specific commodities are created so that they will not last and enforce the need to buy new ones. But this is just a quantitative instance of what is at stake. The point, for Marcuse, is that the system is structured by the creation and satisfaction of "false needs" even as new ones are produced. Bereft of alternatives, lacking in reflexivity, individuals caught within what Heidegger might have termed the "whirl" of such an existence will find the repressive values of the production process "reproduced" in their own consciousness.[25] Surplus repression is, for these reasons, also qualitative insofar as its effects are introjected into the psychological "infrastructure" of society's members. Thus, the transformation of objective conditions becomes all the more difficult as social controls enforce guilt when a transgression of the existing order is attempted.

Metapsychology provides an understanding of this condition and situates the experience of guilt under capitalism within an anthropological framework.[26] Marcuse, engaging in a critical interpretation of Freud, starts with the claim that human history does not begin with the revolt of the sons and brothers against the primal father. It begins instead with the original ascension of the father who, in monopolizing the mother(s), limits enjoyment to himself alone as he imposes labor on the sons. Exploitation and domination result from the unequal distribution of work and satisfaction, which ultimately drives the sons to revolt.[27] That revolt, however, results in guilt. And so, following their victory, the sons imitate the father and develop their own forms of punishment to relieve their guilt. Institutions such as religion fulfill that function. In the process, however, they also perpetuate guilt to the extent that they evidence an organizational and material interest in the continuation of repression even under conditions in which it is no longer necessary.

Coming to terms with this anthropological situation is rendered more difficult insofar as the past is shrouded in mist. Too terrible to recall, its effects remain since "the essence of repression lies simply in the function of rejecting and keeping something out of consciousness."[28] Humanity thereby loses control of its history since repression fosters unconscious and undirected activity. Such activity will result less in a demand for liberation than in destruction, the intensification of guilt, and a desire for punishment. Nondirected libidinal activity of the sort normally identified with progress stands in sharp contrast to the "sublimated" practice engendered by art. Sublimation is, after all, based on a previously desexualized libido that is directed toward a specific object. In contrast to the acts spurred by repression, sublimation is thus necessarily creative since it will always "retain the main purpose of Eros—that of uniting and binding insofar as it helps towards establishing the unity or tendency to unity which is particularly characteristic of the ego."[29] The emphasis on creation, however, is not juxtaposed with happiness. Quite the contrary. Indeed, just as surely as he breaks with the teleological notion of progress forwarded by German idealism, Marcuse contests its emphasis on duty by introducing happiness as the goal of politics. [30]

Marcuse does not believe that the crucial psychological problem of advanced industrial society involves the primacy of the ego. Quite the contrary. His claim is that advanced industrial society weakens the ego and that it does so through the culture industry and its attendant institutions.[31] With their pursuit of profit and the widest possible audience, their commitment to commercial simplification and the lowest common denominator, their unending concern with the new and the fad, a conformism is instituted that actually deforms the ego. The strength of the culture industry enables it to supplant the "father" as the superego against which the ego of the child tests and strengthens itself. Pliant, unconcerned with quality or purpose, equally tolerant of all positions, the child becomes incapable of contesting the existing "reality principle." Myths give way to concrete achievements while stars and sports figures achieve the status of heroes with whom the consumers of mass industrial society compare themselves.[32] Ceaseless competition, anxiety, and an increasingly weakened ego consequently drive historical progress and become the pillars of advanced industrial society. The performance principle, with which the reality principle is now identified, is strengthened insofar as all creative attempts to vent libidinal energy result in its absorption once the object is made popular by the culture industry. In keeping with Adorno's critique of jazz,[33] for example, it becomes possible to suggest that whatever its nonconformist intention, the repetition of the basic rhythm and the noise level of rock music serve "to break down the ego to permit the diffuse release of sexual and aggressive energy, thus substituting annihilation and explosion—escape from the self—for discovery and integration."[34]

Opposition in this way becomes integrated. The aesthetic "truth" of the object is turned against itself as sublimated activity is channeled into socially acceptable and ultimately repressive forms. This is what Marcuse calls "repressive desublimation,"[35] which is another way of speaking about the manipulation of the ego through a perversion of the aesthetic.[36] His position, however, has nothing in common with the deconstructionist assault on representation and aesthetic "truth." He notes the vacuity of a stance in which "the oeuvre drops out of the dimension of alienation, of *formed* negation and contradiction, and turns into a sound game, a language game—harmless without commitment [while employing a] shock which no longer shocks."[37] Nevertheless, he was mistaken in suggesting that "the passing of anti-art [will result in] the re-emergence of form. And with it, we find a new expression of the inherently subversive qualities of the aesthetic dimension, especially beauty as the sensuous appearance of the idea of freedom."[38]

Marcuse follows Kant in suggesting that the aesthetic form subjects "reality to another order, subjects it to the 'laws of beauty.'"[39] But in defining that form, he radically reinterprets Kant's *Critique of Judgment* by claiming that:

[The] aesthetic form in art has the aesthetic form in nature (*das Naturschöne*) as its correlate, or rather desideratum. If the idea of beauty pertains to nature as well as to art, this is not merely an analogy, or a human idea imposed on nature—it is the insight that the aesthetic form, as a token of freedom, is a mode of existence of the human as well as the natural universe [and so retains] an objective quality.[40]

The ability to transform a purely subjective experience into a utopian reordering of existence, according to Marcuse, is predicated on an anthropologically repressed form of solidarity. This, is what provides emancipation with its inherently social character. The argument derives from Schiller's *Letters on the Aesthetic Education of Man*.[41] Fueled by fantasy, according to Schiller, the aesthetic form is estranged from an inherently repressive reality.[42] But it also embodies humanity's "inner truth." The "play impulse" within fantasy mediates between an ethereal passive "sensuous impulse" and a "form impulse," which seeks to exert mastery over nature. What Kant originally considered the "purposeful purposelessness" of the artwork now projects a new emancipated order committed to actualizing "all aesthetic qualities of phenomena and—in a word—what we call *Beauty* in the widest sense of the term."[43] Or, put another way, aesthetic experience calls for its transfiguration into a "living shape."

A utopian transformation of life becomes the objective of the artwork. Segregating art from the real, contesting instrumental notions of work and progress, results not merely in the preservation of subjectivity but in the projection of what Schiller originally saw as the essential quality of play: "lightness" (*Leichtheit*). "Blackness," in the sense of Adorno, no longer serves as the "ideal." Every genuine artwork, according to Marcuse, provides the audience with the hint of a repressed happiness "common to art and reality." The vision is one of abundance and solidarity, and a world in which

> Techniques would then tend to become art, and art would tend to form reality: the opposition between imagination and reason, higher and lower faculties, poetic and scientific thought, would be invalidated. Emergence of a new Reality Principle: under which a new sensibility and a desublimated scientific intelligence would combine in the creation of an aesthetic ethos.[44]

A world defined by the aesthetic form and the "play principle" is seen as engendering a new science with a new logos. Progress takes on a new character. Technology no longer produces products for the sake of producing them, and humanity finally becomes the true master of the machine. The operationalist rationality along with the division between technology and art will disappear with the creation of a "new sensibility." Biologically averse to cruelty and domination, light and free, this sensibility will inform a new rationality in which art's "ability to project existence, to define yet unrealized possibilities would be envisaged as validated by and functioning in the scientific transformation of the world."[45] Indeed, within such a world, humanity will finally recognize nature as a subject in its own right and initiate new modes of interaction to foster the "pacification of existence."

An anthropological break, is seen as taking place. Aesthetic purposes invade the logos, and reason is combined with sensuality. History assumes a new meaning since, in this utopian future, realizing the unrealized possibilities of the past becomes the aim of activity in the present. Marcuse's vision reaches into the darkest recesses of human experience and highlights the transformation of time. No longer conceived in unilinear terms but rather as an internal circular process, a liberating "eternal recurrence" (Nietzsche) enables humanity to confront death itself by abolishing the notion of an "end" to life waiting in the future along with the angst that is ontologically anchored in an "existence" whose being is, by definition, a "being unto death" (Heidegger).[46] Only by abolishing the fear of death, according to Marcuse, will reality genuinely manifest the "attained and sustained fulfillment" of the aesthetic form. The experience of reality will be changed by breaking the "tyranny of becoming over being."[47]

The anthropological break with progress presupposes the break with time. Marcuse's utopia speaks to the existential transformation of reality, and it rejects Marx's view of the human being as *homo faber*. Perhaps the need for a "limited" mastery over nature will remain. But, ultimately, a merging of labor and "play" will take place to the point where "in this utopian hypothesis, labor would be so different from labor as we know it or normally conceive of it that the idea of the convergence of labor and play" would become a possibility.[48] This would result in a "new science" and a "new technology." But it is unclear whether Marcuse was actually calling for the type of apocalyptic transformation capable of bringing about anthropological change. Part of the problem is that he never delineated what a new science or technology might look like. Given his belief in the liberating possibilities of automation, moreover, his break with scientific rationality may actually have been predicated on maintaining the existing technological infrastructure.[49] Finally, his most radical arguments tended to conflate the critique of "science" with the uses to which it is put.

Under any circumstances, however, Marcuse initiated a major debate over whether work has ontological constituents that militate against its utopian transformation into play.[50] In the same vein, even if his analysis of surplus repression lacked an objective referent, it engendered a controversy over the character of progress and happiness no less than the aims of psychology.[51] Opposing the reduction of social repression to questions of private psychology and seeking to anchor social transformation in the transformation of the instincts,[52] Marcuse expanded our understanding of how flexible the human character might prove to be and argued that a transformation of the relation between nature and humanity was fundamental to the formation of an emancipated order.

Divorcing Freud's metapsychology from any practical or clinical referent, however, is a perilous undertaking. The lack of an empirical referent makes it impossible to differentiate between suppression and psychological repression or recognize those elements of the unconscious and human experience that deserve to be repressed. Then too, in seeking the harmonious reconciliation between "subject" and "object," the individual with his world, Marcuse ignores what Geza Roheim—just as surely building upon Freud—called the "dual unity situation." [53] As society becomes the mother who will equally distribute her bounties to a universe of brothers freed from the repression and guilt experienced by their relation to the father, any truly private realm becomes a threat to the sense of community that has been achieved. Even the desire to create an individual personality can be seen as involving the reimposition of that guilt originally stemming from the primordial attempt to overthrow the father. Pacifying existence might therefore lead less to making the tension between subject and object "non-aggressive" and "non-destructive" than to the lowering of ego boundaries, which is for both Freud and Roheim "a characteristic feature of schizophrenia."[54] The ultimate result might even produce that state of "psychological misery" (Freud) in which the identification between members of a society is so close that there can be no ego reward for any activity whatsoever.[55]

All this is necessary, however, in order to recapture the repressed erotic possibilities of existence and a host of unrealized utopian possibilities. The point is to render humanity capable of becoming "playful" and "beautiful," no longer ashamed of sensuousness or intent upon punishing itself for the atrocities committed in the past. The guilt of the primal crime would, according to Marcuse, be expiated through the newly found and liberating potential of memory. In this utopia, people would be "biologically" incapable of committing violence.[56] Evil would be banished, and Thanatos, the death instinct, would be conquered. Sexuality would turn into sensuality as the erogenous zones began to spread over the whole body, abolishing genital sexuality in favor of a new "polymorphous perversity."[57] Thus, quoting Baudelaire, Marcuse envisioned a truly new world where *"tout n'est qu'ordre et beauté: Luxe, calme, et volupté."*

*   *   *

Eros would now manifest itself politically in a desire to destroy repressive institutions and make people conscious of their "irrationality." By the same token, however, the transcendence of art inherently makes for a self-criticism of the revolution and its historical limitations. The political issue revolves around freeing its erotic content so that art can guide the new revolutionaries, imbued with a "new sensibility,"[58] in combating surplus repression. Marcuse never clarified the new organizational forms through which this might occur any more than the manner in which "false" needs could be distinguished from "true" ones. He became caught in the snares of utopian politics. There is no place for any notion of transition or compromise: the anthropological rupture with progress must prove complete. At the same time, however, revolution is expelled into the aesthetic realm that inherently resists its concrete manifestation. Content to delineate the utopian truth of the "aesthetic dimension" rather than formulate an aesthetic, moreover, the artwork is stripped of its technical particularity and its specific liberating content. The artwork becomes subsumed within what a general philosophical category claims it *must* project. There is, in short, no "determinate" way of either investigating the work or defining the relation between art and political revolt. The interpretation of art vacillates between the belief that art inherently manifests what André Breton called the "great refusal" of all reality and the claim that the dream it projects "must become a force of changing rather than dreaming the human condition: it must become a political force."[59]

Demanding a "negation" of the status quo, while continuing to insist that the aesthetic form remain "opposed" to reality, Marcuse seeks to achieve a Hegelian purpose with a Kantian form of presentation. An internal contradiction within the theory combines with what Hegel might have termed an "abstract," or one-sided, characterization of art's utopian potential. Art may provide a sensuous experience of freedom. According to Hegel, however, this form is always bound to an empirical content and stands in need of external mediation for freedom to become reflexively appreciated by individuals. Thus, in contrast to Marcuse, Hegel is unwilling to speak of an inherently abstract aesthetic form and capable of arguing that art is able to supply "out of the real world what is lacking to the notion."

Extracting the critical and utopian elements from a work of art presupposes a link between aesthetics and social theory. But this is precisely what the break offered by art, according to Marcuse, must deny. Fantasy alone is what provides art with its autonomy and its critical character. He often finds what he seeks. Simply positing the liberating potential or "erotic truth" within art, however, blurs the distinction between utopia as "the wholly other" and utopia as a regulative idea. It is also mistaken to believe that a work of art inherently calls forth a critical indictment of the status quo or some political imperative. Even if art does arise from the urging of the repressed life instinct, it is one thing to maintain that Eros provides a psychological moment in the creative process and quite another to identify that urging with the object created. This may become evident in specific works like *Tristan and Isolde*, while in others, like those of Georges Bataille or the Marquis de Sade, it need not become evident at all. Qualitative differences between works exist, and interpretive categories are necessary to extract their diverse contributions. Transcendence is not an immanent characteristic of "art," Marcuse's claims notwithstanding, but a complex material phenomenon based upon the interaction between given *artworks* and a changing set of audiences.

Divorcing "art" from popular culture and ignoring the need for evaluative criteria leave the empirical works hanging in the abstract. This same inability to deal with the concrete becomes readily apparent in Marcuse's ideas on censorship. Willing to argue that censorship of certain ideas is imperative where "the pacification of existence, where freedom and happiness are at stake,"[60] even if there are certain extreme situations imaginable in which censorship is perhaps imperative, Marcuse comes close to turning what might prove an unfortunate necessity into a virtue. His point is that the culture industry, with its inherent desire to reduce all phenomena to the lowest common denominator and eradicate qualitative differences between ideas, has turned the original liberating and critical character of tolerance against itself. It has now become "repressive" insofar as tolerance hinders the ability of individuals to develop their critical faculties and contributes to a climate of thoroughgoing relativism.[61] His awareness of the danger seems less political than aesthetic. Thus, he can emphasize that:

[C]ensorship of art and literature is regressive under all circumstances. There are cases where an authentic oeuvre carries a regressive political message—Dostoievski is a case in point. But then the message is canceled by the oeuvre itself: the regressive political content is absorbed (*aufgehoben*) in the artistic form: in the work as literature.[62]

Marcuse can claim that the regressive political message is "canceled" by the artistic form. But this is simply an assertion. Whether the reactionary content is absorbed depends upon who is judging the work and the conditions under which such a judgment is taking place. Aesthetic mastery, when considering Celine or Jünger, need not cancel a reactionary political content: the two can happily coexist. Even more important, however, is Marcuse's lack of any institutional understanding of censorship or the mechanisms by which it works. Censorship must function through a bureaucracy that, following Max Weber, always seeks to expand itself and its domain. Real censors have never discriminated between art and politics precisely because the lack of democratic accountability, inherent in the enterprise of censoring, makes it unnecessary to do so. Arbitrariness is endemic· to censorship. Only in the most general terms is it possible to determine whether works that carry an explicit political appeal should be regarded as propaganda or as works of art. Thus, if Marcuse is willing to accept the authoritarian logic of censorship in the realm of philosophy and politics, it is illogical for him to ignore a similar threat to freedom and the "pacification of existence" when it is leveled from the artistic realm.

His claims regarding the autonomy of aesthetic form are abstract. Hegel already knew that form is always the form of a content and that the limitations of a given content will not disappear even if, as an "objectification" (*Vergegenständlichung*), the work can contest the original intentions and prejudices of the artist who produced it. Nor is there anything intrinsically progressive in the choice of one form or style over another; the radical utopian images projected by the assault on representation are not necessarily any more "liberating" than the concrete historical indictments of realism. From such a perspective, in fact, emancipation loses its concreteness. And that is also true of transcendence. Art is, again, not transcendent. Some *works* become transcendent and others do not for a variety of reasons. But Marcuse refuses to offer an explanatory apparatus for investigating the phenomenon. Transcendence is not considered a social act. And for good reason. Viewing the concept in this way would involve recognizing some determinate connection between transcendence and the historical order that is being transcended. The concept of progress would then, once again, enter the theory.

Different works express different needs, different hopes, and different possibilities. The liberating potential of each becomes concrete only when it is grasped by what Marx termed an "audience of art lovers." It is impossible to simply presuppose the perception of an artwork's utopian potential. An act of conscious appropriation is necessary, which might well set audiences of different political persuasions against one another. Progressive critics will subsequently find themselves engaged in a continuous battle to elucidate, preserve, and potentially redefine the *promesse de bonheur* that the work may harbor. Censorship will only inhibit an undertaking of this sort. And the reason is clear. Aesthetic interpretation cannot be rigidly divorced from a social theory capable of justifying its normative values and views of political transformation in a free discourse.

*   *   *

Utopia, aesthetics, and revolution. Herbert Marcuse fused them in an almost seamless manner. His thinking evidenced every influence deriving from "critical theory" in its most radical phase. His social theory is predicated on the notion of reification developed by the young Marx and Lukács; his negative anthropology is powered by the metapsychology of Freud; and his commitment to utopia, both practically and existentially, builds on Schiller as well as the radical implications of Hegel's speculative historicism. None of his comrades in the Frankfurt School ever so fully expressed the revolutionary intent of the dialectical method or so radically contested the predominant understanding of progress.[63]

Horkheimer and Adorno had, of course, already analyzed advanced industrial society as part of an anthropological development defined by instrumental rationality and the domination of nature in *Dialectic of Enlightenment*. According to them, however, the point of reference and the culmination of this development was totalitarianism and the concentration camps. They viewed the future in terms of what Benjamin called that single catastrophe which keeps piling up debris. Without forgetting the past, however, Marcuse gave the argument a new and far more radical twist. He brought critical theory in from the cold by highlighting the devil's bargain wherein a "pacification of existence" is exchanged for affluence and genuine autonomy for the sham freedom offered by the culture industry. And this transformed the political stakes.[64] It was one thing for Adorno to assert the subjectivity of the subject against a totalitarian or bureaucratic world of gray and for Horkheimer to indulge in a "yearning for the wholly other." It was quite another for Marcuse to articulate a positive utopian conception and call for revolutionary solidarity under conditions of previously unimaginable affluence and democratic rule in which the "happy consciousness" seemed dominant.[65] He never sacrificed solidarity to subjectivity and always remembered that freedom is connected with an enterprise engineered by the masses in motion. Similarly, in the most radical expressions of his thought, culture is more than a set of emancipatory resources for preserving subjectivity in the face of reification. It also projects the explosion of everyday life by a new movement with a "new sensibility."

Marcuse inherited that concern less from Freud or Marx than from Schiller. Just as the *Aesthetic Letters* from 1793 constituted an attempt to preserve the spirit of emancipation from the political Thermidor of the French Revolution in 1793, similarly, the utopian speculation of *Eros and Civilization* and *One-Dimensional Man* can be seen as an attempt to maintain the hope for an alternative in response to the increasing dominance of technological rationality and the failure of the working class to realize a new emancipated political order. The chief writings of Marcuse, however, did not constitute a rearguard action. Published in 1955 and 1964, respectively, they anticipated the concerns of 1968. The adherents of the new movement identified themselves with new forms of expression, free sexuality, and cultural politics. They too believed, with Marcuse, that "the fight for Eros is a political fight."

Western ideals became the popular subject of radical criticism. Marcuse spoke to the victims of progress as surely as those who retained an "unhappy consciousness" or what Hegel viewed as the ability to recognize new possibilities for emancipation without any clear idea of how to realize them. Both were among those considered marginal to the functioning of advanced industrial society. They were the minorities in the ghettos, women, the students bristling under the conformity of university life in the early 1960s, the colonized suffering under the yoke of imperialism.[66] These groups would serve as "catalysts" for a working class increasingly seduced by the new affluence and the growing integrative power of the culture industry. Indeed, considering the remarkable French strike wave of 1968 inspired by uprisings at Nanterre and elsewhere, Marcuse's analysis was not far off the mark.

His view of these marginal groups was romantic.[67] Marcuse ignored their lack of revolutionary tradition, their political inexperience, the lack of institutions uniting them, and the dynamics of what would become identity politics. But the commitment to liberation and resistance remained firm. Marcuse argued that immediate economic interests could not serve as the primary motivation for a radical political undertaking in the modern era. And that was precisely the reason for his influence. Given the degree of material affluence during the 1960s, after all, this standpoint was anything but illogical. Affluence, mass democracy, and a new "non-conformist conformity" (Adorno) had called into question the old motivations for social transformation. Revolution lost its identification with the seizure of power and the creation of new institutions. It took on a new, more peaceful, and more existential definition. But whatever the idealism of the new position, it is impossible to maintain—with Lukács—that Marcuse like other members of the Frankfurt School was content to watch the decay of civilization from the "grand hotel abyss." Marcuse knew that the revolutionary negation of repression would demand new modes of cultural expression. The important part of his legacy deals not with misguided attempts to realize the aesthetic,[68] but the way his thinking anticipated attempts to contest the culture of capitalist society. Indeed, within certain boundaries, these were successful.

"Legitimation" became an issue in the 1960s. A new empathy with the victims of imperialism was forged. What had previously been private problems like spousal abuse and incest became open to public scrutiny and legislation. Mores concerning relations between the races and sexes changed. The "quality of life" and nature emerged as new matters of fundamental concern. And there is little doubt that aesthetic perceptions changed as well. The excluded took center stage. These were the practical results of the ways in which the thinking of Herbert Marcuse tended to converge with the spirit of a student movement intent on transforming the everyday life of advanced capitalism.

Of course, in basic ways, the marriage of the abstract and the concrete was never really happy, even during the honeymoon. Marcuse distrusted the populism of the movement, its irrationalist tendencies, and he had little use for rock music and popular culture. He was also highly critical of "sexual liberation" and rejected those who believed in the possibility of merging art with reality as it exists. That would result only in "barbarism at the height of civilization." In contrast to many of his old colleagues from the institute, however, he never withdrew his support from the movement.[69] Even in his last effort, Marcuse argued that if art "cannot change the world . . . it can contribute to changing the consciousness and drives of the men and women who could change the world."[70] By the same token, however, *The Aesthetic Dimension* reflected his ongoing desire to undermine the subordination of art to politics. "Socialist realism" appealed, and his critical analysis of soviet ideology illuminated the conflict between the liberating imperatives of artistic creation and government-sponsored styles of this sort.[71] Marcuse had always maintained the impossibility of drawing the consequences from a genuine artwork and then mechanically seeking to actualize them in political practice. But this book identified him far more with the thinking of Adorno. Indeed, the aesthetic analysis was less political than in any of his previous works.[72]

The Aesthetic Dimension appeared when the movement was over and advanced industrial society had—seemingly—absorbed its gains. Progress had triumphed once again. The critical individual stood isolated and perhaps in more danger than before, while the "new sensibility" vanished. Probably as a consequence, Marcuse emphasized even more strongly the need for a total break of the aesthetic from the real. An abstract aesthetic "life-world" became the rather poor substitute for the rich utopia elaborated in *Eros and Civilization*, while the moment of solidarity implicit within the original *promesse de bonheur* was surrendered in favor of subjective redemption through aesthetic experience. *The Aesthetic Dimension* is a work of defeat that portrays the impotence of art when confronted with the victory of reaction. Thus, in a way, it serves as a corrective for the power that Marcuse originally vested in art and that the aesthetic does not—and arguably should not—possess.

Despite everything, however, Herbert Marcuse was the critical theorist of the "cultural revolution" of the 1960s. And his achievements were real. He was the pivotal figure in introducing the Frankfurt School to the United States, and it is no exaggeration to say that the young intellectuals used footnotes from *One-Dimensional Man* to learn more about Theodor Adorno, Walter Benjamin, Max Horkheimer, and the rest. Marcuse's friends were still untranslated and a world apart. Initiating the debates over consumerism, the environment, the malleability of science, the content of progress, the value of work, the role of ideology, the impact of mass media, and the character of revolutionary agency fell to him. Philosophical idealism, which he transmitted through a host of classic essays and works like *Reason and Revolution*, received new intellectual legitimacy. It became an antidote to the stultifying dominance of behaviorism in the social sciences and "new criticism" in literary theory. And Marcuse did not simply forget the moment of practice; indeed, his "marginal groups" theory provided a foundation for the analysis of the "new social movements" by thinkers like Lucien Goldmann, Jürgen Habermas, Claude Lefort, and Alain Touraine. His utopian conception and call for an anthropological break, furthermore, gave intellectual work a needed sense of radical purpose and motivated people to once again think of happiness and beauty as social concerns.

Marcuse's concept of "one-dimensional man" is arguably more applicable today than when it was first articulated.[73] But the fortunes of the left have changed radically. Marcuse's influence has waned, and only specialists now read his writings. There is no longer much sympathy for his attempt to articulate a utopian alternative. Between the international triumph of conservatism during the 1980s, the failure of the communist experiment, and the later fluctuation of the business cycle, cultural radicalism itself has given way to a new concern with the welfare state and the principles underpinning it. With this shift, indeed, Marcuse's speculative concerns of the 1960s have essentially vanished from the public discourse. There should be no mistake: he helped dig his own intellectual grave. Marcuse undervalued the liberal and social democratic traditions. His metapsychological and anthropological critique of advanced industrial society obscured the qualitative differences between the various forms it could take. His assumptions about affluence and, by implication, the end of the business cycle were simply incorrect. He woefully neglected institutional and organizational questions of power even as he exaggerated the emancipatory alternative any revolution could possibly provide. His works were never able to generate categories for making logical distinctions between systems or artworks. For all that, however, the pragmatism of the present is hollow, and with the conservative upsurge, a deadening of the spirit has taken place. Consequently, whatever the limitations of his thought, Herbert Marcuse still sparks the imagination and elicits reflection about what has been forgotten.

⌁ 12 ⌁

Jürgen Habermas
and the Language of Politics

C ritical theory has received a new and powerful formulation from, unquestionably, the most encyclopedic thinker of the postwar period: Jürgen Habermas. A student of Max Horkheimer and Theodor Adorno, born in 1929, he grew up under the Nazi regime and experienced the economic dislocation of reconstruction. It is thus little wonder that he was never attracted by vitalist criticisms of reason and science. There was never much room in his thought for Nietzsche. His writings were—from the very first—always firmly anchored within the tradition of Kant, Hegel, Marx, and Weber. They are often esoteric and burdened with an unnecessarily cumbersome style. But those who would suggest that this renders him relevant only to a small group of academics are sorely mistaken. Habermas has been an exemplary public intellectual.[1] He has taken positions on the major issues of his time: calling for more democracy in the educational system, dealing with student protests,[2] confronting conservatives who considered it time to wash their hands of the Nazi past,[3] challenging the postmodernist advocates of relativism and experientialism, championing the contributions of the welfare state, opposing the deployment of nuclear missiles in Germany, warning against the easy optimism generated by the prospect of reunifying his country, expressing his uncertainty while supporting the war in the Persian Gulf, and rejecting the new nationalism in the name of a "constitutional patriotism" (*Verfassungspatriotismus*). His political convictions have remained constant beyond any changes his philosophy has undergone. Nevertheless, for all the scholarly controversy his work has produced, too rarely has it been observed that Jürgen Habermas has become *the* great exponent of political liberalism in Germany.

His understanding of socialism is indebted to this tradition and the "unfinished" character of the enlightenment enterprise. Practical commitments of a political nature underpin his theory from the early works to the "linguistic turn" and "postmetaphysical" elaboration of his "discourse ethics" in his most recent efforts. A concern with the "legitimation" of the state, the rational adjudication of grievances, the public role of language, and the unfettered use of reason explain his well-founded mistrust of postmodernism. His fear of irrationalism and relativism, in fact, provides an insight into his preoccupation with providing a positive foundation for the normative claims of critical theory.

Habermas has not completely broken with its original tenets. He remains committed to reflexivity, the critique of reification, and the "emancipation" of individuals from all forms of domination. But he has clearly pointed critical theory in a new direction. Habermas has given it a new democratic impulse by fusing it with American pragmatism and linguistic philosophy. He has solidified its connection with liberalism and insisted upon its becoming more "reconstructive" and sensitive to the requirements of social scientific validation. There is some question whether the original enterprise has been narrowed or whether its critical character has been undermined. Indeed, his penchant for procedural and systematic thinking often works to the disadvantage of his emancipatory objectives.

Criticism has been directed against Habermas from almost every academic angle. The champions of Marxist orthodoxy wrote him off long ago: he may have originally sought to develop an immanent "reconstruction" of historical materialism, but it is legitimate to ask whether his more recent forays into language philosophy have gutted the earlier attempt.[4] Conservatives have castigated him unmercifully. He has also been the target of postmodernists and the advocates of "identity politics," uncritical defenders of the new social movements, and communitarians. Within the tradition of critical theory, however, political criticism has mostly been displaced by highly esoteric and technical differences of opinion.[5] The importance of his unique brand of discourse theory is usually accepted at face value. One popular criticism, however, is particularly odious. It condemns his general approach, though it even recognizes the danger of equating communicative competence with a single "best" form,[6] for its "totalizing" ambitions and its privileging of the "intellect" and the power of the word: "as if," remembering the words of Thomas Mann, "there were the slightest danger of too much intellectualism on earth."[7]

Very different issues are at stake. There are the assumptions about consensus, and the willingness to abstract from the ways in which the imperatives of accumulation impact upon the institutional subsystems of an increasingly complex society. There are the suspect claims concerning the "postmetaphysical" character of his linguistic philosophy,[8] and its attempts to substitute an abstract vision of moral evolution for a philosophy of history. There is the paralysis of his discourse ethics when forced to confront questions concerning the way in which power shapes the agenda for discussion, and the existence of *intractable interests.* There is his metaphysical appropriation of pragmatism. There is his refusal to admit that the effectiveness of his linguistic philosophy and democratic theory depends upon the prior institutional realization of their liberal assumptions. There is also a question whether his excursions into linguistic and analytic philosophy have hardened his thought into a system and blunted the radical character of his early work. To this extent, it is necessary to ask whether what has made him popular among the mainstream of philosophers and social scientists has, in fact, tended to undermine the critical character of critical theory.

Before the Turn

The Structural Transformation of the Public Sphere was Habermas's first book. The "public sphere" was seen as mediating between the state and the economic forces of civil society. Its components were understood as ranging from the free press to the town meeting, from the family to salons, from the educational system and the cheap production of books to the liberal assumptions underpinning an open exchange of views.[9] The public sphere emerged from the humanistic tendencies of the Renaissance and became part of the bourgeois response against feudalism and its hierarchy. It presupposed equality and the ability to employ "common sense" on the part of the "common man." The public sphere was, moreover, understood as the arena in which civil liberties are put into practice; its viability is the real proof of a democratic order. Indeed, with its emphasis upon free speech and universal values, the public sphere becomes the sociological starting point for what would ultimately become a more expansive philosophical inquiry into the role of discourse in advanced industrial society.

The study was written as a *habilitation*. It is indebted to *Dialectic of Enlightenment* and the Marxist method.[10] The work emphasizes the increasing power of instrumental reason and the commodity form in undermining social conditions capable of protecting the individual from the arbitrary power exercised by regimes still wavering between monarchy and republicanism. The decline of the public sphere is seen as generated by the growing identification between "public opinion" and "publicity,"[11] and this, in turn, reflects the inability of liberalism to contest the incursions of the commodity form. Horkheimer and Adorno were suspicious from the beginning of any pretensions concerning the public sphere and essentially maintained that "only the word coined by commerce" can prove familiar to the mass of the populace.[12] Habermas also recognized the dangers for communication implicit in the extension of the commodity form. But he was interested in confronting reification with more than "impotent rage."[13] Habermas juxtaposed the unrealized promise of liberalism against a wrecked world emerging from Nazism, still burdened by Stalinism, and rife with neofascist impulses. And so, where his mentors were obsessed with the subjectivity of the subject, Habermas became concerned with the institutions of advanced industrial society and the possibilities for what he would later call "democratic will formation." An altered civil society might yet contest the march of instrumental reason through "reorganisation of social and political power under the mutual control of rival organizations committed to the public sphere in their internal structure as well as in their relations with the state and each other."[14]

Habermas had a background different from that of the original advocates of critical theory. He was the first to have grown up under a totalitarian regime. He was also the first whose work was framed by the postwar experience in a country that lacked the resistance tradition of France or Italy and wherein Marxism was basically identified with the German Democratic Republic. It only makes sense that Habermas should have been far more circumspect than the early members of the institute in appropriating even the most radical strands of Western Marxism and more inclined to take the liberal tradition seriously.[15] The Weimar Republic was widely known as "the republic without republicans," and it suffered the consequences. Attitudes among citizens or, better, what Pierre Bourdieu would call their "habitus," seemed not very different in the postwar reconstruction with its "unmastered past" (*unbewältigte Vergangenheit*). Even academics tainted by Nazism like Arnold Gehlen and Martin Heidegger who helped shape Habermas's early development,[16] no less than Ernst Rothacker and Oskar Becker who were his first teachers, refused to engage in a political and philosophical self-criticism.[17] Thus, for Habermas, the political point was to secure criticism as a moral imperative extending beyond mere self-interest.

But with the introduction of mass media, and the generation of consensus from the top down rather than through the discursive engagement of participants, the public sphere was being increasingly defined by the same forms of instrumental reason exhibited in the state and the economy. Its mediating character was becoming lost, its ability to project systemic criticism rationalized, through the transformation of the public sphere into institutions buttressing the existing order. A concern with counteracting this development explains the later support extended by Habermas to the "new social movements" of the 1960s and the "sub-institutional" changes in everyday life demanded by them no less than their ability to turn previously "private" issues ranging from discrimination to incest into matters of "public" concern.[18] Indeed, the belief in rationalizing power through public discussion as well as the tension between "system" and "life-world" are rooted in his original discussion of the public sphere.

Habermas recognized that the high point of the public sphere lay in the eighteenth century when the bourgeoisie was on the rise. He knew that it was impossible to turn back. Of importance were thus the normative underpinnings of the concept rather than the public sphere itself. The bourgeois public sphere received its democratic definition insofar as debate took place without regard to rank and "in accord with universal rules"; its participants produced the idea of a "common" humanity in the "implicit law of the parity of all cultivated persons" even as they rejected any authority beside that of the "better argument." The achievement of consensus in class or group terms was thus capable of generating a universal interest.[19] An increasingly instrumental use of language, however, was now threatening the suppositions which had rendered this possible. The occupation of the public sphere by the nonpropertied led to the increasing interconnection between state and society, which essentially eradicated the bourgeois public sphere without supplying a new one.[20] The new task was to preserve reflexivity and maintain the conditions for discourse; indeed, with the sociological constriction of the public sphere, such an undertaking could only proceed from the standpoint of "critical philosophy." Epistemology would secure in thought what practice was destroying in action. Thus, *Knowledge and Human Interests* would justify the move from "traditional" to "critical" theory in a new way.

Habermas wished to provide a foundation for the emancipatory norms of critical theory by using the "critique of ideology" (*Ideologiekritik*) to explore the hidden relation between theory and practice or knowledge and interest. Just as it was necessary to preserve the promise of liberalism from what liberal society had become, however, so was it necessary to employ ideology critique against its "dissolution" first into the philosophy of history and then, more completely, into the neutral methodology of positivism and empiricism. Simply relying on historicism, according to Habermas, makes dialectical thinking as guilty as traditional theory of liquidating an "interest in reason."[21] "Historically oriented" sociological criticism must now step back behind the teleological subsumption of epistemology by Hegel and Marx in order to retrieve the insights of Kant.

A rejection of teleology and "stages of reflection" takes place. Habermas recognizes that the attempts by positivists to reduce the theory of knowledge to the philosophy of science was interrupted by Charles Peirce and Wilhelm Dilthey who sought to defend the self-reflexive character of knowledge from the ambitions of the "natural" and "cultural" sciences. Each after his fashion begged the question concerning the "knowledge-constitutive" interest in inquiry. Neither was aware of the manner in which his methodology reflected the assumptions of "science" or the importance of defining the point at which knowledge and interest conjoin. And so, reconstructing a "buried hermeneutic dimension," Habermas sought to emphasize that every form of knowledge with a human interest must concern itself less with "facts" than with "statements about facts."[22] He also sought to specify the connection between theory and practice by exploring the relation between the human species as the self-constituting subject of knowledge and the interest in knowledge itself as constituted by the objective needs derived from such an enterprise.[23]

The "systematic intention" of his work becomes apparent in the delineation of three different anthropological forms of interest. The first, which arises from the interaction with nature, involves prediction and control through "monological" knowledge; the second, which produces historical and hermeneutic forms of knowledge, rests on the need for consensual understanding without which cooperative work becomes impossible; while the third form of emancipatory knowledge, which involves the ability to question previous assumptions, derives from the interest in learning and becoming free from coercively induced forms of dependency.[24] Each of these needs is always open to linguistic interpretation and symbolically affixed to potential actions.[25] They retain a social character even as they express cognitive desires. Habermas thus draws a radical separation between symbolic interaction and instrumental activity or work. He may not have been clear about how to reunite them, but their existence was never meant to reflect a Kantian divorce between "practical" and "pure" reason. Habermas was as critical of idealist attempts to divorce symbolic action from social reality as of Marxist attempts to reduce symbolic action to labor.[26] Indeed, *Knowledge and Human Interests* and *Theory and Practice* both express a marked sympathy for Fichte who rendered reason immediately practical in the original self-reflection of the subject on its own activity.[27]

Habermas defined the three variants of interest as "quasi-transcendental" insofar as each presupposed a life context in which cognition is situated.[28] The concept of interest thereby becomes a "bridge" between the constitutive context of knowledge and the different forms its application can take.[29] Illuminating its normative content, however, involves moving from the "monological" discourse of science to "communicative competence" along with the norms it presupposes. The critical theory of society, in contrast to traditional thinking, will thus incorporate an emancipatory interest in knowledge beyond its mere practical application and employ reflexivity in order to decide how any given interest fosters autonomy. An inherently reflexive "interest in reason" contests how language is employed to create unrecognized forms of dependency and justify interests in domination. Coming to terms with "distorted" forms of communication is thus possible only by positing an "undistorted" mode of communication.

Psychoanalysis is a case in point.[30] Through this dialogic method, which presupposes an analyst devoid of personal interest in the outcome and an analysand willing to treat his own concerns objectively, a common interest in furthering the autonomy of the subject presents itself through self-reflection.[31] Insofar as autonomy is the goal of self-reflection, however, the "meaning of knowledge, and thus the criterion for its autonomy as well, cannot be accounted for without recourse to a connection with interest in general."[32] Any rational justification for autonomy necessarily presupposes such a connection since, without reference to the concept of reciprocity, it turns into license and the arbitrary exercise of power. Indeed, from the standpoint of philosophical rationalism and political liberalism, this is precisely what reason seeks to constrain. The critique of ideology, for this reason, can "identify the normative power built into the institutional system of a society only if it starts from the model of the suppression of generalizable interests and compares normative structures existing at a given time with the hypothetical state of a system of norms formed, *ceteris paribus*, discursively."[33]

Already in this early work, however, Habermas finds the root of critique no less than its object within language. Even "legitimacy" is already defined in terms of the validity accorded the claims of justice offered by any given political order.[34] Knowledge must consequently serve as an instrument for an ongoing practice and prove capable of calling that practice into question, which suggests that it must retain the quality of transcendence. Indeed, from the standpoint of practical discourse, democracy is unique precisely insofar as its "formal properties of justification themselves obtain legitimating force."[35] Knowledge and interest, from the perspective of self-reflection, thereby become unified. But this can only occur through a historical process, and, for this reason, the transcendental subject must dissolve into the natural history of the human species. Thus, the unity of knowledge and interest will become manifest in the linguistic reconstruction of what has been historically suppressed.[36]

Insofar as reason is embedded in the natural history of the human species, however, Habermas finds himself with an indeterminate foundation for the philosophy of history and a contingent justification for rationality. The connection between theory and practice remains suspect. The "philosophy of consciousness," which presupposes a subject mechanically confronting an object, cannot overcome the gap between simply positing discursive norms or generalizable interests and viewing them as empirically constructed. Nor is Habermas able to bridge the gap. For example, within the framework of *Knowledge and Human Interests*, reflection must simultaneously exist as a value-neutral determinant of thinking and as a value-laden ability to illuminate what has been suppressed. Nor does defining interests as "quasi-transcendental" help matters. It only leaves them stranded between serving as transcendental conditions for knowledge as such, which are value-neutral, and appearing as value-laden expressions of empirical action.[37]

Habermas came to the conclusion that overcoming these inadequacies would demand a new "phenomenology of the moral domain" capable of encompassing the rigid division between instrumental and speculative reason while surmounting the need for what some came to consider an artificially created tripartite analysis of "interest."[38] Embedding a general theory of rationality in language thus became the object of construction. The philosophy of language might ultimately be considered epistemology by an other name, but it nonetheless emphasizes the forms of utterance. Meaningful communication, which is itself predicated on "communicative competence," thereby becomes a way of linking theory and practice.[39] Refusing to reduce norms to prescriptive decisions, seeking to elucidate both the general presuppositions of discourse and the way in which language contributes to the reproduction of social life,[40] Habermas would consequently highlight the "performative" aspect of language.[41] The pragmatic rather than the metaphysical discussion of language was what interested him. Indeed, through the development of a "universal pragmatics," Habermas believed it possible to uncover the "ground" for freedom, truth, and justice in the very structure of communication.

An Excursus on Pragmatism

The appropriation of pragmatism for the critical project by Habermas marks probably the first time that a major proponent of critical theory looked away from Europe for genuine philosophical inspiration. It was believed that pragmatism, unreservedly condemned for its utilitarian and decisionist impulses by Max Horkheimer, might prove valuable for problems connected with justifying the values of critical theory. Ironically, however, the use of this uniquely American philosophy by critical theorists has perpetuated the very form of sterile academic theorizing that pragmatism sought to combat. It was originally directed against metaphysical speculation and the various forms of what Marx would have called "vulgar" materialism. Pragmatism sought to dispense with vague abstractions, streamline concepts, and make philosophy participate in the world of action. Concepts like the consensual "community of investigators" postulated by Charles Peirce were embraced by Habermas. But this was done in the name of a discourse ethics encumbered by a seemingly endless set of subtle categorical distinctions, which could stand a cut from Occam's razor, and a standpoint incapable of dealing with strategic problems. Indeed, whatever the "post-metaphysical" claims, pragmatism became employed for the purpose of fashioning what is actually little more than a new metatheory.

Habermas would ignore both the most progressive strain within pragmatism and its most severe weakness. He viewed this philosophy as somehow mirroring the type of "ameliorism" supposedly indicative of the American experience, which is why Habermas called it the "radical democratic" offshoot of Hegelianism. Such a view, however, somewhat exaggerates the pragmatist commitment to change; it forgets that the saying "if it ain't broke don't fix it" is as much in accord with the practical thrust of pragmatism as the call for change. The progressive commitments of men like Charles Peirce, William James, George Herbert Mead, and John Dewey were actually less a matter of "philosophy" than of the fact that they were fundamentally decent men with liberal instincts and an expansive intelligence seeking new combinations of communitarianism and individualism. More conservative theorists could also employ the insights of pragmatism, and its admirers in Europe included Henri Bergson and Mussolini.

Pragmatism harbors not merely utilitarian but also vitalist and even irrational components. Only because its major American representatives were content to assume a liberal milieu could their decisionism, so understandably feared by the modern continental advocates of discourse ethics, prove relatively harmless. There are important differences, of course, between them. The contrast between the philosophies of Charles Peirce and William James is particularly well known. But the "pragmaticism" of the former was never rigidly divorced from the "experientialism" of his friend with its criteria of "usefulness" and the "vital good." Even the architect of semiotic transcendentalism, in contrast to Habermas, ultimately believed that the conception of an object depends upon the clarification of its practical "effects."

Pragmatism is based on experience. The notions of consensus and participation offered by John Dewey were predicated not on categorical preconditions of language like the "life-world" but on the vision of face-to-face interactions by citizens in the equivalents of those New England "town meetings" so well described by Tocqueville. Pragmatism never had much use for a priori constructs. It derived from a critique of Kant, which sought to overcome traditional dualisms, like those posited by Habermas between truth and justice or theory and practice. Its original concerns had little in common with contemporary attempts to "ground" reflexivity, consensus, or emancipatory norms in the structure of "communication." The point was not to secure a given set of normative presuppositions. It was to make philosophy useful for issues of "public" debate and, in even more radical terms, render its academic usage irrelevant. In fact, according to the famous formulation of Peirce, the aim of pragmatism was not to "solve" problems but to show why "supposed problems are not real problems."

Doubt, for example, was always open to termination once a given approach seemed "workable" (James), and it is stretching the boundaries of the framework to maintain that pragmatism can embrace the famous phrase of Descartes that "every definition is a denial." There is indeed no reason to believe that pragmatism is inherently "critical." Pragmatism was intended as an antiphilosophy. Korsch, in particular, liked its antimetaphysical impetus, its emphasis upon action and "concreteness" (*Diesseitigkeit*). What Josiah Royce might have termed the "spirit" of pragmatism, rather than its more stultifying academic rituals, can perhaps prove useful for critical theory. Nevertheless, this would be the case only if pragmatism were related to a transformative project rather than with metaphysical questions in the guise of postmetaphysical philosophy.

The Linguistic Turn

The "universal pragmatics" of Habermas is an important contribution to debates internal to the philosophy of language.[42] It reformulates the relationship between subject and object by stressing concepts like intersubjectivity and the "life-world." Its emphasis on symbolically mediated forms of interaction, which link communicative action with argumentation, projects a "reconstruction of philosophy" (Dewey) predicated on the claim that "reaching understanding is the inherent telos of human speech."[43] This attempt to ground rationality within language and to define the preconditions for meaningful discourse is concrete in its aims. Only if this attempt is successful, according to Habermas, can everyday speech—even of the most distorted sort—both anticipate and presuppose an undistorted form of communication. "Communicative reason," in this regard, "operates in history as an avenging force."[44] An ideal speech situation, precisely because it must confront a counterfactual reality, grounds reflexivity in language. The question is whether its anthropological assumptions are sound and whether they allow for translation into categories capable of clarifying the historically determinate ways in which reality is constituted. Thus, it only makes sense that Habermas should have begun *The Theory of Communicative Action* with a brilliant critique of Max Weber for assuming the epistemological division between subject and object in his views on rationalization and the "iron cage."[45]

Habermas never disputed the claim of Weber concerning the progressive erosion of meaning caused by rationalization. He is aware of the way in which Durkheim's anomie is a function of the "disenchantment of the world." But he refuses to equate science with the domination of nature; Habermas was sharply critical of the attempts by Herbert Marcuse and others to offer an alternative without specifying its character or categories.[46] The thinking of Habermas is essentially devoid of "romantic impulses."[47] He is willing to entertain the validity of scientific reason within delineated boundaries and thus, following Kant, draws a distinction between the subject-centered reason underpinning instrumental rationality and speculative reason or reflexivity. The new "pathologies of the life-world" fostered by instrumental rationality are consequently only one aspect of modern society. An increase in moral and cognitive learning capacity also occurs along with potentially new forms of meaning-giving activity inspired by the democratic ethos of communicative humanism. Weber is seen as having ignored this, however, insofar as he identified purposive rationality with reason as such. The "philosophy of consciousness" with its assumptions concerning the division between subject and object, according to Habermas, lay at the root of his reduction of reason to the instrumental manipulation of the object. But, insofar as critical theory also uncritically carried over these assumptions, what resulted was less a confrontation with this position than a transition from the positive to the negative reading of reason and its power. Critical theory thereby became caught in the "iron cage":[48] it would stand defined by what it opposed.

The argument of Habermas is persuasive. In principle, after all, *Dialectic of Enlightenment* agreed with the belief of Weber that liberation through reason is as negative as it is positive.[49] Or to put it another way, according to Habermas, Weber and Nietzsche reinforce each other in eroding the regenerative possibilities of reason. This is what Habermas seeks to avoid by grounding rationality within the intersubjective structure of language. Neither subject nor object exists for Habermas in the abstract. But the "concrete" takes anthropological rather than historical form. Communicative action of any sort presupposes a shared "life-world" (*Lebenswelt*), which is apodictic or preconceptual, and thus a certain degree of consensus. Reification or the "colonization of the life-world" occurs insofar as the realm of experience is narrowed and, more important, there is a diminishing ability to question the consensus achieved. The speculative element within reason is thus precisely what Habermas wishes to preserve, and he argues his case by claiming that language inherently makes reason regenerative.

Discourse becomes the ground of critique. Indeed, even when it seeks to disturb the prevailing consensus, discourse assumes a commitment to truth whose determination will once again demand consensual validation. This can occur in any number of ways depending on the referential domain of interaction. Validity claims can take communicative, strategic, normative, and dramaturgic form. Communication, however, must receive conceptual primacy in order to supplant the traditional reliance of critical theory on the philosophy of consciousness and ground its normative assumptions.[50] The philosophy of language must consequently present itself as a theory of rationality and *break with all contingent forms of strategic action* pertaining to the pursuit of particular interests.[51] Norms must ultimately be seen as emerging from the rational use of procedures rather than by making reference to specific outcomes.

The necessity follows, in keeping with Charles Peirce and John Dewey,[52] of presupposing what Karl-Otto Apel termed a "communicative community" (*Kommunikationsgemeinschaft*) ideally predisposed to illuminate instrumental and illegitimate forms of domination. The issue is not some equitable adjudication of interests or any systematic imperatives. Theory itself, according to Habermas, can never directly justify political action.[53] Of primary concern for theory is instead the pursuit of the "best argument" and, for this reason, the central problem of democracy is not the discovery of some optimal solution or standard for ranking incommensurate values; it is instead the formation of a somewhat vaguely defined "post-conventional" identity through which everyone affected by a decision must be able to participate in reaching it.[54] Thus, for Habermas, norms receive validity only insofar as all potential participants in a practical discourse will agree to them.[55]

Many proponents of discourse ethics maintain that there is nothing utopian in any of this since transcendence, or the need to project a "counterfactual" condition of undistorted communication against the particular discourses in which distortion takes place, is built into the very structure of language.[56] Communication requires that the discourse be open to all, mutual respect be given to each, needs be linguistically interpreted, and the claim of every disputant be supported by an "informal logic" of argumentation predicated on a moral principle whose function is equivalent to the principle of induction in the empirical sciences: "universalizability."[57] It is impossible to transcend these presuppositions of discourse. This led Apel to claim an "ultimate justification" (*Letztbegründung*) for the rules of discourse ethics,[58] and Albrecht Wellmer to speak about a "pluri-dimensional foundation" of ethics.[59] Habermas, however, secured the middle position by noting the manner in which discursive presuppositions constitute a "weak transcendental necessity" and that there are no alternatives to them.

Habermas retains the skepticism of critical theory with respect to all ontological or quasiontological formulations.[60] More important, in keeping with critical theory, his discourse ethics makes no concession to either positivism or irrationalism. Discourse ethics, after all, insists upon the ability to decide upon ethical principles without demanding that such cognition coincide with knowledge of any given set of facts even while its emphasis upon the principle of "universal reciprocity" contests particularism, relativism, and the recourse to intuition. The normative expectations regulating ideal speech are implicit in the telos of communication as such and thus constitute a prima facie refutation of ethical skepticism. The theory of communicative action, building on Kant, connects three spheres of rationality: the cognitive-instrumental, the moral-practical, and the aesthetic-judgmental.

"Discourses," writes Habermas, "are islands in the sea of practice."[61] Their ethical emphasis on impartial procedures and universalized reciprocity is seen as offering a "regulative idea" for dealing with concrete situations and criticizing repression.[62] The philosophy's "post-metaphysical" character derives principally from its willingness to employ an intersubjective framework, with the "life-world" as its referent, in which norms are made and the search for truth is generated. The theory of communicative action does not posit a self-sufficient subject confronting an object but begins instead with a symbolically structured notion of everyday life in which reflexivity is constituted. Subjectivism and the "negative metaphysics" of Adorno no less than the neopositivism of Karl Popper, with its inability to provide knowledge with a determinate status or foundation, are surmounted by the new standpoint.[63] Just as every hermeneutic understanding must refer to a given historical context, however, so must every moral position refer to a "shared ethos."[64] Here, it is the ethos of the Enlighten-ment. Underpinning strategic forms of discursive interaction with commu-nicative rationality presupposes certain political forms of association that guar-antee the possibility of emancipation from dependency. The theory of communicative action, in fact, is really a "scarcely concealed translation of the requisites for ideal political democracy."[65] It is less concerned with developing a substantive notion of the "good" than affirming a procedural notion of jus-tice.[66] Thus, the "linguistic turn" becomes an attempt to further the struggle for political liberalism evident in Habermas's earlier works.

Showing the practical implications of discourse ethics calls forth an encounter with the state and law. Earlier, in *Legitimation Crisis*, Habermas drew the distinction between various social and institutional spheres. Given the manner in which civil society is "patronised" by the state, however, his point was not to resurrect some new relation between the "base" and "super-structure." It was rather to develop a critique of capitalist society as an integrated whole and demonstrate how "legitimation" serves as the precondi-tion for the proper functioning of the existing order along with its various subsystems.[67] This work emphasized the limits of "formal" democracy and the manner in which needs generated by the system tended to undercut the moti-vations for economic performance. But, whatever the various disruptive ten-dencies of advanced industrial society, only when effective learning within a system is no longer possible will "crisis" shake the existing order.[68] "Con-sciousness," in keeping with the spirit of the Frankfurt School and the New Left, becomes the decisive factor in social transformation. Economics also plays a role insofar as it has an impact upon consciousness. Politics, however, drops out or becomes a mere "reflex."[69] Habermas recognized the role capital and private control over investment play in the formation of policy; he sup-ported making private investment decisions publicly accountable. Neverthe-less, analyzing the state and the economy must take place without reference to the working class as a revolutionary subject intimately linked to the actual production and reproduction of the system.

What Niklas Luhmann termed "*autopoesis*," or the self-generating character of the system and its particular subsystems, has rendered anachronistic the attempt to thematize the existing order from the "macro" standpoint of class.[70] The autopoetic development of increasingly complex bureaucratic sys-tems is a practical reality for economic growth, and according to Luhmann, preserving them from the effects of participatory "will formation" is unavoid-able.[71] Habermas, however, insisted upon the need for legitimation. It became ever more apparent that rendering the legal order "positive" was increasingly leading to the *displacement* of all substantive problems beyond the purely technical concerns internal to the administration of law.[72] Thus, the original question of legitimation came to take on ever greater urgency.

A cogent argument justifying the worthiness of a given political regime and the extent to which it deserves recognition would depend, according to Habermas, upon its ability to differentiate between what can be conceived as a legitimate political order and the claims to legitimacy forwarded by a given form of institutional association.[73] This, in turn, presupposes a connection between morality and law along with the ability of legal procedures to differentiate between particular and generalizable interests.[74] Such a stance, however, makes it necessary to contest the positive theory of law developed by Max Weber who, in keeping with his attempt to develop a value-free social science, sought to divorce morality from law.[75] And this involves more than a merely academic disputation. For, if the purpose of law is less to secure justice within the society than to affirm the neutral understanding of the legal system, then its interconnection with the welfare state becomes suspect.[76] Instrumental rationality, which is purely formal, inherently militates against the material interests generated by those making particular and substantive claims on the state.

Franz Neumann and Otto Kirchheimer, who were both involved with the Institute for Social Research in the 1930s, claimed that liberal legal systems are not "fully rational" if they fail to deal with the concentration of social and economic power in particular capitalist interests.[77] Habermas, in keeping with their views, is willing to argue that the rationality and autonomy of the legal system is not guaranteed simply because extralegal concerns are translated into the language of positive law; latent power structures can invade the seemingly self-referential legal subsystem.[78] Thus, the attempt by Habermas to redefine the ethical character of law is actually an attempt to deal with how law can remain rational even while the "juridification" (*Verrechtlichung*) of social life increases.[79]

Weber recognized how law was losing its traditional legitimating foundations in religion or custom. Identifying it with the predictability and calculability of instrumental rationality seemed the only way to prevent its descent into arbitrariness.[80] Morality, from this perspective, is reduced to an "ethical minimum" while behavior is regulated in accord with the rights individuals possess in the formation of contracts. The point of Habermas, however, is to show that neither decisionism nor scientific objectivity can provide a foundation for legal practice. His claim, in keeping with the anthropological assumptions of discourse ethics, is that procedural rationality generates the norms and values "worthy" of legitimation. The functionalist theory of law elaborated by Max Weber therefore becomes open to rational justification only in the light of moral principles.[81]

Law is seen by Habermas as mediating the idea of human rights with that of popular sovereignty in such a way that the moral purpose of law becomes the extension of political autonomy. This purpose is, in turn, secured through "the communicative form of discursive formation of will and opinion."[82] Law is consequently more than the codification of injunctions or moral impulses; it is not merely a system of symbols, but a system wherein action takes place.[83] It is a form of social integration in which the moral imperatives behind the rule of law are in a constant state of tension with the various forms of instrumental activity pertaining to power and money.[84] And, precisely to that extent, the internal dynamics of law are capable of becoming embedded in those existing between communicative and strategic action.[85] The object of law converges with the implications of discourse theory;[86] the anthropological meets the ethical. The issue for Habermas is less the outcome of legal decisions than, in keeping with liberal understandings of state power, the manner in which they are derived. Predictability and calculability, which are seemingly embedded within the law, give way before the primacy of procedures capable of preventing lawmaking from becoming arbitrary.[87] These procedures, in turn, derive from particular forms of legal reasoning or discursive argumentation. They prescribe neither any given form of behavior nor any given norm. They make no identification between justice or morality and the given order, but instead provide a construct and criteria wherein the rational pursuit of justice and morality becomes possible: the procedures involved in distributing burdens of proof, defining the requirements of justification, and setting the path of argumentative vindication.[88] Reducing law to politics, in this way, becomes illegitimate.[89] Nevertheless, the linguistic turn provides its practical political justification.

The rationality of law becomes impossible to understand without reference to the structure of legal discourse.[90] But where language structurally subsumes object and subject, its materialization in law enables it to "interface" between the systems identified with objective or strategic forms of interaction and the "life-world" in which the apodictic experiences of subjectivity and everyday intercourse are stored.[91] The two spheres may have been "uncoupled" by the differentiation process of modernity. But law must presuppose a life-world even if its sphere of "just" regulation is confined to systems defined by power and money. It thus retains a "double function." Law must simultaneously regulate particular forms of strategic action even as it projects generalizable interests and the possibility of a critical discourse. Given the manner in which strategic action is predicated on monological communication, and both the economy and the state apparatus presuppose an orientation toward "success," discourse is circumscribed within the life-world by definition. The extent to which law trespasses into the life-world is thus the extent to which reification or its "colonization" takes place. Some have emphasized, in this vein, the need to employ the "symbolic" resources of the life-world or civil society against the encroachments of the state and the economy.[92] For Habermas, however, the aim is more concrete: the development of institutions capable of binding systemic processes to the substantive moral implications of law. This pushes his understanding beyond purely formal concerns. His vision indeed is not only of a public life free from arbitrary interference by the state but also of an egalitarian society in which the poorest and the weakest can participate.

Democracy should foster a plethora of views.[93] The emphasis on consensus, and differentiating general from particular interests, should not interfere with either pluralism or individualism.[94] Democracy is the process by which generalizable interests are constituted and, insofar as its formal freedoms give it substantive legitimation, liberalism is seen as generating what, in considering his consensual community of scholars, Charles Peirce called "logical socialism." This type of socialism, according to Habermas, will survive "only if it takes seriously the utopian element within democratic procedures themselves. The procedural utopia focuses on the structures and presuppositions for a radical pluralistic, largely decentralized process that produces complexity and is certainly costly, a process the content and outcomes of which no one can—or should want to—anticipate."[95]

Utopia is retained. It is—correctly—severed from teleology or ontology but—unfortunately—narrowed in its conception and stripped of substance. As for socialism, if it is to retain any salience at all, it must break with the fatalism and economism of times past. Habermas is surely correct in noting how socialism must now rely on democratic will formation. There is a sense in which he is consequently concerned with defending "the belief in progress, in a world-historical evolution toward the realization of reason in the world."[96] Progress is a modern concept, and in anticipation of Marxism, idealist philosophy fused it with history. Teleology, in this way, became part of the effort to develop a philosophy of history. No less than with the critical theory of society, however, Habermas seeks to ground the philosophy of history within a general anthropological vision of which the philosophy of language is the primary component. A "reconstruction" or, better, transvaluation of historical materialism thus takes place wherein the evolution of symbolic action or the structures of communication complement the development of modes of production or the "instrumental" spheres of action.[97]

Work ultimately gives way, following Jean Piaget and Lawrence Kohlberg, to the "moral responsibility" and role differentiation learned within the family as the central criterion distinguishing the human from the animal. Morality is rendered autonomous, and an independent anthropological dynamic becomes present in the normative orders, which appear at given historical conjunctures and provide an "organizational principle" for all social relationships.[98] Kingship, with its initial differentiation of roles and formal "equality" extended to the nonaristocratic, is seen as giving way before what C. P. Macpherson termed "possessive individualism," which, in turn, generated the need for a new moral order predicated on the rational or discursive adjudication of grievances. This typology is meant to serve as a substitute for the "functionalist" notion of development predicated on the tension between forces and relations of production. As with the original view of the young Marx, which already becomes evident in the interpretation provided by Lukács,[99] the motor of change lies in the symbolic and the communicative rather than in the instrumental and strategic spheres of action.

Universal and critical thought is seen by Piaget and Kohlberg as becoming manifest in the normal development of the mind. Socialization is identified with learning to become rational and independent. Extrapolating this moral development upon humanity thus becomes tempting. But the problem is that the evolutionary process is reversible.[100] There is also no apparent motor of development, and questions arise regarding its identification with either ontogenetic or phylogenetic development.[101] Nor is there any way of deriving the manner in which events are actually constituted from the evolutionary categories of what seeks to substitute for a philosophy of history. Humanity as the universal agent of moral evolution is a weak substitute for the proletariat. The vision of traditional idealism lurks in the background: language seems the "spirit" behind the rehabilitation of a new universal subject.

Perhaps this takes matters too far. One thing, however, is certain. Habermas refuses to juxtapose subjectivity against a seamless bureaucratic order in the manner of Adorno. Instead, following Talcott Parsons and Niklas Luhmann,[102] Habermas asserts that modernization involves the generation of systems with increasingly complicated subsystems whose reproduction depends upon their capacity to secure universalistic processes of adaptation against the "life-world." If the life-world stands distinct from the instrumental logic of state and economic systems, however, it is not divorced from all integration mechanisms. New social movements have supplanted the proletarian "macrosubject" of history by translating "latently available structures of rationality" into social practice.[103] They are radical insofar as they assail the given systems logic through their attempts to redeem the sense of solidarity and subjectivity anthropologically embedded in the life-world.[104] How well these movements succeed, however, is open to determination only by employing the concept of universalism they so often oppose and in judging the cultural traditions influencing their actions. This is only logical since advanced industrial society, with its strategically defined economic and state institutions, provides the material foundations for regenerating the life-world.[105] The "illegitimate" extent to which these materials are employed, of course, is the extent to which anomie and "colonization of the life-world" take place. This is obviously not open to determination a priori. The future, for that reason, remains open. Indeed, whatever the reliance of Habermas on systems logic and ahistorical criteria for making social judgments, the dialectic continues on course in this most prominent contemporary representative of critical theory.

Rethinking Habermas

Habermas has always been a radical proponent of the Enlightenment heritage. His "universal pragmatics" seeks to ground its norms and cement the connection between a philosophy and a sociology of law. Habermas is justified in placing himself within the tradition of Lessing and Kant insofar as he prizes the search for truth over its definition; so too, has he been consistent in refusing to identify the socialist project with any particular institutional form of life.[106] Nor have his critics been able to specify alternatives to his prerequisites for communicative interaction. His standpoint need not buttress the existing consensus or smother pluralism. It merely offers a framework for discourse and even solidarity among the new social movements in a period characterized by a logic of fragmentation. His desire to overcome the "philosophy of consciousness" is tempered by a healthy resistance to positivism despite his concern with institutions capable of rationally adjudicating between conflicting claims and interests. Habermas has gone the furthest in making critical theory, once again, shoulder a sense of political responsibility. Nevertheless, it is impossible to take at face value either the "post-metaphysical" pretensions of his new philosophy of language or his claim that "the theory of communicative action is not a meta-theory but the beginning of a social theory concerned to validate its own critical standards."[107]

Liberalism is founded on the rule of law and the right to property, both of which rest on the concepts of the universal underpinnings of the rule of law and the accountability of institutions to the populace. If the conflict between democracy and capital has been noted often enough,[108] however, liberal theory has never been able immanently to conceptualize the relation between political institutions and the capitalist accumulation process from within its own categories. Nor has it ever been able to present itself as a historical theory with categories capable of comprehending the totality or the manner in which events receive their meaning within it. The original advocates of liberalism were either utilitarians or idealists. This division underpins what would become the great schisms between subject and object, fact and value, theory and practice.

"Abstract" antinomies of this sort were what Hegel sought to abolish. Nor were the concerns of Habermas very different in his attempt to supplant the "philosophy of consciousness" with his universal pragmatics. But the question lingers in terms of how well he succeeded. And success is not merely a matter of framing philosophical questions in a new way: it requires coming to terms with the practical weaknesses of earlier arguments. The problem for Habermas, however, was never the practical implications of the "categorical imperative" or even the willingness to divorce theoretical from practical and normative from instrumental questions. It was rather the manner in which the formulation of such dualisms and the emphasis on the transcendental subject precluded an emphasis on communicative interaction between individuals. The issue for Habermas was never really ethics; it was a matter of metaethics all along.

The old dualisms remain even if they are articulated differently. Communicative is now divorced from strategic interaction and the life-world is poised against the system. The structure of language predicated on an intersubjectively constituted life-world serves as the underpinning of both. But universalism remains incapable of dealing with intractable material interests. The theory of communicative action aims to overcome the relativism associated with the hermeneutics of Hans-Georg Gadamer or Hannah Arendt. But it offers no criteria for moving from a description of the whole to a critique of its oppressive parts. History as the unfolding of political institutions, or even the social development of everyday life, is less subsumed within the philosophy of language or the discourse theory of law than defined out of existence through the use of static categories and questionable anthropological assumptions. This takes place in three ways. It occurs structurally by dividing the life-world from the system. It occurs analytically by divorcing dialogic communication, which is confined to the life-world, from the strategic forms of monologic bargaining and compromise identified with acting in a system. It, finally, occurs normatively insofar as liberation from "hunger and misery" becomes qualitatively different than liberation from "servitude and degradation."[109]

Making distinctions between concepts and levels of argument can prove useful. But this does not justify placing them in what is often an antinomial relation to one another. Just as every moral norm can be employed for strategic purposes, which is precisely why Kant identified ethical action with intention, so are political and economic activities often inspired by morality and ideology. Habermas, however, is not content with intention. He wishes to give the norms girding communicative action a practical function without reducing theory to any form of instrumental exigency. That is why he seeks to employ the discourse ethic for resurrecting the moral foundations for a theory of law. Nevertheless, the building blocks remain the same: the life-world, the discursive community, and the moral commitment to autonomy.

The life-world provides an intersubjective context for all speech situations and interpretive possibilities. But its character remains vague. The category is defined both ontologically as the apodictic construct in which values are shared and, simultaneously, as the anthropological background underpinning any given systemic or strategic forms of differentiation. Part of the problem derives from the fact that whatever the claims concerning the manner in which strategic forms of action are grounded in genuine communication, instrumental activity always presupposes categories from the philosophy of consciousness, which the linguistic turn wished to supersede.[110] Indeed, the distinction between activity oriented toward success and discourse directed toward achieving an understanding becomes undermined in this way. The problem is not solved merely by claiming that the "rationalisation of the life-world must adjust to the extent that the rational potential for communicative action is provided and discursively set free within the structures of the life-world."[111]

Concepts like the life-world have an obvious relevance for phenomenological inquiry. Husserl used it in terms still indebted to the "philosophy of consciousness." Heidegger made the break and secured his category of "being-in-the-world" with the notion of "care"(*Sorge*). While rejecting the "philosophy of consciousness," however, Habermas never anchors his concept of the life-world in "Being" or seeks to determine the manner in which it interlocks with an existential analysis of human existence. The apodictic background has no grounding; it thus turns into little more than a vague anthropological postulate for understanding the noninstitutional features of everyday life. While the existential analysis remains truncated, however, no categories are provided for unlocking the historical character or development of this life-world and its correlative systems. The categories of life-world and system are neither ontologically grounded nor historically articulated. Thus, it makes little sense to claim that a new interpretive position is being presented in which events and actors are no longer primary.[112]

Habermas has not supplanted the "philosophy of consciousness"; its dualisms have merely been shifted onto a different plane. The *chasm*, so evident when dealing with the phenomenological ontology of Martin Heidegger, also looms in the new "phenomenology of moral intention." The linguistic theory cannot perform the tasks of a critical social theory, while the anthropological conception of moral evolution inherited from psychology can offer neither insights into the constitution of social reality nor the categories necessary for conceptualizing events with respect to their historically determinate quality. The bifurcations between communicative and strategic action, system and life-world, are belied in practice. Habermas recognizes that certain spheres of communicative action exist within systems and knows the practical dominance of strategic action. But the matter must be framed more starkly. The political and economic systems of advanced industrial society are obviously intertwined with the myths and symbols of the market and individualism, while social movements, even if they originate in the life-world, have always been *fundamentally* inspired by strategic interests. Finally, on the apodictic level, symbolic action is open to various forms of semiotic organization and capable of influencing other strategic areas of life.[113]

"Communication" lies at the root of the undertaking. It is seen as presupposing an unrestrained discourse, the willingness of each to place himself or herself in the position of the other, the discipline to engage in a rational justification of claims, and a willingness to bracket self-interest so that the "better argument" can win out. Concretely, however, every discourse is necessarily "constrained" both in terms of the agenda and those participating in the discussion. Also, if each is able to put himself or herself in the place of the other then, perhaps even more surely than with the "monological" forms of strategic action, there will remain very little to discuss. Finally, if participants are sometimes willing to engage in a rational justification of claims, history suggests that there is no reason whatsoever why the "better argument" should intrinsically prove victorious without extradiscursive activities being brought into play; indeed, "better" arguments often emerge victorious for nonrational reasons.

"Postmetaphysical" claims to concreteness for the new linguistic perspective make sense only from the standpoint of academic philosophy. It is possible to argue, of course, that communicative practices are constitutive of social relations, which, in turn, reveal given forms of ethical commitment. But this provides only an illusory notion of concreteness.[114] No sooner is the question of social or historical specificity raised than the most fundamental categories lose their analytic power; "general interests" can conflict, for example, when directed to a host of issues—often unique to Western societies—like growth and environmental protection. Cutting back growth could impede not only the development of productive forces but the "material level of culture" (Marx) within a society and the range of choice or autonomy of its members. Choosing among generalizable concerns is always a political question. The linguistic category of "universalizability" is incapable of specifying priorities among competing general concerns, and it makes little difference whether discourse ethics can "ground" the rationality behind morality, law, and politics in language when it cannot confront what are often generalizable, if mutually exclusive, claims.[115] The problem, in this same vein, does not derive from the claim of linguistic philosophy that even strategic interaction presupposes communicative foundations. It stems rather from an inability to generate categories capable of reconstructing the reasons why "genuine" communication has shriveled or the ways in which distorted forms of speech are constantly reproduced.[116]

A real "postmetaphysical" philosophy of a critical sort would concern itself not with the deconstruction or reconstruction of "truth" but with the specification of those *material* constraints on its pursuit.[117] Neither the legal nor the linguistic theory of Habermas can link the prerequisites for communicative competence or the stages of moral evolution with the reality of compromise, violence, and the structural imbalance of power. The plight of Marx's "holy family" of young Hegelians is reproduced: the "idea" of autonomy is "disgraced" since, once again, it is divorced from material "interest."[118] There is indeed something ironic about the manner in which "discourse" is becoming ever more fashionable in theory just as its political effectiveness is appearing ever more questionable in practice. The influence of public opinion and opinion makers is, of course, still very real. But its implications for the extension of genuine democracy is truncated if the extraordinary complexity of the system closes its subsystems to participatory impulses. Just how democracy actually applies with respect to such subsystems, or how fragmented interests might further conditions of unity to engage in extending it, always seems absent from the agenda. That is because the emphasis on "participation" by Habermas is defined by what it opposes. The concern with extending participation and "equalizing power" in the discourse is perhaps the philosophical expression of the practical assault on hierarchic and bureaucratic organization by the new social movements. Nevertheless, it is precisely the institutions of the state—and, in particular, the courts—that the new social movements have employed in securing the claims of their constituents.

Accountability rather than *participation* or *autonomy* may well prove the primary political category for a new critical theory willing to recognize that the great battles of the future will take place in what are still burgeoning international and regional institutions.[119] The linguistic turn of Habermas recoils from dealing with the manner in which individuals may not wish to participate in any given discourse as well as how "experts" can shape an argument or set an agenda.[120] Coming to terms with the experts demands their accountability and, while such demands are strengthened with expanded participation in the decision-making process, differentiated information costs exist, and this matter becomes more important the more complex and differentiated society becomes. Because, precisely to that extent, capital will secure its investment decisions from popular accountability. Since the publication of *Legitimation Crisis*, in this vein, Habermas has stressed the impossibility of conceptualizing the "totality" from the perspective of any macrosubject or structural interest like the working class.[121] He is certainly aware of the implications deriving from the conflicting imperatives of capital and its victims concerning the welfare state, and he is cognizant of the opposition generated by private investors against every attempt to implement a radical social program.[122] But nowhere does this receive expression in the philosophical elaboration. Structural problems of this sort no less than the ways in which "compromises" are substantively affected by existing imbalances of power inherently stand outside the discourse ethic.[123] It is not enough for Habermas to speak of "equal treatment" as the normative bias beyond a purely contemplative notion of law.[124]

Participants in a collective bargaining agreement can receive "equal treatment" in the formal terms of a discourse. They can even share a general interest in keeping any given firm profitable, which might even call upon the disputants to put themselves in the shoes of their adversaries in order to "reach an understanding." From within the parameters of this discourse, whatever the substantive imbalance of power between employers and employees, the "better argument" might even win out. It remains impossible, however, to consider the manner in which the dependency of workers upon the investment decisions of capitalists impacts upon the agenda and the ensuing discourse. In the same vein, for the most part, discursive rules are accepted by practitioners in the American legal system. But, still, one in nearly three African American males is either in jail, awaiting trial, or on probation. Rigidly divorcing procedures from outcomes is simply inadequate. Real relations of power disappear, and the external impingements on the discourse become "invisible."[125] Theory loses its critical edge, and takes a step back behind Hegel and Marx in the name of its "reconstruction."

Truth is never reducible to interest. But simply breaking the connection between them is just as objectionable. Commitment to universals like the rule of law or even the psychoanalytic discourse is always connected with a particular form of practice generated by particular interests. Critical theory, if only for this reason, cannot employ a consensual foundation for establishing truth claims or for analyzing society and its institutional subsystems without impairing its identification with the struggles of the exploited. Such an approach preserves theory from dealing with the real imbalances of power it wishes to judge. Presupposing the interest in equitable judgment leaves it powerless to distinguish between particular interests.[126] Critical theory, in this way, becomes as esoteric and lifeless as the bureaucratic thinking it originally sought to oppose. The life-world confronts the system, and the crisis of the system is defined by the crises pertaining to its structurally demarcated subsystems, while contingent interests and organizational prerequisites for action vanish within the "universal pragmatics."

Enough critics have noted the lack of motivational impulses in the theory of Habermas.[127] But the simple commitment to procedural "justice" can sometimes serve as motivation for action, and in fact, the work of his critics often suffers from the same problem. The real problem has less to do with motivation than with the inability to develop a standpoint through which the efforts of disparate actors can be linked with reference to real struggles. Without making reference to organizational questions, the actual constraints on unity, the bureaucratic concerns with autonomy by various groups, or the regulative principles capable of uniting class interests with those of social movements, such calls become nothing more than pious phrases. Radical political action is predicated on coming to terms with how the concerns of particular groups are raised and made relevant to the exercise of freedom within given institutional arrangements. Habermas is content to note that the quality of a society depends largely upon the nonauthoritarian character of its everyday mores and customs (*Sittlichkeit*).[128]

His concept of the life-world is seen as projecting resistance to its "colonization" by the commodity form and bureaucratic rationality: spontaneity is seen as as repulsing reification. But this is spontaneity of a particular sort. Habermas knows that the life-world is not somehow "more innocent" than the bureaucratic institutions of modernity;[129] he has been consistent in confronting the remnants of *völkisch* ideology with what he has termed a "constitutional patriotism," and it is completely logical to maintain that the regressive character of such premodern prejudices becomes illuminated by the discourse ethic. Habermas is also correct in noting how the colonization of the life-world tends to turn citizens into clients incapable of contesting or criticizing bureaucratic structures. This speaks to the issue of accountability. But framing the matter in this way renders the discussion unnecessarily abstract. At issue is less the instrumental "colonization of the life-world" than the ability to make judgments concerning various types of systemic relief for particular groups with often mutually exclusive claims. Contesting intractable interests cannot occur simply through conceptual recourse to an indeterminate discursive community "without definite limits, and capable of definite increase in knowledge."[130]

Consensus is a linguistic prerequisite for the articulation of competing views. It need not stifle pluralism;[131] but it can. There is also nothing simply "self-generating" about either the economy, the state, or the public sphere. All are dependent on the tug of conflicting interests and ideologically motivated forms of strategic action. Discussion of consensus removed from such matters offers little fascination. It tends to distort the analysis of how will formation is constituted, and it can easily contribute to the self-reinforcing ideology of "bipartisan" politics.[132] Unless such issues are confronted, it becomes impossible to consider the "community of investigators" (Peirce) as anything more than yet another logical postulate devoid of practical relevance. Habermas knows the danger in identifying this community with a community of experts. But the autopoetic nature of subsystems makes it difficult for him to understand it in any other terms. The problem is reflected in the evolution of the "public sphere." Once seen as an arena in which it was possible to question consensual assumptions, the concept is indeed still indispensable for developing a concrete analysis of "actually existing democracy."[133] Nevertheless, there is something strange about how the emphasis upon achieving consensus has grown.

The bourgeois public sphere has witnessed the elimination of discussion. It has been extended among the excluded and exploited without any commensurate ability to increase the accountability of institutions with respect to their material grievances, interests, and aims. The point is not to judge the discussions taking place among different publics by an abstract standard of utopian discourse, but to judge the movements by their actual achievements. Habermas has himself spoken often of the "autonomous" and "multiple" publics produced by the new social movements. In highlighting such progressive developments, however, he has said little about the manner in which they are being undermined by the staggering decline in literacy, with its attendant impact upon newspapers and television, and swamped by the extraordinary centralization of media power.[134] Without reference to any of this, "communication" becomes an inflated concept and the "community of investigators" little more than the "life of the scholar" writ large. It is completely irrelevant whether or not this is just another example of the famous "hermeneutic circle" in which truth claims are seen as incapable of escaping the contextually generated assumptions on which they are based. The discourse ethic makes a phenomenological claim to concreteness. But it presupposes—for both its validity and effectiveness—the historically contingent conditions it claims to further. The discourse ethic is useless where democratic institutions and values are not already extant.

The linguistic theory of Habermas is not one for either uniting the exploited against the whip of the market or confronting what might be termed the moral economy of the separate deal among different interest groups in anything other than the most abstract terms. His "phenomenology of moral intention" is actually metaphysics in a new guise. None of this, however, justifies ignoring his often trenchant political insights or extraordinary contributions to social theory and intellectual life. There is nothing illegitimate about developing the philosophical foundations for a reinvigorated public sphere in which political debate can spur an ever greater form of democratic will formation.[135] This concern is what allows him to claim that "the liberal interpretation is not wrong. It just does not see the beam in its own eye."[136] Indeed, whatever the criticisms of his thought, the attempt to capture that beam is what makes Jürgen Habermas the thinker of our time.

Critical Theory and Civil Society
Political Interests, Private Passions, and the Public Sphere

Civic Virtue and Civil Society

All forms of democratic order assume that authority is somehow based on public consent and a concern with the common good rather than mere tradition and the self-interest of the sovereign.[1] Beginning with the Greeks and the Romans, over Machiavelli and Rousseau, civic virtue has spoken to the willingness and ability of individuals to participate in that order. Most of the new thinking on this subject, however, has highlighted the decline in participation and the need to strengthen voluntary associations in civil society.[2] Fears regarding the atomization of the populace are, of course, themselves derivative of a long tradition within political theory suspicious of the corruption of public life by private interests. The Frankfurt School employed this tradition in its structural analysis of the cultural industry and the ways in which the bureaucratic character of a "one-dimensional society" threatens the subjectivity of the subject. Resistance in the name of "genuine" aesthetic, existential, or religious experience has served as the accepted response to a commercial reality increasingly drained of spiritual meaning.

Civil society is usually seen as encompassing everything from nongovernmental organizations to sports clubs to religious organizations and informal community groups. This creates the temptation for taking the sheer number of groups and the degree of participation as an indicator of democratic vitality. But, then, Weimar Germany was marked by the vitality of its civil society, though, unfortunately, most of the organizations constituting it were profoundly reactionary and helped undermine the democratic character of the regime.[3] Mainstream analysts of civil society, naturally, wish to avoid this kind of situation. In so doing, however, they highlight the need for consensus rather than genuine ideological debate, the participation of individuals and single-issue advocacy groups rather than social movements with their own spheres of public life, articulated political programs, and organizations. Nevertheless, this preoccupation has infected mainstream critical theory as well.

Various critical theorists may have correctly anticipated the way in which advertising shapes private needs, and a new merger of religion and television, politics and entertainment, is taking place. Their interpretations of the culture industry have also helped explain how an impoverishment of the popular imagination has accompanied the expansion of individual choices. No less than the the proponents of "traditional" theory, however, critical theorists have had little positive to offer in terms of either providing a political critique of existing civil society or envisioning a new one. Their rejection of instrumental reason, their identification of society with a seamless bureaucratic whole, and their preoccupation with alienation have made it difficult for critical theory to provide any ideas for meaningful change. It is no longer enough to contest the public life of advanced industrial society only in terms of what escapes its grasp: MTV and the like have given "nonconformist conformity"— to use the term originally introduced by Theodor Adorno—a whole new meaning.

The *political* issue regarding civil society must begin less with the distortion of genuine subjectivity, whatever that may be, than with the need to rehabilitate civic virtue and liberate "public opinion" from an increasingly bipartisan consensus concerning the dangers of "big government," the benefits of the free market, and the threat from outside. Partisans of critical theory have, for their part, mostly chosen to understand apathy as a function of "alienation" or the abstract incursion of instrumental reason on an equally abstract "life-world,"[4] rather than as the result of boredom with an increasingly bipartisan approach to social issues coupled with the quite legitimate cynicism regarding the possibility of translating innovative ideas into effective policy. The contempt for any expression of "public opinion" is implicit in concepts like the "culture industry" and the "one-dimensional" society. Apathy is not seen as the result of real interests succeeding in imposing their will upon other interests. There is little sense that the erosion of civic virtue and the degeneration of politics are part of the same process.

Critical theory can contribute to reversing this process only insofar as it begins initiating positive demands within the alienated framework of modern civil society. But this is precisely what its more literary and subjectivist advocates have failed to do. In fact, many have even been supportive of fashionable attempts to jettison the difference between "public" and "private" entirely. They insist that that these categories have lost all analytic utility. And, in fact, traditional lines of demarcation have grown blurry. But it is not a matter of defending them in empirical terms or by finding fixed analytic definitions. "Public" and "private" are heuristic categories with a referent in everyday life. Without them, ego boundaries collapse and the distinction between reflection and experience vanishes. Without them, the understanding of power becomes impaired, its arbitrary exercise more difficult to define, and its imbalance in civil society harder to combat. Without the categories of public and private, in short, critical theory loses its critical edge.

The relation between them is also not completely contingent. The character of public life affects the quality of private virtues, and, it is important to consider the ways in which neoconservative and neoliberal forces have engaged in a sustained assault on public obligations in the name of private interests. The critique of a secular and multicultural public sphere by the former has accompanied the critique of democratic participation and social justice by the latter. Indeed, for this reason, the willingness of a new critical theory to struggle for a radical public sphere intertwined with its commitment to progressive politics.

The Public Sphere and Its Origins

The public sphere arose in conjunction with the rise of "public opinion" and liberal politics.[5] This arena was initially understood as austere, simple, and egalitarian. Its models were the polis, the Roman idea of the res publica, the medieval free town, and later the New England "town meeting," which so impressed Alexis de Tocqueville on his journey to America. The public sphere's more uncritical proponents tend to ignore the way in which men of property predominated and women and people of color were excluded.[6] But the reflexive and critical principles informing the liberal public sphere allow for the correction of its limitations in practice. The class interests of the liberal public sphere were always intertwined with universal ideals, and the tension between them generated the possibility of meaningful political dialogue. The liberal public sphere emerged, after all, in concert with the bourgeois struggle against the aristocracy during what R. R. Palmer called "the age of democratic revolution." The subversive quality of this bourgeois public sphere indeed initially derived from its assault on rank and its willingness to assume an ability on the part of the "common man" to employ public reason or what Thomas Paine called "common sense."

Ignored in contemporary discussions is the way in which the public sphere was once connected with a vibrant political movement. More recent discussions instead focus upon it as the arena in which "citizens" essentially speak their mind and press for their interests. The public sphere thereby becomes implicated in the broader attempts to develop a "discourse ethic" in which, unfortunately, questions of how the agenda is set and other issues stemming from the exercise of power often give way before an inquiry into the conditions of "communicative competence" and the search for consensus. A conflation tends to occur between the public sphere and either the institutions of the liberal state or what is usually understood as "civil society,"[7] the realm mediating between the state and the market. This creates confusion, but it also imbues the concept with an aura of harmony. The allure of public life becomes intense only when political or social movements exist intent on influencing "public opinion" and transforming society.

The public sphere is the *crucible of consciousness:* it is the cultural arena through which a movement becomes aware of its aspirations, its options, and its character. The public sphere is therefore reducible neither to the formal political structure of the movement nor to its economic interests. This realm of social action is not predicated on a consensual attachment to the prevailing regime or economic system, and it is not inclusive of all interests. Thus, it only makes sense that the bourgeois public sphere should have emerged in conjunction with the political project of that same class or that the "proletarian public sphere" should have arisen in concert with the labor movement or a feminist public sphere in relation to a women's liberation movement. The vitality of the given movement and its political enterprise, in each instance, depends upon the vitality of its public sphere and the degree of commitment it can inspire.

Institutional expressions of the bourgeois public sphere ranged from the voluntary association to the free press, from the family to the salon, and from the educational system to the cheap production of books.[8] Its partisans sought freedom from censorship, the right of assembly, and a critical spirit of toleration. But even more than that, they wished to influence popular opinion concerning the need to ensure that the burden of proof for intervention in private life always rested with the state, that the only means of securing such proof was reference to the liberal rule of law, and that the decision reached should be a product of law.[9] The new bourgeois public sphere in principle, if not in fact, was open to all. Its supporters evidenced contempt for the posturing of the aristocracy along with its customs—and, what had already become evident in earlier works like *Les précieuses ridicules* by Molière—its language as well.

The heroes of the bourgeois public sphere were people like Beaumarchais, Hume, Franklin, Newton, and Voltaire. These were the intellectuals who anticipated or identified with what became known as the "third estate," defended those arbitrarily accused under feudal law by an increasingly corrupt aristocracy, and criticized the dogmatism of tradition and church. These intellectuals were committed to an open exchange of ideas among equals and were intent on rejecting all authority other than the "better argument." Here indeed was the crucible in which the notion of the "people" and "common humanity" was forged. The public sphere initially evidenced a certain unity of interest when it represented the revolutionary interests of a class or movement on the rise. But the bourgeois emphasis upon the liberal rule of law, notions of reciprocity, and respect for the rights of the individual against the state would also hold a certain practical affinity for the struggles of the unjustly excluded and exploited. Thus, it follows that the legacy of the bourgeoisie should have informed the public sphere connected with the political movement of the proletariat.

Marxism may have ultimately congealed into an authoritarian dogma. But the European labor movement, which arose during the last quarter of the nineteenth century, certainly did not abolish what was most democratic about the liberal public sphere. The new socialist parties were grounded in the working class, and in contrast to future vanguard organizations, which would ultimately build on a premodern peasantry, they sought to make good on the republican heritage of the revolutionary bourgeoisie rather than dispense with it.[10] These socialist parties were the first mass democratic parties on the continent, and they were built upon the unrealized political legacy of the class enemy and its slogan of "liberty, equality, and fraternity." Each after its fashion generated what Alexander Kluge and Oskar Negt termed a "proletarian public sphere." This sphere provided a response to "society" whose liberal potential had been abandoned following the Revolutions of 1848 and that was still politically dominated by the aristocracy. The burgeoning proletarian public sphere fueled solidarity and the confidence of its members in a socialist future. The astounding electoral successes of the labor movement and the loyalty it generated were very much indebted to this new creation.

Social democratic parties were engaged in far more than conducting elections or lobbying for legislation. This was particularly the case in Germany where the Social Democratic Party literally created a life for its members: a women's movement, a youth movement, party schools, day camps, card clubs, choral groups, and the like. An extraordinary degree of debate took place, and a whole array of publications ranging from the highly theoretical *Neue Zeit* to the satirical *Wahre Jakob* and the *Buch der Jugend* were subsidized by the parties.[11] Lending libraries and paperbacks contributed to literacy, and an ethos of solidarity was generated in the proletarian neighborhoods of the great cities. It is simply appalling that the great majority of "democratic" theorists concerned with "community" and civic engagement should ignore the form of public life constituted by the early labor movement.

Socialists sought to extend the idea of popular sovereignty beyond those purely political institutions wherein liberalism had confined it and render seemingly extrapolitical institutions like the market accountable. And so, if the bourgeoisie and the proletariat had their antagonisms, they also stood in a type of symbiotic relationship with each other. These were the two dominant classes of modernity, and whatever the differences between them, they shared a similar commitment to the value of scientific rationality, moral universalism, and progress. Their respective understandings of the public sphere were also fundamentally modern insofar as they opposed aristocratic elitism and arbitrary authority, the village and the clan, fixed traditions and customs.

Usually ignored is the way in which both the liberal and the socialist public spheres did not simply seek to express a universal interest but rather sought to link a general with a particular class interest. Partisans of both believed that they could bring pressure upon the state; but it was not in the name of abstractions. Each sought to render government accountable to its concerns and support economic policies conducive to its constituency. For these same reasons, however, both expressions of the public sphere became implicated in what many have called the "alienation" of modernity. Romantics of the early nineteenth century condemned it for squashing individuality in the name of equality. These thinkers provided an impetus for the more subjectivist forms of critical theory and various neoromantic, communitarian, and postmodernist criticisms. Today, too, public life is seen as somehow endangering authentic forms of private experience. The same sentiments come into play, but in a new form that demands a new criticism.

Individuality and Community

Alexis de Tocqueville had already suggested in *Democracy in America* that the egalitarian spirit of democracy was generating a new form of mediocrity. But he considered it the wave of the future, and for better or worse, he believed that the various privileged strata must acclimatize themselves to the new conditions and make the best of what the new system had to offer. Tocqueville viewed the impending triumph of democracy with a certain air of aristocratic resignation. But his sophistication and his genuine interest in the new experiments with democracy were not shared by the coming generation of conservatives and neoromantics. Most were unambiguously intent on contesting modernity, the revolutionary heritage of the bourgeoisie, the philosophy of the rising working class, and the egalitarian and critical foundations of the new democratic public sphere.

Similarities exist between their arguments and those developed by certain representatives of the Frankfurt School.[12] Its members, too, were pessimistic about the future of modernity and an alienated mass society whose culture industry prizes the lowest common denominator. Also, their views sometimes reflected the values of what Lukács originally termed "romantic anti-capitalism." They, too, were elitist and condemned public life for distorting the "authentic" sense of subjectivity, if not the experience of finitude, of the individual. But there were important differences of nuance, intent, and substance. Critical theory was never purposefully conservative or neoromantic in its concerns. The pessimism of critical theory derived from its unfulfilled utopian expectations. Its proponents had no illusions about "community," they were contemptuous of anti-intellectualism, and they had no interest in maintaining tradition for its own sake. Furthermore, they upheld reflexivity, and their defense of subjectivity lacked the pathos and the "heroic" connotations of the neoromantics. Indeed, whatever their shortcomings, their critique of modernity inspired a radical response from the students of 1968 whose aims involved expanding the experiential possibilities of individuals, demythologizing the past, including the excluded, and fostering essentially progressive political values.[13]

Their critique had little in common with the conservative assault upon the liberal tradition following the French Revolution. Where Burke was preoccupied with the refusal of radicals to view society as a delicate and artificial complex of institutions and customs, for example, Marcuse feared the "closing of the political universe" and the elimination of a radical alternative. In the same vein, though Adorno may have sought to highlight the moment of subjectivity, it was not at the expense of universal rights. Even the religious views of the late Horkheimer were never intended to justify any existing church or dogma. Unlike Gustave le Bon, moreover, the critique of cultural mediocrity and "the crowd" was undertaken not in the name of established authority or the existential security of aristocratic elites but rather in terms of their unfortunate impact upon freedom. No member of the Frankfurt School was a reactionary in the sense of Joseph de Maistre or Louis Bonald who considered criticism of supposedly God-given institutions like marriage and the demand for institutional accountability expressive of barbarism.

The Frankfurt School was closer to Nietzsche, the *cultural* revolutionary rather than the *political* reactionary, who decried the "decadence" of Victorianism with its puritanical conformism and hypocrisy, its dead materialism and stultifying rationalism, in which "the higher spirit" was doomed to misunderstanding or worse by a "herd" incapable of intellectually mastering its "will to power." The school's critique of capitalist society had nothing in common with that of the neoromantic intent upon forging a homogenous community or the anti-intellectual speaking in the name of the peasantry. The Frankfurt School was, in short, hyperintellectual in its assault on public life, and more than the narcissism of small differences divides its style from what Ernst Cassirer appropriately termed "mythopoetic" thinking. Indeed, whatever the subjectivism or metahistorical notions of resistance articulated by its members, their approach was quite different from those of two important thinkers with whom they are sometimes associated but who are both reflective of an existentialist tradition with which critical theory had little sympathy.

Martin Heidegger offered a challenge to the public sphere in what remains probably the most dramatic fashion. He is surely among the most difficult of modern philosophers and, ironically, the patron saint of much contemporary bohemian culture. Certain subjectivist implications of his philosophy are fairly obvious and bear a superficial affinity to those of Theodor Adorno. But the differences are real.[14] Heidegger saw "public life" (*Öffentlichkeit*) as an "inauthentic" (*uneigentlich*), if ineradicable, part of human "existence" (*Dasein*). His critique was, however, predicated less on the repression of critical or utopian thinking by the public sphere than on the belief that it obscured the "unthought."[15] Public life is thereby seen as generating "chatter" (*Gerede*) rather than "speech" (*Rede*), "indifference" rather than an attuned state of mind (*Befindlichkeit*), mediocrity rather than uniqueness, and "indifference" rather than "concern" for the lived life of the individual. The public world is, for Heidegger, one in which "they" do this and "they" do that.[16] So far so good. Nevertheless, in contrast to Adorno, the critique is fueled by a notion that public life diverts the individual from what "authentically" matters most: the intuitive "disclosure" of his or her "own" mortality.

Contesting public life alone, for Heidegger, makes it possible to experience the manifest possibility of death and evidence the "decisiveness" (*Entschlossenheit*) necessary for mastering one's fate. Public life can, in his opinion, only trivialize such an encounter. Authentic personal life is thus ontologically pitted against an inauthentic public existence and historicity, or the experience of existence, against the objective interests generated by a historical process. There are no criteria for judgment, and there is no willingness to speak about the effect of external conditions on freedom. Individuation replaces individuality while reified categories ignore the workings of advanced industrial society and its commodity form. Experience is thereby divorced from the context that renders it determinate.[17] It becomes impossible to distinguish the "authentic" experience from what is merely a product of ideology. Judgment becomes a totally self-referential enterprise. Thus, in contrast to even the most radically subjectivist forms of critical theory, Heidegger's approach paves the way not merely for dogmatism but for self-deception, and that is perhaps the greatest danger of all.

Existential contempt for bureaucracy, uniformity, and instrumental expressions of self-interest can however be expressed in a very different form. Some former students of Heidegger indeed maintained much of his approach without sharing his antidemocratic inclinations. Dispensing with his mystification of death and his enchantment with the inner experience, they attempted a more legitimate "public" response to the alienated character of modern public life. They sought to reaffirm models of democracy where participation is valued for its own sake and used them to contest the liberal vision with its individualism and its universalistic presuppositions. They indeed looked back approvingly to a simpler time and sought to understand public action within a tradition extending from the polis to the town meeting and the council or soviet. The most sophisticated proponent of this communitarian view is, indeed, Hannah Arendt.

She never had much use personally, politically, or philosophically for Horkheimer and Adorno.[18] Certain superficial similarities between her approach and that of critical theory, however, again manifest themselves. Genuine "politics" is, for Arendt, divorced from questions of economic power and material interest. It is the response to a bureaucratic condition dominated by "the rule of nobody" in which technology undercuts individual "experience" and fosters alienation. Her understanding of politics is also less concerned with matters of economic inequality or the institutional resolution of griev-ances, or resisting "society," than with a form of existential "self-exhibition" by which each can show his or her worth to the community.[19] There is something aristocratic about all this along with her disdain of mass society. The objects of her criticism, no less than her pessimism, are reminiscent of the Frankfurt School. Nevertheless, in contrast to them, she was concerned with the reinvig-oration of democracy and the formation of a language appropriate to it.

Arendt looked to the polis and the town meeting as images of resistance against an alienated bureaucratic state standing over and against the populace. She understood their utopian character in the present context, but, in her view, that did not detract from their regulative character. Her admiration for the councils associated with the Hungarian uprising of 1956, which she pro-claimed in *The Human Condition*, was logical, and, later, she would keep these regulative images in mind when speaking about the virtues of local commu-nity in *On Revolution*. In contrast to most members of the Frankfurt School, moreover, Arendt was always clear about her support for the constitutional principles on which the United States was founded, and she particularly admired John Adams. Nevertheless, she identified even more strongly with Thomas Jefferson and the "anti-federalist" commitment to "states' rights" against the authors of *The Federalist Papers*, Alexander Hamilton, John Jay, and James Madison.

There is a populist streak in Arendt's work totally lacking in the Frankfurt School. Preoccupied with "participation" and wary of centralized state power, which made some sense given her experiences of Europe during the 1930s, Arendt seemed unaware of how her attack on bureaucracy might lend itself to manipulation. She never seriously considered the exceptional opportuni-ties for the abuse of power by highly organized interests in decentralized localities any more than the impact of economic power on political action. She also left the institutional manner of arbitrating between such interests hanging in the abstract. Grant McConnell was more sober when, in his classic study of American government, he wrote that "far from providing guarantees of liberty, equality, and concern for the public interest, organization of politi-cal life by small constituencies tends to enforce conformity, to discriminate in favor of elites, and to eliminate public values from effective political consid-eration."[20]

Communitarians like Arendt choose to ignore the way in which modern forms of public life are predicated on interaction between strangers: the pub-lic is not a family or some communities of neighbors.[21] They also ignore the ways in which the small community of neighbors envisioned by Rousseau and

Thomas Jefferson were never quite as liberating in practice as they were in theory. Provincialism, religious dogmatism, patronage, and a general traditionalism are part and parcel of small town life. The great advances in racial equality and social justice were, moreover, not the work of small communities struggling against the leviathan, but—especially in the United States—the product of legislation and the language of "rights" rather than the rhetoric of the community. It was the same with the revolutions of 1989.

New forms of solidarity in public life demand new cosmopolitan ideals and categories of "right." An indeterminate notion of the subject alone anchors the possibility of individuals' pursuing both their private and their public interests. Decrying the alienation of modernity and trumpeting the need for participation without placing primary emphasis on linking principle and interest lead nowhere. Critical theory, therefore, must highlight its differences with those embarked upon the inward turn as surely as those in search of the lost community. Its partisans must contest the pretensions of authenticity as surely as the provincial consensus underpinning traditional understandings of community. A radical function of critical theory in the future will involve facilitating communication between different communities of meaning among the excluded and the exploited.

Intervention and Resignation

The Frankfurt School interpreted modernity as a dynamic in which technology generated under capitalism and its peculiar form of instrumental or scientific thinking increasingly undermines the reflective exercise of subjectivity.[22] Moral judgment is understood as becoming increasingly subordinate to instrumental thinking, and, as a consequence, individuals appear threatened with the loss of their capacity for normative judgment. Once autonomous realms of practice like art, with its projection of utopian alternatives, are viewed as ineluctably becoming integrated into the status quo. Alternatives are ever more surely defined by the fundamentally repressive rationality of the whole. But these partisans of critical theory also recognized certain fissures in the system of "total administration." Most were able to distinguish between democratic and authoritarian, liberal and conservative, in any number of particular circumstances. Max Horkheimer became more conservative during the 1950s, for example, and he had little use for the attempts of Jürgen Habermas to develop a radical philosophy of praxis intent on challenging the liberal state for inhibiting the extension of democracy from the purely formal to the substantive, the political to the economic, and the ideal to the real.[23] Herbert Marcuse became one of the most important political intellectuals of the 1960s and 1970s. Erich Fromm, a consistent supporter of social justice, international human rights, and the abolition of nuclear weapons, became a leading influence on the New Left. As for Habermas, his willingness to take political stands has only grown with his fame. Even Adorno was a public presence: he provided dozens upon dozens of radio interviews seeking to make his ideas clear, and he concerned himself with criticizing astrology in essays like "The Stars down to Earth." The question is the extent to which their perception of fissures and their practical "interventions" stand in coherent relation to the assumptions underpinning their broader social theory. It is quite possible that the distinctions they drew were more intuitive and implicit than derivative of anything in especially the more modern versions of classical critical theory. Indeed, when dealing with such issues, two works deserve consideration.

The Authoritarian Personality, edited by Theodor Adorno and numerous other collaborators, emphasized the existence of psychological differences between individuals and sought to provide the possibility for "re-educating" not merely the anti-Semitic but the parochial and bigoted personality in general. Using empirical techniques like the famous "f-scale," or "fascism scale," its authors highlighted the traits of this particular character structure, castigated its effects, noted its contempt for the outsider no less than the new and the different, feared its penchant for violence, and pleaded for policies to foster tolerance. The seamless bureaucratic definition of advanced industrial society is seen as evidencing some ideological tears, and there are even possibilities for intervention. On closer inspection, however, that is not entirely the case. The difference between the authoritarian and nonauthoritarian personality is interpreted as a difference of degree rather than of kind.[24] This indeed stands in accord with a position, perhaps justified at the time, regarding the fundamental similarity between different expressions of mass society. Crucial are also the ways in which authoritarianism and bigotry appear as rooted in the personality structure of the individual rather than in particular forms of opinion formation. Thus, for example, anti-Semitism can be understood as part of a more general attitude predicated on powerlessness in the face of a bureaucratic society that generates the need for a false sense of power.[25]

Education has its limits. Expunging prejudices is only possible through the transformation of everyday life and changing the preoccupation with instrumental rationality into a new reverence for the sensibilities of living human beings.[25] There is an obvious utopian element to all of this that would later inspire Herbert Marcuse in identifying the radicalism of the 1960s with a "new sensibility" in An Essay on Liberation. But the utopian preconditions for abolishing the authoritarian personality were precisely what heightened the pessimism of Adorno. His work reflects a certain resignation regarding the triumph of instrumental rationality and a sense that modern man is no longer even capable of "spontaneous" anti-Semitism: industrial killing has become a substitute for the pogrom.[26] Adorno, in any event, never offered any proposals for waging a war on bigotry. In spite of its liberal interventionist intentions, therefore, *The Authoritarian Personality* actually reinforces the same combination of resigned pessimism and utopian thinking evidenced in other major works of the Frankfurt School. The logic of its broader social theory no less than its lack of connection with practice remains intact.

A different way of approaching the same problem of tolerance appears in a notorious essay by Herbert Marcuse, "Repressive Tolerance," which claims that advanced industrial society has changed the character and function of once radical values. This essay maintains that the classical liberal notion of tolerance has now become a tool of repression insofar as it projects nothing more than the refusal to judge between progressive and reactionary arguments of disparate intellectual worth.[27] Marcuse exhibits the usual pessimism of critical theory with regard to the eradication or mitigation of "repressive" tolerance no less than the anticipation of a growing conservative hegemony. In contrast to the reactionaries, of course, Marcuse was not critical of liberal tolerance in the name of traditional communitarian or religious values. He was instead concerned with how liberal tolerance undermines the commitment to emancipation, critical thinking, and the illumination of utopian possibilities. Unfortunately, however, his view is defined by what it opposes. His position blends nicely with arguments by neo-conservatives denouncing the liberal rejection of censorship and by communitarians criticizing the indeterminate character of citizenship and universal rights.[28] The breakdown between theory and practice in this essay is reflective of the other seminal works of modern critical theory.

"Repressive Tolerance" makes virtually no mention of the bureaucracy required for censorship. It exhibits no sense of how bureaucracies inherently seek to expand their domain of authority, no concern for minority views, and no feeling for the arbitrary character of the entire enterprise. Marcuse's primary concern is an assault upon the "happy consciousness," and this can only derive from the "great refusal" of a bureaucratic reality guided by instrumental reason that is ever more committed to liquidating "critical" thinking. Such resistance is possible, if at all, only through the actions of a minority. Intellectuals and students, women and minorities—all those at the margins of what John Kenneth Galbraith called "the affluent society"—can indeed serve as "catalysts" for a working class whose radical consciousness has been defused even as its subordinate position in the capitalist accumulation process has been maintained.[29] The "marginal groups theory" of Marcuse anticipated the new emphasis upon the displacement of institutionally organized political action by radical social movements critical of the "system" and inspired by a more expansive view of subjective possibilities. Nevertheless, Marcuse's critique of the one-dimensional society is itself one-dimensional: modernity is not some linear development of instrumental rationality intent on eliminating subjectivity.

This position is perhaps best articulated by Ulrich Beck who, while not a disciple of the Frankfurt School, nonetheless gives many of their themes a unique twist. He celebrates the appearance of new movements engaged with the quality of life, and the experimentation with modernity, that are less concerned with revolution than reform. Beck considers these movements "sub-political" in character.[30] They are principally concerned with previously unacknowledged issues, though perhaps always intuitively recognized, such as the right to forge one's own lifestyle and to die with dignity and various other matters of this sort. Modernity is therefore seen as retaining a *reflexive,* rather than merely an instrumental, component that is capable of contesting fixed ways of thinking, correcting institutional limitations, and fostering the liberation of subjectivity.[31] Indeed, according to Beck, "reflexive modernization" transforms the relation between public and private as surely as that between the political and the nonpolitical. [32]

Reflexive modernization also supposedly dispels old-fashioned differences of "left" and "right."[33] It explodes traditional constraints on the individual, makes administrative problems ever less discrete, and thereby leaves bureaucrats unable to confront the increasingly incalculable risks accompanying supposedly calculable policy options. Spontaneity from below combines with paralysis from above. Parliamentary institutions and political parties now give way before new social movements capable of liberating subjectivity from traditional constraints and furthering multiplicity. What was "public" and "political" now becomes "private" and "apolitical."[34] Public life is ever more surely defined by the interplay of private passions, and subjectivity is seen less as an expression of "negativity" than as an expression of the modernity itself. This is what, according to Beck, obliterates the need for revolution. The "system" itself is conceived of as inherently revolutionary, and progressives need now only draw the always ambivalent and complicated implications.

Structural imbalances of power, however, are increasingly permeating the different spheres of society: economic inequities not only between nations but between regions and territories within nations have grown and will grow further as transnational monetary organizations seek to insulate themselves from public accountability. Informational and resource constraints militate against "sub-political" movements while, in the same vein, their success in transforming the culture of everyday life must be measured against the marked failure of progressive forces over the last quarter of a century in the political arena. Their "micro-publics" have, furthermore, been falling subject to the same logic of the commodity form as the state and the economy that they initially intended to resist: the language of the expert is becoming ever more complex while that of the public is becoming ever more impoverished. Thus, no less than for the more traditional interpretations of modernity offered by the Frankfurt School, the connection between theory and practice breaks down in Beck's thinking as surely as the relation between public and private.[35]

Critical Theory and Civil Society

The purposes of any new critical theory with respect to civil society are far less complex than many would care to believe. Its advocates should resist "thick" notions of consensus by fostering what might be termed *creative tensions* between progressive movements and existing institutions, democratic ideals and repressed interests, the goals of liberation and the instrumental means employed to achieve them. All of this, however, requires a preliminary commitment to liberal political institutions and policies that would allow time for cultural or political participation by the disempowered. Thus, the dual task of critical theory: it must simultaneously defend the liberal public sphere from those provincial and religious organizations—whose prime purpose lies in constricting discourse and diversity by censorship and social pressures to conform—and criticize the undue influence exerted over it by elites who wish to employ profit as the sole criterion for cultural production.[36]

Institutional accountability becomes more difficult and participation easier to manipulate when, though the market for culture might be free in principle, the public sphere is dominated by a few dozen firms in fact. Corporate control over museums and theaters, public broadcasting stations and publishing houses, has only grown over the years. The great bulk of information worldwide is now dominated by roughly two dozen international firms, and fewer than twenty control most of the national media in the United States.[37] Rendering such powerful corporate institutions accountable is possible only through the use of other, countervailing institutions. An unqualified rejection of bureaucracy or instrumental rationality is, therefore, counterproductive. Only the state can break up the media monopolies. Government intervention can also be employed to expand the number of channels, limit "pay per view" programming, tax commercial use of public air space, and support alternative cultural undertakings.[38] Ironically, then, the possibility of fostering private interests depends upon maintaining the divorce, or alienation, between the state and civil society.

Monopoly control over media has standardized production and narrowed the ability to experiment with everyday life. Too many counterproposals, however, begin with the idea of limiting the mass media rather than unleashing their potential: we constantly bewail the insults to this group or that religion. The worst mistakes made by the left have stemmed from its decisions to curtail freedom rather than expand it. Resisting hegemonic values and combating the conservative reaction is possible only by embracing the most radical possibilities of modernity. The mass media may atomize society, but they also breed a continuous encounter with the new. Even works of cultural "quality" must now employ the technology developed by mass media,[39] and it is shortsighted to maintain that the communication infrastructure is somehow overburdened. The role for critical theory is to offer categories and values by which people can better evaluate the information they receive. And disseminating them will involve the use of media technologies: Internet innovations, new computer technologies, digital developments, holograms, and new modes of travel. The cultural technologies of international civil society are still in their infancy, and resisting globalization will call for relinquishing our antitechnological biases.

All of these technologies will, for better or worse, change the landscape of civil society in extraordinary ways. They may have an even greater impact on television than television had on movies or photography on painting. Technologies are increasingly competing with one another, and, as a consequence, new political possibilities for participation may present themselves: the Internet has already linked people together in new ways, and "interactive" television can conceivably give referenda and voting a new character.[40] Intervention by progressives will increasingly depend upon their ability to foster—rather than constrain—innovation both inside and outside the prevailing forms of cultural production and distribution. And such talk is not merely posturing. Intervention has already taken many forms: popular programs have had a profound impact on the acceptance of gays and minorities by the mainstream, and many of them have consistently trashed traditional forms of intolerance, the fanaticism of religious zealots, and the naked ambitions of establishment politicians. This may all take place in simplistic ways through moralizing, sloganeering, and the use of stereotypes. What's more, when one considers the news and the windbag pundits who rose to fame during the Reagan Revolution, no less than the new direct and indirect constrictions on dissent following September 11th, it becomes clear that the balance of power is still tilted toward conservatism.

But there remains a sense in which mass media constitute a contested terrain. The struggle for tolerance and diversity is not a luxury. Trotting out idealized versions of earlier institutional forms to engage the battle, however, won't help matters. Civic virtue must take on a new character: it can no longer be predicated on the abstract participation of an abstract individual in some idealized public arena. Critical theory must begin thinking seriously about new bureaucratic forms and, following Montesquieu,[41] how curbing the ambition of one bureaucracy requires action by others that itself is possible only through the exertion of pressure from below. It also remains an open question whether any movement can educate its members to read the small print in the larger contract, look for the material interests hidden beneath the technical jargon of administrative experts, or find the sleight of hand in so much policy formation. But new technologies like the Internet have generated radically new possibilities for public scrutiny. Critical theory must, for its part, regain its commitment to deal with the ways in which economic inequality and political imbalances of power privilege the access of some groups over others.

The uncritical assault on instrumental reason by critical theory has outlived its usefulness. Better to become clear about the ethical values a progressive public sphere should foster in the political battle over the future of public life. Partisans of such a sphere *should* employ media to broaden the lives of everyday people, enable them to gain experiences of other cultures, and combat parochialism. Such a sphere *should* attempt to alter the nature of "community" by exploding arbitrary limits on geographical space and personal relations. New communications and media technologies *should* help break down the barriers of color and gender. They *should* help render anachronistic the idea of "ethno-solidarity," which is a pet phrase of Richard Rorty, and seek to undermine the idea that nationalism or religion is the only possible response to the anomie of modern life. Media *should,* in short, help generate a new cosmopolitan sensibility and offer alternatives to outworn customs.[42]

Perhaps it is true that the left—if not the right—is shattering into what Gilles Deleuze has called "micro-publics," each with its own interests and concerns, and few with any connection to a social movement with a political purpose. But this is precisely the situation that calls for resistance by the partisans of critical theory. Any progressive public sphere *should* proclaim the need for engagement in the battle against irrationalism, prejudice, and intolerance. Such a sphere *should* provide a place for those seeking truths rather than those bent upon establishing them. It *should* seek ways of making power visible. It *should* engage in the battle for legislation capable of expanding choices equitably and creating conditions wherein each might more freely determine the content of his or her life. Such a sphere indeed *should* recognize the dignity of each person insofar as it presupposes the capacity for rational dialogue and public reason by every individual. And it *should* do so not because it is possible to "prove" or "ground" such claims but because democracy and the constraint of arbitrary power are impossible without making these kinds of assumptions.

Nothing is more dangerous than seeking the elimination of the public in the name of the private or, like those totalitarian systems now in the garbage can of history, attempting to abolish the private in the name of the public. Placing a premium on the supposedly authentic realm of private experience is just another way of avoiding responsibility for the choices generated by public life. The radicalism of this stance is a false radicalism, a form of quietism with a heroic posture, which narrows the realm of experience as surely, if more slyly, than the authoritarian attempts to assure conformity. Public life can inhibit or foster the pursuit of new experiences and, from the perspective of a reinvigorated critical theory, the purpose of a radical public sphere is to expand the options and possibilities of private life for those who do not, to use the phrase of Bert Brecht, "sit at golden tables." In any event, public life withers with the obliteration of private life: it becomes nothing more than ritual, a form of obeisance to the masters, and a self-conscious denial of autonomy.

The tension between public and private is the mark of liberty. But the quality of this tension is determined by politics. The viable public sphere is one in which instrumental action receives its normative justification and freedom becomes more than a word for nothing left to lose. Only public rights, for this reason, can anchor the pursuit of private virtues.

$$\mathcal{C}\!\sim 14 \sim\!\mathcal{O}$$

Points of Departure
Sketches for a Critical Theory with Public Aims

Introduction

C ritical theory began with its own *promesse de bonheur*. It offered an interdisciplinary perspective seeking to inform the struggle against oppression in all its guises. It rejected the priority accorded political economy by Marxism, and it subverted the "privileged position" of the proletariat. Critical theory called the domination of nature into question and any identification of the subject with existing institutional arrangements. It championed the reflexive subject against totalitarianism and the "happy consciousness." It defended hope and the concept of utopia. The greatest representatives of critical theory produced works of enduring intellectual quality on a remarkable range of subjects and themes. They dared progressive intellectuals to reject the verities of positivism and teleology. They radicalized the use of psychology and anthropology; they linked Marx with Freud and Nietzsche. They proclaimed that "the whole is false" and transformed the debate over culture. They raised the banner of a "negative dialectic" and profoundly influenced the ideology of the 1960s in Europe as well as, in varying degrees, all over the world.

Horkheimer, Adorno, Benjamin, and others associated with the Institute for Social Research forged a radical tradition. Over the last decade, however, critical theory began to lose much of its allure. The triumph of conservativism was not alone to blame. Neither was the continuing lack of a universal "agent" for radical change. The fact is that critical theory had become increasingly domesticated. The success of its enterprise, in good dialectical fashion, generated the conditions for its decline. Apolitical literati turned it into the subject of a deadening scholasticism and embraced its most elitist tendencies while social scientists partitioned its insights for mainstream research. Jürgen Habermas and other innovative thinkers of the "second generation" saw the warning signs. They tried to reinvigorate critical theory, place it on a new "positive" footing, and reaffirm its connection with the most progressive elements of the Enlightenment legacy. Nevertheless, its "great refusal" has withered.

Philosophical differences, shifting political allegiances, and personal conflicts sometimes make it difficult to get an overall sense of what critical theory was originally meant to convey. Basically, however, it was a normative perspective, generated from the traditions of philosophical idealism and historical materialism, that sought to inform empirical research and the struggles of the working class after the initial euphoria of the Russian Revolution had passed. Critical theory was a form of Marxism without organizational attachments or dogma. It emphasized the question of consciousness and the manifold threats to individual autonomy. It also sought to restore the connection between theory and practice, which had been perverted by Stalinism. That purpose has eroded and, indeed, it is somewhat difficult to agree with the famous claim of Leo Lowenthal that it was not the critical theorists who abandoned praxis, but praxis that had abandoned them.

A metaphysical veil has fallen over critical theory. Negative dialectics and discourse theory both use it to hide from the reality of conflicting interests and institutions defined by structural imbalances of power. A new identification with the disadvantaged can help lift this veil. Providing critical theory with a new positive direction of this sort, however, is possible only by reaffirming its forgotten political component and reinvesting it with a practical interest in public affairs. Critical theory was originally inspired by a commitment to freedom and the need for ongoing revision in order to confront new questions posed by new historical circumstances. It was never a set of fixed claims or ironclad proscriptions. Critical theory is perhaps best understood as what Theodor Adorno termed a "force-field," a problem complex, composed of certain intersecting concepts.

The future of critical theory depends upon their fate. This problem complex falls under a set of rough rubrics. The first speaks to the theoretical status of the enterprise and questions concerning its foundations, its view of society, and its conception of tradition. The second deals with immanence and the categories necessary for translating theory into meaningful forms of practice: solidarity, accountability, and autonomy. The last involves transcendence and the concern with emancipation exhibited by aesthetics, nature, and utopia. Only sketches of these concepts and their implications will be given in the following sections. Nevertheless, should they provide an insight into the possibilities of the critical method, this undertaking will have fulfilled its aims.

PART I

Foundations

Foundations were precisely what critical theory sought to deny. They smacked of "traditional theory" with its finished claims, fixed systems, and attempts to subsume the particular within the general. In rejecting the "grounding" impulse, however, critical theory found itself torn by other competing impulses: positive and negative, objective and subjective, anthropological and historical, sociological and aesthetic, material and metaphysical. Innovative attempts to analyze phenomena from within a determinate historical context confronted the radical projection of freedom beyond any context. Critical theory had, in this vein, once inspired radical experiments in the sociology of knowledge. Gradually, however, its focus shifted. The "negation" of society was undertaken so that potentiality might explode actuality, and the integrative power of the culture industries seemed to justify this new preoccupation with transcendence against immanence. Emphasizing the "nonidentity" between subject and object thus became a way of preserving freedom and reflection from necessity and instrumental rationality.

Every system and ideology assuming an identity between the subject and his or her world became open to challenge. But the failure of the revolutionary proletariat generated concerns with the purposes and foundations of this challenge. Theodor Adorno and Ernst Bloch, in keeping with the thrust of the original enterprise, sought to resist traditional forms of ontological thinking. They believed that by transvaluing ontology they might overcome its limitations. Both the ontology of "false conditions" developed by the former and the utopian ontology of the latter presupposed the existence of "latent" experiences and possibilities resisting definition by reified forms of instrumental thinking. Each called upon reflexivity to deal with "what is not." Each stressed the unfinished character of reality. Each provided an opening to the *novum*. Categories were lacking in both cases, however, for making distinctions between traditions or translating the latent into the real. Mediations vanished, institutions too, as these critical attempts to employ traditional ideas conflated the difference between utopia as an other and as a regulative idea. The philosophical attempt to define reality a priori became separated from the practical need for categories capable of dealing with contingent situations. Ontology rendered indeterminate the moment of resistance it promised to deliver. Distinguishing the "false" utopia or negation from the "true" thus became an ever more arbitrary exercise.

Supplanting the teleology of a failed movement and contesting the philosophical mainstream involved rejecting the positive moment of "synthesis" or the "negation of the negation" in favor of "negativity" and a new antinomial form of thinking. Antinomies, when properly set in motion, were seen as fueling the "dialectical" tension within phenomena, thereby maintaining their "nonidentity" and utopian potentiality. The new emphasis on negativity, however, made the falsification of claims impossible, and critical theory found itself simultaneously detached from the empirical sciences and in danger of creating its own form of dogmatism. Critical theory became content to identify its project with resistance to oppression. This purely negative formulation was seen as manifesting the materialist content latent within the idealist concept of reason. Nevertheless, interpreting the "materialist" impulse of idealism in this manner left the negation of injustice and the commitment to freedom divorced from practical interests, institutions, and actual movements. Freedom and necessity, subjectivity and the objective world, no longer reciprocally defined each other. The negation was left to contemplate the world of positivity. The contestation of reality would take place without reference to the political implications of ideas. Emancipation became its own justification. But the problem was less a matter of "grounding" in the abstract than the inability to deal *politically* with concepts like democracy and the rule of law, socialism and equality, internationalism and cosmopolitanism.

Critical theory never had much use for liberalism, and social democracy was derided for its economic reductionism, cultural provincialism, and reformism. The new philosophy was influenced instead by the "dialectical" works of Karl Korsch and Georg Lukács, whose "theory of praxis" reflected the "heroic phase" of the Russian Revolution. These thinkers were principally concerned with analyzing the mediations linking base and superstructure along with the various cultural and psychological impediments to radical change. Their followers in the Institute for Social Research essentially saw the weakness of liberal and social democratic traditions as creating the preconditions for the rise of authoritarianism. Little speculation was wasted on their relevance for an emancipated social order. Indeed, with the exception of Erich Fromm, the "inner circle" never showed much support for the Weimar Republic.

History had seemed to invalidate the original liberal vision of the bourgeoisie as well as that of its social democratic inheritors. And so, when the communist experiment turned sour, it only made sense that Horkheimer and Adorno should have placed a new emphasis on Nietzsche. Marx never vanished from critical theory. But criticism of the commodity form was now leveled in the name of an increasingly imperiled subjectivity and its incommensurability with any objective system. The "subject," once historical and determinate, now became philosophical and abstract. The attempt to explode all "systems" left it stranded beyond any particular institutional conditions capable of securing its existence.

Foundations are a matter for political and social theory rather than philosophy. Horkheimer already intuited in his youth that happiness requires no philosophical justification. But he never extended his insight to issues concerning reflection or the primacy of liberal values. It is now necessary to radicalize the original claim. Neither linguistic philosophy nor a scientific theory, neither epistemology nor a theory of moral evolution, is necessary or sufficient in order to justify accountability or the rule of law. It is enough to look back at *real political systems* and see that, with few historical exceptions, the extent to which the liberal rule of law was employed was the extent to which grievances were open to consistent forms of equitable redress. It is enough to note that the extent to which reciprocity was denied was the extent to which popular sovereignty was subverted, inequality legitimated, and security lost. It is enough to know from the past that the arbitrary exercise of power is the foundation of terror.

John Dewey would probably have agreed that these are "warranted assertions." Engaging in ontological, phenomenological, and epistemological forms of justification—or using the "ungrounded" character of such philosophical approaches to justify the most nihilistic implications of postmodernism—is all nothing more than an academic exercise. The question over whether the public realm is really "better" or merely "differently" served by accountability and the rule of law as against the arbitrary exercise of power should be more than a matter of semantic debate. Refusing to make a practical judgment, in the name of resisting the "domination" supposedly implicit in such a choice, is merely an abdication of responsibility. Judgment is then always exercised by others.

Critical theory is partisan, if not blindly so. It recognizes the existence of diverse constituencies with different ideological commitments. It does not speak only to the converted. But, in practical terms, it recognizes the idealism inherent in seeking to convince the oppressor about the exploitation of the oppressed or, in terms of pure theory, attempting to provide "neutral" justification of its claims before "society" as a whole. The interests of critical theory in justice and happiness are validated by those who suffer from their denial. These people need not "justify" their experience of oppression, *only the manner in which they respond to it and seek to mitigate it*—and that because, in fact, they will assuredly bear the burden for its failure. Constraining the arbitrary exercise of power and emphasizing the universal constructs underpinning the rule of law are thus legitimated not simply from the standpoint of linguistic rules. Their justification derives from a judgment concerning the *practical* needs of the disadvantaged for equitably adjudicating their grievances, overcoming their lack of unity, and developing a sensible view of the institutional conditions capable of fostering their public well-being.

Karl Mannheim liked to speak about "styles of thought" whose internal consistency and relevance for solving practical problems might provide ways of judging between them. Ontology, epistemology, and narrowly linguistic forms of validation become irrelevant from this perspective. The extent to which power is abused becomes the extent to which the "negation" retains its determinate validity. Justifying claims of this sort should occur by reflecting on the past and, from the standpoint of the present, speculating on the practical consequences for the future of a given idea. Controversy will obviously arise on the status of such claims; the counterfactual can confront the real, and conflict among various universal interests, or rights, will also surely occur. Politics will prove primary in reaching a decision. Such, however, is the practical reality.

Immanent criticism is sufficient for judging the conduct of any given order in relation to the ideas most consistent in the given context with social equality, democracy, and internationalism. A critical theory with practical commitments and a public purpose will recognize that these ideals extend beyond the purely formal. Liberalism presupposes certain substantive judgments about the character of "human dignity" and individual responsibility, socialism holds certain substantive views on the value of competition, and internationalism makes certain assumptions about the value of "community" and ethnic forms of solidarity. Critical theory cannot ignore substance in the name of form. If it is to retain its salience, then, it must prove willing to confront power and offer criteria for judging how one response to exploitation or oppression might work better for the exploited and oppressed than another.

Old-fashioned dualisms between truth and justice, consciousness and being, and knowledge and interest have grown stale. Critical theory must anchor itself in the structural imbalances of power defining the manifold contexts wherein subjectivity is put into practice. Only then can discussion regarding the grounding of values lose its metaphysical character. Illuminating and confronting the repressed possibilities for freedom defining particular forms of ideological and material production can alone provide the critical enterprise with concreteness and the ability to anticipate the practical concerns over which future struggles will take place. Seeking to expose the interests of the disadvantaged and the institutional constraints inhibiting their articulation can alone—once again—render critical theory relevant for the coming century.

Society

"Society" remains the cornerstone of the critical enterprise. Through the concept of "totality," it was used to contest the separation of the empirical from the formal mode of analysis. Recently, however, this category in particular has become the object of violent criticism, and much of it is legitimate. "Totality" resonates with absolutist ambitions. It threatens the integrity of the particular; it has been compromised by association with outmoded forms of historical teleology; and it conjures up the image of totalitarianism. But the concept situates the particular and provides it with determination; it turns history into a mutable human product; it explodes paradoxical formulations and makes irrelevant rigid distinctions between facts and values or truth and justice. Totality reflects the dynamism of reality, makes the perception of contradictions possible, and projects the transformation of the status quo.

Idealism, with its commitment to reflexivity, first introduced the category into the modern discourse. Western Marxists like Lukács and Korsch then rejected its neutral epistemological and ontological status. Its objective character, they maintained, was comprehensible only from the standpoint of a proletarian class subject generated by the very society it was destined to transform: the *moment of decision* became inextricably linked with the concept. The neutral truth criteria of the natural sciences, for their part, were seen as excluding the "emancipatory interest" (Habermas) in changing existing social relations. Thus, totality was conceived as an inherently social category, and it made possible the identification of critical theory as an interdisciplinary enterprise informed by revolutionary norms.

Conceiving of "society" still requires such an interdisciplinary stance. This was a fundamental contention of both Western Marxism and critical theory; indeed, even Jürgen Habermas could legitimately maintain that his theory of communicative action retains a thematic connection with the whole. But the justification for an interdisciplinary stance does not merely derive from the intellectual enrichment that can occur through the interchange between scholars in different fields. More important is the recognition that neither reflection nor ethical judgment can arbitrarily grind to a halt even when disciplinary boundaries are "consensually" raised. Thus, whatever the necessary heuristic boundaries separating the various fields of scholarly endeavor, Theodor Adorno was correct in emphasizing that no *social fact* exists beyond the determinations of society as a whole.

Totality opens the "whole" to ethical judgment. It makes visible the structures of production and reproduction in which reification and alienation are generated. It makes thematizing the various contradictions of society possible and, insofar as they are always "mediated," the various factors inhibiting their resolution as well. It undermines economic determinism and renders the theory of Marx receptive to contributions by thinkers concerned with psychological, anthropological, cultural, and a host of other issues. It articulates the constraints on revolutionary commitment and lets repression assume a manifold guise. With the failure of the working class to fulfill its revolutionary mission, however, the category of totality lost its constitutive subject, its potential for transformation, and its dynamism. The integrity of distinct moments within it, no less than the contradictions defining their reproduction, became smothered by reification; the "whole" now confronted the individual in a new way. No longer could the subject receive its determination within a preformed construct. Theory and practice, subject and object, form and content, transcendence and immanence, fell asunder. It was now necessary to introduce a new category capable of recognizing this reality while keeping the subjectivity of the subject "nonidentical" with objective reality and all reified systems of thought.

"Constellation" sought to contest the "totalitarian" tendencies of the parent category. It would restore a sense of what had been forgotten, whether the sacrifices of the past or the repressed elements of subjectivity in the present, and dynamize the understanding of phenomena without reference to the teleological assumptions of Hegelian dialectics. It would also confront reification by continuing to insist that society is a product of human action and that the particular receives its definition only within a context. Proponents of the new category like Walter Benjamin and Theodor Adorno never relinquished the traditional concern of Western Marxism with thematizing a context. Both theorists rejected relativism and maintained a notion of truth. Indeed, the whole remained a point of reference for their respective notions of "negativity" as well as a category for analyzing history or the social reality being negated.

Systematically emphasizing the "nonidentity" between subject and object, however, became the price for rejecting systematic thinking. Its usefulness in constituting an object of inquiry, or interpreting a given event, became evident in the work of its authors. In terms of a transformative project, however, it surrendered any historical or institutional referent for freedom. Solidarity lost its concreteness; it became anchored in art, theology, or anamnesis. Withdrawing from any positive relation to the empirical world in this manner undermined the ability of critical theory either to justify its status or provide determinations for what requires change and why. Immanently deriving the moments of the whole, or the internal dynamics animating them, thereby became ever more difficult. Concern with reconstructing the relation between theory and practice faded, and use of the constellation became ever more involved with the articulation of aesthetic or historical experience.

The totality and the constellation serve different functions, and they are usually juxtaposed against one another. But that opposition has become ever less valid. Political action still requires a sense of the way in which economic conflicts of interest, political imbalances of power, and ideological differences interact. A cultural or historical inquiry, similarly, still requires the intervention of the subject in giving it purpose and arranging its elements. Or, to put it another way, where the totality has lost its proletarian agent, the constellation requires an objective referent if it is not to become the object of self-referential play. If "society" can no longer present itself as prefigured in Hegelian fashion, it is still the case that its understanding requires a sense of different levels of interconnected analysis. In the same vein, society is not an arbitrary collection of fragments whose construction is purely a matter of subjective choice. The totality and the constellation are subsequently in the position of reinvigorating one another: that certainly occurred with respect to narrative and montage, also usually juxtaposed against one another in the work of an artist like John Heartfield. That a tension should exist between the implications of two such different concepts within the given inquiry is less a problem than a benefit so long as the reasons for the tension within this "force-field" are made clear through the analysis itself. The point for any form of new critical theory, after all, is to specify the conditions under which the object of inquiry is constituted and the dynamics defining its potential for radical transformation. These will differ depending upon the object under consideration. Thus, the object must generate its unique categories of inquiry.

Categories engaged in the task of resurrecting "society" can therefore claim neither "scientific" validity nor ontological status. They exist within a hermeneutic frame of reference. Just as social scientific inquiry will always retain a contingent moment, however, hermeneutics cannot dispense with social scientific constructs. An exclusive reliance on either hermeneutic formalism or empirical immediacy can only hinder serious analysis. Again, however, the explanatory status of the interpretive construct need not diminish so long as its particular knowledge-constitutive interests are made explicit. "Society" will always elude the categories seeking to comprehend it. But the need to make sense of it still remains. Grand narratives remain necessary precisely because the economy and mass media are breaking down national barriers, transnational institutions are on the rise, and problems ranging from the environment to the economy are becoming planetary in character. History is taking a global form, and for this reason, viewing society both from the standpoint of its potential for change and as constituting a referent for resistance is less a theoretical issue than a practical one.

Traditional relations between theory and practice, of course, have broken down. But this does not justify withdrawal or dogmatism. There is no philosophical or evolutionary trick with which to compensate for the collapse of teleology. There is nothing with which to cancel the cunning of history or overcome the contingency of progress. Critical theory, for this reason, needs to grasp freedom in the constraints and concrete alternatives making for its *practical exercise.* In this way, philosophy remains both its "epoch comprehended in thought" (Hegel) and the possibility of calling that epoch into question. Critical theory, whatever its commitment to transcendence, cannot escape immanence or the constraints of historical reality.

Tradition

Struggle is always embedded in tradition. Its presence is the response to injustices inherited from a past that shapes anticipations regarding their amelioration in the future. Proponents of the new are always situated in time. Tradition is, for this reason, inescapable. It becomes manifest in the values inspiring their enterprise. Tradition appears in the questions they ask and the assumptions they make. Communitarians and conservatives maintain that actions gain their moral value only in the context of lived traditions. But tradition is not simply handed down to the present in a one-dimensional manner. It needs construction and reconstruction in order to exploit the unrealized "surplus" of the past for progressive ends.

Tradition provides history with coherence. With the new power of the culture industry, however, the past is ever more surely becoming a buffet from which the gourmet can select a bit of this and a touch of that. The culture industry celebrates the fad, immediacy, cynicism, and the "happy consciousness." It loosens the bonds of tradition and, in keeping with the claims of postmodern thinkers, creates juxtapositions whose arbitrary character is limited only by the dictates of profit. Liquidation of the past, or the inability to give it coherence, is a principal way of chaining the disadvantaged to the ideologies of their oppressors. Critical theory must confront this situation by utilizing the seemingly limitless possibilities for signification without surrendering to relativism. Lukács once warned against attempts to pursue left-wing politics with right-wing philosophy. A new understanding of this insight has become necessary. It does not suggest that conservative traditions, and their most outstanding representatives, have nothing to teach. Ideas obviously project beyond the historical context in which they originated and the simplistic reduction of transcendence to immanence impoverishes culture. Nevertheless, even in the greatest of works, there remains a *historical residue* of the prejudices and beliefs of its context.

Walter Benjamin was aware how every document of civilization retains an element of barbarism. Traces of concrete repression, whatever the forms of symbolic and institutional mediation, never completely disappear from an idea. Difficulties arise, however, insofar as not every impulse from the past is reactionary and not every document retains traces of barbarism to the same degree. Gradations exist, freedom and repression intermingle, and a conceptual framework is necessary for making determinations. Cultural works do not simply speak to the present in a self-evident fashion. The critical meaning is constituted, and this requires a sense of its connection with any given genre and style as well as the context in which it was created. Each forwards a certain relation between the transcendent imperatives of theory and the historical limitations of practice. Each also generates a multitude of contradictions in search of resolutions: a given tradition or work can simultaneously prove progressive for artistic creation and regressive with respect to the political or social ideals it embraces. Different traditions of theory and practice can prove useful in different ways for different forms of inquiry, and it becomes incumbent upon critical theory to distinguish between different investigative domains.

Dialectic of Enlightenment never took any of this into account, and, consequently, its authors were never able to deal coherently with the historical residue, the political values, and the social implications of either the Enlightenment or their own age. Refusing to recognize any disciplinary boundaries, unwilling to provide its radical concerns with any institutional referents, critical theory ever more surely began to conflate philosophical with political and aesthetic with social forms of resistance. And this is where the current problem arises. Critical theory can contribute further to developing a theory of modernism or a "negative" philosophy of history. It can also inquire more deeply into the commodity form, deepen the critique of technology, and illuminate new forms of discourse theory. Its possibilities are unlimited. But it cannot do everything at the same time or ignore the distinctions between the manifold spheres of social action. Its emphasis upon negativity is inherently abstract. Its "inversion" of concepts is satisfying to the spirit of neither Marx nor Nietzsche. A new commitment to political struggles has become necessary in order to provide critical theory with a degree of determination. This means its partisans must begin to situate themselves in relation to the past, identify what they wish to transform in the present, and articulate their vision of a liberated future. It means, in short, identifying critical theory with a reconstructive project grounded in concrete forms of solidarity.

PART II

Solidarity

Max Horkheimer once wrote, perhaps with a bit too romantic a flourish, that "the anonymous martyrs of the concentration camps are the symbols of a humanity that is striving to be born. The task of philosophy is to translate what they have done into language that will be heard." But, of course, there are other martyrs as well. Solidarity is just a word unless anchored in a political project. Such projects take different forms. The most dangerous, however, is one that breaks the connection between the universal and the particular. Solidarity is too easily manipulated when delimited in terms of purely racial or sexual as well as ethnic or national feelings and experiences. André Schwarz-Bart recognized this. *The Last of the Just*, wherein he depicted the loss of his family and his own experiences in the camps, is among the greatest evocations of the holocaust and its connection with the fabric of Jewish history. After moving to Guadeloupe, however, he wrote *A Woman Named Solitude*, in which he reconstructed a lost part of Caribbean history through the story of a slave who becomes a revolutionary. A recurrence of images and motifs takes place, and the novel ends with the thought of a modern tourist walking near the unmarked grave of the rebels. Thus, with a certain whimsy, the author can write: "If he is in the mood to salute a memory, his imagination will people the environing space, and human figures will rise up around him, just as the phantoms that wander about the humiliated ruins of the Warsaw ghetto are said to rise up before the eyes of other travelers."

Solidarity involves linking historical events, constituting a tradition of rebellion and suffering. His ability to do just that enables Schwarz-Bart to turn solidarity into more than simply an immediate feeling of compassion or an anthropological abstraction. But those were precisely the parameters in which the most famous proponents of critical theory defined it. Following Schopenhauer, for example, the young Horkheimer rooted solidarity in empathy for human suffering. An instinctual conception of solidarity underpins Herbert Marcuse's notion of the "new sensibility," Ernst Bloch's utopian category of the "we," and the subjectivity seen by Adorno as inherent within an artwork. The combination of immediacy and anthropology also plays a role in the anamnestic view of history developed by Walter Benjamin, more fruitfully in the humanism of Erich Fromm, and in all forms of "negative theology." Even Jürgen Habermas presupposes this combination of the two in his theory of moral evolution and communicative action. And all that has its place. But lacking are any derivative categories for coordinating action and, perhaps more important, any sense of the struggles deserving linkage. Solidarity becomes a matter of practical concern only when it informs a political judgment concerning conflicting public interests.

Habermas has tried. Communicative action in terms of the need for justifying claims discursively can be understood as presupposing empathy or solidarity. Empathy appears in the willingness of each to place himself or herself in the position of others in the communicative discourse. Solidarity is rendered equivalent with the "generalisable interests" and universalist assumptions located in the structure of language. The "moral point of view" is predicated, after all, only on what is common to all. Certain rules for communicative competence can be understood as existing within the structure of language. Simply denying this is foolish. The problem is that the salience of these rules is dependent upon the *prior commitment* to an equitable resolution of differences. In the same vein, the issue is not whether people *can* put themselves in the place of others, but whether they *will*. The "communicative" use of language conveys little when faced with intransigent interests, and making reference to the resulting "performative contradiction," when certain participants in the discourse do not follow its rules, serves as nothing more than a weak moral chastisement. Simply divorcing communication from instrumental concerns, or positing formal equality as a precondition for discourse, is insufficient for challenging their argument concretely.

Claims about the grounding provided by a "universal pragmatics," or any other such category, are illusory: they are nothing more than a retreat into metaphysics by a supposedly "postmetaphysical" philosophy. No "phenomenology of moral intuition" can speak to the ways in which substantive issues of exploitation and the imbalances of institutional power impinge upon contingent discourses. None have been able to deal with the fact that adhering to the normative implications of discourse is a matter of political and existential *choice*. None have much to say about the possibilities for translating solidarity or reciprocity into empirical reality. Even with a universal pragmatics, the need to choose between often mutually exclusive universal demands will not disappear simply by making reference to the rules of communicative action.

Contingency reasserts itself in practice if not in theory. Invocations about the need for reciprocal identification with the other in discourse, no less than concepts like what John Rawls termed the "veil of ignorance," render theory unable to understand the clash of interests and their effects. Idealistic categories of this sort always rest on the idealistic assumption, so sharply contested by Pierre Bourdieu and his followers, that the exploited is somehow merely the exploiter without riches or advantages. Uncritical preoccupation with what Nietzsche termed the "all too human" creates a situation in which, while identifying with the suffering of all, it becomes impossible to distinguish between the suffering of each. Reciprocity and solidarity become lifeless assumptions rather than *material interests in their own rights* capable of being denied or advanced. Indeed, this is what creates the nagging thought that perhaps the liberating implications residing within communicative interaction are seriously pursued only in the breach and that discourse ethics must quietly presuppose the very institutions in which its assumptions gain validity.

Solidarity is, of course, not simply reducible to matters of social or historical interests. It always harbors an element of transcendence. Were this not the case, according to Erich Fromm, people could never have confronted the values embedded in the dominant personality patterns of an epoch and united for radical aims. From the dominant standpoints of contemporary critical theory, however, solidarity loses its connection with reality. The concrete is either subsumed within the covering category or defined by the freedom it denies. Solidarity is left either hanging in the realm of metaphysical abstractions or drowning in empirical immediacy. It lacks reference to the choices informing action because the public interest recedes before the private sentiment. Critical theory must oppose this trend in the future. Solidarity becomes material only when consideration is given to competing views, policies, interests, and ideas on ending misery. That is why it cannot be imposed by philosophical fiat.

Accountability

Solidarity is no guarantee against the abuse of power. Issues concerning liberty must always make reference to the organizational arrangements through which interests might be rendered tractable and social institutions could be held accountable. Empowerment is consequently less a discursive concept than a political one. It is always the product of strategic action even if its aim involves the creation of institutions capable of reproducing norms consonant with an ongoing discourse among equals.

Accountability is the lynchpin for any institutional notion of empowerment. It connects knowledge and interest, and it binds the communitarian notion of popular sovereignty with liberal ideas of individual responsibility. It reflects a concern not only with the production but with the reproduction of relations empowering the disadvantaged. It rejects identifying democracy with the will of the majority or even participation. Accountability tempers such concern with respect for the rights of the minority and the problems pertaining to representation. It recognizes the positive role bureaucracies can play in furthering democracy and insists on confronting their petrifying tendencies so well analyzed by Max Weber. Accountability is not merely a metaphysical or discursive concept but the *practical fulcrum* for making judgments concerning the democratic character of existing institutions.

Empowerment is a process. It can take different forms and call for the primacy of different "standpoints" under different circumstances. New social movements have furthered equality under the law and transformed previously "private" issues like spousal abuse into matters of public concern. Indeed, they have challenged and changed the realm of everyday life. Unions and labor parties, by the same token, have historically waged the battle for economic equality and republican institutions. The priority accorded social movements and interest groups in relation to unions and organized parties will vary according to the given institutional context. No single organization like the labor movement of the nineteenth century, after all, is able any longer to extend both universality in the political domain and class-specific interests in the economic realm. Nevertheless, only in terms of this dual burden inherited from the labor movement is it possible for critical theory to deal with empowerment from the standpoint of both form and content.

Accountability speaks to this dual burden. Whatever the obvious contributions of the new social movements in the cultural realm, insofar as their identity claims have been created by particular interests, they have also generated a certain logic of political fragmentation along with an inability to contest the deteriorating economic conditions of working people. Unions, by the same token, have become increasingly fragmented, and preoccupied with the narrow economic concerns of their constituencies, while most labor parties have entered the mainstream and ignored issues dealing with identity or the quality of life under advanced capitalism. The whole has thereby become less than the sum of its parts. Coordination of "crosscutting" interests—class is obviously what they "cut across"—among the exploited has therefore become a matter of paramount concern. Capital and labor remain the two basic categories of the existing economic system. But they are either turned into simple interest groups by important pluralists like Robert Dahl who ignore the imbalance of structural power between them, or dismissed from the political discussion entirely by theorists like Hannah Arendt.

Empowerment requires a concern with the accountability of all social, political, and economic institutions. The exclusion of capital is purely arbitrary, and a class concept is necessary to contest its power as well as its ability to overcome the divisions between different *subaltern* groups and organizations. Such a category must link the formal equality sought by most of the new social movements with the interests specific to the working people within each; it must also confront petrifying labor organizations with their original reason for being. Politics must take precedence in bringing any worthwhile society into being. Neither economics or teleology can guarantee the employment of a *class ideal.*

No longer is it sensible to think of class in terms inherited from the nineteenth century. Working people may still serve as the precondition for any successful attempt to transform the accumulation process or restructure the political order. There is no longer a single organization capable of expressing their interests; indeed, their identities have been both fractured and broadened in a multitude of ways. Class conflict has, certainly for the time being, been "suspended" (Habermas); it has been pushed or displaced to the margins of society. Labor is no longer identifiable with the industrial working class, and stratification has helped shatter "class consciousness." The structural, empirical, and normative elements within the concept of class are, in short, no longer unified as they were during the last quarter of the nineteenth century. And the same holds true for the values of liberal democracy, economic justice, and internationalism. But these values remain necessary for developing any project concerned with increasing the public accountability of institutions, and future forms of critical theory must seek to reconnect them in a coherent fashion. This is possible only by confronting, once again, the issue of class. Empirical and structural inquiries are insufficient for such a task. More important is political judgment since the primacy accorded any constituent element of the class ideal will change from one set of contingent circumstances to another.

Formulating standards of accountability for differing institutional systems and subsystems, illuminating repressed contradictions within what Niklas Luhmann called the "autopoetic" processes of a complex bureaucratic society, can alone make empowerment concrete. Realizing accountability is possible only through democratic institutions. Commitment to the formal and universal elements of democracy must, for this reason, serve as the precondition for realizing substantive and particular aims. Only in this way is it possible to reject the trade-off, so reminiscent of cold war thinking, between civil rights and economic equity. A self-enforced blindness to questions of class and the structural imbalances of economic power, in this vein, will result in an abstraction not only from the accumulation process and its differentiated effects but from the constituting practice of various other institutional systems and subsystems as well. Opening the various subsystems of society to public pressure requires contesting the various hegemonic interests embedded within them.

A critical theory with public aims must deal with issues of this sort. Such a theory, however, must also be willing to speculate about the freest possible conditions in which individuals can reach intelligent decisions concerning the quality of their lives. A public philosophy has its limits. It can never decide on the existential "meaning" of life or a host of private issues ranging from sexual practice to euthanasia. But this need not simply relegate ethics to matters of procedure. Substantive judgments concerning dignity and the integrity of the individual are crucial for rendering judgments about conflicting generalizable concerns. A public philosophy cannot simply rest on the formal character of its claims but must recognize the way in which ideological controversy and the clash of interests is the stuff of democracy. A public ethic is, consequently, as little concerned with ontological questions of truth as with theological questions of grace. Contingency marks the new epoch. Too much is at stake, however, for using the concept to justify some poststructural reduction of philosophy into "play." Confronting the triumph of uncertainty means substituting an ethic that is contingent in its appeal and utility for any form of teleology and developing a new relation between theory and practice. There is no artificial substitute for an "agent," and for this reason, theory can now do nothing more than present the prerequisites for its realization.

An emancipated future is no longer appearing in the present. Opposing teleology consequently calls for tempering optimistic theories of moral evolution and discourse ethics as surely as the predictions of an outworn Marxism. There is no longer anything legitimate about metaphysically presupposing a fixed understanding of reflexivity, conscience, or the inherent desire of people to reconcile contradictions. New approaches in critical theory must squarely confront this reality without resorting to set categories of moral evolution, the "cunning of history," or inflexible economic laws. Judgment remains a "practical" necessity, and if only for this reason, theory still has a task. But it can function only if ethical questions are provided with a practical referent and practical questions with a normative framework for judgment. Therein lie its limits and possibilities. Thus, for the time being, connecting theory and practice can occur only from the standpoint of theory itself.

Autonomy

Autonomy was, for critical theory, the response to alienation and reification. It was, from the start, a reflexive concept with ethical connotations. Autonomy never had anything in common with license. Increasingly, however, the preoccupation with autonomy has begun to evince ever stronger affinities with what the young Hegel called "bad reflection," or the fear of entering the real. It has become self-referential, coterminous with the "totally other," the "great refusal," "higher praxis," or genuine "communication." Such exercises in "bad reflection" make it impossible to specify *what* tendencies are inhibiting the *exercise* of autonomy in *which* particular spheres. Thus, autonomy has turned in upon itself.

Concern with autonomy should exhibit a material component insofar as the exercise of human faculties depends upon certain economic, political, and social preconditions. Even Kant used the concept to anchor his theory of "practical reason," and, politically, its identification with individual responsibility made autonomy the core justification for republicanism. Civil liberties and the rule of law, human rights and popular sovereignty, all presuppose autonomy even as they seek to secure it universally through a public realm capable of protecting the weak from the arbitrary exercise of power by the privileged. For this reason, from the standpoint of practice, universalism and particularism do not stand in some rigidly antinomial relation with one another. The same is true of solidarity and autonomy. Following this line of thought, in fact, the partisans of democratic socialism pursued material equality precisely so that economic "necessity" would not intrude on the exercise of "freedom." Thus, Henry Pachter could identify a genuinely socialist order with "the highest stage of individualism."

Autonomy only makes sense with reference to accountable institutional forms capable of realizing reciprocal conditions for the free play of the faculties. But critical theory has had trouble conceiving of it in these terms, and part of the problem derives from identifying alienation and reification with objectification. The increasing dominance of instrumental reason was seen by various members of the Institute for Social Research as creating a situation in which any social or political action poses a threat to subjectivity. Only the aesthetic or philosophical inversion of public life was considered capable of redeeming authentic experience in the "totally administered society." Both for Marx and Lukács, however, coming to terms with reification involved empowering the exploited and disadvantaged through political action. They may have assumed that the proletariat was the revolutionary agent of history. But they assumed something else as well: the existence of responsible people with determinate political aims. Neither meant to imply that working people *are* things and that subjects *are* objects. Crucial for their understanding of the commodity form were how working people were treated by dominant institutions and treat one another, the values of the existing order, and the extent to which workers are defined as a mere cost of production by capital.

Focusing on this concrete referent for reification produces the preoccupation with empowerment and the accountability of institutions. Contesting reification requires the image of a world in which no subject is treated as an object or means to an instrumental end. This indeed is the point on which the *critical* theories of Kant and Marx converge. Such a world is one in which the institutional space and material conditions are created for the constant enrichment and the permanent revolution of subjectivity. Certain forms of political activity can help bring us closer to such a world, and for this reason, reification is not interchangeable with objectification or the mere externalization of subjectivity. Indeed, for this same reason, neither concept is identifiable with alienation. Alienation generates little interest in reforms or revolution. It lacks a determinate referent and, for this reason, creates a concern with the apocalypse and utopia.

Alienation expresses the "poverty of the interior" (Benjamin). It is not concerned with externalization at all. Alienation is existential in character and speaks to issues like loneliness, death, and the lack or source of ultimate meaning. These are real concerns, and there is no sense in simply condemning them as mystical or irrational. Arguably, in fact, the radical purpose of abolishing reification is so that each can come to terms with private matters of this sort in his or her own way without the intrusion of institutional dogmas like the fear of hell or the economic needs of everyday life. Indeed, there is a sense in which autonomy does involve becoming sovereign over what Martin Heidegger called "one's ownmost possibility."

"*Ecrasez l'infâme*," the famous words flung by Voltaire at religious fanaticism must now receive a new and expanded meaning. Old prejudices and provincial beliefs, along with the institutions profiting from them, must receive a new form of criticism. Sensitivity for existential problems must combine with a commitment to broaden the public space in which autonomy is exercised. For all that, however, the proponents of critical theory cannot deceive themselves. No theory can offer magic remedies for alienation. Loneliness and death will not disappear. Dealing with them through the mores of a "new sensibility" might indirectly temper the experience of alienation. But subjectivity will always recede behind the veil of politics, and the longing for utopia or the "wholly other" will remain. There is an obvious danger in burdening political action with limitless expectations or viewing empowerment as a series of steps on the road to utopia.

Alienation and reification speak to different domains of existence, and dealing with the one does not invalidate the importance of the other. There are even points of overlap. To consider the commodity form, for example, qualitative differences between objects are still ever more surely being reduced to quantitative ones and the "labor power" sold by individuals on the market is ultimately still being evaluated by the employer no differently than any other resource. But this is all taking a new and more radical form insofar as the subversion of reflexive capacities is increasingly becoming fused with the expansion of choices. Amid a staggering literacy crisis, and an invasion of the private sphere by mass media in ways even Balzac and Flaubert could never have imagined, the subject now faces an expanding number of material decisions with existential import. Violence, environmental decay, the difficulties in accessing scores of new information, and making choices about matters ranging from cloning to euthanasia, impinge on the existential experience of existence. It is the task of critical theory to judge just how well society is preparing the subject for this expanded realm of decision making.

Autonomy means being able to choose between cultural and political options. Its public exercise still presupposes reflexivity, which depends upon education. For this reason, critical theory has an important role to play in developing new forms of pedagogy and contesting both the narrow ways in which "culture" is transmitted and the avoidance of questions concerning "quality" in modern life. Without making reference to education and reflexivity, in fact, speaking of autonomy makes no sense at all. Indifference undermines its exercise. One choice will become the same as another even as alternatives increase. Autonomy will, under these circumstances, ever more surely degenerate into cynical forms of anomie. Inhibiting choices by which the individual might enhance the control of his or her destiny, by the same token, is not a viable option: it only fosters the arbitrary exercise of power and resentment. The point is rather to develop secular rules of conduct linked with a sense of human possibility. Critical theory will soon have to begin thinking about how new advances in parapsychology, space travel, cybernetics, and holograms might affect the existential encounter of the subject with his or her world. Notions like the "end of history" and the "end of art" all entail metaphysical judgments. Technology continues to develop, and coming to terms with it will demand a rejection of the assumptions formed in the postmodern night in which all cats are gray. Indeed, conceiving of the future as unfinished is less a theoretical problem than a practical one.

PART III

Aesthetics

John Dewey once said that aesthetics involves the "ultimate judgment on the quality of civilization." It only makes sense then that virtually every major representative of critical theory should have produced studies on art and the ways in which given works and styles of music, poetry, film, and literature reflect certain historical and anthropological experiences. The contextual referent never entirely vanished from the cultural criticism of the Frankfurt School, and it remained dominant in the work of Leo Lowenthal. But it clearly grew less important in the aesthetic theory of Adorno, Benjamin, Marcuse, and even Siegfried Kracauer. Especially following World War II, in keeping with philosophical developments, a preoccupation with form over content marked the greatest aesthetic achievements of critical theory. Both its unequivocal allegiance to modernism and its famous analysis of the culture industry were anchored in the emphasis on form. And that only makes sense. The history of modernism coincides with an elimination of the representational object in the name of color or line; consider, for example, the dynamic leading from the haystacks of Monet to the fauves and Kandinsky as well as the road leading from Cézanne's Mont Sainte-Victoire and Chateau Noir to the cubists and the constructivists. Subjectivity affirms its autonomy from the objective world precisely insofar as form vanquishes representation in an effort to capture an "authentic" content.

Autonomy and the unique experience generated by modernism are, by the same token, precisely what the culture industry is seen as subverting through its emphasis on the lowest common denominator and its desire to assure the greatest possible profits. Classicism and realism, with their contemplative concern for the representational object and commitment to narrative, offer no resistance. Their formal conservatism makes their more radical elements particularly susceptible to "nullification" by the culture industry. According to Lowenthal's interpretation of classical French drama, in fact, the "realist" critique of society is seen as occurring simultaneously with the gradual elimination of unique subjective experience. Adorno recognized that the radical elements of modernism are also open to absorption. With its affirmation of subjectivity and formal innovations like montage, however, modernism was seen as providing the only bulwark against the conformism generated by the extension of the commodity form into the cultural realm. The future looked bleak. Aesthetic resistance to the culture industry would now require the commitment either to utopia or ambiguity.

According to Herbert Marcuse, whose views were based on a tradition extending from Schiller to Breton, aesthetic resistance was predicated on the projection of utopia. Cultural norms would inform a new sensibility capable of envisioning the emancipated life-world, and the "pacification of existence" would serve as the critical referent for contesting advanced industrial society and the commodity form. A confusion between political and cultural practice, however, takes place. The aesthetic projection of utopia winds up substituting for the determination of emancipatory social or political institutions even while the particular work of art and the categories for dealing with it vanish from critical inquiry. By contrast, Theodor Adorno provides the work with primacy to the point where its inner dynamics actually generate the categories, or characteristics, making for its interpretation. Reception is no longer an important category of aesthetic understanding precisely because the culture industry has already impinged upon the autonomous exercise of subjectivity. The work with its paradoxical ability to resist the conditions of its own genesis preserves subjectivity in an objective fashion, forges a mimetic content through reflexive means, and creates a unique inner language through technique. It resists the omnivorous culture industry, in short, by producing an inversion of sociological categories. Thus, the identity of the artwork lies in its ability to strengthen the tensions underlying the nonidentity between subject and object.

Both Marcuse and Adorno essentially begin with a metacritique of the culture industry. Its products are essentially dismissed a priori. Neither provides categories for making qualitative distinctions between different works developed within different traditions, styles, and genres. Sociologically, of course, it is legitimate to forward general claims concerning the negative effects of the culture industry. Aesthetically, however, it is mistaken to simply deny the culture industry and to reject its numerous works of high quality. With the exception of Benjamin and Kracauer, however, an unyielding emphasis on aesthetic form and complex techniques combined with old-fashioned elitism made most proponents of critical theory blind to this possibility. A metacritique of the culture industry makes no sense if it must assume that the dove of Picasso or any other "popular" work can produce enlightenment only in the form of "mass deception." Works of popular culture deserve the same serious treatment as those generally interpreted from the perspective of high art. They too exist within a context and manifest its contradictions; they too are defined within genres and influenced by manifold traditions; indeed, they too *can* evidence critical and emancipatory elements. None of this calls for a suspension of critical judgment. Quite the contrary. Precisely because the culture industry is eradicating perceived differences in quality, which is in keeping with the imperatives of the commodity form, aesthetics must privilege the category of judgment.

Aesthetics can only reassert its salience by applying its methods to practical problems. Old concerns about the nature of aesthetic "experience" have lost their relevance given the ability of the culture industry to create and fulfill a variety of existential needs. Subjectivity is now less threatened than overwhelmed. Arguing for modernism over realism, or nonrepresentation against representation, is irrelevant given the dominance of an industry capable of generating a plethora of styles in any number of genres. Nor is it any longer legitimate to maintain that "art" inherently projects freedom or a vision of emancipation. This assumes what the interpretation must demonstrate. Art has no predetermined purpose, and neither its "meaning" nor its "potential" nor its "contribution" is usually self-evident. Fostering resistance or reflexivity, for example, no more defines music than the limitless ways in which popular songs give rise to various dances or become associated with an equally limitless set of personal memories. There is a place for the *private*, or what Kant called the "purposefully purposeless," experience of an artwork in which *public* judgment is simply irrelevant.

But the two should not be confused. Radical aesthetics must recognize that the work of art does not generate the norms for either its application or its appropriation. A work of art, just like a particular tradition, can simultaneously offer progressive impulses for cultural production and regressive implications for politics, and vice versa. Critical aesthetics should respect the tensions between different spheres of activity even as it seeks to expand the alternatives of cultural experience. This cannot occur, however, by obsessing over the autonomy of art or the technical complexity supposedly required for "resistance." Better to distinguish between works and the radical possibilities that they *may or may not evidence*. Resistance is meaningful only insofar as the subject is able to make meaningful choices among an ever-increasing variety of cultural products. Or, put another way, a genuine commitment to diversity involves judgment. The problem is that the culture industry *tends* to crowd out works that militate against the lowest common denominator. Working people learn little about the "classics" or their salience, and, in turn, this narrowing of aesthetic experience is justified through relativism. Critical aesthetics must consequently eject both its more elitist and its more populist tendencies. It must commit itself to increasing diversity while, in Benjamin's phrase, "never forgetting the best." That is a difficult task, and it requires a return to the work. By the same token, however, what Marx termed "the material level of culture" remains a genuine issue. Raising it will always involve criticism by bohemians, nonconformists, and those whom reactionaries like Maurice Barrés liked to call "rootless cosmopolitans." Aesthetics will always have a special place for such people. Indeed, therein lies its special power.

Nature

The harnessing of nature once seemed closely linked with the philosophical promise of the good life. Technology projected both empowerment and the transformation of dead nature into a live world of commodities. Critical theory played an important role in dispelling such illusions. Its willingness to emphasize the human price of progress, the costs of alienation and reification, the implications of scientific reason for moral capacities, and the potential "revenge of nature" were all major contributions. The increasing fear of everything associated with instrumental rationality, however, sundered whatever fruitful interchange Max Horkheimer had originally envisioned between critical theory and the empirical sciences. Nature increasingly became pitted against technology, while "science" was engaged either sociologically or from the utopian perspective of a "new" type whose categories and criteria were never fully articulated. But there was a kernel of truth in the often exaggerated criticisms of empiricism and positivism. Skepticism concerning the technological definition of progress was also surely warranted, and if the proponents of critical theory generally ignored new theoretical developments in the philosophy of science, they surely anticipated many contemporary concerns of the ecology movement.

Each age defines its problems. Ecology first became an issue in advanced industrial society just as "society" only appeared as an object of concern in the industrial age. Coming to terms with either becomes merely a metaphysical exercise without this kind of historical perspective. The institutions of modernity remain necessary for dealing with what modernity has produced. A degree of bureaucracy and planning is unavoidable in mitigating what is rapidly becoming an environmental nightmare. What makes the process so difficult, however, is that an ever more complex division of labor has seemingly bedeviled administrative decision making. Linear notions of scientific development have fallen before the new preoccupation with "paradigm shifts." There is also little consensus concerning what values and political priorities are intrinsically connected with developing sustainable forms of ecologically sound production.

There are new risks for planetary society. Without even considering purely metaphysical questions of grounding the "scientific method," which is less important in practice than many theorists might believe, specialists in different fields of scientific endeavor increasingly find themselves unable to communicate with one another on the most advanced planes of research. Consequences of previously unimaginable ecological horror now seem attendant on the most routine decisions of an administrative apparatus defined by what Hannah Arendt originally called the "rule of nobody." The impact of an oil spill is incalculable. The very dynamism of modern technology, the geometrically increasing set of unintended consequences for every technological act, fosters a growing refusal to accept responsibility, which has itself become ever more difficult to assign due to the proliferation of institutional subsystems, committees, and the like. Technological change is transforming the existential character of decision making by forcing individuals to deal with issues ranging from cloning to personal appearance. Movements can raise issues and pressure existing institutions. Ultimately, however, adjustment will depend upon the ability of the organizations generating ecological and other forms of risk to reform themselves through what Ulrich Beck described as "reflexive modernization."

Critique should, however, no longer be limited to particular institutions or subsystems. Commodities like oil link them together: they affect planetary society from the foreign relations undertaken by its most industrially developed governments to the ways we breathe, and the spills that devastate the environment, to the derivative products produced by economic subsystems. Perhaps there is an ongoing "reflexive" or self-critical moment to modernization. But certain institutions clearly profit by the production of risk, and are usually the most seminal and powerful industries of society, while working people and the poor will suffer from it the most. There is no reason to believe that the mere recognition of future risks will somehow cause the oil industry or nuclear energy to "reform" themselves. Class interests insinuate themselves into the new society and organizational pressure is required to curb them. There is ultimately no way around it: achieving accountability with respect to nature requires achieving accountability with respect to production.

Utopian plans for rolling back technology or offering unformulated versions of a "new science," by the same token, don't help matters. New bureaucratic institutions and new forms of technology will, ironically, become necessary to constrain ecologically devastating forms of production *before they are introduced*. New developments in critical theory must therefore enter into the discussion about the direction of technology and the social character not of science but of the ethical implications generated by particular forms of research. Practical matters will come into play concerning the ways in which government can influence ecologically sound production, provide subsidies or tax benefits for particular industries, fund particular forms of knowledge creation, and make risks a matter of public debate. But there are also ethical matters pertaining to the status of humans in nature and animal rights. Advocates of critical theory must invigorate the commitment to turn ecological spoilage and cruelty to sentient beings into political issues. It will also have to revise older definitions of "evidence" and culpability in order to meet the needs of a society whose interaction with nature is ever more defined by complex developments in science, technology, and administrative management. Nature projects the need for new understandings of responsibility and accountability as well as the importance of forging a "new sensibility." Indeed, if the critical engagement with progress is to continue, it will have to generate a new perspective beyond the prevailing forms of anthropocentrism.

Progress has always worked behind the backs of the masses. Imprisoned within the private realm of the subject, ethics could not respond to a scientific method whose extension seemed to permit of no alternatives. The complexity of science and its neutrality with respect to means, which seemingly justifies a closed debate among experts, became the basis for an often uncritical acceptance of purposive ends generated without reference to democratic will formation. Focusing on internal issues pertaining to the methodological conduct of research thus actually perpetuates the reification of society. The issue is less the scientific method than the manner in which technology crystallizes social goals. It is incumbent upon critical theory to prevent the scientific enterprise from remaining identified with the discourse of experts.

A new understanding of progress will develop only insofar as the public has an input into its definition. A democratic critique of technology is, following André Gorz, the basis for any "revolutionary reform" of society. But too much time has been spent, especially by those who lack any genuine scientific expertise, on deconstructing the scientific method. More important are sustained critical inquiries into the institutional complexes, with their particular balance of forces, wherein the scientific method receives its purposive aims and social content. Retreating into the realm of scientific procedure is too often a way of avoiding questions concerning the normative content of social choices. Dealing with such issues *critically* is impossible without a substantive interest in reasserting the lost connection between critical theory and the empirical sciences no less than with the movements and political organizations seeking to effect ecological change.

Instituting new technological priorities and ethical parameters for the human interchange with nature is inherently what Ernst Bloch would have called a "world experiment." Ecology serves the new motor for internationalism precisely because a disaster like Chernobyl is limited neither by time nor space. The very difficulty of assigning responsibility or providing compensation calls forth a cosmopolitan commitment as surely as the need to control a rapacious set of multinationals. Ongoing despoliation of the planet may not ultimately bring about the final crisis of capitalism. Ecological concerns will, however, surely help set the parameters for any new progressive views on the accumulation process in a democratic polity as well as any future definition of social equity or internationalism. They raise the need to reconsider the notion of progress and human well-being. Indeed, precisely to that extent, confronting the domination of nature immanently raises the question of utopia.

Utopia

History has not been kind to utopia, perhaps because there is no way ever to deliver on what it promises. Utopia is the response to alienation, and for that very reason, it always retains an element of otherness. But that doesn't obliterate its practical importance. Utopian longing has inspired the most extraordinary sacrifices and the grandest undertakings. These have always given way to resentment following their betrayal, and with every failed experiment in liberation, of which communism is only the most recent example, utopia has been buried anew. But then it seems again to rise from the dead. Utopia is "nowhere." But its traces appear every time solidarity triumphs over self-interest. Speaking about "the end of utopia," like Judith Shklar, thus simply misses the point.

Every experiment in social change presupposes a certain notion of the "best life." Each assumes, in its own way and after its own fashion, that things can be different. Glowing like the biblical "burning bush," with which Manés Sperber associated it in his great novel *Like a Tear in the Ocean*, utopia constantly rekindles the dreams of the lowly and the insulted. It forms the underside of history, and in this regard, the preoccupation of critical theory with the concept was only logical. The utopian imagination opened materialism to a host of repressed and unrealized possibilities. It offered a certain standard with which to judge the repression of the present and provided the future with an emancipatory legacy from the past.

Transcendence is not inimical to immanence. Both are moments of revolutionary practice. Fantasy and happiness, beauty and wonder, have often inspired what in the moment of execution can only have appeared as inherently "anticipatory" enterprises of social or political change. Karl Mannheim was aware that the neglect of utopia constituted a serious failing of all "realistic" theories. Even a critical theory reinvigorated by the insights of pragmatism cannot afford to ignore the practical role of the *novum*. Marx, of course, was always justifiably wary of attempting to depict the emancipated communist society of the future. He had only contempt for the "system builders" and moralists concerned with making dogmatic claims about the "good." Marx could indulge in such irony, however, because he considered his own theory capable of "objectively" explaining how an alternative to the prevailing course of history would arise within history itself. Perhaps there is still a place for such forms of "scientific" endeavor. But the teleology of times past is no longer plausible. Ernst Bloch probably has the most to offer for the development of a new philosophy of history in which transcendence is linked with immanence. Even his utopian theory, however, is still grounded in the ontological and teleological assumptions of an earlier time.

"Negative dialectics" sought to break the connection between utopia and teleology. Its points of reference for any new understanding of utopia were the previously unimaginable horrors of the 1930s and 1940s. Just as Auschwitz was seen as the final and most compelling reason for the Jewish injunction against depicting God, or the absolute, the ability to depict utopia was denied. The fungible quality of utopia and its sensuous appeal remain. In projecting utopia beyond the realm of even symbolic action, however, transcendence became turned into an inexpressible quality of the individual imagination. "Otherworldliness" (*Jenseitigkeit*) became an end unto itself through notions of the "totally other" and the "yearning" for God no less than in the fleeting moment of aesthetic experience and anamnestic remembrance. Reification as the mutable experience of exploitation thereby became ignored in favor of the unrealizable apocalyptic response to alienation. Utopia turned its back on history and, for once, it really was exiled to "nowhere." Utopia became a content devoid of form.

Others within the tradition of critical theory would view the matter differently. They would interpret utopia as a regulative ideal that is asymptotically connected with any given form of practice as a complex of procedural rules for communication. Democratic institutions and values obviously serve as preconditions for this understanding of utopia. Its character is, by the same token, considered irreducible to any particular substantive aim or public good. That is because, as Habermas correctly noted, progress achieved in one systemic domain can produce regression in another, and there is a danger of dogmatism in venturing substantive judgments on the relative merits of one culture or set of traditions against another. The image of a "best" order, in any event, appears immanent within the sense of "justice" rather than transcendent in its assumptions about the "good." Conditions for the reproduction of utopia thus define the understanding of it: utopia is left as a form without a content.

What unites both of these positions is the recognition that utopia is always *more* than what the real can offer. Unfortunately, however, both also ignore the way in which everyday life under the commodity form both prefigures its character and generates its usually unacknowledged appeal. It is in everyday life that utopia confronts the reality of death, inner and outer poverty, ugliness, and the destruction of nature. Utopia can conceptually illuminate repressed needs and even help provide insights into what Ernst Bloch termed the ratio of the irratio. But the paradox concerning utopia derives from the way in which attempts to render impulses toward the "best life"concrete always push it further away. The pursuit of social change— inspired, whether consciously or unconsciously, by utopian visions—generates new, if often qualitatively different, forms of alienation. Perhaps that is because no matter what the connection between principle and interest—and that connection is real—the tension between them remains always incapable of complete resolution.

This indeed calls for understanding utopia in a new way: it should be considered as the "totally other" even as its totalizing aspirations should be denied. Utopia must be seen as existing in a state of tension; every struggle and every theory must remain content with indicating its asymptotic relation to reality. Utopia always eludes the real. But following Jacques Derrida, its absence indicates its presence. Utopia is not an anthropological break. It is not merely pacification, it is also growth. It is not simply play, it is also *l'esprit serieux*. It is not just spontaneity, but order. It is not only a higher form of intuition, but also knowledge. It is not only the future or anticipations of space travel and parapsychology, but remembrance and logic. It is not merely mimesis, but reflexivity. It is freedom and it is license. Thus, utopia should perhaps be seen.

The "best life" can never be encompassed by a fixed and finished system. It is always closer to a sketch than a painting or a drawing. Both the painting and the drawing are complete; they integrate their diverse components, place them in motion against one another, and project beyond the context. Sketches are always incomplete. They are often little more than half-visible outlines of a seemingly indeterminate content. That is why the sketch cannot dictate how an artist *must* employ contrasts of tone, shadow, and color in a painting. Each is open to employment in a different way, in one part of the sketch or another, and each is open to being redrawn or withdrawn. Sketches, however, retain their inner logic. The best offer constructive insights into the problems internal to a particular artistic undertaking and the terms in which the struggle to resolve them will be waged. The indeterminacy of a sketch can actually provide the future work with a degree of determination. It lets the eye play, gives a sense of direction, and offers a set of coordinates. Only the sketch can make visible the unfinished painting of the future.

NOTES

NOTES TO CHAPTER 2

1. Modern idealist philosophy, in short, "sets itself the following problem: it refuses to accept the world as something that has arisen (e.g. has been created by God) independently of the knowing subject, and prefers to conceive of it instead as its own product." Georg Lukács, *History and Class Consciousness: Studies in Marxist Dialectics*, trans. Rodney Livingstone (Cambridge, 1971), 111.

2. Kant believed he had "indicated the limits of reason with regard to all cognition of mere beings of thought. Now, since the transcendental ideas have urged us to approach them and thus have led us, as it were, to the spot where the occupied space (viz. Experience) touches the void (that of which he can know nothing, viz. Noumena) we can determine the bounds of pure reason." Immanuel Kant, *Prolegomena to Any Future Metaphysics*, trans. Paul Carus and revised by James W. Ellington (Indianapolis, 1977), 94.

3. "Thus we shall have to investigate purely *a priori* the possibility of a categorical imperative, for we do not have the advantage that experience would give us the reality of this imperative, so the [demonstrations of its] possibility would be necessary only for its explanation and not for its establishment. In the meantime, this much at least may be seen: the categorical imperative alone can be taken as a practical law ... This is because what is necessary merely for the attainment of an arbitrary purpose can be regarded as itself contingent, and we get rid of the precept once we give up the purpose, whereas the unconditional command leaves the will no freedom to choose the opposite. Thus it alone implies the necessity which we require of law ... It is: Act only according to that maxim by which you can at the same time will that it should become universal law." Immanuel Kant, *Foundations of the Metaphysics of Morals*, trans. Lewis White Beck, ed. Robert Paul Wolff (Indianapolis, 1969), 43–44.

4. Ibid., 52.

5. Immanuel Kant, "Idea for a Universal History with a Cosmopolitan Purpose," in *Kant's Political Writings*, trans. H. B. Nisbet and ed. Hans Reiss (Cambridge, 1970), 42.

6. "Confronted by the sorry spectacle not only of those evils which befall mankind from natural causes, but also of those which men inflict upon one another, our spirits can be raised by the prospect of future improvements. This, however, calls for unselfish good will on our part, since we shall have been long dead and buried when the fruits we helped to sow are harvested." Immanuel Kant, "On the Common Saying: 'This may be True in Theory, but it does not Apply in Practice' in *Kant's Political Writings* 89; Kant, *Foundations of the Metaphysics of Morals*, 11ff.

7. Immanuel Kant, "An Answer to the Question: 'What is Enlightenment?'", in *Kant's Political Writings*, 59.

8. "For Kant the moment to rebel is the moment when freedom of opinion is abolished." Hannah Arendt, *Lectures on Kant's Political Philosophy*, ed. Ronald Beiner (Chicago, 1982), 50.

9. Theodor Adorno, *Aesthetic Theory*, trans. C. Lenhardt, ed. Gretel Adorno and Rolf Tiedemann (London, 1984), 247, 320, 467, and passim.

10. J. G. Fichte, *Addresses to the German Nation*, trans. R. F. Jones and G. H. Turnbull (Chicago, 1922), and *Der geschlossene Handlesstaat* (Tübingen, 1800). For an overview of Fichte's philosophy, Frederick Copleston, S. J., *A History of Philosophy*, vol. 7, part I (New York, 1963), 50–120, and Frank Thalirdas, *German Political Idealism* (New Jersey, 1980), 107–49. Also of interest, G. W. F. Hegel, *Geschichte der Philosophie, 3 Bde.* (Leipzig, 1971 ed.), vol. III, 547–82.

11. J. G. Fichte, "*Über den Begriff der Wissenschaftslehre*," in *Werke*, vol. 1 (Berlin, 1845), 434; *The Science of Ethics*, trans. A. E. Kroeger (London, 1889). For a superb discussion, cf. Jürgen Habermas, *Knowledge and Human Interests*, trans. Jeremy J. Shapiro (Boston, 1972), pp. 205–10.

12. Ernst Cassirer, *Kant's Life and Thought*, trans. James Haden (New Haven, 1981), pg. 365.

13. Ernst Bloch, *Das Materialismusproble, Seine Geschichte und Substanz* (Frankfurt, 1972); Georg Lukács, *Der junge Hegel*, 2 Bde. (Frankfurt, 1973 ed.); G. V. Plekhanov, *Fundamental Problems of Marxism* (New York, 1971); Alfred Schmidt, *The Concept of Nature in Marx*, trans. Ben Fowkes (London, 1972).

14. Friedrich Schelling, *Ideen zu einer Philosophie der Natur* (Leipzig, 1797) and, above all, his *System der transzendentalen Idealismus* (Tübingen, 1800). For an overview, Ernst Cassirer, *Das Erkenntnisproblem in der Philosophie und Wissenschaft der neueren Zeit*, vol. III (Berlin, 1920), and Copleston, *History of Philosophy*, vol. 7, part I, 121–82.

15. Jürgen Habermas, *Theory and Practice*, trans. John Viertel (Boston, 1970), 261.

16. While coediting the *Critical Journal of Philosophy* with Schelling, Hegel was originally considered as a follower of his younger friend when he wrote his first important work, "Differenz des Fichte'schen und Schelling'shen Systems der Philosophie," in *Werke*, vol. 1 (Frankfurt, 1970 ed.). For Hegel's mature evaluation see Hegel, *Geschichte der Philosophie*, vol. III, 582ff. On the background, Horst Althaus, *Hegel und die heroischen Jahre der Philosophie* (München, 1992), 36ff and 59ff.

17. In particular, see Karl Jaspers, *Schelling: Grösse und Verhängnis* (München, 1955).

18. "What distinguishes Hegel's mode of thought from that of all other philosophers was the tremendous sense of the historical upon which it was based. Abstract and idealist though it was in form, yet the development of his thought always proceeded parallel with the development of world history and the latter is really meant to be only the test of the former. If, thereby, the real relation was inverted and stood on its head, nevertheless the real content entered everywhere into the philosophy." Karl Marx, "Contributions to the Critique of Political Economy," in Karl Marx and Frederick Engels, *Selected Works*, 3 vols. (Moscow, 1969), vol. 1, 512.

19. The most important partisans of critical theory would ultimately understand Marxian methodology in these terms; each after his fashion would attempt "the application of the materialist conception of history to the materialist conception of history itself." Karl Korsch, *Marxism and Philosophy*, trans. Fred Halliday (London, 1970), 92.

20. Karl Lowith, *From Hegel to Nietzsche: The Revolution in Nineteenth Century Thought*, trans. David Green (New York, 1967 ed.), 50–135 and passim.

21. "But, what must, in fact, be said here is this: that in Hegel the views developed above are not so sharply delineated. They are a necessary conclusion of his method, but one which he himself never drew with such explicitness. And this indeed for the simple reason that he was compelled to make a system and, in accordance with traditional requirements, a system of philosophy must conclude with some sort of absolute truth. Therefore, however much Hegel, especially in his *Logic*, emphasized that his eternal truth is nothing but the logical, or the historical process itself, he nevertheless finds himself compelled to supply this process with an end, just because he has to bring his

system to a termination at some point or other . . . But at the end of the whole philosophy a similar return to the beginning is only possible in one way. Namely by conceiving of the end of history as follows: Mankind arrives at the cognition of this selfsame absolute idea and declares that this cognition of the absolute is reached in Hegelian philosophy. In this way, however, the whole dogmatic content of the Hegelian system is declared to be absolute truth, in contradiction to his dialectical method, which dissolves all dogmatism. Thus the revolutionary side is smothered beneath the overgrowth of the conservative side. And what applies to philosophical cognition applies also to historical practice. Frederick Engels, "Ludwig Feuerbach and the End of Classical German Philosophy," in *Selected Works*, vol. 3, 340.

22. Löwith, *From Hegel to Nietzsche*, 84.
23. Alexandre Kojéve, *Introduction to the Reading of Hegel*, trans. James H. Nichols, Jr., ed. Allan Bloom (New York, 1969), 232.
24. Georg Wilhelm Friedrich Hegel, *The Philosophy of History*, trans. J. Sibree (New York, 1956), 19.
25. "As long as the things-in-themselves were beyond the capacity of reason, reason remained a mere subjective principle without power over the objective structure of reality. And the world thus fell into two separate parts, subjectivity and objectivity, understanding and sense . . . The Kantian philosophy left a gulf between thought and being, or between subject and object, which the Hegelian philosophy sought to bridge. The bridge was to be made by positing one universal structure for all being." Herbert Marcuse, *Reason and Revolution: Hegel and the Rise of Social Theory* (Boston,) 23,63.
26. G. W. F. Hegel, *The Phenomenology of Mind*, trans. J. B. Baillie (New York, 1967), 228ff.
27. Theodor Adorno, *Negative Dialectics*, 406.
28. George Lichtheim, "Reason and Revolution," in *Collected Essays* (New York, 1973), 356.
29. Marcuse, *Reason and Revolution*, 110.
30. Karl Marx, *Economic and Philosophic Manuscripts of 1844*, ed. Dirk J. Struik (New York, 1964), 140.
31. Ibid., 67.
32. Karl Marx, *Capital: A Critique of Political Economy*, 3 vols., trans. Samuel Moore and Edward Aveling (New York, 1967 ed.), vol. 1, 71–84.
33. Marx, *Economic and Philosophic Manuscripts*, 110.
34. Marx, *Capital*, 1:621.
35. V.I.Lenin, *Collected Works* (London, 1963), vol. 38, 276.
36. Lukács, *History and Class Consciousness.*, 1ff.
37. Ibid., 83ff.
38. Note the superb review of the *Economic and Philosophic Manuscripts* written on their publication by Herbert Marcuse in *Studies in Classical European Philosophy* (Boston, 1973), 1–48.
39. Lukács, *History and Class Consciousness*, 46ff.
40. Ibid., 295ff.
41. Later in his career, Lukács would suggest that there were certain ontological prerequisites of labor that, while contributing to alienation, were ineradicable: the argument underpins his self-critical "Preface to the New Edition" of 1967 regarding the idealism and utopianism of *History and Class Consciousness*. Also note the unfinished last work of Georg Lukács, *The Ontology of Social Being: Labour*, trans. David Fernbach (London, 1978).
42. Stephen Eric Bronner, *Socialism Unbound*, 2d ed. (Boulder, 2001), 84ff.
43. Leon Trotsky, *Literature and Revolution*, trans. Rose Strunsky (Ann Arbor, 1960), 256.
44. Georg Lukács, *Die Zerstörung der Vernunft*, 3 Bde. (Neuwied, 1974 ed.), vol. II, 7–152, vol. III, 7–39; Barbara Drygulski Wright, "Sublime Ambition: Art, Politics, and Ethical Idealism in the Cultural Journals of German Expressionism," in *Passion and Rebellion:*

The Expressionist Heritage, eds. Stephen Eric Bronner and Douglas Kellner (New York, 1988), 82ff; Andrew Arato, "The Neo-Idealist Defense of Subjectivity," in *Telos* 21 (Fall 1974), 108–61.

45. Martin Heidegger, *Being and Time*, trans. John Macquarrie and Edward Robinson (New York, 1962), 32ff.

46. Martin Heidegger, *Hegel's Concept of Experience* (New York, 1970).

47. Herbert Marcuse, *One-Dimensional Man: Studies in the Ideology of Advanced Industrial Society* (Boston, 1964).

48. Theodor W. Adorno, *Negative Dialectics*, trans. E. B. Ashton (New York, 1973), 3.

49. For the most lucid general overview of his work, see Martin Jay, *Adorno* (Cambridge, 1984).

50. Henry Pachter, "The Idea of Progress in Marxism," in *Socialism in History: Political Essays of Henry Pachter*, ed. Stephen Eric Bronner, (New York, 1984), 65ff.

51. A place to begin might be the approach, which has little in common with critical theory, embraced by Amartya Sen, *Development as Freedom* (New York, 1999).

52. Note the general discussion of this theme by Karl Korsch, *Kernpunkte der materialistischen Geschichtsauffassung: Eine quellenmässige Darstellung* (Berlin, 1922).

53. Note the relevant sections in Theodor W. Adorno et al., *The Positivist Dispute in German Sociology*, trans. Glyn Adey and David Frisby (London, 1976).

54. The matter is put succinctly in the phrase "there is no compromise between science and speculative philosophy." Hans Reichenbach, *The Rise of Scientific Philosophy* (Berkeley, 1951), 73.

55. "The productive forces appear as a world for themselves quite independent of and divorced from the individuals, alongside the individuals: the reason for this is that the individuals, whose forces they are, exist split up and in opposition to one another, whilst, on the other hand, these forces are only real forces in the intercourse and association of these individuals. Thus, on the one hand, we have a totality of productive forces which have, as it were, taken on a material form and are for the individuals no longer the forces of the individuals, but of private property and hence of the individuals only insofar as they are owners of private property themselves. Never in any earlier period, have the productive forces taken on a form so indifferent to the intercourse of individuals *as* individuals, because their intercourse itself was formerly a restricted one. On the other hand, standing over and against these productive forces, we have the majority of individuals from whom these forces have been wrested away and who, robbed of all real-life content, have become abstract individuals, but who are, however, only by this fact put into a position to enter into relation with one another as individuals." Karl Marx and Friedrich Engels, *The German Ideology* (Moscow, 1964), 82–83.

56. "History is nothing but the succession of the separate generations, each of which exploits the materials, the capital funds, the productive forces handed down to it by all preceding generations, and thus, on the one hand, continues the traditional activity in completely changed circumstances and, on the other, modifies the old circumstances with a completely changed activity. This can be speculatively distorted so that later history is made the goal of earlier history, e.g., the goal ascribed to the discovery of America is to further the eruption of the French Revolution. Thereby history receives its own special aims . . . while what is designated with the words 'destiny,' 'goal,' 'germ,' or 'idea' of earlier history is nothing more than an abstraction formed from later history, for the active influence which earlier history exercises on later history." Ibid., 59.

57. Bronner, *Socialism Unbound*, 2d ed. (Boulder, 2001), 165ff.

NOTES TO CHAPTER 3

1. A bibliography of Korsch's writings can be found in *Jahrbuch der Arbeiterbewegung 1: Über Karl Korsch*, hrsg. Claudio Pozzoli (Frankfurt am Main, 1973).

2. On his early life, Michael Buckmiller, *Karl Korsch und das Problem der materialistischen Dialektik: Historische und theoretische Voraussetzungen seiner ersten Marx-Rezeption (1909–1923)* (Hannover, 1976); on the later years, Gian Rusconi, "Korsch's Political Development," in *Telos* (fall 1976).

3. Georg Lukács, *History and Class Consciousness: Studies in Marxist Dialectics*, trans. Rodney Livingstone (Cambridge, Mass., 1970), 1ff.

4. Martin Jay is correct in noting that "Korsch was clearly rejecting the idealist indifference to empirical reality that Lukács had defended immediately after his conversion to Marxism," in *Marxism and Totality: The Adventures of a Concept from Lukács to Habermas* (Berkeley, 1984), 144ff.

5. "[Marx] created the theoretical-scientific expression adequate to the new content of consciousness of the proletarian class, and thereby at the same time elevated this proletarian class consciousness to a higher level of being." Karl Korsch, "The Marxist Dialectic," in *Karl Korsch: Revolutionary Theory*, ed. Douglas Kellner (Austin, 1977), 136.

6. Note the historical introduction by Douglas Kellner to his edition of *Karl Korsch: Revolutionary Theory*, 3ff.

7. For a more complete discussion, see Andrew Arato and Paul Breines, *The Young Lukács and the Origins of Western Marxism* (New York, 1979), 176ff.

8. Richard Lowenthal, "The Bolshevization of the Spartacus League," in *International Communism* (London, 1960), 23–71.

9. For a historical overview, Paul Breines, "Praxis and Its Theorists: The Impact of Lukács and Korsch in the 1920's," in *Telos* (spring 1972).

10. Note the description of Korsch in the "Autobiographical Fragment" of Henry Pachter, *Weimar Etudes* (New York, 1984), 1ff.; also note the interview with Heinz Langerhans in *Jahrbuch der Arbeiterbewegung*, 267ff., and his poem "Der Lehrer," in *Zur Aktualität von Karl Korsch*, hrsg. Michael Buckmiller (Frankfurt, 1981), 150ff.; also, in this regard, see the insightful, touching, yet ironical piece by Bertolt Brecht, "Über meinen Lehrer," in *Gesammelte Werke*, 20 vols. (Frankfurt, 1967), 20:65ff.

11. On the influence he exerted in the decades following World War II, see Frank Dingel, "Das Symposium über Karl Korsch vom 20. Bis 21 Juni 1980 an der Universität Frankfurt," *Internationale Wissenschaftliche Korrespondez zur Geschichte der Deutschen Arbeiterbewegung*, vol. 16, no. 3, (1980), 404–12.

12. Buckmiller, *Karl Korsch und das Problem der materialistischen Dialektik* (Hannover, 1976), 103.

13. Note his letter to Paul Mattick of 20 November 1938 included in *Karl Korsch: Revolutionary Theory*, 283ff.

14. Kellner, *Karl Korsch*, 33ff.

15. Jay, *Marxism and Totality*, 144.

16. Karl Korsch, *Karl Marx* (New York, 1938), 24ff.

17. Karl Korsch, *Marxism and Philosophy*, trans. Fred Halliday (London, 1970), 92.

18. An extension of this position appears in the view that modern philosophy is defined by three fundamental "moments" corresponding to the rise of the two dominant classes of the modern production process: that of Descartes and Locke, Kant and Hegel, and Marx. Intriguing is the claim that the attempt to forge a new moment of thought, while bypassing the dominant philosopher of the given moment, will necessarily result only in a retreat into the thinking of an earlier philosophical framework. Jean-Paul Sartre, *Search for a Method*, trans. Hazel Barnes (New York, 1963), 7.

19. "In the middle of the nineteenth century [the bourgeoisie] ceased to be revolutionary in its social *practice*, and by an inner necessity it thereby also lost the ability to comprehend in *thought* the true dialectical interrelation of ideas and real historical developments, above all of philosophy and revolution." Korsch, *Marxism and Philosophy*, 40.

20. An interesting example of this appears in the thought of Lukács, whose *History and Class Consciousness* of 1923 forwarded a utopian conception of subject-object unity and a radical attack on alienation and reification. These concerns essentially vanish from his uncompleted *Ontology*, which emerges as an acceptance of the Soviet Union and its limits. Gaspar M. Tamas, "Lukács' Ontology: A Metacritical Letter," in *Lukács Reappraised*, ed. Agnes Heller (New York, 1983), 155.

21. Russell Jacoby, "The Inception of Western Marxism: Karl Korsch and the Politics of Philosophy," *Canadian Journal of Political and Social Theory*, vol. 3, no. 3 (fall 1979), 7ff.

22. Note the critique of his historicism by Jay, *Marxism and Totality*, 137ff.

23. For a differing interpretation of this development, see the new preface to the second edition of my *Socialism Unbound* (Boulder, 2001), xviiff.

24. Korsch, *Marxism and Philosophy*, 59.

25. A debate over the idea of socialism as an "other" and the salience of workers' councils was begun with my article "Red Dreams and the New Millennium: Remarks on Rosa Luxemburg," in *New Politics*, vol. 8, no. 3 (summer 2001), 162–67, which received replies from David Camfield and Alan Johnson, to which I then replied with "Rosa Redux: A Reply to David Camfield and Alan Johnson," in *New Politics*, vol. 8, no. 4 (winter 2002), 35–52.

26. Georg Bammel, "Vorwort zu *Marxismus und Philosophie*," in *Zur Aktualität von Karl Korsch*, 71ff.

27. Note Korsch's essays "Lenin and the Comintern," as well as "State and Counterrevolution," in Kellner, *Karl Korsch*, 149ff. and 237ff.

28. "Some Fundamental Presuppositions for a Materialistic Discussion of Crisis Theory," in Kellner, *Karl Korsch*, 181ff.

29. Ibid., 212ff.

30. Note the critique of Karl Mannheim's *Ideology and Utopia* for its hidden metaphysical assumptions and relativism, by Max Horkheimer, "Ein neuer Ideologiebegriff," in *Archiv für die Geschichte des Sozialismus und der Arbeiterbewegung*, vol. 15 (1930).

31. Some go so far as to say that "few doubts remain as to Korsch's total rejection of the Marxian perspective," in Leonardo Ceppa, "Korsch's Marxism," *Telos* (winter 1975–76), 118; also, see Paul Piccone, "Korsch in Spain," *New German Critique* (fall 1975).

32. The central texts used to justify Korsch's abandonment of his old theoretical commitments are "The Crisis of Marxism" (1931), which was translated and reprinted in *New German Critique* (fall 1974), 7ff. and the "Zehn Thesen über Marxismus Heute" (1950), in Karl Korsch, *Politische Texte*, hrsg. Erich Gerlach und Jurgen Seifert (Frankfurt, 1974), 385ff. In the first piece, Korsch does say that "Marxism as an historical phenomenon is a thing of the past," but goes on to state, "Yet, in a more fundamental historical sense, the theory of proletarian revolution, which will develop anew in the next period of history, will be an historical continuation of Marxism" (11). This, of course, conforms with the present interpretation. Although a similar mode of argumentation occurs, that is arguably less clear in the case of the "Ten Theses." In this regard, however, it is important to mention a conversation with Hedda Korsch shortly before her death. She told me then that the "theses" were less a reflection of her husband's own views than notes to spark discussion in a course for workers that he was teaching in Zurich. Of course, such ad hoc information is independent of their impact and relevance. Nevertheless, Hedda Korsch requested that at some point I express her sentiments for the historical record, and I take this opportunity to do so.

33. Cf. Oskar Negt, "Theory, Empiricism, and Class Struggle: On the Problem of Constitution in Karl Korsch," *Telos* 26.

34. Naturally, according to Korsch, self-criticism need not take the form of Eduard Bern-

stein's "revisionism" of orthodox Marxism into a theory of social reform. Still, it is interesting to note that Korsch saw Bernstein as historically correct in his attack on the Marxism of the Second International insofar as his was the theory that the SPD was actually following in practice. Meanwhile, in her famous debate with the revisionists, Rosa Luxemburg—who Korsch obviously found otherwise much more sympathetic—is seen as neglecting actual practice and arguing purely on the level of theory. Note his essay "The Passing of Marxian Orthodoxy," in Kellner, *Karl Korsch*, 176ff; also cf. Bronner, *Socialism Unbound*, 50–52.

35. For "economic ideas themselves only appear to be related to the material relations of bourgeois society in the way an image is related to the object it reflects. In fact, they are related to them in the way that a specific particularly defined part of the whole is related to the other parts of the whole." Korsch, *Marxism and Philosophy*, 84.

36. "It might be observed that irrespective of whether or to what extent the 'unity of theory and practice' thus understood was a reality, [Marxist orthodoxy] was quite compatible with the traditional or transcendental conception of truth as consisting in the conformity of our judgment with a state of affairs completely independent of our cognitive activity. In other words, the unity of theory and practice, thus understood, did not conflict with what Marx called the 'contemplative' conception of knowledge." Kolakowski, *Main Currents of Marxism*, 3 vols., trans. P. S. Falla (New York, 1978), 3:311.

37. Karl Korsch, *Die materialistische Geschichtsauffassung und andere Schriften*, hrsg. Erich Gerlach (Frankfurt, 1971), 3–130.

38. Thus, Korsch can claim that those who dissociate the "truth" of economics from the "falsity" of ideology will "universally transfer the dialectic into Object, Nature and History and [so] present knowledge merely as the passive mirror and reflection of this objective Being in the subjective consciousness. In so doing they destroy both the dialectical interrelation of *being* and *consciousness* and, as a necessary consequence, the dialectical interrelation of *theory* and *practice*." Korsch, *Marxism and Philosophy*, 117; he is consequently not simply engaged in some variant of "reflection theory, which is the position argued by Leonardo Ceppa, "Korsch's Marxism," *Telos* 26 (winter 1975–76), 96ff.

39. "[So] long as that material foundation of the existing bourgeois society is only attacked and shaken, but not completely over-thrown, through the revolutionary proletarian struggle, the socially entrenched thought-forms of the bourgeois epoch can only be criticized and not definitely superseded by the revolutionary theory of the proletariat. The critique of political economy, which Marx began in *Capital*, can therefore only be completed by the proletarian revolution, that is, by a real change in the present bourgeois mode of production and of the forms of consciousness pertaining to it." Korsch, *Karl Marx*, 157.

40. Rolf Wiggershaus, *Die Frankfurter Schule: Geshichte, Theoretische Entwicklung, Politische Bedeutung* (Frankfurt, 1988), 70.

41. For an alternative view, see Kolakowski, *Main Currents of Marxism*, 3:308ff.

42. Korsch, *Karl Marx*, 84.

43. "*Materialistic criticism of religion* is aware of the fact that the ideological reflection of the real world cannot be totally dissolved until the practical conditions of everyday [life] offer to the human beings concerned, a continuous display of perfectly intelligible and reasonable relations both between man and nature and between men and men. Similarly, the life process of society, i.e., material production does not strip off its mystical veil until it is transformed into the result of the conscious and self-controlled activities of freely associated men." Ibid., 161.

44. On the councils and their role, Korsch' *Schriften zur Sozialisierung*, hrsg. Erich Gerlach (Frankfurt am Main, 1969), as well as his *Arbeitsrecht für Betriebsräte*, which appeared

in a special edition by IG Metall under the title *Auf dem Wege zur industriellen Demokratie* (Frankfurt, 1968).

45. Ceppa, "Korsch's Marxism," 110.

46. Korsch, *Marxism and Philosophy*, 64.

47. "Neither 'dialectical causality' in its philosophical definition nor scientific 'causality' supplemented by 'interactions' is sufficient to determine the particular kinds of connections and relations existing between the economic 'basis' and the juridical, political and ideological 'superstructure' of a given socio-economic formation." Korsch, *Karl Marx*, 227. For a sophisticated analysis of the relation between "base" and "superstructure" that builds on Korsch's perspective, see Franz Jakubowski, *Ideology and Superstructure in Historical Materialism*, trans. Anne Booth (London, 1976).

48. In contrast to the "three-level" approach to reality offered by orthodox Marxists, Korsch forwards a completely different view. Roughly speaking, where certain sciences lie in direct immediate relation to material production, their relation to those means of production will necessarily be mechanistic. On the other hand, there are also sciences and processes that lie in indirect, mediated relation to material production but that simultaneously lie in direct, unmediated relation to the production of social relations; these grow out of material production and in them material production itself extends—as in the case of the "culture industry." Finally, as with the fine arts, there are processes which do not lie in direct relation with either material production or with the direct production of social relations; instead, they only stand in direct relation with overriding cultural production as such. Thus, Korsch does achieve a certain differentiation of forms, even while—as is to be expected—these interrelations can appear in qualitatively different combinations in differing stages of production. Karl Korsch, "15 Thesen über wissenschaftlichen Sozialismus," in *Politische Texte*, 51ff.

49. No less than for Lukács, humanity for Korsch is at once bound to nature and yet separated from it. Though it is possible to explain how scientific changes occurred and how science is employed from the historical perspective of social theory, this is not the same as saying that social theory has the last word in terms of the specific results achieved by a scientific formulation. Korsch warns against such vulgar misuse of social theory—which, for Marxism, can lead to nonsense like the "dialectics of wheat"—in his *Kernpunkte der materialistischen Geschichtsauffassung: Eine quellenmässige Darstellung* (Hamburg, 1973). Lukács also reacted against the attempt to present Marxism as a single unified theory of nature and society when he critically noted "that Engels—following Hegel's mistaken lead—extended the dialectical or sociohistorical method to apply also to nature," which lacks all those reflexive aspects that "form the crucial determinants of dialectics." Lukács, *History and Class Consciousness*, 24. This point is badly misinterpreted by Kolakowski, *Main Currents of Marxism*, 314ff.

50. Korsch, *Karl Marx*, 150.

51. Korsch, *Kernpunkte*, 9

52. Kellner, *Karl Korsch*, 232ff.

53. Note the essay "The Revolutionary Commune," in Kellner, *Karl Korsch*, 201.

54. Bronner, *Socialism Unbound*, 167ff.

55. Kellner, *Karl Korsch*, 232ff; also, "Brief von Amadeo Bordiga an Karl Korsch," in Pozzoli, *Jahrbuch der Arbeiterbewegung*, 243–47.

56. Henry Pachter, "The Idea of Progress in Marxism" in *Socialism in History: Political Essays of Henry Pachter*, ed. Stephen Eric Bronner (New York, 1984), 65ff.

57. According to Korsch, "vulgar" Marxism recognizes three "levels" of reality. The first, the economy, is the only objective and totally nonideological reality, while the second—law and the state—is somewhat less "real" or "objective" since it is clad in ideology. The third level, that of pure ideology, is putatively objectless and unreal or—as

Kautsky would have it—"pure rubbish." Korsch, *Marxism and Philosophy*, 73. Kolakowski mistakenly identifies the position that is being attacked with the standpoint Korsch supports in *Main Currents of Marxism*, 3:313.

58. Korsch, *Marxism and Philosophy*, 42.

59. "In social affairs, the act of investigation coincides with its object—such is the Hegelian interpretation adopted by Marxism. From this point of view Korsch likens the Marxist theory of society to the view of Clausewitz (also a Hegelian) that the theory of war is not a matter of external observation but is part of war itself . . . The dialectic is not simply a 'method' applicable at will to any object. It would seem that in Korsch's view it is altogether impossible to expound the materialistic dialectic as a collection of statements or precepts of investigation. As an expression of the revolutionary movement of the working class it is part of that movement and not a mere theory or 'system.'" Kolakowski, *Main Currents of Marxism*, 313.

60. Brecht, "Über meinen Lehrer," 65.

61. Note the fine essay by Michael Buckmiller, "Aspekte der internationalen Korsch-Rezeption," in *Zur Aktualität von Karl Korsch*, 9ff.

62. Korsch, "Zehn Thesen," 386.

63. Oskar Negt, "Zurück zu Marx und Engels! Oder: Was konnen wir von Korsch lernen?" in *Zur Aktualität von Karl Korsch*, 39.

64. Brecht, "Über meinen Lehrer, 66.

65. The joke went around that in the midst of an important political conflict, someone asked: "Where is Korsch?" Someone else then supposedly answered: "He is taking the correct position—while sitting in his room." Klaus von Beyme, *Theorie der Politik im 20. Jahrhundert: Von der Moderne zur Postmoderne* (Frankfurt am Main, 1991), 107.

66. Negt, "Zurück zu Marx und Engels," 43.

67. Korsch can thus note that in contrast to the late Adorno, "Karl Marx was a *positive dialectician and revolutionary* and the magnificent character of his spirit is very evident in the *Critique*: he never allows his critical work to become a mere *negation* of the errors and superficialities analyzed . . . He always goes on to expound or briefly indicate the *positive* and *true* concepts which should replace the error and illusion he criticizes." Korsch, *Marxism and Philosophy*, 140.

68. Bronner, *Socialism Unbound*, 164ff.

NOTES TO CHAPTER 4

1. "Let us assume for the sake of argument that recent research had disproved once and for all every one of Marx's individual theses. Even if this were to be proved, every serious 'orthodox' Marxist would still be able to accept all such modern findings without reservation and hence dismiss all of Marx's theses *in toto*—without having to renounce his orthodoxy for a single moment. Orthodox Marxism, therefore, does not imply the uncritical acceptance of the results of Marx's investigations. It is not the 'belief' in this or that thesis, nor the exegesis of a 'sacred' book. On the contrary, orthodoxy refers exclusively to *method*." Georg Lukács, *History and Class Consciousness: Studies in Marxist Dialectics*, trans. Rodney Livingstone (Cambridge, Mass., 1971), 1.

2. Max Adler, *Marx und Engels als Denker* (Frankfurt am Main, 1972).

3. Martin Jay, *Marxism and Totality: The Adventures of a Concept from Lukács to Habermas* (Berkeley, 1984), 84, 102.

4. Note the chapter entitled "Rosa Luxemburg and Western Marxism," in Stephen Eric Bronner, *Rosa Luxemburg: A Revolutionary for Our Times* (New York, 1987), 96ff.

5. Lukács, *History and Class Consciousness*, xxiiiff.

6. Istvan Mészaros, *Marx's Theory of Alienation* (London, 1970), 28–33.

7. "The infinitive of alienation (*Entfremden*) is an ancient word, which had a social con-

notation from the beginning. Abalienare, according to the Romans, meant to external-
ize (*entäussern*) oneself in something meant for sale. Grimmelshausen may have still
called exchange the process of alienating (*veralienieren*). But, in contrast to French
and English, this foreign word otherwise disappeared from everyday speech. It was
almost the same with the German 'to alienate' (*Entfremden*), at least in its original reference to the implications of exchange: People have alienated themselves from one
another in the sense of becoming cool to one another." Ernst Bloch, *Verfremdungen*, 2
Bde. (Frankfurt, 1968), 2:81.

8. Paul Ricoeur, *The Symbolism of Evil* (Boston, 1980).
9. "The infinitive of estrangement (*verfremden*) is, however, not ancient. But it is difficult
to translate. Remarkably, according to Grimm, Berthold Auerbach is the first to give it
literary definition in his novel of 1842 "New Life." There the parents feel themselves
estranged, that is to say deeply hurt, because their children speak French, which they
cannot understand, in their company. Apparently the children are talking about them.
They are absent and, like servants who are not supposed to listen, feel estranged." It is
from the perspective of this original feeling of distance that Brecht would develop his
"estrangement-effect" (*Verfremdungseffekt*). Bloch, *Verfremdungen*, 2:82.
10. Friedrich Holderlin, *Hyperion* in *Gesammelte Werke*, ed. Friedrich Beissner (Stuttgart,
1957), 3:153.
11. Georg Lukács, *Der junge Hegel*, 2 Bde. (Frankfurt, 1973), 2:826ff.
12. "The chief defect of all hitherto existing materialism—that of Feuerbach included—is
that the thing [*Gegenstand*], reality, sensuousness, is conceived only in the form of the
object [*Objekt*] or of contemplation [*Anschauung*], but not as human sensuous activity, practice, not subjectively." Karl Marx, "Theses on Feuerbach," in Karl Marx and
Frederick Engels, *Selected Works*, 3 vols. (Moscow, 1969), 1:11
13. Ibid., 1:13-15.
14. Georg Lukács, *Der junge Marx: Seine philosophische Entwicklung von 1840 bis 1844*
(Pfullingen, 1965).
15. Note the comparison between Lukács and Marx by Istvan Mészaros, "Kontingentes
und notwendiges Klassenbewusstsein," in *Aspekte von beschichte und Klassenbewusstsein*, ed. Istvan Mészaros (Munchen, 1972), 124ff.
16. Ibid, 193.
17. Georg Lukács, "Das Zerschellen der Form am Leben: Soren Kierkegaard und Regine
Olsen," in *Die Seele und die Formen* (Neuwied, 1971), 44ff; also, Arpad Kadarkay, *Georg
Lukács: Life, Thought, and Politics* (London, 1991), 56ff.
18. On the revolutionary character of Lukács's analysis, which reinserted dialectics into
Marxism, cf. Lucien Goldmann, "Reflexionen uber Geschichte und Klassenbewusstsein," in *Aspekte von Geschichte und Klassenbewusstsein*, 96ff.
19. It is only once society has become fully demystified or rational, which occurs through
the extension of the commodity form, that the rational reconstruction of the past
becomes possible; indeed, Marx already knew that the human is incomprehensible
from the standpoint of the ape and that the ape is only comprehensible from the
standpoint of the human. This subverts the objection raised by Josef Revai who
argued that if only the proletariat alone can "know" the conditions of its creation, it
becomes impossible to speak of conscious historical agents in the past. Dialectical
notions of history, after all, basically emerge with the entry of the bourgeoisie upon
the world stage. See the reprint of the 1924 review of *History and Class Consciousness*
by Josef Révai in *Theoretical Practice* 1 (January 1971).
20. Ibid., 149.
21. Ibid., 161.
22. Ibid., 178.
23. Marx, "Theses on Feuerbach," 15; Lukács, *History and Class Consciousness*, 262ff.

24. Andrew Arato, "Lukács Theory of Reification," *Telos* 11 (spring 1972), 26ff.; also Andrew Feenberg, *Lukács, Marx, and the Sources of Critical Theory* (Oxford, 1986).
25. Andrew Arato, "The Neo-Idealist Defense of Subjectivity," in *Telos* 21 (fall 1974), 108ff.
26. Georg Lukács, "Emil Lask," in *Kant-Studien* (1917–18), 349ff.
27. Karl Marx, *Capital*, 3 vols. ed. Frederick Engels and trans. Samuel Moore and Edward Aveling (New York, 1973), 1:71ff.
28. The critique of Nikolai Bukharin's *Historical Materialism*, written in 1922, would emphasize that "Technique is a *part*, a moment, naturally of great importance, of the social productive forces, but it is neither simply identical with them nor . . . the final or absolute moment of the changes in these forces. This attempt to find the underlying determinants of society and its development in a principle other than that of the social relations between men in the process of production . . . leads to fetishism." Georg Lukács, *Political Writings 1919–1929*, ed. Rodney Livingstone and trans. Michale McColgan (London, 1972), 136.
29. Lukács, *History and Class Consciousness*, 103.
30. Ibid., 94.
31. "Vulgar socialism . . . has taken over from the bourgeois economists the consideration and treatment of distribution as independent of the mode of production and hence the presentation of socialism as turning principally on distribution." Karl Marx, "Critique of the Gotha Programme," in *Selected Works*, 3:20.
32. Class consicousness and "self-administration" (*Selbsttätigkeit*) were the goals she and her followers sought to further. Note in particular her reflections written in early February 1906 on the mass strike in *The Letters of Rosa Luxemburg*, ed. Stephen Eric Bronner (Atlantic Highlands, 1993), 2d ed., 112ff.
33. Lukács, "Tactics and Ethics," in *Political Writings*, 6ff.
34. Georg Lukács, *Selected Correspondence 1902–1920*, ed. and trans. Judith Marcus and Zoltan Tar (New York, 1986), 148 and passim.
35. Lukács, *History and Class Consciousness*, 91.
36. Ibid., 87.
37. Ibid., 79; also, Iring Fetscher, "Zum Begriff der 'Objektiven Moglichkeit' bei Max Weber und Georg Lukács," *Revue Internationale de Philosophie* 106 (1973).
38. Lukács, *History and Class Consciousness*, 169.
39. Ibid., 3.
40. Ibid., 155.
41. "If, then, the standpoint of the proletariat is opposed to that of the bourgeoisie, it is nonetheless true that proletarian thought does not require a *tabula rasa*, a new start to the task of comprehending reality and one without any preconceptions. In this it is unlike the thought of the bourgeoisie with regard to the medieval forms of feudalism—at least in its basic tendencies. Just because its practical goal is the *fundamental* transformation of the whole of society it conceives of bourgeois society together with its intellectual and artistic productions as the point of departure for its own method." Ibid., 163.
42. Instrumental rationality "by concerning itself with the formal calculability of the contents of forms made abstract, *must define* these contents as *immutable*—within the system of relations pertaining at any given time." Ibid., 143–44.
43. Isaak Ilych Rubin, *Essays on Marx's Theory of Value*, trans. Milos Somardziga and Fredy Perlman (Montreal, 1982); and Roman Rosdolsky, *The Making of Marx's Capital*, trans. Pete Burgess (London, 1977).
44. Lukács, *History and Class Consciousness*. 93.
45. Ibid., 88.
46. Heidegger would surely have agreed, albeit from an ontological perspective, with the

claim of Lukács that "thus time sheds its qualitative, variable, flowing nature; it freezes into an exactly delimited quantifiable continuum filled with quantifiable 'things' (the reified, mechanically objectified 'performance' of the worker, wholly separated from his total human personality); in short, it becomes space." Ibid., 90.

47. Lucien Goldmann, *Lukács et Heidegger*, ed. Youssef Ishaghpour (Paris, 1973).

48. "But Engels' deepest misunderstanding consists in his belief that the behavior of industry and scientific experiment constitutes praxis in the dialectical, philosophical sense. In fact, scientific experiment is contemplation at its purest. The experimenter creates an artificial, abstract milieu in order to be able to *observe* undisturbed the untrammelled workings of the laws under examination, eliminating all irrational factors both of the subject and the object." Lukács, *History and Class Consciousness*, 132.

49. Ibid., 89.

50. Ibid., 184.

51. Ibid., 186–87.

52. Arpad Kadarkay, *Georg Lukács: Life, Thought, and Politics* (London, 1991), 192ff.; Michael Löwy, *Georg Lukács: From Romanticism to Bolshevism* (London, 1979).

53. Georg Lukács, "The Old Culture and the New Culture," in *Marxism and Human Liberation*, ed. E. San Juan Jr. (New York, 1973).

54. Lukács, *History and Class Consciousness*, 327.

55. Lukács, *Political Writings*, 227ff.

56. David Kettler, "Culture and Revolution: Lukács and the Hungarian Revolution," in *Telos* 10 (winter 1971).

57. The point was not simply to proceed without reference to the facts since ". . . what is decisive is whether this process of isolation is a means toward understanding the whole and whether it is integrated within the context it presupposes and requires or whether the abstract knowledge of an isolated fragment retains its 'autonomy' and becomes both an end in itself." Lukács, *History and Class Consciousness*, 73.

58. Ibid., 71.

59. Ibid., 198.

60. "Every momentary interest may have either of two functions: either it will be a step towards the ultimate goal or else it will conceal it. Which of the two it will be depends *entirely upon the class consciousness of the proletariat and not on victory or defeat in isolated skirmishes.*" Ibid., 73.

61. Ibid., 171.

62. Kadarkay, *Georg Lukács*, 270.

63. Andrew Arato and Paul Breines, *The Young Lukács and the Origins of Western Marxism* (New York, 1979), 142ff.

64. Samuel Farber, *Before Stalinism: The Rise and Fall of Soviet Democracy* (London, 1990).

65. Kadarkay, *Georg Lukács*, 280ff.

66. Lukács's response to the attacks launched during this congress appears in the just recently discovered manuscript titled *A Defense of* History and Class Consciousness: Tailism and the Dialectic, trans. Esther Leslie (New York, 2000).

67. "The foundation of our whole policy must be the widest possible development of productivity," it was already possible to claim in 1918, "everything else must be subordinated to this one task." Nikolai Bukharin and Evgenii Preobrzehnsky, *The ABC of Communism: A Popular Explanation of the Program of the Communist Party* (Ann Arbor, 1967), 74.

68. Lukács, "The Old Culture and the New Culture," 5.

69. It is probably correct to suggest that in the 1920s, Lukács "incessantly tried to reveal the 'ideal type' of the system as opposed to its empirical reality, a procedure barely tolerated by the system itself (hence the constant conflicts between Lukács and the cultural bureaucracy), but this same procedure also entailed acceptance of the final prin-

ciples of the regime." Ferenc Fehér, "Lukács in Weimar," in *Lukács Reappraised*, ed. Agnes Heller (New York, 1983), 79.
70. Lukács, *History and Class Consciousness*, xviii.
71. Paul Breines, "Praxis and Its Theorists: The Impact of Lukács and Korsch in the 1920s," *Telos* 11 (spring 1972), 102ff.
72. Ernst Bloch, *Das Prinzip Hoffnung*, 3 vols. (Frankfurt, 1973) 3:1628.
73. Jürgen Habermas, *The Theory of Communicative Action*, 2 vols., trans. Thomas McCarthy (Boston, 1984), 1:355ff.

NOTES TO CHAPTER 5
1. Ernst Bloch, *Geist der Utopie* (Frankfurt am Main, 1973), 217.
2. Ernst Bloch, "A Jubilee for Renegades," *New German Critique* 4 (winter 1975).
3. Ernst Bloch, *Das Prinzip Hoffnung*, 3 Bde. (Frankfurt am Main, 1973), 1:163.
4. Bloch, *Das Prinzip Hoffnung*, 2:620.
5. Ernst Bloch, *Verfremdungen* (Frankfurt am Main, 1964), 181.
6. Bloch, *Das Prinzip Hoffnung*, 1:230.
7. Ernst Bloch, *Erbschaft dieser Zeit* (Frankfurt am Main, 1962), 104–60.
8. Bloch, *Das Prinzip Hoffnung*, 2:590.
9. Ibid., 1:170.
10. Ernst Bloch, *Die Kunst, Schiller zu Sprechen* (Frankfurt am Main, 1969), 67.
11. Bloch, *Das Prinzip Hoffnung*, 1:249.
12. Ibid., 1:101.
13. Ibid., 1:285.
14. Ibid., 1:274.
15. Ibid., 1:226.
16. Ibid., 1:351.
17. Ibid., 1:143.
18. Ernst Bloch, *Spuren* (Frankfurt am Main, 1969), 127.

NOTES TO CHAPTER 6
1. Helmut Gumnior und Rudolf Ringguth, *Max Horkheimer: in Selbstzeugnissen und Bilddokumenten* (Hamburg, 1973), 7–27; Rolf Wiggershaus, *Die Frankfurter Schule: Geschichte, Theoretische Entwicklung, Politische Bedeutung* (München, 1988), 55–67.
2. Judith Marcus and Zoltan Tar, "The Judaic Element in the Teachings of the Frankfurt School," in *The Leo Baeck Institute Yearbook* (London, 1986), 344.
3. Max Horkheimer, *Dawn and Decline: Notes 1926–31 & 1950–69*, trans. Michael Shaw (New York, 1978).
4. "If today the subject is vanishing, aphorisms take upon themselves the duty to consider the evanescent itself as essential. They insist, in opposition to Hegel's practice and yet in accordance with his thought, on negativity." Theodor Adorno, *Minima Moralia: Reflections from a Damaged Life*, trans. E. F. N. Jephcott (London, 1974), 16.
5. "Metaphysical pessimism, always an implicit element in every genuinely materialist philosophy, had always been congenial to me. My first acquaintance with philosophy came through Schopenhauer; my relation to Hegel and Marx and my desire to understand and change social reality have not been obliterated by experience of his philosophy, despite the political opposition between these men. The better, the right kind of society is a goal which has a sense of guilt entwined about it." Max Horkheimer, "Preface" to *Critical Theory: Selected Essays* (New York, 1982), ix.
6. Horkheimer, especially toward the end of the 1920s, "understood himself as an advocate of Marxist theory in the sense that he viewed his position as an extension of a line that went from the French Enlightenment over Hegel and Marx." Wiggershaus, *Die Frankfurter Schule*, 66.

7. Frank Hartmann, *Max Horkheimers materialistischer Skeptizismus: Frühe Motive der Kritischen Theorie* (Frankfurt, 1990).

8. The idea for the institute emerged from a meeting—"the first marxist work week"—of about two dozen intellectuals who sought to determine the character of "true" Marxism in the aftermath of the war when new philosophical perspectives were emerging amid the more obvious battles between social democrats and communists. Participants in this work week, nearly half of whom would later work with the institute in one capacity or another, included such prominent thinkers as Karl Korsch, Georg Lukács, Paul Massing, Julian Gomperz, Karl Wittfogel, and Friedrich Pollock. Wiggershaus, *Die Frankfurter Schule*, 23ff.

9. It is important to note that from the beginning, the institute was directly associated with Frankfurt University and the director had to hold a chair (*Lehrstuhl*). Grünberg's chair was given to the political economist Adolph Löwe, while Paul Tillich used his influence to establish a chair in social philosophy for Horkheimer. Ibid, 50.

10. In the final analysis, "institutionally and cognitively, Max Horkheimer occupied the dominant position within the circle . . . [N]ot every member could play an equally influential role within the group, suggesting an overall structure in which a figure of cognitive leadership systematically integrated the various disciplines. This group structure was in turn based on the Circle's institutional substructure—on the "dictatorship of the director" that was anchored in the Institute's statutes and often invoked by Horkheimer." Helmut Dubiel, *Theory and Politics: Studies in the Development of Critical Theory*, trans. Benjamin Gregg (Cambridge, Mass., 1985), 184.

11. For the text, see Max Horkheimer, "The State of Contemporary Social Philosophy and the Tasks of an Institute for Social Research," in *Critical Theory and Society: A Reader*, ed. Stephen Eric Bronner and Douglas Mackay Kellner (New York, 1989), 25–36.

12. "Horkheimer attempted to overcome the crisis of Marxism by attempting to link it to modern developments in the realm of 'bourgeois' science and philosophy. Max Weber's refusal to speculate about any predefined meaning for the world was combined with Heidegger's rejection of any transhistorical essence for humanity; the attempt by Lukács and Korsch to preserve the philosophical elements in Marxism were combined with Scheler's integration of empirical knowledge into philosophy." Wiggershaus, *Die Frankfurter Schule*, 53; also, Alfons Sollner, *Geschichte und Herrschaft: Studien zur materialistischen Sozial-wissenschaft 1929–1942* (Frankfurt, 1979), 30ff.

13. Hauke Brunkhorst, "Dialektischer Positivismus des Glücks" in *Zeitschrift für philosophische Forschung*, Bd. 39, Heft 3, 1985, S. 353ff.

14. Also, for a basic analysis of the concept, Herbert Marcuse, "Philosophy and Critical Theory," in *Critical Theory and Society*, 58–73.

15. In 1932, Horkheimer could also still see technological rationality as value-neutral. Crucial for him in overcoming the "crisis" brought on by the Great Depression was the need to redirect productive forces from the perspective of a new set of sociopolitical relations. Max Horkheimer, "Notes on Science and the Crisis," in *Critical Theory*, 3–10.

16. Douglas Kellner, *Critical Theory, Marxism and Modernity* (Cambridge, 1989), 22ff.

17. Leszek Kolokowski, *Main Currents of Marxism*, 3 vols. (New York, 1978), 3:341ff; Howard, *The Marxian Legacy*, 100–101.

18. Karl Korsch, *Marxism and Philosophy*, trans. Fred Halliday (London, 1970), 92.

19. Note the essay of 1933 by Max Horkheimer, "Materialism and Morality," *Telos* 69 (fall 1986), 85–118; also, Herbert Schnädelbach, "Max Horkheimer and the Moral Philosophy of German Idealism," *Telos* 66 (winter 1985–86), 81–104.

20. Max Horkheimer, "The Latest Attack on Metaphysics," in *Critical Theory*, 132ff.

21. Jürgen Habermas, "Max Horkheimer: Zur Entwicklungsgeschichte seines Werkes," in *Texte und Kontexte* (Frankfurt am Main, 1992), 92.

22. Horkheimer, "Materialism and Metaphysics," in *Critical Theory*, 45–46.
23. Heidrun Hesse, *Vernunft und Selbstbehauptung: Kritische Theorie als Kritik der neuzeitlichen Rationalität* (Frankfurt, 1986), 137ff.
24. Dick Howard, *The Marxian Legacy* (New York, 1977), 91.
25. Kellner, *Critical Theory, Marxism and Modernity*, 83ff.
26. Dubiel, *Theory and Politics*, 13.
27. Horkheimer, "Authority and the Family," in *Critical Theory*, 47–128.
28. These essays are translated and reprinted in *Critical Theory and Society*, 77–94, and *Telos* 15 (spring 1973), 3–20;.
29. A similar line of reasoning, stressing the weakening of the ego produced by the modern substitution of television for the patriarchal father, would recur in Herbert Marcuse, "The Obsolescence of the Freudian Concept of Man," in *Five Lectures: Psychoanalysis, Politics, and Utopia,* trans. Jeremy J. Shapiro and Shierry M. Weber (Boston, 1970), 44ff.
30. Following the seminal essays of Pollock, Horkheimer and Adorno could ultimately come to view "state socialism" as one variant within a broader trend toward bureaucratic domination and—with the belief that the preservation of profitable accumulation rested on the transformation of the state into a capitalist in its own right—an "economic justification for considering an economic analysis of society no longer necessary or even possible." Dubiel, *Theory and Politics*, 81. Also, Friedrich Pollock, "State Capitalism: Its Possibilities and Limitations," in *Critical Theory and Society*, 95ff; "Is National Socialism a New Order?" *Studies in Philosophy and Social Science* 9 (1941).
31. "According to Hegel, the stages of the World Spirit follow one another with logical necessity and none can be omitted. In this respect Marx remained true to him. History is represented as an indivisible development. The new cannot begin before its time. However, the fatalism of both philosophers refers to the past only. Their metaphysical error, namely that history obeys a defined law, is cancelled by their historical error, namely that such a law was fulfilled at its appointed time." Horkheimer, "The Authoritarian State," 11.
32. Thus, not only will Horkheimer compare the Western working-class organizations with those of the Soviet Union, which is defined in terms of "integral statism"; the "integral state" of course, is originally a concept employed by the far right. Ibid., 7–8.
33. Also, Herbert Marcuse, "The Struggle against Liberalism in the Totalitarian View of the State (1934)," in *Negations: Essays in Critical Theory* (Boston, 1968).
34. Admittedly, Horkheimer believes that the form of political regime matters to the individual and that the degree to which the state remains dependent on private capital is crucial. But actual criteria for *political* differentiation are external to the theory; they recede before the emphasis placed on bureaucratic rationalization and the belief that state capitalism is creating the conditions for its own demise. Interestingly enough, however, this same indeterminacy allows Horkheimer to envision a situation in which "two friend-enemy blocs of states . . . will dominate the world . . . and (find) in their reciprocal threat to each other new grounds for an arms race." Howard, *The Marxian Legacy*, 111.
35. This definition of totalitarianism as the absence of intervening institutions to protect the individual from the state is already indicated in Horkheimer's "The End of Reason," in *The Frankfurt School Reader*, ed. Andrew Arato and Eike Gebhardt (New York, 1982), 36–39.
36. Thus, in spite of his obvious antifascism, Horkheimer could mirror the sentiments of his circle for the duration of the war by writing on the day of its outbreak that "the frightful thing about this situation is that given the present constellations and rallying cries, there is not a single one toward which one could feel even distantly sympathetic." Cited in Dubiel, *Theory and Politics*, 76. Also, Horkheimer, *Dawn and Decline*, 152.

37. Thus, for Horkheimer and other major proponents of the Frankfurt School, the fascist form of state capitalism merely completes the historical logic of late capitalism, itself a product of liberal capitalism, that Hitler's Germany reflects the basic tendency inherent in all Western industrial nations. Dubiel, *Theory and Politics*, 44ff. and passim.

38. Horkheimer seeks to provide a material foundation for this claim by stating that "European history is finished and therefore positivism is right. There is no escape except machinery. All concepts that are irreducible to facts are meaningless." Horkheimer, *Dawn and Decline*, 173.

39. "The research program of the 1930s stood and fell with its historical-philosophical trust in the rational potential of bourgeois culture—a potential that would be released in social movements under the pressure of developed forces of production. Ironically, however, the critiques of ideology carried out by Horkheimer, Marcuse, and Adorno confirmed them in the belief that culture was losing its autonomy in postliberal societies and was being incorporated into the machinery of the economic-administrative system. The development of productive forces, and even critical thought itself, was moving more and more into a perspective of bleak assimilation to their opposites. In the totally administered society only instrumental reason, expanded into a totality, found embodiment: everything that existed was transformed into a real abstraction. In that case, however, what was taken hold of and deformed by these abstractions escaped the grasp of empirical inquiry." Jürgen Habermas, *The Theory of Communicative Action*, trans. Thomas McCarthy, 2 vols. (Boston, 1987), 2:382.

40. Jürgen Habermas, "Nachwort" to *Dialektik der Aufklärung* (Frankfurt, 1986).

41. Sollner, *Geschichte und Herrschaft*, 190ff.

42. It is important to note that the concept of enlightenment has two meanings. Horkheimer made this point clearly in his lectures of 1959–60 at Frankfurt when he wrote: "On the one hand, it means the philosophical tendencies in England, France, and Germany which developed a specific theory of knowledge in opposition to the dominant theological views . . . On the other hand, and more decisively, one understands under enlightenment the total philosophical thinking which, in contrast to mythology, has led the battle to achieve clarity over its own ideas and make concepts as well as judgments visible to everyone. Clarity, hence the name enlightenment: philosophy as struggle with error and superstition is also and always enlightenment . . . Both concepts are bound with one another." Max Horkheimer, "Die Aufklärung," in *Gesammelte Werke* (Frankfurt, 1989), 13:571.

43. Dubiel, *Theory and Politics*, 71.

44. In a work written for Horkheimer's fiftieth birthday, Adorno could note: with the dissolution of liberalism, the truly bourgeois principle, that of competition, far from being overcome has passed from the objectivity of the social process into the composition of its colliding and jostling atoms, and therewith as if into anthropology." Adorno, *Minima Moralia*, 18, 37, 27.

45. Horkheimer's view thus comes down to the claim that "Everything that is not reducible to numbers becomes illusion for the Enlightenment. This answer provides the unity from Parmenides to Russell. It stands on the destruction of the gods and qualitative differences." Predig Vranicki, *Geschichte des Marxismus*, 2 Bde. (Frankfurt, 1974), 831; Horkheimer and Adorno, *Dialectic of Enlightenment*, 6ff.

46. "Anti-semitic behavior is generated in situations where blinded men robbed of their subjectivity are set loose as subjects. For those involved, their actions are murderous and therefore senseless reflexes, as behaviorists note—without providing an interpretation. Anti-semitism is a deeply imprinted schema, a ritual of civilization; the pogroms are the true ritual murders. They demonstrate the impotence of sense, significance, and ultimately of truth—which might hold them within bounds . . . Action becomes an autonomous end in itself and disguises its own purposelessness." Max

Horkheimer and Theodor W. Adorno, *Dialectic of Enlightenment*, trans. John Cumming (New York, 1972), 171–72.

47. Ibid., 9; also, 87.

48. Note the seminal essay by Alfred Schmidt, "Aufklärung und Mythos im Werk Max Horkheimers," in *Max Horkheimer Heute: Werk und Wirkung*, hrsg. Alfred Schmidt und Norbert Altwicker (Frankfurt, 1986), 180ff.

49. "In the innermost recesses of humanism, at its very soul, there rages a frantic prisoner who, as a Fascist, turns the world into a prison." Adorno, *Minima Moralia*, 89.

50. "The permanent sign of enlightenment is domination over an objectified external nature and a repressed internal nature . . . Horkheimer and Adorno [thus] play a variation on the well-known theme of Max Weber, who sees the ancient, disenchanted gods rising from their graves in the guise of depersonalized forces to resume the irreconcilable struggles between the demons." Jürgen Habermas, "The Entwinement of Myth and Enlightenment: Max Horkheimer and Theodor Adorno," in *The Philosophical Discourse of Modernity: Twelve Lectures*, trans. Frederick Lawrence (Cambridge, Mass., 1987), 110.

51. Horkheimer summarized the position nicely when, in an aphorism from 1957–58, he wrote: "the destruction of the inner life is the penalty man has to pay for having no respect for any life other than his own. The violence that is directed outward and called technology, he is compelled to inflict on his own psyche." Horkheimer, *Dawn and Decline*, 161.

52. Note the rather pale historical discussion of 1926 by Max Horkheimer, "Vorlesung der deutschen idealistischen Philosophie von Kant bis Hegel," in *Gesammelte Werke* (Frankfurt, 1990), 10:12–23.

53. "The claim that democracy and aristocracy are different possibilities for a republic ultimately becomes irrelevant with the self-conscious turn of the nobility against the Enlightenment after 1815 and the inherently democratic political implications of most Enlightenment theorists." Horkheimer, "Die Aufklärung," 593.

54. Note the discussion in Stephen Eric Bronner, "The Great Divide: The Enlightenment and Its Critics," *New Politics*, volume 5, no. 3 (summer 1995), 65–86.

55. A very different view of the Enlightenment, which locates utopian resources in past philosophical traditions and movements seemingly leveled by an omnivorous instrumental reason, is provided by Ernst Bloch, *Natural Law and Human Dignity*, trans. Dennis J. Schmidt (Cambridge, Mass., 1986).

56. Note the historical argument developed by Ernst Nolte, *Three Faces of Fascism,* trans. Leila Vennewitz (New York, 1965); also, the philosophical argument, concerning the role of "non-synchronous contradictions" in analyzing fascism, by Ernst Bloch, *Erbschaft dieser Zeit* (Frankfurt, 1973), 45ff.

57. Neither Horkheimer nor Adorno ever took to heart the insight from Nietzsche with which they putatively agreed: "He who seeks to mediate between two bold thinkers . . . stamps himself mediocre: he has not the eyes to see uniqueness: to perceive resemblances everywhere, making everything alike, is a sign of weak eyesight." Adorno, *Minima Moralia*, 74.

58. ". . . liberal theory is true as an idea. It contains the image of a society in which irrational anger no longer exists and seeks for outlets. But since the liberal theory assumes that unity among men is already in principle established, it serves as an apologia for existing circumstances." Horkheimer and Adorno, *Dialectic of Enlightenment*, 169.

59. The willingness to treat any opponent of the communist movement as providing an "objective apology" for capitalism or fascism, as the case may be, emerged during the infamous "third period" of the Comintern and became routine under Stalinism. See Georg Lukács, *Die Zerstorung der Vernunft*, 3 Bde. (Darmstadt, 1962) 3:196ff.

60. Note the somewhat questionable claim that given how the argument highlights the

question of "organizational form," it has little in common with the "social fascist" thesis of the Communist Party. Dubiel, *Theory and Politics*, 71.

61. Habermas, "Max Horkheimer," 97.
62. It is revealing that in a commentary on Leo Lowenthal's *Prophets of Deceit*, Horkheimer could write: "I still do not quite understand your extreme caution about discussing the relation between democracy and fascism. Why should it be so daring to point to the trend of democracy towards fascism? In my opinion, this trend is one of the most important theses—nay, presuppositions—of any critical theory of present-day society." Cited in Leo Lowenthal, *Critical Theory and Frankfurt School Theorists: Lectures, Correspondence, Conversations* (New Brunswick, N.J., 1989), 206–7.
63. Nietzsche will later be termed by Horkheimer "the most radical enlightenment figure in all of philosophy." And in the general indeterminate sense of the term *enlightenment*, of course, that is arguable; in terms of the values and political ideas deriving from the movement, however, it is obviously nonsense. Here, the unfortunate consequences of using one term in two ways become obvious. Horkheimer, "Die Aufklärung," 574.
64. Horkheimer and Adorno, *Dialectic of Enlightenment*, xiii.
65. Note the discussion in Stephen Eric Bronner, *Ideas in Action: Political Tradition in the Twentieth Century* (Lanham, Md., 1999), 1ff.
66. Horkheimer and Adorno, *Dialectic of Enlightenment*, 120ff.
67. The notion that "high art" provided a critical and emancipatory alternative to that of the "popular" variety was already argued in the 1941 essay by Horkheimer, which anticipates much of the cultural argument in *Dialectic of Enlightenment*, titled "Art and Mass Culture," in *Critical Theory*, 273.
68. Martin Jay, "Mass Culture and Aesthetic Redemption: The Debate between Max Horkheimer and Siegfried Kracauer," in *Fin de Siecle Socialism and Other Essays* (New York, 1988), 82ff.
69. Adorno, *Minima Moralia*, 25.
70. "Mass culture in its different branches," Horkheimer could write to Leo Lowenthal, "reflects the fact that the human being is cheated out of his own entity which Bergson so justly called "durée." Cited in Lowenthal, *Critical Theory and Frankfurt School Theorists*, 203–4; also, Horkheimer, "Art and Mass Culture," 274–78.
71. Horkheimer, *Dawn and Decline*, 230.
72. While Adorno, Horkheimer, and Pollock returned, there were others like Marcuse and Lowenthal who decided to remain in the United States. "This permanently destroyed the possibility of re-establishing the sort of multidisciplinary research program begun in the early 1930s and continued to some degree or another in the 1940s. For, while Horkheimer talked in his inaugural address of merging American social science research methods with speculative social theory, the Institute undertook few multidisciplinary projects, and never really returned to serious work on developing a systematic social theory of the current epoch." Kellner, *Critical Theory, Marxism and Modernity*, 119–120.
73. Max Horkheimer, et al., *Aspects of Sociology*, trans. John Viertel (Boston, 1972).
74. "Democracy in the age of mass propaganda will not respect the constitution. Poor human rights that are anchored in it, poor freedom which democracy is meant to protect. But democracy exists for the sake of the majority, and human rights apply to the individual. Has there ever been a time when the individual was secure? Relatively so in the industrialized countries of the nineteenth century perhaps, but only perhaps. And freedom after all is the freedom of the so-called people, not of the individual. So don't worry as long as it is the majority that opts for constitutional change—change against the individual. That's why democracy leads to its opposite—tyranny." Horkheimer, *Dawn and Decline*, 159; also, 137, 141, 153, 179, 186–87, 233, and passim.
75. Horkheimer, "Traditional and Critical Theory," 245.

76. Note the interview with Max Horkheimer titled "Die Preis der Aufklärung," in *Gesammelte Schriften* (Frankfurt, 1989) 13:225ff.
77. Horkheimer, *Dawn and Decline*, 225
78. Ibid., 193ff.
79. Wiggershaus, *Die Frankfurter Schule*, 479ff.
80. "Philosophy is the futile attempt to achieve recognition for a kind of knowledge which is more than merely instrumental. It is the attempt to produce truth which not only has no practical purpose but cannot even be used in the ordering and application of the knowledge one has . . . Recourse to the immanent logic of the work of art is useless, for philosophy lays claim to a different kind of truth. What remains is insight into the impotence of all that is spirit and is not content with mere power. That is the truth, and at this point materialism and serious theology converge." Horkheimer, *Dawn and Decline*, 159–60.
81. "Horkheimer's theoretical and political decline represents one of the enigmas of the history of Critical Theory." Kellner, *Critical Theory, Marxism and Modernity*, 113.
82. The elder Horkheimer "begins with the assumption that truth cannot exist without an absolute . . . Without *ontological* anchoring, so he believes, the concept of truth must fall back into the innerworldly contingency of the mortal person." Jürgen Habermas, "Zu Max Horkheimers Satz: 'Einen unbedingten Sinn zu retten ohne Gott, ist eitel,'" in *Texte und Kontexte* (Frankfurt am Main, 1992), 119. A somewhat different view is offered in Max Horkheimer, *Sozialphilosophische Studien: Aufsätze, Reden, Vorträge 1930–1972* (Frankfurt am Main, 1972), 143.
83. Max Horkheimer, *Die Sehnsucht nach dem ganz Anderen* (Hamburg, 1970), 70.
84. Hans Günther Holl, "Religion und Metaphysik im Spätwerk Max Horkheimers," in *Max Horkheimer Heute*, 140ff.
85. "The state itself must regulate views and attitudes, must become totalitarian, for religion is finished. I mourn the loss of the superstitious belief in a Beyond. For the society that gets along without it, every step that brings it closer to paradise on earth will take it further from the dream which makes earth bearable." Horkheimer, *Dawn and Decline*, 223.
86. Max Horkheimer, "Die Aktualität Schopenhauers" and "Schopenhauers Denken," in *Gesammelte Schriften*, 7:136ff., 252ff. Also see Rudolf Siebert, *Horkheimer's Critical Sociology of Religion: The Relative and the Transcendent* (Washington, D.C., 1979); Schmidt, "Aufklärung und Mythos im Werk Max Horkheimers" in *Max Horkheimer heute*, 180ff.
87. Matthias Lutz-Bachmann, "Humanität und Religion: Zu Max Horkheimers Deutung des Christentums," in *Max Horkheimer Heute*, 108ff.; Joseph Maier, "Jüdisches Erbe aus deutschem Geist," in *Max Horkheimer Heute*, 146ff.
88. Horkheimer, *Die Sehnsucht nach dem ganz Anderen*, 62.

NOTES TO CHAPTER 7

1. Walter Benjamin, *Briefe*, 2 Bde., hrsg. Gershom Scholem und Theodor W. Adorno (Frankfurt am Main, 1966), 2:505.
2. Note the evaluations regarding its incomprehensibility by Hans Cornelius and Franz Schutz in *Walter Benjamin 1892–1940: Eine Austellung*, bearbeitet von Rolf Tiedemann et al. für den *Marbacher Magazin* 55 (1990) 72–73; also note the similar reception of Karl Kraus regarding Benjamin's laudatory essay on his work, 120ff.
3. On its proposed structure, Susan Buck-Morss, *The Dialectics of Seeing: Walter Benjamin and the Arcades Project* (Cambridge, 1991), 47ff.
4. Decisive for the reception of Benjamin in America was Hannah Arendt's article, which originally appeared in *The New Yorker* and then served as the introduction to her edition of Benjamin's *Illuminations*, trans. Harry Zohn (New York, 1969); it was also included in her own essay collection *Men in Dark Times* (New York, 1973).

5. Gershom Scholem, "Walter Benjamin and His Angel," in *On Jews and Judaism in Crisis*, ed. by Werner J. Dannhauser (New York, 1976), 198.

6. This produced a response from the right. In a superficial piece of intellectual biography, which confronts none of Benjamin's important works other than a single essay, an insulting and unscholarly attempt to debunk his influence and achievements was undertaken by Richard Vine, "The Beatification of Walter Benjamin," *The New Criterion* (June 1990), 37ff.

7. Ottmar John, "Fortschrittskritik und Erinnerung: Walter Benjamin, ein Zeuge der Gefahr," in *Erinnerung, Befreiung, Solidarität: Benjamin, Marcuse, Habermas und die politische Theologie*, ed. Edmund Arens et al. (Düsseldorf, 1991), 13ff.

8. Note the discussion by Eugene Lunn, *Marxism and Modernism: An Historical Study of Lukács, Brecht, Benjamin, and Adorno* (Berkeley, 1982), 188ff; Gershom Scholem, *Walter Benjamin: The Story of a Friendship*, trans. Harry Zohn (New York, 1981), 121ff., 227ff.

9. It was primarily in order to visit Lacis, who had fallen ill, that Benjamin made his only trip to the Soviet Union. His stark description of life in the increasingly authoritarian workers' state, along with the difficulties of following the official line in his work, led him to decide against joining the German Communist Party. Walter Benjamin, "Moscow Diary," trans. Richard Sieburth in *October* 35 (winter 1985), 9–121.

10. It is interesting that Benjamin should already have published a somewhat stilted review of the Lenin-Gorky correspondence in 1924. Walter Benjamin, *Gesammelte Schriften*, III, hrsg. Rolf Tiedemann und Hermann Schweppenhauser (Frankfurt am Main, 1972), 51ff.

11. That there is no simple break between the early and the mature Benjamin is emphasized by Sandor Radnoti, "The Early Aesthetics of Walter Benjamin," *International Journal of Sociology*, vol. VII, no. 1 (spring 1977), 76, as well as in Rolf Tiedemann's "Nachwort" to Walter Benjamin, *Charles Baudelaire: Ein Lyriker im Zeitalter des Hochkapitalismus* (Frankfurt am Main, 1969).

12. Note the letter to to Scholem of June 1917 in which Benjamin describes romanticism, which reproduced the inner unity between the religious and the historical in thinking and life experience, as the last movement seeking to explore the transcendent element of tradition. Walter Benjamin, *Briefe*, 1:137ff.

13. Benjamin, "Über das Programm der kommenden Philosophie," 27.

14. Benjamin could thus approvingly note that when children think about a story they become "directors" and do not bother about what makes sense in conventional terms. The concern with play and the attempt to free objects from "use" are utopian themes that recur throughout his writings. Walter Benjamin, "Aussicht ins Kinderbuch," in *Angelus Novus: Ausgewahlte Schriften*, 2 (Frankfurt am Main, 1966), 151ff.

15. Somewhat simplifying the issue and exaggerating the similarity, one important critic could claim that "Benjamin's intellectual dilemma was essentially the same as Adorno's: how could he reconcile his Marxist commitment with his Kantian effort in philosophy, especially when, furthermore, he considered religio-mystical and philosophical experience as one?" Susan Buck-Morss, *The Origin of Negative Dialectics: Theodor W. Adorno, Walter Benjamin, and the Frankfurt Institute* (New York, 1977), 21ff.

16. Note, in this regard, the beautiful essay that links memory to the experience of eating, or that of smoking hashish. Walter Benjamin, "Essen," in *Angelus Novus*, 161–69; also, Walter Benjamin, "Hashish in Marseilles," in *Reflections*, ed. Peter Demetz, and trans. Edmund Jephcott (New York, 1979), 131ff.

17. Theodor W. Adorno, *Über Walter Benjamin* (Frankfurt am Main, 1968), 11.

18. Ernst Bloch, "Erinnerung," in *Über Walter Benjamin*, 17.

19. Terry Eagleton, *The Ideology of the Aesthetic* (London, 1990), 328.

20. Walter Benjamin, *The Origins of German Tragic Drama* (London, 1977), 34; Buck-Morss, *The Origins of Negative Dialectics*, 96ff.
21. Eagleton, *The Ideology of the Aesthetic*, 334.
22. "Metaphors are the means by which the oneness of the world is poetically brought about. What is so hard to understand about Benjamin is that without being a poet he *thought poetically* and therefore was bound to regard the metaphor as the greatest gift of language." Hannah Arendt, "Walter Benjamin," in *Men in Dark Times*, 164.
23. It is subsequently legitimate to claim that "for all his renunciation of system, his thought, presented as that of a fragmentarian, yet retains a systematic tendency. He used to say that each great work needs its own epistemology just as it has its own metaphysics." Gershom Scholem, "Walter Benjamin," in *On Jews and Judaism in Crisis*, 182.
24. It makes sense that history should have been viewed by him as early as 1915 as "the objective element in time, something *perceptibly* objective." Scholem, *Walter Benjamin*, 13.
25. Ibid., 113.
26. Walter Benjamin, "On Language as Such and on the Language of Man," in *Reflections*, 321.
27. Benjamin, "Über das Programm der kommenden Philosophie," in *Angelus Novus*, 321.
28. Benjamin, *The Origins of German Tragic Drama* (London, 1977), 178ff.
29. "Allegory is always a symptom that, in a certain respect the subject-object distance has been sublated (*aufgehoben*), that the object-world has been transformed in its singification, that it has been worked through by the subject . . . Thus we approach the essence of allegory only then when we recognize it as a possibility which lies in the depths of the essence of language." In Hans Heinz Holz, "Prismatisches Denken," *Über Walter Benjamin*, 77.
30. Ibid., 76.
31. Georg Lukács, *Aesthetik*, 4 Bde. (Darmstadt, 1972), 4:164.
32. Scholem, "Walter Benjamin and His Angel," 203; Scholem, *Walter Benjamin*, 135.
33. Walter Benjamin, "Eduard Fuchs, der Sammler und der Historiker," in *Angelus Novus*, 302ff.
34. Walter Benjamin, "The Technique of the Critic in Thirteen Theses," in *Marbacher Magazin*, 112.
35. Restoration as the function of commentary is made evident in the Talmud; note the superb essay by Jürgen Habermas, "Gershom Scholem: The Torah in Disguise," in *Philosophical-Political Profiles*, trans. Frederick G. Lawrence (Cambridge, Mass., 1985), 201ff.
36. Again, in Talmudic terms, the redemptive power of language comes into play. See the intelligent discussion by Susan A. Handelman, *Fragments of Redemption: Jewish Thought and Literary Theory in Benjamin, Scholem, and Levinas* (Bloomington, 1991), 25ff.
37. Walter Benjamin, "The Task of the Translator," in *Illuminations*, trans. Harry Zohn (New York, 1969), 69ff.
38. Walter Benjamin, "Goethes Wahlverwandtschaften," in *Schriften*, 2 Bde. (Frankfurt, 1955), 1:56.
39. Michael Löwy, *Redemption et Utopie: Judaisme libératrice en Europe Central* (Paris, 1988).
40. His ties were to a "mystical tradition and to a mystical experience which nevertheless was a far cry from the experience of God, proclaimed by so many oversimplifying minds as the only experience deserving to be called mystical. Benjamin knew that mystical experience is many-layered and it was precisely this many-layeredness that played so great a role in his thinking." Scholem, "Walter Benjamin and His Angel," 201; also note the discussion by Irving Wolfarth, "On Some Jewish Motifs in Benjamin," in

The Problems of Modernity: Adorno and Benjamin, ed. Andrew Benjamin (London, 1989), 157ff., and Michael Löwy, "Religion, Utopia, and Counter-modernity: The Allegory of the Angel of History in Walter Benjamin," in *On Changing the World: Essays in Political Philosophy, From Karl Marx to Walter Benjamin* (Atlantic Highlands, N.J., 1992), 164ff.

41. Handelman, *Fragments of Redemption*, 137ff.
42. Scholem, *Walter Benjamin*, 56; also Benjamin, "Programm der kommenden Philosophie," 41.
43. Walter Benjamin, "Theses on the Philosophy of History." In *Illuminations*, 258.
44. Ibid., 254.
45. Ibid., 257.
46. Ibid., 261.
47. Ibid., 255.
48. Theodor Adorno, "Walter Benjamin," in *Prisms*, 236.
49. Walter Benjamin, "Zur Kritik der Gewalt," in *Angelus Novus*, 42ff.
50. Rolf Tiedemann, "An Interpretation of the Theses 'On the Concept of History'" in *The Philosophical Forum* 2:1–2 (fall to winter, 1983–84), 91ff.
51. Benjamin's actual political commitments are rarely discussed, and when they are, even in the otherwise superb study by Susan Buck-Morss, an uncritical stance incapable of relating them to his metaphysics is generally the norm. Buck-Morss, *Dialectics of Seeing*, 317ff; also, see the chapter titled "Léon Blum and the Legacy of the Popular Front," in Stephen Eric Bronner, *Moments of Decision: Political History and the Crises of Radicalism* (New York, 1991), 57ff.
52. Benjamin, "Theses on the Philosophy of History," 264.
53. Note the discussion by Richard Wolin, *Walter Benjamin: An Aesthetic of Redemption* (New York, 1982), 213ff; also, Arendt, "Walter Benjamin," 164.
54. It is logical, in a way, that Carl Schmitt—the brilliant legal thinker and Nazi collaborator—should have expressed his admiration for Benjamin's essay on Sorel. Jürgen Habermas, "The Horrors of Autonomy: Carl Schmitt in English," in *The New Conservatism: Cultural Criticism and the Historians' Debate*, trans. and ed. Shierry Weber Nicholson (Cambridge, Mass., 1992), 137.
55. Scholem, "Walter Benjamin," 187.
56. Rolf Tiedemann, "Historical Materialism or Political Messianism?", 91.
57. Note the discussion by Karl Korsch, *Karl Marx* (New York, 1938), 84; also note Karl Marx, "Theses on Feuerbach," in Karl Marx and Friedrich Engels, *Selected Works*, 3 vols. (Moscow, 1969), 1:13; Handelman, *Fragments of Redemption*, 163ff.
58. The belief that it is impossible to confront the proletariat with preconceived utopian tasks is a constant in the work of Marx; the remark about the proletariat's not having goals of its own to realize must be set in the context of the young Marx's concern with extending democracy from the realm of the state into civil society in works like *On the Jewish Question* and *The Holy Family*.
59. Alluding to this point, Horkheimer stated the obvious when he chastised his friend in a letter: "The injustice, the terror, the pains of the past are irreparable"; cited in Buck-Morss, *The Origins of Negative Dialectics*, 57.
60. Christian Lenhardt, "Anamnestic Solidarity: The Proletariat and Its *Manes*," in *Telos* 25 (fall 1975), 136ff, 141ff.
61. Löwy, "Revolution against 'Progress': Walter Benjamin's Romantic Anarchism," in *On Changing the World*, 143ff.
62. Walter Benjamin, "Goethes Wahlverwandtschaften," 131.
63. Leo Lowenthal, *An Unmastered Past*, ed. Martin Jay (Berkeley, 1987), 227.
64. "How misery, and not just social misery but rather architectonic misery as well, the misery of the interior turns enslaved and enslaving things into revolutionary nihilism, of that

no one before these seers and astrologers has been aware . . ." Benjamin, "Der Surrealismus: Die letzte Momentaufnahme der europäischen Intelligenz," in *Angelus Novus*, 204.

65. "Whereas earlier interpreters have seen his pessimism regarding the course of history as a late characteristic of his thinking, coming as a response to the Nazi-Soviet Non-Aggression Pact or the impending war, the *Passagen-Werk* makes it clear that it was his long-standing (if intensifying) concern." Buck-Morss, *The Dialectics of Seeing*, 79.

66. Eugene Lunn, *Marxism and Modernism*, 166.

67. Walter Benjamin, "What Is Epic Theatre?," in *Understanding Brecht*, trans. Anna Bostock (London, 1973), 2, 4, 8.

68. Lowenthal, *An Unmastered Past*, 224.

69. "The construction of life at the moment lies far more in the power of facts than in convictions." Walter Benjamin, *Einbahnstrasse*, in *Schriften*, 2:515.

70. Obvious problems arise if it is true that Benjamin "charts philosophical ideas visually within an unreconciled and transitory field of oppositions that can perhaps best be pictured in terms of coordinates of contradictory terms, the 'synthesis' of which is not a movement toward resolution, but the point at which their axes intersect." Buck-Morss, *The Dialectics of Seeing*, 210.

71. Lukács, *Aesthetik*, 4:169.

72. If this desire along with the importance attributed to montage appears in the collection of letters by historical personalities, which appeared individually in the *Frankfurter Zeitung* in 1931/2 and were then published by Benjamin under the pseudonym Detlef Holz in 1936, the need for introductions to them—no less than their importance—evidences the difficulty of having aesthetic or historical objects speak for themselves. Walter Benjamin, *Deutsche Menschen: Eine Folge von Briefen* (Frankfurt, 1984).

73. Max Horkheimer, "Notes on the Crisis," in *Critical Theory and Society: A Reader*, ed. Stephen Eric Bronner and Douglas Kellner (New York, 1989), 52.

74. Cited in *Marbacher Magazin*, 45.

75. Löwy, "Fire Alarm: Walter Benjamin's Critique of Technology," in *On Changing the World*, 175ff.

76. It appears in an earlier essay titled the "Short History of Photography," for example, where Benjamin notes that early photographs by Eugene Atget retain elements of the aura they would later lose owing to commercial exploitation. Note the critique of Benjamin's mechanical juxtaposition of the auratic against the mass produced in T. W. Adorno, *Aesthetic Theory*, trans. C. Lenhart, ed. Gretl Adorno and Rolf Tiedemann (London, 1984), 82–83.

77. Walter Benjamin, *Charles Baudelaire: A Lyric Poet in the Era of High Capitalism*, trans. Harry Zohn (London, 1973), 148.

78. Adorno is correct when, concerning Benjamin's compilation of historical letters, he observes that "a historical judgment over the letter as form [has been rendered]. It is anarchronistic; who is still able to write them highlights capacities grown archaic; actually, letters can no longer be written. Benjamin provided them with a monument." Theodor Adorno, "Afterword" to *Deutsche Menschen*, 95.

79. Walter Benjamin, "The Work of Art in the Age of Mechanical Reproduction," in *Illuminations*, 221.

80. Walter Benjamin, "The Author as Producer," in *Understanding Brecht*, 89.

81. Ibid., 101.

82. Benjamin, *Charles Baudelaire*, 105.

83. This is why Adorno could attack the notion of "dialectical images" and further claim that Benjamin's Baudelaire manuscript "lacks one thing: mediation," in "Letters to Walter Benjamin," *New Left Review* 81 (September–October, 1973), 70; also note the evaluation of the dispute by Wolin, *Walter Benjamin*, 163ff.

84. Benjamin, *Charles Baudelaire*, 103.
85. Buck-Morss, *The Dialectics of Seeing*, 221.
86. Ibid., 142.
87. Benjamin, "The Technique of the Critic in Thirteen Theses," 112.
88. Walter Benjamin, "Die politische Gruppierung der russichen Schriftsteller," in *Angelus Novus*, 193
89. Benjamin, "The Author as Producer," 86.
90. Ibid., 98.
91. Walter Benjamin, *Der Begriff der Kunstkritik in der deutschen Romantik* (Frankfurt, 1973), 67.
92. Lowenthal, *An Unmastered Past*, 110.

NOTES TO CHAPTER 8

This is a revised version of an article originally entitled "Expressionism and Marxism: Towards an Aesthetics of Emancipation," in *Passion and Rebellion: The Expressionist Heritage*, ed. Stephen Eric Bronner and Douglas Kellner (2d ed., New York, 1988).

1. An excellent collection on socialist realism has been edited by Hans-Jürgen Schmidt and Gödehard Schramm, *Sozialistische Realismuskonzeption: Dokumente zum 1. Allunionskongress der Sowjetschriftsteller* (Frankfurt, 1974).

2. The articles constituting the debate have been collected by Hans-Jürgen Schmidt, *Die Expresionismusdebatte: Materialen zu einer marxistischen Realismuskonzeption* (Frankfurt, 1973). Sections of the debate also comprise the anthology by Frederic Jameson, *Aesthetics and Politics* (London, 1978), while many of Brecht's contributions are included in "Brecht on Social Realism," in *New Left Review* 84, and in *Brecht on Theatre*, ed. John Willet (New York, 1975).

3. Note the 1967 introduction to Georg Lukács, *History and Class Consciousness: Studies in Marxist Dialectics* (Cambridge, Mass., 1971), ix.

4. George Lukács, "Es geht um den Realismus," in *Marxismus und Literature*, 3 Bde., hrsg. Fritz Raddatz (Hamburg, 1969), 2:64.

5. "The formative depth (*Gestaltung*), the breadth and durability of a realistic writer's effectiveness depends largely on the extent of his formal (*gestalterisch*) awareness of what the manifestations described by him actually represent. This conception of the relation of a significant writer to reality does not in any way exclude, as Bloch believes, the realization that the surface of reality manifests ruptures (*Zersetzungen*) and accordingly reflects itself in the consciousness of men." Ibid.

6. The aesthetic position developed in the expressionism debate prefigures the philosophical assault on irrationalism launched in 1954 by Lukács, *Die Zerstörung der Vernunft*, 3 Bde. (Darmstadt, 1974 ed.)

7. Georg Lukács, "'Grösse und Verfall' des Expressionismus," in *Marxismus und Literatur*, 2:17.

8. Perhaps the real instigator of the entire debate, Alfred Kurella, argued that expressionism directly led to fascism. Lukács was never in accord with this far more crude interpretation. He argued only that expressionism—perhaps even unintentionally—helped create the climate in which fascism could thrive. Note the discussion by Kurella in "nun ist dies Erbe zuende . . . ," in *Marxismus und Literatur*, 2:43ff.

9. Lukács, "Grösse und Verfall," 13.

10. Lukács, 'Es geht um den Realismus,' 70.

11. Georg Lukács, *Realism in Our Time*, trans. John and Necke Mander (New York, 1964).

12. Note the evaluations of Fadeyev, Makarenko, and Sholokov in Georg Lukács, *Russische Revolution, Russische Literatur* (Berlin, 1969), 166ff; also Georg Lukács, "Briefwechsel mit Anna Seghers," in *Marxismus und Literatur*, 2:118.

13. Henry Pachter, "Orthodox Heretic, Romantic Stalinist: On the Ninetieth Birthday of

George Lukács," in *Socialism in History: Political Essays of Henry Pachter*, ed. Stephen Eric Bronner (New York, 1984), 295ff.
14. Lukács, "Es geht um den Realismus," 83.
15. Ernst Bloch, *Erbschaft dieser Zeit* (Frankfurt, 1973), 149.
16. Ibid., 270.
17. Ibid., 266.
18. Ernst Bloch, *Geist der Utopie* (Frankfurt, 1974 ed.), 20.
19. Georg Lukács, "Narrate or Describe?", in *Writer and Critic and Other Essays* (New York, 1971).
20. Ernst Bloch, *Die Kunst, Schiller zu Sprechen* (Frankfurt, 1974 ed.), 65.
21. Bloch, *Erbschaft dieser Zeit*, 258.
22. Ibid., 270.
23. Ibid., 267.
24. Bloch, *Geist der Utopie*, 43.
25. Ernst Bloch, *Das Prinzip Hoffnung*, 3 vols. (3d ed., Frankfurt am Main, 1973), 1:257.
26. The diary notation of Walter Benjamin speaks to this concern: "The publication of Lukács, Kurella *et al.* are giving Brecht a good deal of trouble. He thinks, however, that one ought not to oppose them at the theoretical level." Walter Benjamin, *Understanding Brecht*, trans. Anna Bostock (London, 1973), 116.
27. Henry Pachter, "Brecht's Personal Politics," in *Weimar Etudes* (New York, 1982), 225ff.
28. Bertolt Brecht, "Über den Dadaismus," in *Gesammelte Werke*, 20 vols. (Frankfurt, 1967), 18:6.
29. Jost Hermand, "Brecht on Utopia," in *The Minnesota Review* NS6 (spring 1976), 96ff.
30. Bertolt Brecht, "Förderungen an eine neue Kritik," in *Gesammelte Werke*, 18:113.
31. Bertolt Brecht, "Praktischen zur Expressionismusdebatte," in *Gesammelte Werke*, 19:327.
32. Bertolt Brecht, "Uber alte und neue Kunst," in *Gesammelte Werke*, 19:314.
33. Bertolt Brecht, "Bemerkungen zum Formalismus," in *Gesammelte Werke*, 18:314.
34. Brecht, "Volkstumlichkeit und Realismus," in *Gesammelte Werke*, 19:326.

NOTES TO CHAPTER 9
1. Theodor W. Adorno, *Minima Moralia: Reflections from Damaged Life*, trans. E. F. N. Jephcott (London, 1974), 16.
2. "Freedom has contracted to pure negativity ... The objective end of humanism is only another expression for the same thing. It signifies that the individual as individual, in representing the species of man, has lost the autonomy through which he might realize the species." Ibid., 38.
3. Theodor W. Adorno, *Negative Dialectics*, trans. E. B. Ashton (New York, 1973), 20ff.
4. Note the discussion in the famous section on "commodity fetishism," in Karl Marx, *Das Kapital*, 3 vols., ed. Friedrich Engels, trans. Samuel Moore and Edward Aveling (New York, 1967), 1:71ff.
5. "The word alienation ... acknowledges by the very tenacity with which it views the alien external world as institutionally opposed to the subject—in spite of all its protestations of reconciliation—the continuing irreconcilability of subject and object, which constitutes the theme of dialectical criticism." Adorno, *Minima Moralia*, 246.
6. Note the excellent discussion by Gillian Rose, *The Melancholy Science: An Introduction to the Thought of Theodor W. Adorno* (New York, 1978), 43ff.
7. Stefan Breuer, "Adorno's Anthropology," in *Telos* 64 (summer 1985), 15ff.
8. Theodor W. Adorno, "Die revidierte Psychoanalyse" and "Zum Verhaltnis von Soziologie und Psychologie," in *Soziologische Schriften* (Frankfurt, 1979), 1:20–85.
9. Drucilla Cornell, "The Ethical Message of Negative Dialectics," in *Social Concept* 4:1 (December 1987), 3ff.

10. Theodor W. Adorno et al., *The Positivist Dispute in German Sociology*, trans. Glyn Adey and David Frisby (London, 1976), 35ff.

11. Ibid., 12ff.

12. Georg Lukács, *History and Class Consciousness: Studies in Marxist Dialectics*, trans. Rodney Livingstone (Cambridge, Mass., 1968), 15ff.

13. Rose, *The Melancholy Science*, 146.

14. Adorno, *Negative Dialectics*, 320; also cf. Theodor W. Adorno, "Fortschritt," in *Stichworte* (Frankfurt, 1978).

15. Arnold Künzli, "Irrationalism on the Left," in *Foundations of the Frankfurt School of Social Research*, ed. Judith Marcus and Zoltan Tar (New Brunswick, N.J., 1984), 140–41; also, Paul Connerton, *The Tragedy of Enlightenment: An Essay on the Frankfurt School* (Cambridge, 1980), 113ff.

16. The critique of ideology, bereft of a practical agent to realize the repressed possibilities of emancipation, can only "*dispute* the *truth* of a suspicious theory by *exposing its untruthfulness*. It advances the process of enlightenment by showing that a theory presupposing a demythologized understanding of the world is still ensnared by myth, by pointing out a putatively overcome category mistake." Jürgen Habermas, *The Philosophical Discourse of Modernity: Twelve Lectures*, trans. Frederick Lawrence (Cambridge, Mass., 1987), 116.

17. "Negative philosophy, dissolving everything, dissolves even the dissolvent. But the new form in which it claims to suspend and preserve both, dissolved and dissolvent, can never emerge in a pure state from an antagonistic society. As long as domination reproduces itself, the old quality reappears unrefined in the dissolving of the dissolvent: in a radical sense no leap is made at all." Adorno, *Minima Moralia*, 245.

18. Hartmut Scheible, *Theodor W. Adorno* (Hamburg, 1989), 55.

19. Theodor Adorno, "Kulturkritik und Gesellschaft," in *Prismen* (Frankfurt, 1955), 27.

20. Karl Marx, "Theses on Feuerbach" in Karl Marx and Friederich Engels, *Selected Works*, 3 vols. (Moscow, 1969), 1:11; Karl Korsch, *Karl Marx* (New York, 1938), 84.

21. T. W. Adorno, *Aesthetic Theory*, ed. Gretl Adorno and Rolf Tiedemann, trans. C. Lenhardt (London, 1972), 30–31.

22. "In the modern administered world the only adequate way to appropriate art works is one where the uncommunicable is communicated and where the hold of reified consciousness is thus broken." Ibid., 280.

23. An indication of this becomes apparent in the following: "What is unique about music, however, is the indeterminate conceptual quality; change and articulation by means typical of music alone are highly determinate. Music gains content because it gives itself a totality of defining characteristics." Ibid., 282.

24. Theodor W. Adorno, "The Actuality of Philosophy," in *Telos* 31 (spring 1977), 128.

25. Rose, *The Melancholy Science*, 13ff. Lambert Zuidervaart, *Adorno's Aesthetic Theory: The Redemption of Illusion* (Cambridge, Mass., 1991), 45ff.

26. Frederic Jameson, *Late Marxism: Adorno, or, The Persistence of the Dialectic* (London, 1990), 179.

27. Adorno, *Negative Dialectics*, 24ff.

28. Adorno, "The Actuality of Philosophy," 129.

29. Adorno, *Negative Dialectics*, 3.

30. Peter Osborne, "Adorno and the Metaphysics of Modernism: The Problem of a 'Postmodern' Art," in *The Problems of Modernity: Adorno and Benjamin*, ed. Andre Benjamin (London, 1989), 23ff.

31. Rose, *The Melancholy Science*, 68ff.

32. Scheible, *Theodor W. Adorno*, 76.

33. Christa Hackenesch, "Erfahrung von Nichtidentität," in *Philosophische Rundschau* 1–2 (1993), 106ff.

34. Adorno, *Negative Dialectics*, 5, 138.
35. Ibid., 153–54.
36. Ibid., 211ff.
37. Jürgen Habermas, "Der Horizont der Moderne verschiebt sich," in *Nachmetaphysisches Denken: Philosophische Aufsätze* (Frankfurt, 1992), 13.
38. Erstwhile defenders of Adorno like Leo Lowenthal tend to dismiss the criticisms of "rebellious youngsters" like the fine scholar Andreas Huyssen and the important activist Hans-Jürgen Krahl with sophistic queries about what disasters would have befallen future culture had Adorno and his colleagues joined the barricades or through caricatured references to the radicalism of the 1960s. The mistake made by Huyssen and Krahl is not one of political evaluation. It derives instead from their inability to deal immanently with Adorno's concepts in their own terms. Cf. Leo Lowenthal, "Adorno and His Critics," in *Critical Theory and Frankfurt Theorists: Lectures—Correspondence—Conversations* (New Brunswick, N.J., 1989), 54ff; Hans-Jürgen Krahl, "The Political Contradictions in Adorno's Critical Theory," *Telos* 21 (fall 1974), 164; Andreas Huyssen, "Introduction to Adorno," *New German Critique* 6 (fall 1975), 3.
39. "No theory, not even the true one, is secure from perversion into madness once its spontaneous relation to the object has been externalized." Theodor W. Adorno, "Kulturkritik und Gesellschaft," in *Prismen*, 29.
40. "For the intellectual, inviolable isolation is now the only way of showing some measure of solidarity. All collaboration, all the human worth of social mixing and participation, merely masks a tacit acceptance of inhumanity. It is the sufferings of men that should be shared: the smallest step towards their pleasures is one towards the hardening of their pains." Adorno, *Minima Moralia*, 26.
41. Adorno, *Negative Dialectics*, 297.
42. Adorno, *Minima Moralia*, 129.
43. Theodor W. Adorno, *Kierkegaard: Konstruktion des Aesthetischen* (Frankfurt am Main, 1979). For a summary of the critique developed in this unnecessarily convoluted work, see Martin Jay, *Adorno* (Cambridge, 1984), 29ff.
44. Adorno, *Aesthetic Theory*, 286; *Negative Dialectics*, 160ff.
45. Theodor W. Adorno, "On the Fetish Character of Modern Music and the Regression of Listening," in *The Essential Frankfurt School Reader*, ed. Andrew Arato and Eike Gebhardt (New York, 1978), 299.
46. "My argument is that precisely because art works are monads they lead to the universal by virtue of their principle of particularization. In other words, the general characteristics of art are more than just responses to the need for conceptual reflection: they also testify to the fact that the principle of individuation has its limits and that neither it nor its opposite should be ontologized. Art works approach this limit by ruthlessly pursuing the principle of individuation, whereas if they pose as universals, they end up being accidental and pseudo-individual like examples of a type or species." Adorno, *Aesthetic Theory*, 259.
47. Ibid., 11.
48. Irving Wohlfarth, "Dialektischer Spleen. Zur Ortsbestimmung der Adornoschen Aesthetik," in *Materialien zur ästhetischen Theorie Theodor W. Adornos Konstruktion der Moderne*, hrsg. Burkhardt Lindner und W. Martin Ludke (Frankfurt am Main, 1980), 318.
49. "*Angst*, that supposed 'existential,' is the claustrophobia of a systematized society. Its system character, yesterday still a shibboleth of academic philosophy, is strenuously denied by initiates of that philosophy; they may, with impunity, pose as spokesmen for free, for original, indeed, for unacademic thinking ... [But] the things philosophy has yet to judge are postulated before it begins. The system, the form of presenting a total-

ity to which nothing remains extraneous, absolutizes the thought against each of its contents and evaporates the content in thoughts. It proceeds idealistically before advancing any arguments for idealism." Adorno, *Negative Dialectics*, 24; note also, what was originally to have been included in this major volume, by Theodor W. Adorno, *The Jargon of Authenticity*, trans. Knut Tarnowski and Frederic Will (London, 1973).

50. Adorno, *Negative Dialectics*, 283.
51. "The more the work of art seeks to liberate itself from external determinations, the more it becomes subject to self-positing principles of organization, which mime and internalize the law of an administered society." Terry Eagleton, *The Ideology of the Aesthetic* (London, 1990), 351.
52. Adorno, *Aesthetic Theory*, 346.
53. Ibid., 20–1.
54. Ibid., 351 and passim; Max Horkheimer and Theodor W. Adorno, *Dialectic of Enlightenment*, trans. John Cumming (New York, 1972), 81ff.
55. Adorno, *Minima Moralia*, 80.
56. Scheible, *Theodor W. Adorno*, 16.
57. Adorno, *Aesthetic Theory*, 334.
58. Ibid., 350.
59. Adorno, *Minima Moralia*, 122.
60. Habermas, "Motive nachmetaphysichen Denkens," in *Nachmetaphysisches Denken*, 45.
61. Ibid., 145.
62. "Knowledge as such, even in a form detached from substance, takes part in tradition as unconscious remembrance; there is no question which we might simply ask, without knowing of past things that are preserved in the question and spur it." Ibid., 54.
63. Adorno, *Aesthetic Theory*, 27.
64. Adorno, *Negative Dialectics*, 63.
65. Adorno, *Negative Dialectics*, 151.
66. Adorno, *Aesthetic Theory*, 189; also, Eagleton, *The Ideology of the Aesthetic*, 361.
67. "Unlike discursive knowledge, art does not rationally understand reality, including its irrational qualities which stem in turn from reality's law of motion. However, rational cognition has one critical limit which is its inability to cope with suffering. Reason can subsume suffering under concepts; it can furnish means to alleviate suffering; but it can never express suffering in the medium of experience for to do so would be irrational by reason's own standards." Ibid., 27.
68. Albrecht Wellmer, *The Persistence of Modernity Essays on Aesthetics, Ethics, and Postmodernism*, trans. David Midgley (Cambridge, Mass: 1991), 5ff.
69. Adorno, *Aesthetic Theory*, 197.
70. Ibid., 6.
71. Ibid., 293.
72. Ibid., 3.
73. The tension between them, in fact, casts doubt on Benjamin's belief that "the adjustment of art to extra-aesthetic technique has always automatically spelled intra-aesthetic progress." Ibid., 310.
74. "[W]e must look not at the sphere of reception, but at the more basic sphere of production. Concern with the social explication of art has to address the production of art rather than study its impact." Ibid., 324.
75. Ibid., 304.
76. Ibid., 207.
77. Nor does it help to claim that "truth content is that which is not illusory in the artistic illusion. Truth content is that which transcends via that which is transcended." Zuidervaart, *Adorno's Aesthetic Theory*, 201ff. This is playing with words. *What*, concretely, is

not illusory in the illusion? *What* mediates transcendence? Technique? The configuration of elements in the artwork? Talk of this sort only turns the products of human activity into human agents. There is, in fact, no mediated transcendence at all in Adorno's thinking since mediating transcendence would involve providing it with a *concrete* and positive historical determination. That, however, is precisely what his notion of illusion cannot provide.

78. Adorno, *Aesthetic Theory*, 22.
79. "Meaning is responsible for producing illusion and therefore contributes in a major way to the illusory quality of art. Still, the essense of meaning is not synonymous with illusion; it is more. Above all, the meaning of a work of art is also the summoning to appearance of an essence that is otherwise hidden in empirical reality. This is the purpose of organizing the work of art in such a way that the moments are grouped 'meaningfully' in relation ot one another." Ibid., 154.
80. Horkheimer and Adorno, *Dialectic of Enlightenment*, xvi.
81. Adorno, *Minima Moralia*, 214.
82. Adorno, *Aesthetic Theory*, 268ff.
83. Ibid., 190.
84. Rüdiger Bubner, "Kann Theorie aesthetisch werden? Zum Hauptmotiv der Philosophie Adornos," in *Materialien zur ästhetischen Theorie Theodor W. Adornos Konstruktion der Moderne*, 108ff.
85. "Relativism, no matter how progressive its bearing, has at all times been linked with moments of reaction, beginning with the sophists' availability to the more powerful interests. To intervene by criticizing relativism is the paradigm of definite negation." Adorno, *Negative Dialectics*, 37.
86. "The less identity can be assumed between subject and object, the more contradictory are the demands made upon the cognitive subject, upon its unfettered strength and candid self-reflection." Ibid., 31.
87. Adorno, *Aesthetic Theory*, 203.
88. "When we say that works undergo changes we mean something more than changes in reception and appropriation: there are objective changes taking place in the works themselves, which must mean that there is a force bound up in them that lives on." Ibid., 276.
89. Ibid., 243.
90. "Becoming aware of the constellation in which a thing stands is tantamount to deciphering the constellation which, having come to be, it bears within it." Adorno, *Negative Dialectics*, 163.
91. Adorno, *Aesthetic Theory*, 325
92. Peter Bürger, "Das Vermittlungsproblem in der Kunstsoziologie Adornos," in *Materialien zur ästhetischen Theorie Theodor W. Adornos Konstruction der Moderne*, 175.
93. "In art, the criterion of success is twofold: first, works of art must be able to integrate materials and details into their immanent law of form; and second, they must not try to erase the fractures left by the process of integration, preserving instead in the aesthetic whole the traces of those elements which resisted integration." Adorno, *Aesthetic Theory*, 10.
94. Ibid., 296–302.
95. Ibid., 274.
96. "The development of artworks is therefore the posthumous life of this inner dynamic. What an artwork expresses by virtue of the configuration of its moments differs objectively from one epoch to the next, and ultimately this change affects its truth content, namely at the point where it becomes uninterpretable." Ibid., 277.
97. "Nietzsche, the irreconcilable adversary of our theological heritage in metaphysics, had ridiculed the difference between essence and appearance. He had relegated the

'background world' to the 'backwoodsmen,' concurring here with all of positivism. Nowhere else, perhaps, is it so palpable how an undefatigable enlightement will profit the obscurantists. Essence is what must be covered up, according to the mischief-making law of unessentiality; to deny that there is an essence means to side with appearance, with the totality ideology which existence has since become. If a man rates all phenomena alike because he knows of no essence that would allow him to discriminate, he will in a fanaticized love of truth make common cause with untruth." Adorno, *Negative Dialectics*, 169.

98. Ibid., 362ff.
99. Adorno, *Aesthetic Theory*, 278.
100. Ibid., 128.
101. Zuidervaart, *Adorno's Aesthetic Theory*, 178ff.
102. Ibid., 147.
103. Ibid., 312.
104. Ibid., 119-20.
105. "Mistrust is called for in face of all spontaneity, impetuosity, all letting oneself go, for it implies pliancy towards the superior might of the existent." Theodor W. Adorno, *Minima Moralia*, 25.
106. Adorno, *Aesthetic Theory*, 236.
107. Adorno, *Minima Moralia*, 70.
108. Ibid., 115.
109. Jameson, *Late Marxism*, 182ff.
110. Adorno, *Minima Moralia*, 51 and passim.
111. References to the influence of Adorno on those concerned with developing an immanent critique of the logic of capital does not help matters; indeed, whatever their quality, investigations of this sort have been notoriously lacking in developing genuine political implications or bridging the gap between the phenomenological and the empirical moments of the analysis. Note the seminal works by Alfred Sohn-Rethel, *Geistige und körperliche Arbeit: Zur Theorie der gesellschaftlichen Synthesis* (Frankfurt am Main, 1970); Roman Rosdolsky, *The Making of Marx's Capital* (London, 1977).
112. "By being different from the ungodly reality, art negatively embodies an order of things in which empirical being would have its rightful place." Adorno, *Aesthetic Theory*, 322.
113. "The social deviance of art is the determinate negation of a determinate society." Ibid., 321.
114. Note his conformist stance on the cold war and his embarrassingly conservative role in the student movement. Scheible, *Theodor W. Adorno*, 131; Rolf Wiggershaus, *Die Frankfurter Schule: Geschichte, Theoretische Entwicklung, Politische Bedeutung* (München, 1988), 676ff.
115. Theodor W. Adorno, "Society," in *Critical Theory and Society*, 275.
116. Adorno, *Aesthetic Theory*, 124.
117. Ibid., 323.
118. Adorno, *Negative Dialectics*, 143.
119. Franz Neumann, "The Concept of Political Freedom," in *The Democratic and the Authoritarian State: Essays in Political and Legal Theory*, ed. Herbert Marcuse (New York, 1957), 160ff; Henry Pachter, "Freedom, Authority, Participation," in *Socialism in History: Political Essays of Henry Pachter*, ed. Stephen Eric Bronner (New York, 1984), 36ff.
120. Adorno, *Aesthetic Theory*, 58–59.
121. "Happiness is an accidental moment of art, less important even than the happiness that attends the knowledge of art. In short, the very idea that enjoyment is of the essence of art deserves to be overthrown." Adorno, *Aesthetic Theory*, 22.

122. Ibid., 154ff.
123. Adorno, *Minima Moralia*, 28, 102.
124. Adorno, *Aesthetic Theory*, 281.
125. Theodor W. Adorno, "Zeitlose Mode. Zum Jazz," in *Prismen*, 144ff.
126. Jameson, *Late Marxism*, 137, 145.
127. Habermas, *The Philosophical Discourse of Modernity*, 123; also, his "Nachwort" to *Dialektik der Aufklärung* (Frankfurt, 1986 ed.).
128. Adorno, "Veblens Angriff auf die Kultur," in *Prismen*, 82ff.
129. Various nontraditional Marxists of the 1968 generation in Germany, including Ulrike Meinhoff in the name of the Red Army Faction, tried to justify the use of terror by making reference to the writings of Adorno. Note the article by Paul Berman, "The Passion of Joschka Fischer: From the Radicalism of the '60s to the Interventionism of the 90s," *The New Republic Online*, 08.27.01, 23ff.
130. Adorno, *Minima Moralia*, 173.

NOTES TO CHAPTER 10

1. It is regrettable that the only full-length study of Fromm's work to appear in English for many years abstracted his arguments from their social and philosophical context and, through a deadening textual critique, often trivialized them. The influence of his religious background in Talmudic studies, critical theory, and the broader intellectual-political milieu of the Weimar Republic was never made clear in John Schaar, *Escape from Authority: The Perspectives of Erich Fromm* (New York, 1961). Notable improvements took place in the succeeding full-length studies by Don Hausdorff, *Erich Fromm* (New York, 1972); Rainer Funk, *Erich Fromm: The Courage to Be Human* (New York, 1982); and Daniel Burston, *The Legacy of Erich Fromm* (Cambridge, Mass., 1991).

2. On his friendship and conflicts within this circle, see Rainer Funk, *Erich Fromm: Selbstzeugnissen und Bilddokumenten* (Hamburg, 1983), 54ff. and passim, and the excellent discussion of the various controversies by Bursten, *The Legacy of Erich Fromm*, passim.

3. Rolf Wiggershaus, *Die Frankfurter Schule: Geschichte, Theoretische Entwicklung, Politische Bedeutung* (München, 1988), 14; also, Erich Klein-Landskron, "Max Horkheimer und Erich Fromm," in *Erich Fromm und die Frankfurter Schule*, hrsg. Michael Kessler und Rainer Funk (Tübingen, 1992), 161ff.

4. Erich Fromm, *Beyond the Chains of Illusion. My Encounter with Marx and Freud* (New York, 1963), 5ff.; Funk, *Erich Fromm: Bildnisse und Zeugnisse*, 28–45; also Wiggershaus, *Die Frankfurter Schule*, 67ff.; Zoltan Tar and Judith Marcus, "Erich Fromm und das Judentum," in *Erich Fromm und die Frankfurter Schule*, 217ff.

5. Rainer Funk, "Der Humanismus in Leben und Werk von Erich Fromm: Laudatio zum 90 Geburtstag," in *Jahrbuch der Internationalen Erich-Fromm Gesellschaft*, Bd. 3 (1992), 133ff.

6. Michael Kessler, "Das Versprechen der Schlange: Religion und Religionskritik bei Erich Fromm und die Frankfurtern," in *Erich Fromm und die Frankfurter Schule*, 131ff.

7. Edgar Z. Friedenberg, "Neo-Freudianism and Erich Fromm," *Commentary* (October 1962), 307.

8. Note the penetrating profile of Hitler drawn by Erich Fromm, *The Anatomy of Human Destructiveness* (New York, 1972), 411ff.

9. Fromm was among those who developed the tools of social theory that would be used by those members who later became more closely associated with Horkheimer's "inner circle." Axel Honneth, "Kritische Theorie: Vom Zentrum zur Peripherie einer Denktradition," *Kölner Zeitschrift für Soziologie und Sozialpsychologie*, vol. 41, no. 1 (March 1989), 2ff.

10. Wiggershaus, *Die Frankfurter Schule*, 298ff.

11. Note the excellent introduction by Wolfgang Bonss to Erich Fromm, *Arbeiter und Angestellte am Vorabend des Dritten Reiches. Eine sozial-psychologische Untersuchung* (Stuttgart, 1980).
12. "The personal relation of Fromm to Marcuse was different than the one he had with Horkheimer and Adorno. There was never a friendly relationship with Adorno. Horkheimer certainly made a strong impression on Fromm in the 1930s. But Fromm began to feel in Horkheimer the effects of Adorno's attempt to 'rephilosophize' the later 'critical theory' or what was called the marxist theory of society. Fromm later interpreted this development on the part of Horkheimer as a retreat into the bourgeoisie and bourgeois society which received its most consequent expression in Horkheimer's rediscovery of established religion ('the longing for the totally other') and in his acceptance of honorary citizenship by the city of Frankfurt." Funk, *Erich Fromm: Bildnisse und Zeugnisse*, 98.
13. Wolfgang Bonss, "Analytische Sozialpsychologie: Anmerkungen zu einem theoretischen Konzept und seiner empirischen Praxis," in *Erich Fromm und die Frankfurter Schule*, 23ff.
14. Erich Fromm, "Psychoanalysis and Sociology" along with "Politics and Psychoanalysis in," in *Critical Theory and Society: A Reader*, ed. Stephen Eric Bronner and Douglas Kellner (New York, 1989), 37–39, 213–18.
15. An indicative view is given in a letter of 13 September 1941 from Leo Lowenthal to Max Horkheimer where he writes: "Mr. Fromm's book . . . is a work of inexpressible boredom. Despite our requests, we didn't receive a review copy, probably due to the author's own wish. Fromm, incidentally, has now landed where he belongs. The courses he is giving at the secessionist psychoanalytic union have been incorporated in the New School's lecture program. Since you enjoy an outstanding memory, you no doubt recall that a few years ago none of us were capable of besting Mr. Fromm in characterizing that institution negatively." Leo Lowenthal, *Critical Theory and Frankfurt Theorists: Lectures, Correspondence, Conversations* (New Brunswick, N.J., 1989), 186.
16. Too often, however, American interpreters have mistakenly argued that Fromm identified the formation of the authoritarian personality with the degree to which capitalist individualism flourished and then criticized him for ignoring the fact that fascism was not successful in the United States or Great Britain. The political issue thus drops out in favor of a prefabricated economistic idea of Marxism with which Fromm never identified himself. Indeed, this standpoint becomes particularly clear in Bruce Mazlish, "American Narcissism," in *The Psychohistory Review*, vol. 10, nos. 3–4 (spring–summer 1982), 192–93.
17. "Every neurosis is an example of dynamic adaptation; it is essentially an adaptation to such external conditions as are in themselves irrational and, generally speaking, unfavorable to the growth of the child." Erich Fromm, *Escape From Freedom* (New York, 1965 ed.), 30.
18. Note the critique of this revisionism by Theodor W. Adorno, "Die revidierte Psychoanalyse," in *Der Stachel Freud: Beitrage und Documente zur Kulturismus-Kritik*, ed. Bernhard Görlich, Alfred Lorenzer, and Alfred Schmidt (Frankfurt am Main, 1980), 119ff; also, Herbert Marcuse, *Eros and Civilization: A Philosophical Inquiry into Freud* (New York, 1962 ed.), 217ff.
19. Moving public opinion to affect institutional decision making was, whatever the "obstacle" posed by the mass media, always considered a "real possibility." Erich Fromm, *The Revolution of Hope: Toward a Humanized Technology* (New York, 1968), 143.
20. Erich Fromm, *The Sane Society* (New York, 1955), 131ff.
21. Erich Fromm, "The Application of Humanist Psychoanalysis to Marx's Theory," in

Socialist Humanism: An International Symposium (New York, 1966), 231.

22. Note the summary of his views in Erich Fromm, *Greatness and Limitations of Freud's Thought* (New York, 1980).

23. A critical psychoanalytic view of this position is offered by Otto Fenichel, "Psychoanalytische Bemerkungen zu Fromms Buch *Die Furcht vor der Freiheit*," in *Der Stachel Freud*, 93ff; also, cf. Bernard Görlich, "'Trieb' und/oder 'Gesellschaftscharakter'? Anmerkungen zu Fromms Versuch einer 'Neubestimmung der Psychoanalyse,'" in *Erich Fromm und die Frankfurter Schule*, 75ff.

24. Erich Fromm, *Man for Himself: An Inquiry into the Psychology of Ethics* (New York, 1947), 21ff.

25. Thus he "emphatically disagrees with [Freud's] interpretation of history as the result of psychological forces that in themselves are not socially conditioned [and] as emphatically with those theories which neglect the role of the human factor as one of the dynamic elements in the social process." Fromm, *Escape from Freedom*, 28–29.

26. Note the excellent discussion by R. B. O'Neill, "Character, Society, and the Politics of Hope: A Comparative Look at the Theories of Wilhelm Reich, Erich Fromm, and Herbert Marcuse," in *The Humboldt Journal of Social Relations*, vol. 2, no. 2 (spring–summer 1975), 39ff.

27. Erich Fromm, *Marx's Concept of Man* (New York, 1961), 133.

28. At stake is "the dialectic character of the process of growing freedom. Our aim will be to show that the structure of modern society affects man in two ways simultaneously: he becomes more independent, self-reliant, and critical, and he becomes more isolated, alone, and afraid. The understanding of the whole problem of freedom depends on the very ability to see both sides of the process and not to lose track of one side while following the other." Fromm, *Escape from Freedom*, 124.

29. Fromm, *The Sane Society*, 40ff.

30. Erich Fromm, *Sigmund Freud's Mission* (New York, 1959), 109–11.

31. Note the intelligent discussion by Honneth, "Kritische Theorie," 22; also, Martin Jay, *The Dialectical Imagination: A History of the Frankfurt School and the Institute of Social Research, 1923–1950* (Boston, 1973), 229ff.

32. Erich Fromm, *The Crisis of Psychoanalysis: Essays on Freud, Marx, and Social Psychology* (New York, 1970), 1–30; also, Erich Fromm, *The Revision of Psychoanalysis* (Boulder, 1992), 1ff.; on the debate with Marcuse, Daniel Burston, "Auf den Spuren Freuds: Fromm und Marcuse," in *Erich Fromm und die Frankfurter Schule*, 61ff.

33. Fromm, *Escape from Freedom*, 159.

34. Note the discussion by Russell Jacoby, *Social Amnesia: A Critique of Conformist Psychology from Adler to Laing* (Boston, 1975), 13–15, 33ff.; also, Bernard Görlich, "Die Kulturismus-Revisionismus-Debatte: Anmerkungen zur Problemgeschichte der Kontroverse um Freud," in *Der Stachel Freud*, 13ff.

35. Martin Jay, "The Frankfurt School in Exile," in *Perspectives in American History*, vol. VI (1972), 351.

36. Fromm, "The Application of Humanist Psychoanalysis to Marx's Theory," 233.

37. Fromm, *The Revolution of Hope*, 32–34.

38. Fromm, *The Sane Society*, 173.

39. Ibid., 12ff., 40ff., 237ff., and passim.

40. Fromm, *Escape from Freedom*, 207.

41. Max Horkheimer, *Eclipse of Reason* (New York, 1947), 184.

42. Leland M. Griffin, "The Rhetorical Structure of the New Left Movement," *The Quarterly Journal of Speech*, vol. L, no. 2 (April 1964), 114.

43. Erich Fromm, *May Man Prevail? An Inquiry into the Facts and Fictions of Foreign Policy* (New York, 1961), 67ff.; also note the articles collected in *Ethik und Politik: Antworten auf aktuelle politische Fragen*, hrsg. Rainer Funk (Basel, 1990) 53–86. On the character

of Soviet foreign policy, see Heinz Pächter, *Weltmacht Russland: Aussenpolitsche Strate-gie in Drei Jahrhunderten* (Oldenburg, 1968). For my own views on the transformation of the Soviet Union , see *Socialism Unbound*, 2d ed. (Boulder, 2001), 77ff.

44. His critique of Soviet repression with respect to its eradication of an independent ethical realm no less than its puritanism and authoritarian attempts to ensure conformism and raise production, interestingly enough, relies heavily on the important study by his principal antagonist in the debate over Freud: Herbert Marcuse, *Soviet Marxism* (New York, 1958).

45. Fromm, *May Man Prevail?*, 57.

46. Ibid., 17ff.

47. Fromm, *Ethik und Politik*, 135ff.

48. Fromm, *May Man Prevail?*, 154ff.

49. Note the debate over Fromm's claim that nonintervention was a necessary cold war policy even if it meant maintaining the status quo, *New Politics*, vol. 1, no. 3 (spring 1962), and vol. 1, no. 4 (fall 1962).

50. Fromm, *Ethik und Politik*, 94ff.; 132ff.; 204ff.

51. Even in Europe, "only with the student movement, which was led back to the writings of the Institute for Social Research while engaged in its own search for an orientation, did [critical theory] enter into the public consciousness as a unified theoretical project." Honneth, "Kritische Theorie," 1.

52. It did, however, have a marked influence on the intellectuals who constitute what has been called "the generation of '68." Martin Jay, *Marxism and Totality: The Adventures of a Concept from Lukács to Habermas* (Berkeley, 1984), 19.

53. Fromm, *The Sane Society*, 263ff.

54. "Marx's concern was man, and his aim was man's liberation from the predomination of material interests, from the prison his own arrangements and deeds had built around him." Fromm, "The Application of Humanist Psychoanalysis to Marx's Theory," 228–29.

55. "Man's drives, inasmuch as they are transutilitarian, are an expression of a fundamental and specifically human need: the need to be related to man and nature and to confirm himself in this relatedness." Fromm, *The Revolution of Hope*, 69.

56. Leszek Kolakowski, *Main Currents of Marxism: The Breakdown*, III, trans. P. S. Falla (Oxford, 1978), 386ff.

57. "The majority of the population in America is well fed, well housed, and well amused, and the sector of 'underdeveloped' Americans who still live under substandard conditions will probably join the majority in the foreseeable future. We continue to profess individualism, freedom, and faith in God, but our professions are wearing thin when compared with the reality of the organization man's obsessional conformity guided by the principle of hedonistic materialism." Erich Fromm, *The Revolution of Hope*, 27.

58. In fairness, however, it is important to note that Fromm did not believe "production as such should be restricted; but that once the optimal needs of individual consumption are fulfilled, it should be channeled into more production of the means for social consumption such as schools, libraries, theaters, parks, hospitals, etc." Fromm, "The Application of Humanist Psychoanalysis to Marx's Theory," 238.

59. "The growing doubt of human autonomy and reason has created a state of moral confusion where man is left without the guidance of either revelation or reason. The result is the acceptance of a relativistic position which proposes that value judgments and ethical norms are exclusively matters of taste or arbitrary preference and that no objectively valid statement can be made in this realm. But since man cannot live without values and norms, this relativism makes him an easy prey for irrational value systems . . . Irrationalism, whether veiled in psychological, philosophical, racial, or political terms, is not progress but reaction. The failure of eighteenth- and

nineteenth-century rationalism was not due to its belief in reason but to the narrowness of its concepts. Not less but more reason and an unabating search for the truth can correct errors of a one-sided rationalism—not a pseudo-religious obscurantism." Fromm, *Man for Himself*, 4–5, ix.

60. "The contemporary human crisis has led to a retreat from the hopes and ideas of the Enlightenment under the auspices of which our political and economic progress had begun . . . The ideas of the Enlightenment taught man that he could trust his own reason as a guide to establishing valid ethical norms and that he could rely on himself, needing neither revelation nor the authority of the church in order to know good and evil." Ibid.

61. Fromm, *The Revolution of Hope*, 143.

62. Fromm, *Escape from Freedom*, 80.

63. "Planning itself is one of the most progressive steps the human race has taken. But it can be a curse if it is 'blind' planning, in which man abdicates his own decision, value judgment, and responsibility. If it is alive, responsive, 'open,' planning, in which the human ends are in full awareness and guiding the planning process, it will be a blessing." Fromm, *The Revolution of Hope*, 55.

64. Ibid., 32–35.

65. Erich Fromm, *To Have or to Be?* (1976), 155–60.

66. "The managerial elite are also different from those of old in another respect: they are just as much appendages of the machine as those whom they command. They are just as alienated or perhaps more so, just as anxious, or perhaps more so, as the worker in one of their factories. They are bored, like everyone else, and use the same antidotes against boredom." Fromm, *The Revolution of Hope*, 32.

67. Fromm, *The Sane Society*, 183ff.

68. Fromm, *The Philosophy of Hope*, 107–13.

69. Note in particular Martin Buber, *Paths in Utopia*, trans. R. F. C. Hull (Boston, 1958).

70. Fromm, *Man for Himself*, 9–10.

71. John Schaar is correct in noting that Fromm's use of alienation lacks the "precision" of Marx's original formulation. Unfortunately, however, he doesn't carry through this insight and focuses his criticism on an exaggerated rendering of Fromm's *lebensphilosophie* rather than any problems caused by the lack of emphasis on class, institutions, and production. Schaar, *Escape from Authority*, 193ff.

72. Augustin Souchy, *'Vorsicht: Anarchist!' Ein Leben für die Freiheit: Politische Erinnerungen* (Darmstadt, 1977), 11.

73. "For if one is not concerned with steps between the present and the future, one does not deal with politics, radical or otherwise." Fromm, *The Revolution of Hope*, 8–9.

74. Ibid., 154–56.

75. Fromm, *To Have or to Be?*, 40–41.

76. Fromm, *Man for Himself*, 230.

77. Jorge Silva Garcia, "Erich Fromm in Mexiko: 1950–1973," in *Jahrbuch der Internationalen Erich-Fromm Gesellschaft*, 3:11ff.; Alfonso Millan, "Die Entwicklung der Mexikanischen Psychoanalytischen Gesellschaft und des Mexikanischen Instituts für Psychoanalyse," in *Jahrbuch der Internationalen Erich-Fromm Gesellschaft*, 3:27ff.; also, Funk, *Erich Fromm*, 116ff.

78. Even the attempt to view this as a "negative theology" places an unwarranted philosophic and systematic character on perspective; Rudolf J. Siebert, "Fromm's Theory of Religion," *Telos* 34 (winter 1977–78), 111ff. Fromm's view of God, his emphasis on spirituality without idols, is beautifully articulated by Ramon Xirau, "Erich Fromm: What Is Man's Struggle," in *In the Name of Life: Essays in Honor of Erich Fromm*, ed. Bernard Landis and Edward S. Tauber (New York, 1971), 150ff.

79. "Even whether there is harmony or conflict, joy or sadness, is secondary to the funda-

mental fact that two people experience themselves from the essence of their existence, that they are one with each other by being one with themselves, rather than by fleeing from themselves. There is only one proof for the presence of love: the depth of the relationship, and the aliveness and strength in each person concerned; this is the fruit by which love is recognized." Erich Fromm, *The Art of Loving* (New York, 1956), 103.

80. "Success, prestige, money, power—almost all our energy is used for the learning of how to achieve these aims, and almost none to learn the art of loving . . . Could it be that only those things are considered worthy of being learned with which one can earn money or prestige and that love, which 'only' profits the soul, but is profitless in the modern sense, is a luxury we have no right to spend much energy on?" Ibid., 6.

81. Jay, "The Frankfurt School in Exile," 343ff.

82. "I want the loved person to grow and unfold for his own sake, and in his own ways, and not for the purpose of serving me. If I love the other person, I feel one with him or her, but with him as he is, not as I need him to be as an object for my use." Fromm, *The Art of Loving*, 28.

83. "The point I want to make is to uphold the principle that a person has an inalienable right to live—a right to which no conditions are attached and which implies the right to receive the basic commodities necessary for life, the right to an education and to medical care; he has a right to be treated at least as well as the owner of a dog or a cat treats his pet, which does not have to 'prove' anything in order to be fed." Fromm, *The Revolution of Hope*, 125.

84. Ibid., 142.

85. "The assumption that the problems, conflicts, and tragedies between man and man will disappear if there are no materially unfulfilled needs is a childish daydream." Ibid., 107.

86. Schaar, *Escape from Authority*, 22.

87. Note my discussion in "Reconstructing the Experiment: Politics, Ideology, and the New Left in America," in *Moments of Decision: Political History and the Crises of Radicalism* (New York, 1992).

88. Note the interesting piece by Neil McLaughlin, "How to Become a Forgotten Intellectual: Intellectual Movements and the Rise and Fall of Erich Fromm," in *Sociological Forum*, vol. 13, no. 2 (1998), 215ff.

NOTES TO CHAPTER 11

1. "The final culmination of philosophy is thus at the same time its abdication. Released from its preoccupation with the ideal, philosophy is also released from its opposition to reality. This means that it ceases to be philosophy. It does not follow, however, that thought must then comply with the existing order. Critical thinking does not cease, but assumes a new form. The efforts of reason devolve upon social theory and social practice." Herbert Marcuse, *Reason and Revolution: Hegel and the Rise of Social Theory* (Boston, 1969), 28.

2. Ibid., 9.

3. Herbert Marcuse, *One-Dimensional Man: Studies in the Ideology of Advanced Industrial Society* (Boston, 1964), 144.

4. Note the fascinating analysis undertaken by Marcuse in collaboration with Franz Neumann, "A History of the Doctrine of Social Change" and "Theories of Social Change," in Herbert Marcuse, *Technology, War, and Fascism* (New York, 1999), 93ff. and 105ff.

5. Marcuse, *One-Dimensional Man*, 19ff.

6. Herbert Marcuse, "The End of Utopia," in *Five Lectures* (Boston, 1970), 68–69.

7. For a provocative argument, which claims that his social theory implicitly projects a theological discourse, see Peter Rottlander, "Philosophie, Gesellschaftstheorie, und die Permanenz der Kunst; Theologische Reflexionen zur Herbert Marcuse," in *Erinnerung, Befreiung, Solidarität: Benjamin, Marcuse, Habermas, und die politische Theologie*, ed. Edumund Arens et al. (Düsseldorf, 1991), 81ff.

8. Herbert Marcuse, "Der deutsche Kunstlerroman," in *Schriften* (Frankfurt, 1978), 1:7ff. In this vein, however, the radical interpretation of what remains the best general biography on Marcuse suggests that his work is basically a critical meditation on Marx and an experiment with the utopian implications of his thought. See Douglas Kellner, *Herbert Marcuse and the Crisis of Marxism* (Berkeley, 1984).
9. Marcuse, "The Obsolescence of the Freudian Concept of Man," in *Five Lectures*, 58.
10. Marcuse, *One-Dimensional Man*, 70.
11. "The authentic utopia is grounded in recollection . . . Forgetting past suffering and past joy alleviates life under a repressive reality principle. In contrast, remembrance spurs the drive for the conquest of suffering and the permanence of joy. But the force of remembrance is frustrated; joy itself is overshadowed by pain . . . If the remembrance of things past would become a motive power in the struggle for changing the world, the struggle would be waged for a revolution hitherto suppressed in the previous historical revolutions." Herbert Marcuse, *The Aesthetic Dimension: Toward a Critique of Marxist Aesthetics* (Boston, 1978), 73. Note also the excellent discussion by Martin Jay, *Marxism and Totality: The Adventures of a Concept from Lukács to Habermas* (Berkeley, 1984), 224ff.
12. Herbert Marcuse, "The Affirmative Character of Culture," in *Negations*, trans. Jeremy J. Shapiro (Boston, 1969), 230.
13. Marcuse, *The Aesthetic Dimension*, 47.
14. Marcuse, *One-Dimensional Man*, 63.
15. Herbert Marcuse, *Counterrevolution and Revolt* (Boston, 1972), 98.
16. Marcuse, "The Affirmative Character of Culture," 118–19.
17. Ibid., 122.
18. "The truth value of the imagination relates not only to the past, but also to the future: the forms of freedom and happiness which it invokes claim to deliver the historical *reality*. In its refusal to accept as final the limiations imposed upon freedom and happiness by the reality principle, in its refusal to forget what can *be*, lies the critical function of fantasy." Herbert Marcuse, *Eros and Civilization: A Philosophical Inquiry into Freud* (New York, 1962), 135.
19. Ibid., 105.
20. Rolf Wiggershaus, *Die Frankfurter Schule: Geschichte, Theoretische Entwicklung, Politische Bedeutung* (Frankfurt am Main, 1988), 398ff.
21. Ibid., 74.
22. Ibid., 41.
23. The attempt to reintroduce a sense of harmony and what has been excluded or repressed from consciousness results, for some, in Marcuse's contributing along with Carl Jung to a "feminization" of political thought by his employment of utopian aesthetics as a form of therapeutic practice. That the concrete character of such a therapy is never disclosed, that Marcuse is explicitly engaging in a metapsychological discourse, that the aesthetic is not a substitute but rather the goal of politics, and that—in contrast to Jung—his politics is predicated on progressive and rationalist assumptions are not entertained by Gertrude A. Steuernagel, *Political Philosophy as Therapy: Marcuse Reconsidered* (Westport, Conn., 1979), 117ff. Also, since the author does not seem clear about why Marcuse never embraced Jung, it is useful to consider the excellent critique of Freud's former disciple from a critical utopian standpoint by Ernst Bloch, *Erbschaft dieser Zeit* (Frankfurt, 1973), 344ff.; *Das Prinzip Hoffnung*, 3 Bde. (Frankfurt am Main, 1973), 1:181ff. A useful overview of the psychological dimension of Marcuse's thought is provided by Edward Hyman, "Eros and Freedom: The Critical Psychology of Herbert Marcuse," in *Marcuse: Critical Theory and the Promise of Utopia* ed. Richard Pippen et al. (London, 1988), 143ff.
24. Marcuse, *Eros and Civilization*, 34.
25. Marcuse, *Counterrevolution and Revolt*, 29ff.

26. Paul A. Robinson, *The Freudian Left: Wilhelm Reich, Geza Roheim, Herbert Marcuse* (New York, 1969), 208; note also Burston.

27. Marcuse, "Progress and Freud's Theory of Instincts," in *Five Lectures*, 37.

28. Sigmund Freud, "Repression," in *General Psychological Theory*, ed. Philip Rief (New York, 1962), 105.

29. Sigmund Freud, *The Ego and the Id*, trans. Joan Riviere (New York, 1960), 35.

30. This becomes apparent in the evaluation of hedonism. In spite of what is often an inability to distinguish between prefabricated and autonomously chosen forms of enjoyment, hedonism maintains that happiness is a moment of truth. Herbert Marcuse, "On Hedonism," in *Negations*, 159ff.

31. Marcuse, "The Obsolescence of the Freudian Concept of Man," 47.

32. "The stars, the consorts of royalty, the kings and champion sportsmen have the function which demigods had in mythology; they are human to a superlative degree and therefore to be imitated, their behavior has a normative character. But as they are not of this world one can only imitate them in a small way, on one's own level, and not presume to match oneself with them in reality." Reimut Reiche, *Sexuality and Class Struggle*, trans. Susan Bennett (New York, 1971), 71.

33. Theodor W. Adorno, "Zeitlose Mode. Zum Jazz," in *Prismen: Kulturkritik und Gesellschaft* (Frankfurt am Main, 1955), 144ff.

34. Marcuse, "The Obsolescence of the Freudian Concept of Man," 55.

35. Marcuse, *One-Dimensional Man*, 73ff.; *Eros and Civilization*, 75ff.

36. "The perversion of the aesthetic: whereas the aesthetic is a totality formed by sublimation of the instincts, the spectacle releases instinctual energies but does not bind them into forms. On the other hand, the spectacle as aesthetic and as consumption prevents the individual from experiencing action and process; he is an actor only as an object and a subject only as a spectator; he consumes rather than makes." Shierry M. Weber, "Individuation as Praxis," in *Critical Interruptions: New Left Perspectives on Herbert Marcuse*, ed. Paul Breines (New York, 1970), 37.

37. Marcuse, "Art and Revolution," *Partisan Review* (spring 1972), 178.

38. Ibid., 179.

39. Marcuse, *Counterrevolution and Revolt*, 99.

40. Ibid., 67.

41. His interest in this extraordinary artist and intellectual already occurred early in life; thus, the research that resulted in Herbert Marcuse, *Schiller-Bibliographie* (Berlin, 1925).

42. This fits with Freud's view of fantasy as the only thought activity still preserved from reality testing and subordinate to the pleasure principle; it inherently wishes "to satisfy those wishes which reality does not satisfy." Sigmund Freud, "The Theme of the Three Caskets," in *Character and Culture* (New York, 1963), 76.

43. Friedrich Schiller, *On the Aesthetic Education of Man* (New York, 1965), 76.

44. Herbert Marcuse, *An Essay on Liberation* (Boston, 1969) 24.

45. Marcuse, *One-Dimensional Man*, 239.

46. Alfred Schmidt, "Existential Ontology and Historical Materialism in the Work of Herbert Marcuse" in *Marcuse: Critical Theory and the Promise of Utopia*, 47ff.

47. Marcuse, *Eros and Civilization*, 110.

48. Marcuse, "The End of Utopia," 78.

49. Still, Marcuse was less clear on the subject than many may believe. Varied statements suggest that his desire to break with the formal principle of progress was predicated on a commitment to maintain its substantive foundations. This, of course, would produce a fundamental contradiction. Note the discussion by Andrew Feenberg, *The Critical Theory of Technology* (New York, 1991), 76ff.; Kellner, *Herbert Marcuse*, 227ff., 326ff.

50. Jürgen Habermas, "Technology and Science as Ideology: For Herbert Marcuse on His 70th Birthday," in *Toward a Rational Society: Student Protest, Science, and Politics*, trans. Jeremy J. Shapiro (Boston, 1970), 81ff.

51. Erich Fromm, *The Crisis of Psychoanalysis: Essays on Freud, Marx, and Social Psychology* (New York, 1970), 1ff.; also Erich Fromm, *The Revision of Psychoanalysis*, ed. Rainer Funk (Boulder, 1992), 111ff.

52. Herbert Marcuse, "Gesellschaftliche und psychologische Repression. Die politische Aktualität Freuds," in *Der Stachel Freud: Beitrage und Dokumente zur Kulturismus-Kritik* ed. Bernard Görlich, Alfred Lorenzer, and Alfred Schmidt (Frankfurt am Main, 1980), 186ff.

53. Geza Roheim, *Magic and Schizophrenia* (Bloomington, 1970), 4.

54. Ibid., 111.

55. Sigmund Freud, *Civilization and Its Discontents*, trans. and ed. James Strachey (New York, 1961), 62–63.

56. Marcuse, *An Essay on Liberation*, 21–28.

57. Vincent Geoghegan, *Reason and Eros: The Social Theory of Herbert Marcuse* (London, 1981), 1–5.

58. "The new sensibility . . . emerges when the struggle is waged for essentially new ways and forms of life," negation of the entire Establishment, its morality, culture, affirmation of the right to build a society in which the abolition of poverty and toil terminates in a universe where the sensuous, the playful, the calm, and the beautiful become forms of existence and thereby the form of society itself." Marcuse, *An Essay on Liberation*, 25.

59. Marcuse, *Counterrevolution and Revolt*, 102.

60. Marcuse, "Repressive Tolerance," in Robert Paul Wolff, Barrington Moore Jr., and Herbert Marcuse, *A Critique of Pure Tolerance*, 88.

61. Richard Lichtman, "Repressive Tolerance" in *Marcuse: Critical Theory and the Promise of Utopia*, 189ff.

62. Marcuse, "Repressive Tolerance," 89.

63. Marcuse, "Progress and Freud's Theory of the Instincts," in *Five Lectures*, 28.

64. He was indeed aware that the crucial problem is that advanced industrial society throws the subject "back upon himself, [so that he or she] learn[s] to bear, and in a certain sense, to love his isolation." Herbert Marcuse, "The Affirmative Character of Culture," 122.

65. Marcuse, *One-Dimensional Man*, 56ff.

66. Ibid., 46ff., 256ff.

67. Marcuse was no political neophyte. As chief of the Central European Branch, Division of Research, of the Department of State, "he exerted an enormous influence in discussion and theory formation" with respect to questions dealing with denazification and organizations like the social democrats and the trade unions capable of contributing to the democratic reconstruction of Germany. Indeed, especially during the postwar years, "this picture of Marcuse as the proponent of Anglo-Saxon democratic constitutionalism or Social-Democratic reform seems to clash with every familiar image of him and his politics—the radical thinker of Weimar, the intellectual precursor of the student movement, the vehement critic of social democratic quietism who grasped the repressive tolerance inherent in American liberalism and its paralyzing of every radical opposition." Alfons Söllner, "Marcuse's Political Theory in the 1940s and 1950s," *Telos* 74 (winter 1988), 69, 73; also Barry Katz, "The Frankfurt School Goes to War," *Journal of Modern History* 59 (September 1987), 439ff.

68. To this extent, even while the general theoretical point is correct, the historical context is not taken into account when a critic of Marcuse claims that politics "must remain until those who continue to profit from an adversary relationship with nature are

deposed; for they are the 'serious ones' who could easily take advantage of individuals committed to aesthetic transcendence. The aesthetic perspective may be crucial to the liberated society; however, it cannot be expected in any way to be responsible for the creation of such a society." Timothy J. Lukes, *The Flight into Inwardness: An Exposition and Critique of Herbert Marcuse's Theory of Liberative Aesthetics* (Cranbury, N.J., 1985), 162.

69. Paul Breines, "Marcuse and the New Left in America," in *Antworten auf Herbert Marcuse*, ed. Jürgen Habermas (Frankfurt, 1968), 134ff.

70. Marcuse, *The Aesthetic Dimension*, 32.

71. Herbert Marcuse, *Soviet Marxism* (New York, 1961), 113ff.

72. Marcuse, *Counterrevolution and Revolt*, 101.

73. Brad Rose, "The Triumph of Social Control? A Look at Herbert Marcuse's *One-Dimensional Man*, 25 Years Later," in *Berkeley Journal of Sociology* 35 (1990), 55ff.

NOTES TO CHAPTER 12

1. Eight volumes of his *Kleine Politische Schriften* had already appeared when this chapter was first written, and more will follow. Much has already been translated in works like Jürgen Habermas, *The New Conservatism: Cultural Criticism and the Historians' Debate*, trans. and ed. Shierry Weber Nicholson (Cambridge, Mass., 1992).

2. Robert Holub, *Jürgen Habermas: Critic in the Public Sphere* (New York, 1991), 78ff.

3. Note the new translation of this important debate in its entirety by James Knowlton and Truett Cates under the title *Forever in the Shadow of Hitler?* (Atlantic Highlands, N.J., 1993).

4. Jürgen Habermas, *Zur Rekonstruktion des Historischen Materialismus* (Frankfurt, 1976), 49ff. and 144ff.; also, for a critique, Tom Rockmore, *Habermas on Historical Materialism* (Indianapolis, 1989), and Richard Roderick, *Habermas and the Foundations of Critical Theory* (New York, 1986).

5. Note, for example, the strained attack by Alessandro Ferrara, "A Critique of Habermas' *Diskursethik*," *Telos* 64 (summer 1985), 45ff.

6. Jürgen Habermas, "Die Krise des Wohlfahrtsstaates und die Erschöpfung utopischer Energien," in *Die Neue Unübersichtlichkeit* (Frankfurt, 1985), 141ff.

7. Thomas Mann, "The Light of Recent History," in *Last Essays*, ed. Richard Winston et al. (New York, 1970), 162.

8. Jürgen Habermas, "Motive nachmetaphysischen Denkens," in *Nachmetaphysisches Denken: Philosophische Aufsätze* (Frankfurt, 1988), 35ff.; Jürgen Habermas, "An Alternative Way out of the Philosophy of the Subject," in *The Philosophical Discourse of Modernity*, trans. Frederick Lawrence (Cambridge, Mass., 1987), 294ff.

9. Jürgen Habermas, *Strukturwandel der Öffentlichkeit: Untersuchungen zu einer Kategorie der bürgerlichen Gesellschaft* (Darmstadt und Neuwied, 1971), 46ff.

10. "*Structural Transformation* moved totally within the circule of a classical Marxian critique of ideology, at least as it was understood in the Frankfurt environment. What I meant to do was to take the liberal limitations of public opinion, publicity, the public sphere, and so on, at their worst, and then try to confront these ideas of publicness with their selective embodiments and even the change of their very meaning during the process of transformation from liberal to organized capitalism, as I described it at that time." Jürgen Habermas, "Concluding Remarks," in *Habermas and the Public Sphere*, ed. Craig Calhoun (Cambridge, Mass., 1992), 463.

11. Ibid., 211ff.

12. Max Horkheimer and Theodor W. Adorno, *Dialectic of Enlightenment*, trans. John Cumming (New York, 1982), 256.

13. Jürgen Habermas, *The Theory of Communicative Action*, 2 vols., trans. Thomas McCarthy (Boston, 1987), 2:333ff.

14. Jürgen Habermas, "The Public Sphere: An Encyclopedia Article," in *Critical Theory and Society*, ed. Stephen Eric Bronner and Douglas Mackay Kellner (New York, 1989), 142.

15. Martin Jay, *Marxism and Totality: The Adventures of a Concept from Lukács to Habermas* (Berkeley, 1984), 464.

16. Habermas's first published work, an indignant response in 1953 to the republication of Heidegger's *Introduction to Metaphysics* from 1935 in which he simply ignored its most compromising portions, now appears in Jürgen Habermas, "Zur Veröffentlichung von Vorlesungen aus dem Jahre 1935," in *Philosophisch-politische Profile* (Frankfurt, 1971).

17. Jürgen Habermas, *Autonomy and Solidarity*, ed. Peter Dews (London, 1992), 192, 43–61.

18. Habermas, *The Theory of Communicative Action*, 2:374ff.

19. Note the fine discussion by Neil Saccamano, "The Consolations of Ambivalence: Habermas and the Public Sphere," *MLN* 106 (1991), 685ff.

20. Oskar Negt und Alexander Kluge, *Zur Organisationsanalyse von bürgerlicher und proletarischer Öffentlichkeit* (Frankfurt am Main, 1977), 106ff.; also, Peter Uwe Hohendahl, "Kritische Theorie, Öffentlickheit und Kultur. Anmerkungen zu Habermas und seinen Kritikern," *Basis* 8 (1978), 60–90.

21. Jürgen Habermas, *Knowledge and Human Interests*, trans. Jeremy J. Shapiro (Boston, 1971), 198ff.

22. Jürgen Habermas, *On the Logic of the Social Sciences*, trans. Shierry Weber Nicholson and Jerry A. Stark (Cambridge, Mass., 1988), 24, 92.

23. Habermas, *Knowledge and Human Interests*, 196.

24. Ibid., 308.

25. Ibid., 285.

26. Richard J. Bernstein, *The Restructuring of Social and Political Theory* (New York, 1976), 197ff.

27. Ibid., 204ff.

28. "The transition to modernity is characterized by a differentiation of spheres of value and structures of consciousness that makes possible a critical transformation of traditional knowledge in relation to specifically given validity claims." Habermas, *Theory of Communicative Action*, 1:340.

29. Jürgen Habermas, *Theory and Practice*, trans. John Viertel (Boston, 1973), 9.

30. "A meaning that, even if it is not indended as such, takes form in the course of communicative action and articulates itself reflexively as the experience of a life history. This is the way in which 'meaning' discloses itself in the course of a drama. But in our own self-formative process, we are at once both actor and critic. In the final instance, the meaning of the process itself must be capable of becoming part of our consciousness in a critical manner, entangled as we are in the drama of a life history. The subject must be able to relate his own history and have comprehended the inhibitions that blocked the path of self reflection." Habermas, *Knowledge and Human Interests*, 260.

31. "Habermas saw [psychoanalysis] essentially as a methodological model of personal ideology critique . . . [and as] a process of heightened insight on the part of the patient, whose self-reflection helped dissolve the pseudo-otherness of his symptoms, which controlled him as if they were externally determined." Jay, *Marxism and Totality*, 479–80.

32. Habermas, *Knowledge and Human Interests*, 289.

33. Jürgen Habermas, *Legitimation Crisis* (Boston, 1975), 113.

34. Jürgen Habermas, *Communication and the Evolution of Society*, trans. Jeremy Shapiro (Boston, 1978), 178.

35. Ibid., 84.

36. Habermas, *Knowledge and Human Interest*, 312–15.
37. Holub, *Jürgen Habermas*, 8ff.; also, Thomas McCarthy, *The Critical Theory of Jürgen Habermas* (Cambridge, Mass., 1978).
38. Bernstein, *The Restructuring of Social and Political Theory*, 219ff.
39. The theory of communicative action "is not a continuation of methodology by other means. It breaks with the primacy of epistemology and treats the presupposition of action oriented to mutual understanding *independently* of the transcendental preconditions of knowledge." Habermas, *On the Logic of the Social Sciences*, xiv.
40. John B. Thompson, "Rationality and Social Rationalization: An Assessment of Habermas' Theory of Communicative Action," *Sociology*, vol. 17, no. 2 (May 1983), 289.
41. Martin Jay, "The Debate over Performative Contradiction: Habermas vs. the Poststructuralists," in *Zwischenbetrachtungen: Im Prozess der Aufklärung*, hrsg. Axel Honneth et al. (Frankfurt am Main, 1989), 171ff.
42. John B. Thompson, "Universal Pragmatics," in *Habermas: Critical Debates*, ed. John B. Thompson and David Held (Cambridge, Mass., 1982), 116ff.
43. Habermas, *The Theory of Communicative Action*, 1:287.
44. Jürgen Habermas, "A Reply to My Critics," in *Habermas: Critical Debates*, 227.
45. Ibid., 1:143ff.
46. Jürgen Habermas, "Technology and Science as 'Ideology,'" in *Toward a Rational Society: Student Protest, Science, and Politics*, trans. Jeremy Shapiro (Boston, 1970), 81ff.
47. Jay, *Marxism and Totality*, 467.
48. Habermas, *The Theory of Communicative Action*, 1:339ff.
49. Habermas, "The Entwinement of Myth and Enlightenment: Max Horkheimer and Theodor Adorno," in *The Philosophical Discourse of Modernity*, 106ff.
50. The break with Kant and subjective idealism is seen as occurring in that "instead of asking what an individual moral agent could or would will, without self-contradiction, to be a universal maxim for all, one asks: what norms or institutions would the members of an ideal or real communication agree to as representing their common interests after engaging in a special kind of argumentation or conversation?" Seyla Benhabib, "Communicative Ethics and Current Controversies in Practical Philosophy," in *The Communicative Ethics Controversy*, ed. Seyla Benhabib and Fred Dallmayr (Cambridge: Mass., 1991), 331.
51. "Whereas in strategic action one actor seeks to *influence* the behavior of another by means of the threat of sanctions or the prospect of gratification in order to *cause* the interaction to continue as the first actor desires, in communicative action one actor seeks *rationally* to *motivate* another by relying on the illocutionary binding/bonding effect (*Bindungseffekt*) of the offer contained in the speech act." Jürgen Habermas, *Moral Consciousness and Communicative Action*, trans. Christian Lenhardt and Shierry Weber Nicholson (Cambridge, Mass., 1990), 58.
52. Jürgen Habermas, "Charles S. Peirce über Kommunikation," in *Texte und Kontexte* (Frankfurt am Main, 1991), 9ff.; Robert J. Antonio and Douglas Kellner, "Communication, Modernity, and Democracy in Habermas and Dewey," in *Symbolic Interaction* 15:3 (1992), 277ff.
53. Habermas, *Theory and Practice*, 36–39.
54. James F. Bohman, "Communication, Ideology, and Democratic Theory," *American Political Science Review*, vol. 84, no. 1 (March 1990), 99.
55. Jürgen Habermas, *The Tanner Lectures on Human Values* vol. VIII (Salt Lake City, 1988), 243.
56. Karl-Otto Apel, "Is the Ethics of the Ideal Communication Community a Utopia on the Relationship between Ethics, Utopia, and the Critique of Utopia," in *The Communicative Ethics Controversy*, 23ff.
57. Habermas, *Moral Consciousness and Communicative Action*, 62.

58. Dietrich Bohler, "Transcendental Pragmatics and Critical Morality: On the Possibility and Moral Significance of a Self-Enlightenment of Reason," in *The Communicative Ethics Controversy*, 111ff.
59. Albrecht Wellmer, *Ethik und Dialog* (Frankfurt, 1989), 10–12, 123ff.
60. Jürgen Habermas, "Discourse Ethics: Notes on a Program of Philosophical Justification," in *The Communicative Ethics Controversy*, 60ff.; also Jürgen Habermas, *Erlauterungen zur Diskursethik* (Frankfurt, 1991).
61. Habermas, "A Reply to My Critics," 235.
62. Note the schema offered in the seminal article by Joshua Cohen, "Deliberation and Democratic Legitimacy," in *The Good Polity*, ed. A. Hamlin and B. Petit (Oxford, 1989).
63. Habermas, "Motive nachmetaphysischen Denkens," 35.
64. Seyla Benhabib, "Communicative Ethics and Current Controversies in Practical Philosophy," in *The Communicative Ethics Controversy*, 333.
65. Alexander, "Habermas' New Critical Theory," 414.
66. "Ethics oriented to conceptions of the good or to specific value hierarchies single out particular *normative contents*. Their premises are too strong to serve as the foundation for universally binding decisions in a modern society characterized by the pluralism of gods and demons. Only theories of morality and justice developed in the Kantian tradition hold out the promise of an *impartial* procedure for the justification and assessment of principles." Habermas, *The Tanner Lectures*, 241.
67. David Held, "Crisis Tendencies, Legitimation and the State," in *Habermas: Critical Debates*, 181ff.
68. Habermas, *Legitimation Crisis*, 7.
69. Richard Lowenthal, "Social Transformation and Democratic Legitimacy," in *Social Change and Cultural Crisis* (New York, 1984), 48.
70. Jürgen Habermas, "What Does Socialism Mean Today? The Revolutions of Recuperation and the Need for New Thinking," in *After the Fall: The Failure of Communism and the Future of Socialism*, ed. Robin Blackburn (London, 1991), 39.
71. Habermas, *Legitimation Crisis*, 36ff., 123ff.; for an opposing view, in which administrative subsystems are seen as capable of taking the leading role in developing society precisely because they are no longer dependent upon profit, Lowenthal, "Social Transformation and Democratic Legitimacy," 54ff.
72. Habermas, *The Theory of Communicative Action*, 1:261.
73. Habermas, *Communication and the Evolution of Society*, 178.
74. Peter Koller, "Moralischer Diskurs und politische Legitimation," in *Zur Anwendung der Diskursethik in Politik, Recht, und Wissenschaft*, hrsg. Karl-Otto Apel and Matthias Kettner (Frankfurt am Main, 1992), 62ff.
75. Habermas, *The Tanner Lectures*, 220ff.
76. Niklas Luhmann, *Rechtssoziologie* (Opladen, 1983).
77. Richard R. Weiner, "Retrieving Civil Society in a Postmodern Epoch," in *The Social Science Journal*, vol. 28, no. 3 (1991), 313ff.; also, Axel Honneth, "Critical Theory," in *Social Theory Today*, ed. Anthony Giddens and J. H. Turner (Cambridge, 1987), 362ff.
78. Habermas, *The Tanner Lectures*, 258–59.
79. Klaus Eder, "Critique of Habermas' Contribution to the Sociology of Law," in *Law and Society Review*, vol. 22, no. 5 (1988), 934.
80. Still, "Weber's denial that values are logically demonstrable—Habermas would say that they are *wahrheitsfähig*—does not imply a denial that in any historical situation a particular set of values is given and binding . . . the cohesion of a complex sociey is never based on its economic division of labor alone, but always also on the norms of conduct that make that division possible." Lowenthal, "Social Transformation and Democratic Legitimacy," 62ff.

81. Habermas, *The Tanner Lectures*, 226.
82. Ibid., 133.
83. Ibid., 137.
84. Ibid., 59.
85. Jürgen Habermas, *Faktizität und Geltung: Beiträge zur Diskurstheorie des Rechts und des demokratischen Rechtsstaats* (Frankfurt, 1992), 41.
86. Ibid., 10.
87. "Legitimacy is possible on the basis of legality insofar as the procedures for the production and application of legal norms are also conducted reasonably, in the moral-practical sense of procedural rationality. The legitimacy of legality is due to the interlocking of two types of procedures, namely, of legal processes with processes of moral argumentation that obey a procedural rationality of their own." Habermas, *The Tanner Lectures*, 230.
88. Ibid., 242; on the different types of proceduralism, John Rawls, *A Theory of Justice* (Cambridge: Mass., 1971), 85ff., 359ff.
89. Ibid., 267.
90. Ibid., 246; also, Eder, "Critique of Habermas' Contribution to the Sociology of Law," 937.
91. Habermas, *The Theory of Communicative Action*, 2:113ff.
92. Claus Offe, "The New Social Movements: Challenging the Institutional Boundaries of the Political," in *Social Research* (winter 1985); also, Jean Cohen and Andrew Arato, "Politics and the Reconstruction of the Concept of Civil Society," in *Zwischenbetrachtungen*, 482ff.
93. Bohman, "Communication, Ideology, and Democratic Theory," 101.
94. It is correct to suggest, in this vein, that "our communicative practices are constitutive of our forms of relationship, and our forms of relationship reveal our ethical commitments. The interest in consensus is just our commitment to recognizing the most important form of relationship—a universal moral community." Jane Braaten, "The Succession of Theories and the Recession of Practice," *Social Theory and Practice*, vol. 18, no. 1 (spring 1992), 98; for an alternative view, which misunderstands the philosophical issues involved and thus criticizes the theory of Habermas for posing a threat to pluralism, see Douglas B. Rasmussen, "Political Legitimacy and Discourse Ethics," *International Philosophical Quarterly*, vol. XXXII, no. 1, issue no. 125 (March 1992), 17ff.
95. Habermas, "Political Culture in Germany since 1968: An Interview with Dr. Rainer Erd for the *Frankfurter Rundschau*," in *The New Conservatism*, 192.
96. Randall Collins, "Habermas and the Search for Reason," *Semiotica* 64 (1987), 157.
97. Note the excellent discussion by Ron Eyerman, "Social Movements and Social Theory," in *Sociology*, vol. 18, no. 1 (February 1984), 75ff.
98. Habermas, *Communication and the Evolution of Society*, 153.
99. Habermas, *The Theory of Communicative Action*, 2:354ff.
100. "It is not evolutionary processes that are *irreversible* but the structural sequences that a society must run through *if* and *to the extent* that it is involved in evolution." Habermas, *Communication and the Evolution of Society*, 141.
101. Habermas is aware of the difficulty in linking the ontogenetic with the phylogenetic. Given that these terms are anthropological in character, however, the "principle of historical specification" still drops from the discussion. It also remains unclear how the connection between ontogenesis and the developmental logic of worldviews becomes concrete given that people of earlier social formations did not all pass through all the stages of ontogenetic development. Habermas, "Individuierung durch Vergesellschaftung. Zu G.H. Meads Theorie der Subjektivität," in *Nachmetaphysisches Denken*, 187ff.; also Michael Schmid, "Habermas's Theory of Social Evolution," in *Habermas: Critical Debates*, 173ff.

102. With regard to analyzing the points of disagreement between Habermas and these more politically conservative sociologists, Habermas, *The Theory of Communicative Action*, 2:199ff.; also Jürgen Habermas und Niklas Luhmann, *Theorie der Gesellschaft oder Sozialtechnologie* (Frankfurt, 1971) and *Theorie der Gesellschaft oder Sozialtechnologie: Beiträge zur Habermas-Luhmann Diskussion*, hrsg. Franz Maciejewski (Frankfurt, 1975), 2 Bde.
103. Jürgen Habermas, "New Social Movements," *Telos* 49 (fall 1981), 33ff.
104. Kenneth H. Tucker Jr., "Ideology and Social Movements: The Contributions of Habermas," *Sociological Inquiry*, vol. 59, no. 1 (February 1989), 30ff.
105. "The contradiction arises between, on the one hand, a rationalization of everyday communication that is tied to the structures of intersubjectivity of the lifeworld, in which language counts as the genuine and irreplaceable medium of reaching an understanding, and, on the other hand, the growing complexity of sub-systems of purposive-rational action, in which actions are coordinated through steering media such as money and power." Habermas, *The Theory of Communicative Action*, 1:342.
106. Habermas, *Faktizität und Geltung*, 12.
107. Habermas, *The Theory of Communicative Action*, xxxix.
108. Habermas's claim that power should come into play only insofar as it furthers rather than constrains the autonomy of the citizen is anchored in the ideology of laissez-faire capitalism. The autonomy of the citizen leaves him or her free to act autonomously in the market—and exploit; it is impossible to give autonomy an emancipatory connotation, which involves demonstrating its connection with solidarity and reciprocity, without explicitly confronting the existing logic of accumulation. Habermas, *Faktizität und Geltung*, 215.
109. Habermas, *Theory and Practice*, 169.
110. Gerhard Wagner and Heinz Zipprian, "Intersubjectivity and Critical Consciousness: Remarks on Habermas' Theory of Communicative Action," *Inquiry* 34 (1990), 54ff.
111. Habermas, *Faktizität und Geltung*, 127.
112. "With a theory of communication, there is no obligation to proceed only according to action theory, to speak only of agents and their fate, acts and consequences. It becomes possible also to speak of the characteristics of life-worlds in which agents and collectives or individual subjects move." Habermas, *Autonomy and Solidarity*, 113.
113. Jeffrey Alexander, "Habermas' Critical Theory: Its Promise and Problems," *The American Journal of Sociology*, vol. 91, no. 2 (1985), 410.
114. "Hence Habermas' methodic fiction that a discourse that was freed from particular interests and elements of domination and oriented only toward truth—according to his own example, a discourse resembling an ideal seminar—could never justify a social order based on structural inequality does not rest on logically compelling arguments, but on the primacy of a utopian vision of equality in his personal order of values; and I dispute that, even in the conditions of an "ideal speech situation" as postulated by him, he could achieve consensus about his thesis—certainly not with Karl Marx." Lowenthal, "Social Transformation and Democratic Legitimacy," 59–60.
115. For a different view, Karl-Otto Apel, "Diskursethik vor der Problematik von Recht und Politik: Können die Rationalitätsdifferenzen zwischen Moralität, Recht und Politik selbst noch durch die Diskursethik normativ-rational berechtfergigt werden?", in *Zur Anwendung der Diskursethik in Politik, Recht und Wissenschaft*, 29ff.
116. Submission to religious practices and various other premodern customs, after all, are not simply based on "coercion"—unless the term is stretched beyond recognition—and, when dealing with such issues, it is simply an evasion to maintain that all distortion in communication "can be seen as the result of the confusion of action oriented to understanding and action oriented to success, of strategic and communicative action." Habermas, *The Theory of Communicative Action*, 1:373.

117. Schmid, "Habermas's Theory of Social Evolution," 180.

117. Schmid, "Habermas's Theory of Social Evolution," 180.
118. Karl Marx and Friedrich Engels, *The Holy Family or Critique of Critical Criticism: Against Bruno Bauer and Company*, trans. Richard Dixon and Clemens Dutt (Moscow, 1975), 96.
119. Stephen Eric Bronner, *Socialism Unbound*, 2d ed. (Boulder, 2001), 151ff.
120. Habermas, "The Scientization of Politics and Public Opinion," in *Toward a Rational Society*, 62ff.
121. The state apparatus and the economy "can no longer be transformed democratically from within, that is, be switched over to a political mode of integration, without damage to their proper systemic logic and therewith their ability to function ... The goal is no longer to supersede an economic system having a capitalist life of its own and a system of domination having a bureaucratic life of its own but to erect a democratic dam against the colonializing *encroachment* of system imperatives on areas of the lifeworld." Habermas, "Further Reflections on the Public Sphere," in *Habermas and the Public Sphere*, 444.
122. Habermas, *The New Conservatism*, 55–56.
123. Cohen, "Deliberation and Democratic Legitimacy," 26ff.
124. Habermas, *Faktizität und Geltung*, 108.
125. Ellen Meiksins Wood, "The Uses and Abuses of 'Civil Society,'" in *The Retreat of the Intellectuals: Socialist Register 1990*, ed. Ralph Miliband and Leo Panitch (London, 1990), 60.
126. Habermas, *Faktizität und Geltung*, 190ff
127. Adela Cortina, "Ethik ohne Moral: Grenzen einer postkantischen Prinzipienethik?", in *Zur Anwendung der Diskursethik in Politik, Recht, und Wissenschaft*, 278ff.
128. Habermas, *Autonomy and Solidarity*, 266.
129. Habermas, *The New Conservatism*, 62–63.
130. Habermas, *Faktizität und Geltung*, 205.
131. Jane Braaten, "The Succession of Theories and the Recession of Practice," 98ff.
132. "While class conflict is not the only form of struggle that characterizes advanced capitalist societies, it would seem imprudent to maintain, as Habermas is inclined to do, that such conflict has been 'dammed up.' Moreover, it is striking—although perhaps not suprising in view of its evolutionary emphasis—that a 'society' or a 'nation-state' remains the *pierre de touche* of Habermas's account. Nowhere does he examine in detail the international system of nation-states, the multi-national alliances which greatly affect economic development and threaten one another's survival with the accumulated means of waging war. It is at best incomplete to interpret the conflicts and protest movements of our societies from within a framework that filters out the confrontation of nation-states and the politics of mass destruction." John B. Thompson, "Rationality and Social Rationalization," 293.
133. Nancy Fraser, "Rethinking the Public Sphere: A Contribution to the Critique of Actually Existing Democracy," in *Habermas and the Public Sphere*, 57.
134. Ben H. Bagdikian, *The Media Monopoly* (Boston, 1992).
135. Habermas, "Further Reflections on the Public Sphere," 441.
136. Habermas, "What Does Socialism Mean Today?," 31.

NOTES TO CHAPTER 13
1. Franz Neumann, *The Rule of Law: Political Theory and the Legal System in Modern Society* (London, 1985).
2. Robert D. Putnam, *Bowling Alone: The Collapse and Revival of American Community* (New York, 2000).
3. Note the fine work on the political culture during the 1920s by Sheri Berman, *The Social Democratic Moment: Ideas and Politics in the Making of Interwar Europe* (Princeton, 1998).

4. Jürgen Habermas, *Theory of Communicative Action*, 2 vols. (Boston, 1987), 2:113ff.
5. Jürgen Habermas, *Strukturwandel der Öffentlichkeit: Untersuchungen zur einer Kategorie der bürgerlichen Gesellschaft* (Berlin, 1962), 112ff.
6. Nancy Fraser, "Rethinking the Public Sphere: A Contribution to the Critique of Actually Existing Democracy," in *Postmodernism and the Re-Reading of Modernity*, ed. Francis Barket et al. (New York, 1992).
7. Jean Cohen and Andrew Arato, *Civil Society and Political Theory* (Cambridge, Mass., 1992); John Ehrenberg, *Civil Society: The Critical History of an Idea* (New York, 1999).
8. Underground literature is seen as "the principal agent of delegitimation" during the ancien régime by Robert Darnton, *The Forbidden Bestsellers of Prerevolutionary France* (New York, 1995).
9. Franz Neumann, "The Concept of Political Freedom," in *The Democratic and Authoritarian State: Essays in Political and Legal Theory*, ed. and preface Herbert Marcuse (New York, 1957), 163ff.
10. "When the International was formed in 1864, the principle of political equality for the working class on a democratic basis had by no means been recognized in a majority of European states. The working classes had as yet gained no measure of political emancipation . . . Parliamentary democracy, founded on universal suffrage and today accepted unquestioningly as a standard requirement for any political system indeed represents one of the achievements of the socialist movement." Julius Braunthal, *History of the International*, trans. Henry Collins et al. (New York and Boulder, 1980), 3:503.
11. James Joll, *The Second International, 1889–1914* (New York, 1966), 65.
12. A particular manifestation of this with respect to all the following trends appears in certain essays—"Kulturkritik und Gesellschaft," "Spengler nach dem Untergang," "Zeitlose Mode. Zum Jazz," "George und Hofmansthal. Zum Briefwechsel"—included in Theodor W. Adorno, *Prismen: Kulturkritik und Gesellschaft* (Frankfurt am Main, 1955).
13. Stephen Eric Bronner, *Moments of Decision: Political History and the Crises of Radicalism* (New York, 1992), 101ff.
14. Theodor W. Adorno, *The Jargon of Authenticity*, trans. Knut Tarnowski and Frederic Will (London, 1973).
15. Martin Heidegger, *What Is Called Thinking?*, trans. Fred D. Wieck and J. Glenn Gray (New York, 1968), 76.
16. "The they" (*das Man*) is everyone in general and no one in particular to whom this mode of speech applies, and thus, in public, a situation results in which "everyone is the other and no one is himself." Martin Heidegger, *Being and Time*, trans. John Macquarrie (New York, 1962), 165.
17. Note the argument in support of this position developed in Martin Heidegger, *Hegel's Concept of Experience* (New York, 1970).
18. She was particularly incensed by what she considered a fleeting attempt by Adorno to make his way in the Germany of 1933 as a half-Jew, who sought to use his mother's Italian name rather than his father's more Jewish-sounding name, Wiesengrund, with an article on *völkisch* music in a Frankfurt student newspaper. Hannah Arendt and Karl Jaspers, *Briefwechsel 1926–1969*, hrsg. Lotte Köhler und Hans Saner (Munich, 1987), 673, 679.
19. Hannah Arendt, *The Human Condition* (New York, 1958), 155ff.
20. Grant McConnell, *Private Power and American Democracy* (New York, 1966), 6.
21. Richard Sennett, *The Fall of Public Man: On the Social Psychology of Capitalism* (New York, 1978).
22. Max Horkheimer and Theodor Adorno, *Dialectic of Enlightenment*, trans. John Cumming (New York, 1972); Herbert Marcuse, *One-Dimensional Man: Studies in the Ideology of Advanced Industrial Society* (Boston, 1964).

23. Rolf Wiggershaus, *The Frankfurt School: Its History, Theories, and Political Significance* trans. Michael Robertson (Oxford, 1994), 554 and passim. Note the radically edited version of Jürgen Habermas, *Theory and Practice*, trans. John Viertel (Boston, 1973).

24. Theodor W. Adorno et. al, *The Authoritarian Personality* (New York, 1950), 656.

25. The fascist character can be summed up in the following way: it includes "a rigid commitment to dominant values, mainly conventional middle-class values, such as outwardly correct, unobtrusive behavior and appearance, efficiency, cleanliness, success along with a pessimistic and contemptuous view of humanity, a readiness to believe that uncontrollable dangerous events were taking place in the world and that sexual depravity could be detected everywhere; extremely hierarchical thoughts and feelings, with submissiveness towards idealized authorities in one's own group and contempt for outside groupings and everything deviant, discriminated against or weak; anti-introversion i.e. defense against self-reflection, sensibility and fantasy, with a simultaneous tendency towards superstition and stereotyped misperception of reality." Wiggershaus, *The Frankfurt School*, 414.

26. Ibid., 423.

27. Herbert Marcuse, "Repressive Tolerance," in Herbert Marcuse, Barrington Moore Jr., and Robert Paul Wolff, *A Critique of Pure Tolerance* (Boston, 1969).

28. Irving Kristol, "Pornography, Obscenity, and the Case for Censorship," in *Conservatism: An Anthology of Social and Political Thought from David Hume to the Present*, ed. Jerry Z. Muller (Princeton, 1997), 358ff.; Michael J. Sandel, "The Procedural Republic and the Unencumbered Self," *Political Theory*, vol. 12, no. 1 (1994), 81ff.

29. Herbert Marcuse, *An Essay on Liberation* (Boston, 1969).

30. Ulrich Beck, *The Reinvention of Politics: Rethinking Modernity in the Global Social Order*, trans. Mark Ritter (Cambridge, Mass., 1997), 94ff.

31. Ulrich Beck, *Risikogesellschaft: Auf dem Weg in eine andere Moderne* (Frankfurt am Main, 1986), 121ff., 254ff.

32. Ulrich Beck, Anthony Giddens, and Scott Lash, *Reflexive Modernization: Politics, Tradition and Aesthetics in the Modern Social Order* (Stanford, 1994), 1ff.

33. Beck, *The Reinvention of Politics*, 148ff.

34. Beck, *Risikogesellschaft*, 306ff.

35. Note the more extended discussion in Stephen Eric Bronner, "Ecology, Politics, and Risk: Considerations on the Social Theory of Ulrich Beck," in *Imagining the Possible: Radical Politics for Conservative Times* (New York, 2002).

36. While organizations like the Christian Coalition obviously have a mass base in various parts of the country, given the existence of businesses like the Christian Broadcasting Network and the wealth of religious institutions, it would be a mistake both to underestimate their influence and to think that they are divorced from the corporate world. The National Endowment for the Arts and the Public Broadcasting System remain targets for many right-wing politicians. Yet, while political censorship also remains important at the state and community levels, "because our entertainment and news are increasingly produced and distributed by large media corporations, the question of government censorship is largely a moot point. More important questions revolve around how corporate media perceive and respond to well-organized Christian Right activists. Censorship in the United States is mostly a matter of silencing dissident voices, not by government edict, but through the power of corporations to stifle or ignore what they deem unprofitable." Sara Diamond, *Not by Politics Alone: The Enduring Influence of the Christian Right* (New York, 1998), 193.

37. Herbert Schiller, *Culture Inc: The Corporate Takeover of Public Expression* (Oxford, 1991); Ben H. Bagdikian, *The Media Monopoly* (Boston, 1992).

38. Douglas Kellner, *Television and the Crisis of Democracy* (Boulder, 1990).

39. "Commitment is a necessary, but never a sufficient, condition for a writer's work

acquiring an organizing function. For this to happen it is also necessary for the writer to have a teacher's attitude. And today this is more than ever an essential demand. *A writer who does not teach other writers teaches nobody.* The crucial point, therefore, is that a writer's production must have the character of a model: it must be able to instruct other writers in their production and, secondly it must be able to place an improved apparatus at their disposal. This apparatus will be the better, the more consumers it brings in contact with the production process—in short, the more readers or spectators it turns into collaborators." Walter Benjamin, "The Author as Producer," in *Understanding Brecht*, trans. Anna Bostock (London, 1973), 98.

40. Benjamin Barber, *Strong Democracy: Participatory Politics for a New Age* (Berkeley, 1984) 274–81.

41. Note the superb introduction to *The Spirit of the Laws* by Franz Neumann, *The Democratic and Authoritarian State: Essays in Political and Legal Theory* (New York, 1957), 96ff.

42. Stephen Eric Bronner, *Ideas in Action: Political Tradition in the Twentieth Century* (Lanham, Md., 1999), 329ff.

INDEX

absolute, the, 17–18, 20, 21, 24; spirit, 53; transcendental, 21
abstract, the, 127, 142, 186
abstraction, 122–23, 125, 243
accountability, 67, 210, 212, 232, 234–35, 243–46, 254; democratic, 183; institutional, 206, 220, 227, 243, 247; of the state, 87; public, 226
accumulation: capital, 16, 44, 79, 206, 225, 303n. 108; logic of, 169; process, 10, 16, 174, 206, 245
action, 19, 28, 163, 207, 221; communicative, 51, 200–201, 206–208, 237, 242–43, 299n. 30, 300nn. 39; political, 38, 211, 222, 238; spheres of, 204–205; strategic, 208–209, 212; symbolic, 194, 204; theory of, 19, 303n. 112
activity, 20, 27, 29, 70
Adams, John, 222
Adorno, Theodor, 3, 4, 6, 7, 9, 13, 16, 18, 21, 24, 33–34, 44, 48, 52, 69, 72, 79, 81, 83–93, 96, 99, 104, 108, 113, 135, 137–55, 156, 158, 160, 175, 177, 179, 184, 186, 187, 189, 191, 200, 205, 215, 220–21, 224, 231–32, 233, 234, 237, 238, 242, 249, 250–51, 267n. 67, 273n. 30, 274nn. 39, 275n. 57, 276n. 72, 278n. 15, 281nn. 78, 285n. 38, 287n. 77, 288n. 111, 289n. 129, 290n. 12, 305n. 18; Dialectic of Enlightenment, 8, 14, 84–85, 86–87, 89–90, 108, 141, 154, 166, 172, 184, 191, 199, 240; The Authoritarian Personality, 8, 153–54, 224–25
advertising, 132, 134, 215
aesthetic: appreciation, 145, 298n. 68; criticism, 74, 119, 132, 134–35, 142; experience, 14–16, 76, 110, 112, 147, 175, 186, 251, 256; feeling, 149–50; forms, 111, 121, 133, 147, 174–75, 178–79, 181–83;

inquiry, 110, 119, 131, 145; inversion, 146–50; realm, 15, 181; the, 16, 125–26, 133, 144–45, 146–47, 172–73, 175, 178, 185, 186–87, 214, 287n. 93, 296n. 36
aestheticism, 134
aesthetics, 4, 6, 8, 10, 90, 93, 142, 147, 150–52, 156, 172–88, 232, 249–52, 295n. 23; critical, 134–36, 252; emancipatory, 130–36; political, 116–36
affluence, 185, 187
alienation, 6, 9, 12, 14, 19, 21, 25–27, 28–31, 32–34, 37, 45, 51–56, 58, 60, 62–63, 65–66, 69, 74, 82, 138–39, 145, 153, 159, 166, 167–68, 171, 172, 178, 215, 219, 222–23, 227, 237, 246, 248, 252, 256–57, 261n. 41, 264n. 20, 267n. 7, 283n. 5, 293n. 71
allegory, 101, 110, 278n. 29
Amnesty International, 163
analysis: aesthetic, 186; concrete, 151; empirical, 158; existential, 208
anamnesis, 238, 242, 256
anomie, 53, 198, 205, 249
anthropology, 4, 8, 62, 151, 166, 231, 242; negative, 175, 184
anti-Semitism, 85, 224, 274n. 46
Apel, Karl-Otto, 199–200
apocalypse, the, 122, 248
Arendt, Hannah, 96, 207, 221–22, 244, 253, 277n. 4, 305n. 18
argumentation, 200, 209–10
aristocracy, 216–18, 220, 275n. 53
Aristotle, 20, 22, 24, 32, 64, 162
arms control, 164–65
art, 23, 53, 74, 76, 93, 112–14, 116–31, 129, 132, 134–35, 138, 145, 146–48, 152, 173, 177, 179, 182–83, 187, 223, 238, 249, 251, 276n. 67, 285n. 46, 286nn. 67, 287nn. 79, 288n. 121;